CAMPAIGNING FOR PRESIDENT 2016

Coming out of one of the most contentious elections in history, Dennis W. Johnson and Lara M. Brown have assembled an outstanding team of authors to examine one of the fiercest and most closely fought presidential elections of our time. Like the 2008 and 2012 editions of *Campaigning for President*, the 2016 edition combines the talents and insights of political scientists who specialize in campaigns and elections together with seasoned political professionals who have been involved in previous presidential campaigns. Campaigning for President is the only series on presidential campaigns that features both political scientists and professional consultants.

This book focuses on the most important questions of this most unusual presidential campaign. What was the appeal of Donald Trump? Have Twitter and social media become the dominant means of communicating? How did fake news, WikiLeaks, and the Russians factor in this election? What happened to the Obama coalition and why couldn't Hillary Clinton capitalize on it? Hundreds of millions of Super PAC dollars were raised and spent, and much of that was wasted. What happened? Is the wild west of online media the new norm for presidential contests? These and many other questions are answered in the provocative essays by scholars and practitioners.

The volume also is packed with valuable appendices: a timeline of the presidential race, biographical sketches of each candidate, a roster of political consultants, the primary and general election results, exit polls, and campaign spending.

New to the 2016 Edition

- The 2016 presidential contest brings a completely new set of players, policies, and electoral challenges. Like the 2008 and 2012 editions, the authors probe the strategies and tactics of the candidate campaigns and the outside organizations.
- The chapters focus on Donald Trump and Hillary Clinton, but also look at the Bernie Sanders insurgency, the collapse of the mainstream Republican candidates, and the dynamics of the general election.
- Chapters also analyze the changes in campaign finance, new technologies, the role of social media, and how fake news and subterfuge might become the new realities of presidential campaigning.

Dennis W. Johnson is Professor Emeritus at the George Washington University Graduate School of Political Management.

Lara M. Brown is Associate Professor and Director of the George Washington University Graduate School of Political Management.

CAMPAIGNING FOR PRESIDENT 2016

Strategy and Tactics

Edited by
Dennis W. Johnson and Lara M. Brown
George Washington University

NEW YORK AND LONDON

Published 2018
by Routledge
711 Third Avenue, New York, NY 10017

and by Routledge
2 Park Square, Milton Park, Abingdon, Oxon, OX14 4RN

Routledge is an imprint of the Taylor & Francis Group, an informa business

© 2018 Taylor & Francis

The right of Dennis W. Johnson and Lara M. Brown to be identified as the author of the editorial material, and of the authors for their individual chapters, has been asserted in accordance with sections 77 and 78 of the Copyright, Designs and Patents Act 1988.

All rights reserved. No part of this book may be reprinted or reproduced or utilized in any form or by any electronic, mechanical, or other means, now known or hereafter invented, including photocopying and recording, or in any information storage or retrieval system, without permission in writing from the publishers.

Trademark notice: Product or corporate names may be trademarks or registered trademarks, and are used only for identification and explanation without intent to infringe.

First edition published by Routledge 2009
Second edition published by Routledge 2013

Library of Congress Cataloging-in-Publication Data
A catalog record for this book has been requested

ISBN: 978-1-138-05846-0 (hbk)
ISBN: 978-1-138-05847-7 (pbk)
ISBN: 978-1-315-16426-7 (ebk)

Typeset in Bembo
by Saxon Graphics Ltd, Derby

CONTENTS

List of Illustrations	*vii*
Notes on Contributors	*ix*
Preface	*xiii*

1	The Election of 2016	1
	Dennis W. Johnson	

PART I
The Primaries   45

2	The Democratic Primaries	47
	Lilly J. Goren	
3	The Republican Primaries	65
	Wayne P. Steger	
4	Trump's Appeal	81
	Mark S. Mellman	

PART II
Money and Communication   103

5	Presidential Candidate Fundraising: An Exception to the Rule?	105
	Anthony Corrado and Tassin Braverman	
6	The Digital Battle	129
	Suzanne Zurn	

vi Contents

7 Political Advertising in the 2016 Presidential Election 145
Peter Fenn

8 #Campaigns2016: Hashtagged Phrases and the
Clinton–Trump Message War 156
Michael Cornfield and Michael D. Cohen

9 The Trump Effect on the Press, the Presidency, Rhetoric,
and Democracy 173
Major Garrett

PART III
The General Election **189**

10 Outside Voices: Super PACs, Parties, and Other
Non-Candidate Actors 191
Stephen K. Medvic

11 Republican Strategy and Tactics During the General
Election 210
Katie Packer

12 Democratic Strategy and Tactics During the General
Election 225
Maria Cardona

13 The Defining Fault Lines in One of the Darkest Campaigns
in Political History 238
Matthew Dallek

Appendix A: Timeline 249
Appendix B: Presidential and Vice Presidential Candidates 256
Appendix C: Campaign Operatives and Consultants 261
Appendix D: Primary and Caucus Results 263
Appendix E: General Election Results 270
Appendix F: Exit Polls 282
Appendix G: Campaign Spending by Candidates, Parties, and
Major Super PACs 284
Index 286

ILLUSTRATIONS

Figures

3.1	Caucus and Primary Vote Shares of the Top Four Candidates in the 2016 Republican Caucuses and Primaries	75
4.1	Clinton Vote Share by National and Individual Economic Indices	84
4.2	Presidential Vote by Views on Government	86
4.3	"Which is More Important to You Personally? 'Order and Stability' or 'Progress and Reform'?"	87
4.4	"Since the 1950s, Do You Think American Culture and Way of Life Has 'Mostly Changed for the Better,' 'Mostly Changed for the Worse,' or 'Not Changed Much at All'?" And Presidential Vote by Views on Cultural Change since the 1950s	88
4.5	Views of Feminists, And Presidential Vote by Views of Feminists	89
4.6	"Which Statement Comes Closer to Your Own Views – Even if Neither is Exactly Right? 'The Number of Newcomers from Other Countries Threatens Traditional American Customs and Values' or 'The Number of Newcomers from Other Countries Strengthens American Society'"	93
4.7	Presidential Vote by Candidate Favorability	97
4.8	Strongest Determinants of a Trump Vote among White Voters	99

Tables

1.1	Republican and Democratic Presidential and Vice Presidential Candidates	6
5.1	Presidential Candidates, Receipts and Disbursements, in Millions	109

viii Illustrations

5.2	Sources of Funds—Individual Donors through June 30, 2016	112
6.1	How Candidate Websites Changed from 2012 to 2016	131
6.2	Clinton and Trump Links on Facebook and Twitter	133
7.1	Top Television Show, by Percentage of Household Share, 1950s–2010s	147
7.2	Television Ad Spending by Candidates and Outside Groups During Primaries	150
8.1	Top Campaign Hashtags of 2016	161

CONTRIBUTORS

Dennis W. Johnson is professor emeritus at the George Washington University Graduate School of Political Management (GSPM). His writings include *Democracy for Hire: A History of American Political Consulting* (2016); *Campaigning in the Twenty-first Century,* second edition (2016); *Political Consultants and American Elections*, third edition (2015; formerly *No Place for Amateurs*); *The Laws that Shaped America* (2009); and *Congress Online* (2004). He is also editor of and contributor to *Campaigning for President 2012* (2013); *Campaigning for President 2008* (2009); and the *Routledge Handbook on Political Management* (2009). He was Fulbright Distinguished Lecturer in China (2010–2011) and was associate dean of the GSPM.

Lara M. Brown is associate professor and director of the GSPM. She is the author of *Jockeying for the American Presidency: The Political Opportunism of Aspirants* (2010) and co-editor of *The Presidential Leadership Dilemma: Between the Constitution and a Political Party* (2012). Along with publishing a number of academic journal articles, she serves as a regular contributor to *U.S. News & World Report*'s "Thomas Jefferson Street" blog. Prior to her work in academia, Brown served as a political appointee in President William J. Clinton's administration in the U.S. Department of Education in Washington, D.C.

Tassin Braverman is a research assistant in the Department of Government at Colby College. His primary areas of interest are presidential campaign finance, the role of Super PACs in federal elections, and sources of Super PAC funding. His previous research work developing a typology of donors to Super PACs was published in *The Landscape of Campaign Contributions* (2016), sponsored by The Committee for Economic Development of The Conference Board. He is currently working on an analysis of contributions to Super PACs in the 2016 election.

x Contributors

Maria Cardona is a principal at the Dewey Square Group, founder of Latinovations, and veteran of Democratic Party politics. She served as a senior advisor for the Hillary Clinton for President Campaign in 2008, a senior vice president for the New Democrat Network, and communications director for the Democratic National Committee. She has been named one of the 100 most influential Hispanics in the country and is currently a political commentator on CNN and CNN Español. She serves on several boards of directors including the U.S. Hispanic Chamber of Commerce, the Centers for Reproductive Rights, and the Latina Advisory Council for Emily's List. She is currently a fellow at the GSPM.

Michael D. Cohen is an assistant professor and deputy director of the Political Management program at the GSPM, where he serves as chief data scientist for the PEORIA Project. In 2004, he founded Cohen Research Group, a Washington, D.C.-based public opinion and market research firm that also published Congress in Your Pocket, the leading mobile app for Capitol Hill. He earned his undergraduate and graduate degrees from the University of Florida in mass communications and political science, where he was inducted into the program's Hall of Fame.

Michael Cornfield is an associate professor of political management at the GSPM and research director of the Global Center for Political Management. He is the author of many articles and reports on presidential rhetoric and online politics, including two books: *Politics Moves Online: Campaigning and the Internet* (2004) and *The Civic Web: Online Politics and Democratic Values*, co-edited with David M. Anderson (2003). In 2012 he contributed a chapter to the previous volume in this series.

Anthony Corrado is a professor of government at Colby College and chair of the board of trustees of the Campaign Finance Institute, a non-partisan research organization focused on the study of money in politics. He formerly served as a non-resident senior fellow of the Brookings Institution. He is the author or co-author of numerous books and articles on campaign finance, including (with Thomas Mann, Daniel Ortiz, and Trevor Potter) *The New Campaign Finance Sourcebook* (2005) and *Campaign Finance Reform: Beyond the Basics* (2000). He is co-editor (with David B. Magleby) of *Financing the 2008 Election* (2011) and (with David B. Magleby and Kelly D. Patterson) of *Financing the 2004 Election* (2006).

Matthew Dallek is an associate professor at the GSPM, a political historian, and a frequent commentator in the news media on politics and history. His most recent book, *Defenseless Under the Night: The Roosevelt Years and the Origins of Homeland Security*, was named one of the *Washington Post*'s fifty notable non-fiction books in 2016. He is also co-author of *Inside Campaigns: Elections through* the *Eyes of Political Professionals* (2016) and author of *The Right Moment: Ronald Reagan's First Victory and the Decisive Turning Point in American Politics* (2004).

Peter Fenn is a long-time Democratic media consultant who has worked on campaigns from president to mayor. Prior to forming his media firm, he was executive director of Democrats for the 80s, founded by Pamela Harriman to help rebuild the Democratic Party. He also served on the Senate Intelligence Committee, chaired by Senator Frank Church, and as Washington chief of staff in his office. He co-founded the Center for Responsive Politics in 1983 and was its first executive director. Peter has been an adjunct professor at the GSPM for the past twenty years. He writes regularly for *U.S. News & World Report*.

Major Garrett is chief White House correspondent for CBS News. Previously, he was White House correspondent for *National Journal*, Fox News, and CNN, and congressional correspondent for *U.S. News & World Report*. He was also congressional correspondent and deputy national editor for *The Washington Times*. Garrett has won news writing awards from the Associated Press and United Press International. He is co-author (with former Minnesota congressman Tim Penny) of *The 15 Biggest Lies in Politics* (2000) and *Common Cents* (1995).

Lilly J. Goren is a professor of political science and global studies at Carroll University, where she teaches American government, the presidency, public policy, politics and culture, and political theory. Her writings include *Mad Men and Politics: Nostalgia and the Remaking of Modern America* (2015, co-edited with Linda Beail); *Women and the White House: Gender, Popular Culture, and Presidential Politics* (2012, co-edited with Justin Vaughn)—winner of both the 2014 Susan Koppelman Book Award and the 2014 Peter C. Rollins Book Award; *You've Come a Long Way, Baby: Women, Politics, and Popular Culture* (2009); and *Not in My District: The Politics of Military Base Closures* (2003).

Stephen K. Medvic is Kunkel professor of government at Franklin & Marshall College. His research and teaching interests include campaigns and elections, political parties, the media and politics, and public opinion. In addition to numerous academic articles and book chapters, he is the author of *Campaigns and Elections: Players and Processes*, second edition (2014); *In Defense of Politicians: The Expectations Trap and Its Threat to Democracy* (2013); and editor of three volumes on American campaigns. He is currently working on a book, *Campaign Finance in the United States*.

Mark S. Mellman is president of the American Association of Political Consultants (AAPC) and chief executive officer of The Mellman Group, a leading polling and consulting firm whose clients have included major political figures, Fortune 500 companies, and some of the nation's most important public interest groups.

xii Contributors

Recently, his firm was named "pollster of the year" by the AAPC, the third time it has won that prestigious award. The Mellman Group has been cited as the most accurate campaign pollster in the country by Nate Silver of the *New York Times*.

Katie Packer is a veteran Republican political consultant and strategist, who has worked in presidential campaigns since 1988. She was deputy campaign manager for Mitt Romney's 2012 presidential campaign, and founding partner of the Michigan-based consulting firm WPP Strategies and the Washington, D.C.-based all-female consulting firm Burning Glass Consulting. In early 2016, she founded Our Principles PAC, an anti-Trump Super PAC. She is an adjunct professor at the GSPM and a fellow at the Georgetown University Institute of Politics.

Wayne P. Steger is a professor of political science at DePaul University. He recently published *A Citizen's Guide to Presidential Nominations: The Competition for Leadership* (2015). Previously he was an editor of the *Journal of Political Marketing* and co-editor of *Campaigns and Political Marketing*. He has published over forty articles, chapters, and essays on campaigns, elections, and the American presidency.

Suzanne Zurn was the vice president of digital strategy at DCI Group, Washington, D.C. She is a former Republican political operative and veteran digital consultant who cut her teeth early in the business at political technology firms. She is best known for her work on award-winning digital public affairs campaigns. Zurn earned an M.A. from the GSPM, where she currently is an adjunct faculty member teaching a course on digital strategy.

PREFACE

This series, Campaigning for President, is unique among those works that analyze presidential elections. It combines the talents and experience of political consultants, both Republicans and Democrats, with the scholarly analysis of political scientists who specialize in campaigns and elections. The book is divided into three parts: the primaries; money and communications; and the general election. In addition there are seven appendices giving valuable information about the candidates, primary and general election results, a timeline of events, and, unique among books on presidential elections, a roster of the most important political consultants and campaign operatives for the candidates.

In the 2008 edition of *Campaigning for President*, the opening chapter was titled "An Election Like No Other." In one of the best-run operations, the campaign staff headed by David Plouffe and David Axelrod, helped propel Barack Obama to victory, first defeating Hillary Clinton in the hotly contested primaries then besting John McCain in the general election. The 2008 election was unique from an historical sense, with the election of America's first black president. From a campaigning perspective, the Obama campaign stood out because of its brilliant implementation of technology and big data, along with its low-keyed, "no drama" execution of electoral strategy execution.

That unique and historic 2008 contest, however, pales in comparison to the gyrations, trash-talking, unorthodox campaigning, and electoral surprises of 2016. This contentious, unpredicted, and truly nasty 2016 presidential election redefines the meaning of "An Election Like No Other."

Several themes emerge from our analysis of this election. Like much of the campaign itself, many of its distinguishing features center on the personality, strategy, and tactics of Donald Trump.

xiv Preface

First, this truly was a historic election. For the first time, a woman became the standard bearer for a major party. Few candidates could match Hillary Clinton in the depth and breadth of her public service experience. At the same time, not since 1940 had a candidate such as Donald Trump been chosen, a public affairs neophyte who lacked any prior elected office, military service, and any public service experience.

Never in modern presidential history had both major parties been torn apart by insurgent candidates; Donald Trump ripping through the Republican primaries, with Republican Ted Cruz and Democrat Bernie Sanders putting up impressive fights in their primaries as well.

Never had a candidate openly and repeatedly charged, without any evidence, that the core element of our democratic system, the election process, had been rigged and that the results would be fraudulent. Further, no presidential aspirant, until Donald Trump, had ever hesitated in accepting the outcome of the election.

This election was also unprecedented for the redefining of the role of the media. For decades, television has been the dominant vehicle for communicating campaign ideas and messages. During this election, we have seen one candidate, again Trump, successfully exploit free media and single-handedly capture the daily news cycle, through his clever and persistent use of Twitter, relaying his highly acerbic remarks, putdowns, and accusations directly to his faithful followers, bypassing the mainstream media. In this new world of political communication, mainstream media was the enemy, not to be trusted, and political reality was revealed in 140 characters on Twitter.

In this election, we have also seen unprecedented spread of fake news. Online platforms have opened up a wild west of communications, allowing anyone to spread rumor, innuendo, and falsehood to millions of viewers. Fake news and rumors are not unique to this election; we've seen all this before. But what is different is the widespread proliferation of fake news, to a degree not seen previously. The combination of an angry, disconnected audience, that was highly suspicious of elite institutions (particularly the mainstream media), that got its information (and at times disinformation) directly from candidates and causes, was the new reality of presidential campaigns.

For the first time, we have seen direct and compelling evidence that another country, Russia, has attempted to influence the presidential election, by its hacking of Democratic Party computers, by leaking damaging information to WikiLeaks, and by attempting to embarrass Hillary Clinton and aid Donald Trump.

Another distinguishing feature of this election was the gutter-level of discourse, again almost exclusively generated by Donald Trump. In past elections, there have been accusations, harsh characterizations, and unfair portrayals. But nothing compared with the insults, putdowns, and general trash-talking found in this campaign. Trump was able to drag down some of his Republican opponents to his rhetorical level, but even the most belligerent (Ted Cruz and Chris Christie) could not match Trump's diatribes. And the more Trump spouted and harrumphed, the more his followers ate it up.

Candidates have always come in for scrutiny as they enter the presidential election ring. But none in modern history has endured the insults, the demeaning and untrue charges, and the visceral hatred leveled against Hillary Clinton. We have never before seen the spectacle of Republican convention delegates shouting "Lock Her Up," or candidate Trump stoking up his faithful followers by promising to prosecute and toss her in jail. Clinton was certainly a flawed and imperfect candidate, but never has such candidate endured that level of ridicule and scorn.

Since the 1960s, presidential campaigns had relied on political consultants and seasoned political operatives to help guide the candidates through the hurdles and landmines of the arduous campaign season. This professional campaign model was carefully followed by Hillary Clinton. Her senior advisors were some of the best and brightest campaign operatives, many of whom previously had worked for the successful Obama campaigns. But not so for Donald Trump. He ran through a series of political consultants, but relied to a great degree on his own instincts and skills, his family members, and bare-knuckle supporters, like Steve Bannon, who also had very little campaign experience, but considerable experience in ideological warfare.

This election was distinctive when looking at campaign finances. Never before had a candidate raised so much money online as had Bernie Sanders, and never before had a candidate earned so much free media, as Trump did, that he did not have to invest heavily in paid media. In this post-*Citizens United* world, we have seen outside groups, both individuals and Super PACs, spend enormous amounts of money on presidential and congressional campaigns. This time was something quite different. Vast amounts of money were spent by wealthy individuals for Super PACs, but particularly on the Republican side, with very little to show for their investments. The Republican winner, Donald Trump, had the best return on his investment, spending far less per delegate won than anyone else, and at the same time eschewing Super PAC help. Just like in 2012, the eventual winner spent less money than his general election opponent. Some of the most active individual donors in past elections, like the Koch brothers, mostly stayed out of the presidential contest and concentrated their spending on congressional races.

Another theme, which follows from much that is written above, was the opportunistic genius of Donald Trump. He defeated what probably was the best qualified field of Republicans, picking them off one by one; he became a media darling by his outrageous behavior, gaining a couple billion dollars in free media. At the same time, he castigated the media as the enemy, cast widespread doubt about its legitimacy, thereby defanging it in the process. He ignored the mainstream press by going directly to his supporters through social media. He fought with his own party's leadership, ran his own campaign without a gaggle of

xvi Preface

consultants, used his own highly attuned instincts for grabbing attention and giving his followers what they wanted to hear. He was out-spent, out-maneuvered, and out-strategized by his well-funded and competent opponent, but still managed to win. He was the deeply flawed candidate, who managed to alienate wide swaths of voters, but who convinced just enough voters in the right states that he was far better than his horrible opponent. His was a dark, dystopian view of the world with its threats and imminent dangers, and a world of incompetent public officials and uncaring and corrupt public institutions. Through his bravado and snake-oil salesmanship he promised to fix difficult and complex problems through quick and bold solutions. He was the bull in the china shop, and his supporters loved him for it. He broke the mold in what we usually think of as a presidential candidate. There may never be another like him, with his swagger, ego, and temperament.

We were also compelled to look more seriously at disaffected voters, their world views, their fears, and their profound sense of distrust of institutions and the political class. It brought into stark contrast the worlds of urban, educated, culturally diverse voters with the world of rural, less educated, conservative, white Americans. For this latter 46 percent of voters, Trump was the answer, and change, not perpetuation of the Obama legacy, was the dominant, successful theme. They overlooked Trump's many faults, banking on his assurance of "draining the swamp" and bringing about fundamental change. The irony, of course, was while this may have been a change election, hardly anything changed in the House of Representatives and the Senate.

Finally, the results caught many people (including us) off guard. Who could have predicted a Trump victory? A variety of national polls showed that, while the election was close, Clinton would undoubtedly win. Was this some sort of conspiracy of the media elite (as Trump would imply), poor polling techniques, or perhaps a misreading of results (thanks in part to the project of results found in aggregation polling sites) and the margins of error? In hindsight there were plenty of signs of trouble, for not only Hillary Clinton and the Democratic Party, but also for continuing the Obama legacy. Several social scientists, using well-developed predictive models, forecast a rocky time for Clinton, and a victory for Trump. Such models discount personality and ego, relying instead on economic trends, social indicators, and incumbency. Perhaps the most prescient observer was not a social scientist, but filmmaker and social advocate Michael Moore, who looking at those who were attracted to Trump saw his own people—disaffected middle-class voters in the industrial heartland of America. They were angry and disappointed, and they were ready for change.

What Follows

In Chapter 1, Dennis W. Johnson presents an overview of the 2016 campaign, particularly putting it in historical context and suggesting the major themes that have unfolded through the arduous primary and general election season.

Part I, on the primaries, begins with Chapter 2 by political scientist Lilly J. Goren. She analyzes the Democratic primary contests, the strategy and tactics of Hillary Clinton, the insurgency of Bernie Sanders, the role of primary campaign financing, and the search for delegates and super delegates. In Chapter 3, political scientist Wayne P. Steger focuses on the much different dynamics and players in the Republic primaries. Steger looks at the strengths and weaknesses of the large field of candidates, the deep divisions within the Republican Party, and how Trump ultimately triumphed. In Chapter 4, Democratic polling consultant Mark S. Mellman focuses on Donald Trump: What was it that he ignited in his fervent followers, what was the role of personality and celebrity, and what motivated voters to give this deeply flawed candidate the benefit of the doubt?

Part II covers money and communication. In Chapter 5, political scientists Anthony Corrado and Tassin Braverman show us how Donald Trump defied conventional wisdom regarding money and politics, was outspent by Clinton and her Super PAC allies, but managed to win. Trump was not the only outlier: Bernie Sanders also took an unusual, and highly successful, approach to raising campaign money. In Chapter 6, former Republican strategist Suzanne Zurn looks at the advances in campaign technology and the use of social media by the candidates and outside groups. Once again, the focus is on Trump: with his mastery of social media and his ability to constantly seize the spotlight. Democratic media consultant Peter Fenn focuses on political advertising in Chapter 7. For Fenn, who has been involved in media politics for thirty years, the fundamental question is, just what is political advertising? Is it the traditional television, radio, or print ads, or is it Facebook, Snapchat, and Twitter? Fenn analyzes what works in advertising, what doesn't, and where elections are headed. Political scientists Michael Cornfield and Michael D. Cohen, in Chapter 8, dig deeper into social media, particularly into the use of Twitter, popular hashtagged phrases, and the message war between Clinton and Trump. Cornfield and Cohen argue that hashtagged phrases enhance the campaigns in four basic ways. In Chapter 9, CBS chief White House correspondent Major Garrett focuses on the press, the candidates, and the coverage of the campaign. Garrett gives us a first-hand account of the frustrations and difficulties of trying to cover Donald Trump.

Part III shifts to the general election. In Chapter 10, political scientist Stephen K. Medvic examines the outside voices: the Super PACs, the national political parties, and other non-candidate actors. Republican consultant Katie Packer, in Chapter 11, analyzes the strategy and tactics of the Trump–Pence campaign during the general election. Similarly, Democratic consultant Maria Cardona, in Chapter 12, focuses on the strategy and tactics of the Clinton–Kaine campaign

xviii Preface

during the general election. In the final chapter, Chapter 13, historian Matthew Dallek takes the long view, focusing on what will be important and what will be remembered about this election fifty years from now.

In addition, there are several appendices that put this election in context. Appendix A is a timeline of the election, going from the beginning of the "invisible primary" nearly two years before Election Day. Appendix B contains biographical sketches of the seventeen Republican and six Democratic candidates for president, in addition to the vice presidential candidates. Next, Appendix C is a roster of the major political consultants and campaign operatives for the Trump and the Clinton campaigns. Appendix D presents the results of the Republican and Democratic caucuses and primaries. Appendix E gives the General Election results. Appendix F presents the exit polls conducted on Election Day. Finally, Appendix G presents the campaign spending by the candidates, political parties, Super PACs, and other outside organizations.

Acknowledgments

We wish to thank each of the authors, political scientists and political consultants alike, for their perspective and analysis as we take this first step toward understanding this historic election of 2016. In addition, we would like to thank Pat Petrash and Sunny Early for their insightful comments. Special thanks to Jennifer Knerr, senior editor (politics), and Ze'ev Sudry, senior editorial assistant (politics), at Routledge. Thanks also to the fine production team at Saxon Graphics Ltd; the copyediting services of Penelope Harper; and proofreading from Sandra Stafford.

Dennis W. Johnson
Denver, Colorado

Lara M. Brown
Washington, D.C.

1

THE ELECTION OF 2016

Dennis W. Johnson

The election of Donald Trump sent shockwaves through the American political system, surprising nearly every political prognosticator (including just about every author in this book), causing jubilation among those 46 percent of voters who chose him, fear among many groups and individuals that Trump either insulted, threatened, or demeaned, and bewilderment among the political class in this country and throughout the world. Trump triumphed, it seems, almost in spite of himself. Most of his wounds were self-inflicted; at times, it looked like Trump would bring disaster to his party and wholesale defeat on an historic level, bringing disrepute to his party and disastrous results in the Senate and House elections. But the voices of millions of disgruntled voters who demanded change in Washington pulled him through.

In the end, Hillary Clinton won the popular vote by nearly 2.9 million, but lost in the Electoral College. Trump won 304 electoral votes (34 more than needed), while Clinton won 227, and an unprecedented 7 electors defected and chose others. During this election, just 55.4 percent of eligible American adults voted, the lowest level since 1992. Clinton won 48.2 percent of those who voted, Trump won 46.1 percent.[1] A total of 138 million votes were cast, but in the end, fewer than 78,000 determined the difference, when Trump beat Clinton in Michigan, Pennsylvania, and Wisconsin. Jill Stein, running as the Green Party's presidential candidate, who barely made a dent in the polls and coming in well behind Libertarian candidate Gary Johnson, collected enough votes in each of these three states to cover the difference between Trump and Clinton.

2 Chapter 1: The Election of 2016

Democrats and Republicans: Advantages and Challenges

The Democrats' Advantage

Democrats came into this election with a built-in advantage: during the past six presidential elections, beginning in 1992, voters in eighteen states and the District of Columbia, with a combined 242 electoral votes, had chosen Democratic presidential candidates.[2] During the same time, voters in thirteen states, with a combined 102 electoral votes, consistently chose Republicans.[3] In addition, from 1992 to 2012, Democrats had won the popular vote in every election except 2004. It would be up to the Republican candidate to chip away at Democratic strongholds, and do better than Romney did in 2012, when he won just 206 electoral votes and 47 percent of the popular vote. For Clinton, winning Florida (twenty-nine electoral votes) would be enough to assure victory; and Democrats had won Florida by small margins in the last two previous elections. All Clinton had to do was hold on to the Obama coalition, and if she couldn't do that, there were still many paths to victory. On the other hand, Donald Trump had a narrow road, one that permitted few mistakes and miscues.

Demographic changes also appeared to be on the Democrats' side. A Pew Research Center report in September 2016 concluded that the Democratic Party was becoming "less white, less religious and better-educated at a faster rate than the country as a whole, while aging at a slower rate." This was just the reverse of the Republican Party. Republican voters were becoming "more diverse, better-educated and less religious at a slower rate than the country generally, while the age profile of the GOP is growing older more quickly than that of the country."[4] Decade after decade, the country was moving demographically in the direction that favored Democrats.

Democrats also seemed to have the issues on their side. More and more people were siding with Democrats on cultural issues, such as increased tolerance for same sex marriages, abortion rights, and emerging transgender issues. On policy matters, more and more voters saw climate change as a major threat, demanded some form of gun control, and wanted immigration reform; they turned to Democrats to fight for change.

Warning Signs for Democrats

But there were also troubling signs. First, during the Obama years Democrats had been losing elective office at an alarming rate, not just at the national level, but at state and local contests as well. In 2010, Democrats suffered a "shellacking" (in Obama's words), when they lost control of the House and saw their majority in the Senate shrink. It only got worse for Democrats in 2012 and 2014 in those chambers. The Republican Party and its affiliated political action committees, 527 and 503(c)(4) groups, and individual donors (like the Koch brothers and

Chapter 1: The Election of 2016   **3**

Sheldon Adelson) poured money strategically into key Senate and House races, helping to turn the majority back to the Republicans. An Obama-friendly 2009 Congress (257 Democrats, 178 Republicans in the House; 57 Democrats, 41 Republicans in the Senate) had shrunk to a 2016 Congress (188 Democrats, 246 Republicans in the House; 44 Democrats, 54 Republicans in the Senate).

During the Obama years, Democrats lost over 800 seats in state legislatures. This all didn't happen by chance: Republicans invested big money in attempts to rebuild their majority at the state legislative levels. In 2010, Republicans spent $30 million (three times the amount invested by Democrats) to gain in state legislatures, with the result of picking up 675 seats and taking control of twelve state legislatures. The big prize: to gain control of the once-a-decade congressional redistricting process, assuring Republicans of the best gerrymandered districts possible. By 2014, Republicans gained control of another ten more state legislatures, pouring $38 million into the election process. Democrats were caught flat-footed.[5]

It is not unusual for a president to leave a hollowed-out party in his wake after leaving office. Professor Larry J. Sabato noted that since Dwight Eisenhower, "every eight-year presidency has emptied the benches for the triumphant party, and recently it has gotten even worse." On average, the eight-year presidents have lost an average of 10 governors, 8 senators, 36 House members, and 450 state legislative seats during their terms. But Obama, through 2014, was doing far worse: losing 11 governors, 13 senators, 69 House members, and 913 state legislative seats. "Barack Obama," wrote Sabato in 2014, "is well on his way to becoming the most harmful to his sub-presidential party of all modern chief executives."[6]

All this matters in presidential politics. Candidates need to rely on robust, healthy state parties and volunteer forces, to help local elected officials identify voters and get out the vote on Election Day.

Another worrisome matter was Hillary Clinton's lack of popularity. In August 2016, despite a solid performance at the Democratic Nominating Convention, Clinton was seen as favorable by only 41 percent of the American public, with 56 percent holding an unfavorable view. Since pollsters began tracking this figure, no presidential candidate—except for Donald Trump—has had such abysmal numbers.[7] Many Democrats had a difficult time warming to her, particularly progressives and millennials who were attracted to Bernie Sanders during the tough primary battles.

Barack Obama was enjoying increasingly favorable evaluations from voters, and by Election Day had reached 52 percent. But that would not guarantee success for his party's successor. Could Obama's appeal (along with his direct campaigning for her) help Clinton? The historical record was surely mixed. In 1960, Eisenhower was at 58 percent approval, yet his successor, Vice President Richard Nixon, could not win the presidency; in 2000, Bill Clinton was at 57 percent approval, but his successor, Vice President Al Gore, could not win office.

4   Chapter 1: The Election of 2016

Ronald Reagan was at 51 percent approval at the end of his term of office, but Vice President George H.W. Bush was able to succeed him (thanks in large part to a very poorly run campaign by his opponent, Michael Dukakis).[8]

Republican Advantages

Long before the first primary, it looked like a good year for Republicans. A number of prominent elected officials had decided to become candidates. Current and past governors, current and former U.S. senators, representing key Republican constituencies put forth their candidacy (see discussion below). This line-up was far more impressive than the weak list of Republican contenders in 2012, which gave Mitt Romney, the solid but distinctly non-Washington candidate, a leg up. But as it turned out, too many traditional Republican candidates vied for the voters' attention, and in the end were each picked off by Trump.

In the zero-sum game of American politics, the Democrats' problem—a hollowed-out party and a president, albeit popular, who could not transfer his popularity to his successor—became the Republicans' opportunity. Moreover, Republicans sensed, particularly as Trump increasingly appeared as their nominee, that this was going to be an election dominated by the need to bring about change. And Trump, flawed and ill-suited as he might be, was definitely the agent of change. In fact, his impulsive, at times, reckless "tell it like it is, no holds barred" style became an asset for his fervent backers.

Republican Problems

For most of the primaries and general election, the biggest problem was Donald Trump. Was he even a Republican, many asked? As journalist Jonathan Rauch pondered, Trump was not,

> in any meaningful sense, a Republican. According to registration records, since 1987 Donald Trump has been a Republican, then an independent, then a Democrat, then a Republican, then "I do not wish to enroll in a party," then a Republican; he has donated to both parties; he has shown loyalty to and affinity for neither.[9]

He trashed and insulted his Republican primary opponents, he picked fights with party leaders, especially Paul Ryan, he balked at working with the party and coordinating campaign strategy, he embarrassed his party by his antics and words, he veered widely from assumed Republican conservative orthodoxy.

Conservative newspapers refused to endorse him, mega-donors backed away, Republican and conservative-leaning opinion writers flailed against him, and in the harshest of terms, the party's 2012 standard bearer called him a fraud and a phony. Several groups of Republican consultants created Super PACs with the vain hope of stopping him. Trump, predictably, lashed out against his Republican critics, leaving no attack or insult unchallenged.

This certainly was not going to be a unified Republican Party, and it was not until the General Election period that the sometime warring, always fractious Trump campaign and Republican Party began coordinating and working together in crucial field operations.

Running for President

The Primary Candidates

The Republican Party boasted a large, strong field of candidates, many of whom have had national and state-wide experience. Four years earlier, the 2012 Republican primary field was especially weak, with only Mitt Romney ultimately emerging as the strong contender and the Republicans' choice. This time around, there were seventeen candidates, seasoned with many elected officials. There were four sitting governors (Chris Christie, Bobby Jindal, John Kasich, and Scott Walker); five former governors (Rick Perry, Jeb Bush, George Pataki, Mike Huckabee, and Jim Gilmore); four sitting U.S. senators (Ted Cruz, Rand Paul, Lindsey Graham, and Marco Rubio); and a former U.S. senator (Rick Santorum). Kasich, Huckabee, Santorum, and Gilmore had run before for their party's nomination. In addition were three outsiders who had no government experience, former business executive Carly Fiorina, retired neurosurgeon Ben Carson, and entrepreneur and television celebrity Donald Trump.

The Democratic Party field of candidates was quite different. Just like in the 2008 primaries, Hillary Clinton was considered the prohibitive favorite. Former Maryland governor Martin O'Malley, who signaled his interest in running when he gave a not very well received address at the 2012 Democratic National Convention, should have been the strongest contender against Clinton, once Vice President Joe Biden decided that he would not run. Former Virginia senator Jim Webb and former Rhode Island governor Lincoln Chafee declared their candidacies and went nowhere. Neither did professor Lawrence Lessig, whose tilt-the-windmill campaign barely got off the ground before it collapsed. The big surprise was Vermont senator Bernie Sanders, the 74-year-old self-described Independent-Socialist who jumped in as a Democrat (see Table 1.1).

In Chapter 2, "The Democratic Primaries," Lily J. Goren analyzes the strategy and plans of the Clinton campaign, explores her weaknesses and strengths, and writes about the unexpected surge and appeal of Bernie Sanders. In Chapter 3, "The Republican Primaries," Wayne P. Steger analyzes the surprising and unorthodox campaign run by Donald Trump, which "resembled a concert tour more than a presidential nomination campaign."

TABLE 1.1 Republican and Democratic Presidential and Vice Presidential Candidates

Office	Party	Name	Year of Birth	Position	State
President	Republican	Jeb Bush	1953	former governor	Florida
President	Republican	Ben Carson	1951	retired neurosurgeon, author, and conservative activist	Maryland
President	Republican	Chris Christie	1962	governor	New Jersey
President	Republican	Ted Cruz	1970	U.S. senator	Texas
President	Republican	Carly Fiorina	1954	former CEO, Hewlett-Packard	Virginia
President	Republican	James Gilmore	1949	former governor; 2008 presidential candidate	Virginia
President	Republican	Mike Huckabee	1955	former governor; 2008 presidential candidate	Arkansas
President	Republican	Bobby Jindal	1971	governor	Louisiana
President	Republican	John Kasich	1952	governor; 2000 presidential candidate	Ohio
President	Republican	George Pataki	1945	former governor	New York
President	Republican	Rand Paul	1963	U.S. senator	Kentucky
President	Republican	Rick Perry	1950	former governor; 2012 presidential candidate	Texas
President	Republican	Marco Rubio	1970	U.S. senator	Florida
President	Republican	Rick Santorum	1958	former U.S. senator; 2012 presidential candidate	Pennsylvania
President	Republican	Donald Trump	1946	business entrepreneur, television personality	New York
President	Republican	Scott Walker	1967	governor	Wisconsin
President	Democrat	Lincoln Chafee	1953	former governor and former U.S. senator	Rhode Island
President	Democrat	Hillary Clinton	1947	former U.S. Secretary of State; former U.S. senator; former First Lady of the United States; 2008 presidential candidate	New York
President	Democrat	L. Lawrence Lessig	1961	professor, Harvard University Law School	Massachusetts
President	Democrat	Martin O'Malley	1963	former governor	Maryland
President	Democrat	Bernie Sanders	1941	U.S. senator	Vermont
Vice President	Republican	Mike Pence	1959	governor; former member of Congress	Indiana
Vice President	Democrat	Timothy Kaine	1958	former governor; former U.S. senator	Virginia

Note: For a thumbnail sketch of each candidate, see Appendix B.

Consultants and Campaigns

Since the 1960s, presidential candidates have increasingly turned to professional political consultants to help steer them through the primaries and general election. While they work in the background, several consultants have become well known to the public in their own right, including Lee Atwater, Roger Ailes, James Carville, Dick Morris, Karl Rove, and David Axelrod.[10] For consultants, the 2016 contest proved to be a bumpy exception. Hillary Clinton, whose 2008 primary campaign operatives were famously at each other's throats, hired virtually an entirely new team, with many coming from the successful Obama 2012 campaign. Among the consultants were chief strategist Joel Benenson, media advisor Jim Margolis, pollsters John Anzalone and David Binder, digital strategist Teddy Goff, and campaign manager Robby Mook. These Clinton operatives were battle-tested in previous presidential and statewide campaigns. (For an expanded list of consultants and key operatives for both Clinton and Trump, see Appendix C.)

The Trump–Pence campaign had a rocky time with consultants. Roger Stone was Trump's original and long-time advisor, but either left or was fired before the campaign began. Little-known consultant Corey Lewandowski was hired as campaign manager, then fired in June 2016, but retained a consulting relationship with the campaign during the general election. Paul Manafort, long-time consultant, whose work dated back to the Reagan years, but who mostly worked on the lobbying and public relations side, became a principal fixture in the campaign, until he resigned in August 2016. For a short period of time Rick Wiley served as political director, until he was fired in May 2016. Trump turned to Kellyanne Conway, veteran Republican pollster, as his campaign manager during the general election. Veteran pollster Tony Fabrizio also assisted the campaign. Trump also turned to Stephen Bannon, former executive chairman of Breitbart News, and David Bossie, head of Citizens United, giving his campaign a decided turn to the right. Neither had much presidential campaign experience. (Bannon was characterized in 2015 as "the most dangerous political operative in America" in a *Bloomberg Businessweek* story.)[11]

Behind the scenes, however, two influential members of the Trump family, daughter Ivanka and son-in-law Jared Kushner provided considerable influence in picking the senior staff.[12] Roger Ailes, one-time political consultant, before becoming a Fox News mogul and then being unceremoniously fired for allegations of sexual harassment, became an unofficial advisor to Trump. In many ways, Trump relied on his own marketing and communication instincts, eschewing tried-and-true professional campaign services. For example, survey research is an integral part of any presidential campaign. But the Trump campaign spent more money purchasing the iconic "Make America Great" baseball caps ($3.2 million) than investing in private polling ($1.8 million).[13]

8 Chapter 1: The Election of 2016

Money Can't Buy You Delegates

Recent U.S. Supreme Court decisions have lifted many of the federal restrictions on campaign finance. In *Citizens United v. FEC* (2010), the Court ruled that the federal government could not curtail independent expenditure spending by corporations (and by extension labor unions) in candidate elections. A second opinion, *SpeechNow.org v. FEC* (2010), issued by a federal district court, permitted unlimited raising of money by independent groups. A third decision, *McCutcheon v. FEC* (2014) struck down a ban on the total amount of money an individual could contribute to a candidate over a two-year election cycle.[14] Together, these three decisions meant that unlimited campaign funds could flow with ease. The money flowed, but with some curious results.

In 1980, Texas governor John B. Connally, running for the Republican presidential nomination, spent $11 million, but was only able to gain one delegate. Connally and his "eleven million dollar delegate" became the butt of Republican Party jokes. But Connally's pile of cash (a little more than $32 million in today's dollars) had a familiar ring in the 2016 Republican primaries.

The "smart money" came out early, and mostly for Jeb Bush and Ted Cruz. And it wasn't coming from the Koch brothers, who spent at least $407 million trying to defeat Obama in 2012 and famously bragged that they would spend some $889 million during the 2016 cycle. David Koch said, after the 2012 defeat, that he and his brother's financial/political network was "not going to roll over and play dead" in 2016.[15] But during the 2015 primaries, the Koch brothers were remarkably silent, and later confined their giving mainly to 2016 U.S. Senate races, the RNC, and their own Super PACs. Sheldon Adelson together with his wife Miriam, who hosted what some derisively called the "Sheldon Primary" the year before the actual primaries, ended up spending some $77.7 million (less than they spent in 2012), mostly on Senate races and later on a pro-Trump Super PAC, Future45.[16]

In a major piece of investigative reporting, journalists from the *New York Times* showed that just 158 families had donated $176 million during the first part of the primaries, accounting for nearly half of all the money raised. Of those, 138 families each had contributed at least a quarter-million dollars to Republican campaigns. Nicholas Confessore, Sara Cohen, and Karen Yourish concluded, "Not since before Watergate have so few people and businesses provided so much early money in a campaign, most of it through channels legalized by the Supreme Court's *Citizens United* decision."[17]

The biggest beneficiary was the Right to Rise Super PAC, which was closely affiliated with the Jeb Bush campaign. But Jeb Bush was a bust; no more successful than John Connally in his day. Altogether, Bush and his Super PAC spent $139 million, with Bush garnering just four delegates in the process ($34.75 million per delegate). Other Republicans were equally unsuccessful: Carly Fiorina spent $25.49 million, claiming just one delegate; Mike Huckabee's one delegate came at the cost of $9.14 million. Trump was far more efficient: during the primaries he spent $76.9 million, much of it his own money, and gathered in 1,543 delegates, at a cost of a little under $50,000 per delegate.[18] Bernie Sanders made it a point of honor not to take Super PAC money, flailing away at the moneyed class, and continually bragging that the average contribution to his campaign, from the millions who supported him, was just $27. For more on the role of money in the 2016 presidential campaign, see Chapter 5 on campaign money (Anthony Corrado and Tassin Braverman) and Chapter 10 on outside voices (Stephen K. Medvic).

During the general election, we find that the Clinton campaign and its allies outspent the Trump forces. Likewise, Mitt Romney and his allies outspent the Obama forces in 2012. In 2012, the Obama campaign spent the money more wisely and strategically; in 2016, the Trump campaign found itself the beneficiary of some $2 billion in free publicity in the primaries alone, obviating the need to match Clinton one-on-one in paid media advertising.[19]

Feelin' the Bern!

How a seventy-four-year-old self-identified Socialist/Independent, who caucuses with Democrats in the Senate, became the darling of progressives, liberals, millennials, and disaffected Democrats is one of the major themes of the 2016 election. It pointed up several truths about our system of politics. First, thanks to the democratic reforms of the 1970s, anyone can run for office and, it seems, without penalty candidates can attach themselves to the major political parties, no matter how little track record they have with it. The prime example, of course, was Donald Trump, not really a Republican, who became the party's standard bearer; another was Ted Cruz, whose principal goal was to tear down the established Republican Party. On the Democratic side, Bernie Sanders joined the race with nary an objection from the party establishment. Second, it also tells us how fragile the Democratic Party (or for that matter, the Republican Party) has been. This was supposed to be the coronation of Hillary Clinton. Sure, Sanders could play the role of willing sparring partner, sharpening Clinton's debate and campaigning skills. But Sanders presented an historic challenge to Clinton, exposing deep schisms in the party and weaknesses in the candidacy of the putative frontrunner.

The Sanders campaign was also remarkable in its ability to gather some $228 million in campaign funds, 99.3 percent of which came from individuals, and 59 percent coming from small amount (less than $200) donations. Many of Sander's 2.5 million small amount donors gave contributions multiple times.[20]

Making Presidential Election History

In some ways, the 2016 election simply amplified the patterns of earlier presidential elections, but in other instances, what happened was historic and unprecedented.

10 Chapter 1: The Election of 2016

And as he has for most aspects of this election, Donald Trump is the reason, for good or ill, for several of the history-making episodes.

A Woman Heading the Ticket of a Major Party

Hillary Clinton certainly is not the first woman candidate for president in the United States. In recent elections, New York representative Shirley Chisholm (1972), Colorado representative Pat Schroeder (1988), and Illinois senator Carol Moseley-Braun (2004) had been unsuccessful candidates for the Democratic presidential nominations. Maine senator Margaret Chase Smith (1964), former cabinet member Elizabeth Dole (2000), Minnesota representative Michele Bachmann (2008), and business executive Carly Fiorina (2016) were unsuccessful candidates for the Republican presidential nomination. Scores of female candidates have run as presidential candidates from third parties or splinter groups, from Belva Lockwood (1884, 1888) through Jill Stein (2016). Hillary Clinton, who ran unsuccessfully for the Democratic nomination in 2008, made history as the first woman to capture the nomination of one of the two major parties.[21]

What would have been new and remarkable in the United States—a woman president—has been accepted for years in many democracies. Currently, there are twenty-one female presidents or heads of state, including German chancellor Angela Merkel (elected 2005), Liberian president Ellen Johnson-Sirleaf (2006), and British prime minister Theresa May (2016).[22]

The Trash-Talking Insult King

> "Every day, this is a candidate who has said things that just four years ago, just eight years ago, twelve, we would have considered completely disqualifying," [Obama] told the audience. "I mean, imagine if in 2008 I had said any of the things that this man said. Imagine if I had behaved in the way this man behaved. Imagine what Republicans would have said! Imagine what the press would have said!"
>
> Barack Obama on Donald Trump (October 2016)[23]

Presidential contests invariably have had rough language, taunts, and insults thrown back and forth between candidates and their supporters. But Trump also has gone where no other modern presidential candidate has gone: full-blown insults of other candidates, former Republican presidential candidates, news organizations, and reporters. Trump made the audacious, blanket claim, never heard before in such raw form by a modern presidential candidate: elected politicians are all corrupt, spineless, clueless, or complicit—and none of those running deserve to be the next president (but surely, when compared to Hillary Clinton, they were all better, he acknowledged; of course, he was better than them all). Only George Wallace, Ross Perot, or Patrick Buchanan would come close to Trump's bombast.

The *New York Times* kept tabs, coming up with 281 persons, places, or things that Trump had insulted, sometimes many times over, just using his Twitter account. A full accounting would fill this book. Other Republican primary candidates tried to keep up, but without the bravado, recklessness, and insensitivity they were not able to keep apace. Trump had a unique gift of honing in on opponents' weaknesses: Lyin' Ted (Cruz), Liddle Marco (Rubio), Low Energy Jeb (Bush), and most pointedly Crooked Hillary (Clinton). And these were only Twitter messages, to say nothing of his speeches or other comments.[24]

It seemed week after week, Trump would say something provocative, offensive, and/or insulting. In past elections, any one of these comments would probably doom a candidate. What would be the tipping point, we asked ourselves week after week, what would be that outrageous comment that would thoroughly turn off large swaths of the electorate, swaying those undecided to turn away from Trump? Calling Mexicans rapists? Demanding a wholesale ban on Muslims? Offending a Gold Star family, whose Muslim son had died in battle serving his country? Dismissing John McCain as something less than a war hero? Disparaging the Pope? Insulting commentator Megyn Kelly, calling women pigs, sniping at Carly Fiorina's looks? Calling Hillary Clinton the devil, promising to put her in jail once he became president? The list appeared endless, but with a devious outcome: boorish, inflammatory comments, that made daily headlines, and always kept Trump in the public eye and deepened his appeal as someone who would shake up the system.

And what did it say about his fervent supporters? Trump wasn't about to give in to political correctness, he repeatedly told his audiences. Like George Wallace before him, he'd tell it like it is. And the more he talked trash, the more his supporters lapped it up. Even the *Access Hollywood* tape, which would have sunk any other candidate, didn't destroy Trump. He characterized it simply as "locker room banter," weathered the criticism and calls for his stepping down, and forged ahead. His response to all the criticism of sexual harassment was to threaten to sue his accusers, parade out Bill Clinton's sexual harassment accusers from the 1990s, and, with a straight face, to assure his followers at the third debate, "Nobody has more respect for women than I do. Nobody."[25]

Systematic Vilification of Hillary Clinton

> Such a nasty woman.
>
> Donald Trump (referring to Clinton) at the third debate

No presidential contender in memory has been subjected to the taunts, visceral hatred, and cruelness that Hillary Clinton has endured. Indeed, she was a flawed candidate, wounded by continual criticism heaped upon her and her husband during the Clinton White House years. She labeled it a "vast right-wing conspiracy." Whether it was vast, right-wing, or a conspiracy, it certainly was

12 Chapter 1: The Election of 2016

persistent. Republicans made it a blood-sport to go after Hillary Clinton, who had the audacity to project both independence and policy expertise. She was not the typical First Lady, but was without doubt the most vilified since Eleanor Roosevelt, another strong and independent First Lady (and hero to Hillary Clinton). The irony is, that while Republicans and conservative ideologues tried to bring her (and especially her husband) down, she was still one of the most admired women in the world. Since 1948, the Gallup Poll has asked respondents to identify the most admired man and woman in the world. Since appearing on the U.S. and world stage as First Lady in 1993, Hillary Clinton has been the most admired woman in each of the last fourteen years, and twenty years overall—far longer than other well-known public figures, like Eleanor Roosevelt, Dwight Eisenhower, or Ronald Reagan.[26]

She gained high marks from the public while serving as senator from New York and, during her service as Secretary of State under President Obama, Clinton averaged 64 percent approval in Gallup polls. Her public approval ratings were still high (at 59 percent) during the Benghazi investigations; it was not until the revelations of using a private email server in March 2016 that her approval rating began to tank. It was definitely affected by Trump and his Republican rivals trying to outdo each other in their contempt for her and Clinton's inability to make a clean acknowledgment of the potential problems and put them behind her.[27]

The spectacle of rabid Trump supporters chanting and screaming for her head (with Trump smiling and encouraging the outrage) led conservative columnist George Will to compare the Republican convention to a "mini-Nuremberg rally for Republicans whose three-word recipe for making America great again was the shriek, 'Lock her up.'"[28]

The contempt and visceral reaction to Clinton, stoked by Trump, his allies, and online conspiracy theorists became Trump's last and most important line of defense. *No matter his sins, no matter his foibles, he would be far better than that monster Hillary Rodham Clinton.*

The Internecine Fights with Trump

There is inevitably tension within a political party as its contenders and factions vie for political power. In 1948, the Democratic Party fell apart, with South Carolina governor Strom Thurmond leading the exit of southerners who then formed the Dixiecrat movement, and Henry Wallace, former vice president, bolting to create a Progressive Party campaign. Barry Goldwater caused heartburn among establishment Republicans when he captured his party's nomination in 1964. And when George McGovern gained the Democratic nomination in 1972, there was widespread concern in the more conservative faction of the party— particularly southern white Democrats (there were such politicians back then). McGovern was simply too liberal, too far removed from the Democratic mainstream. Some bolted the party and many were resigned to defeat, but nothing compares to the anguish caused by Trump.

But just as Donald Trump laid into his opponents with scorn and ridicule, many struck back. The sniping came from all corners; never before had there been this level of angst coming from establishment conservatives. First, came the harsh criticism from commentators and ideological foes. Conservative columnists, like George Will and Charles Krauthammer, were particularly critical of Trump and his operation. Will wrote that Trump was the GOP's "chemotherapy," a "nauseating but, if carried through to completion, perhaps a curative experience."[29] Krauthammer wrote that there was a "dazzling array of ... reasons for disqualification [of Trump]: habitual mendacity, pathological narcissism, profound ignorance and an astonishing dearth of basic human empathy."[30] Influential talk show host Erick Erickson found himself in a battle over conservative loyalties, arguing that Trump was not a true conservative. (Trump denounced Erickson on Twitter as a "major sleaze and buffoon.") Trump also battled conservative firebrand Laura Ingraham, while getting the support of loyalists Sean Hannity and William Bennett.[31]

Elected officials also denounced Trump. The most prominent was former presidential candidate Mitt Romney, who in a blistering speech called Trump a "phony," and a "fraud" who is "playing the American public for suckers." "Here's what I know," Romney said at a major speech at the Hinckley Institute of Politics at the University of Utah, March 2, 2016,

> Donald Trump is a phony, a fraud. His promises are as worthless as a degree from Trump University. He's playing the members of the American public for suckers. He gets a free ride to the White House and all we get is a lousy hat.[32]

(Weeks after Trump won the election, Romney met several times with Trump, raising the prospects that he would be chosen as Secretary of State, or perhaps getting the sucker's treatment from Trump, who eventually chose business executive Rex Tillerson instead.)

Normally, retired generals and ambassadors, and other former high-ranking officials do not endorse or condemn presidential candidates. This election year was the exception. During the primary season, over a hundred Republican national security officials said they would never work for Trump, even before Trump won the Republican nomination. In August 2016, fifty Republican senior officials, including former cabinet members, signed a letter stating that Trump would be "the most reckless president in American history." In September 2016, another seventy-five former ambassadors and foreign affairs experts, serving in both Democratic and Republican administrations, signed a letter stating their opposition to Trump, saying that Trump "is ignorant of the complex nature of the challenges facing our country, from Russia to China to ISIS to nuclear

14   Chapter 1: The Election of 2016

proliferation to refugees to drugs, but he has expressed no interest in being educated" and declaring that each would vote for Clinton and Kaine.[33]

Newspapers and magazines, particularly those considered well-entrenched in the mainstream, were sometimes ruthless in their assessments of Trump. *The Atlantic*, which in its 159-year history had previously endorsed just two candidates, Abraham Lincoln in 1860 and Lyndon Johnson in 1964, endorsed Clinton and lambasted Trump. It noted that if Clinton had faced George W. Bush, or Mitt Romney, or John McCain, or any of the leading candidates during the Republican 2016 nomination process, the magazine would not have considered an endorsement.

> We believe in American democracy, in which individuals from various parties can advance their ideas and compete for the affection of voters. But Trump is not a man of ideas. He is a demagogue, a xenophobe, a sexist, a know-nothing, and a liar. He is spectacularly unfit for office ...[34]

The *Dallas Morning News* broke a 50-year tradition and supported Clinton, the *Arizona Republic* had never in its 125-year history supported a Democrat until this year, while the *Cincinnati Enquirer* broke a 100-year spell, and supported Clinton as well.[35] Their beef with Trump: he wasn't a true, rock-ribbed conservative.

The Role of the First Lady and President Obama

At no other time during modern presidential elections has the First Lady been so vocal and outspoken in a presidential election supporting the successor to her husband. Perhaps the closest would be Eleanor Roosevelt, who as former First Lady, enthusiastically supported Adlai Stevenson in his campaigns against Dwight Eisenhower. Michelle Obama, probably the most popular person in Washington, spoke out forcefully on behalf of Hillary Clinton at the Democratic Convention, and most noticeably on the campaign trail in response to Trump's behavior toward women.

At a Clinton rally in New Hampshire just four weeks before the election, Michelle Obama lit into Donald Trump:

> I can't believe that I'm saying that ... a candidate for president of the United States has bragged about sexually assaulting women... . And I have to tell you that I can't stop thinking about this. It has shaken me to my core in a way that I couldn't have predicted.
>
> So while I'd love nothing more than to pretend like this isn't happening, and to come out here and do my normal campaign speech, it would be dishonest and disingenuous to me to just move on to the next thing like this was all just a bad dream.[36]

Past presidents have at times assisted the candidates in their own party at election time. Eisenhower, late in the 1960 campaign, appeared with presidential candidate Richard Nixon, and even cut a commercial stating that he considered his vice president to be most qualified for the job.[37] Vice President Hubert Humphrey's relations with retiring president Lyndon Johnson were strained, particularly when Humphrey in 1968 tried to distance himself from the quagmire of Vietnam. Ronald Reagan in a short announcement endorsed Vice President George H.W. Bush (managing to mispronounced Bush's name), but Reagan's statement lacked spark and enthusiasm.[38] When Vice President Al Gore ran in 2000, he distanced himself from President Bill Clinton, who earlier had endorsed him for president.[39] George W. Bush, whose popularity was headed toward historic lows, gave an awkward endorsement of Senator John McCain, who was late to the White House for the announcement.[40]

But Obama came out strongly for Hillary Clinton. In the assessment of political analyst Domenico Montanaro, "no president has campaigned so strongly for his chosen successor in at least 100 years."[41] Obama gave a forceful speech at the Democratic National Convention, endorsing Clinton, with these words: "there has never been a man or a woman, not me, not Bill, nobody more qualified than Hillary Clinton to serve as president of the United States of America ..."[42]

The Rigged Election

Certainly there have been electoral shenanigans in past elections, especially during some of the turbulent times in the nineteenth century. But in modern times, no presidential candidate has ever called into question the fundamentals of American democracy like Trump. Long before Election Day, Trump was charging that the elections were going to be rigged against him, that the results would be fraudulent. With just three weeks remaining, Trump claimed that the 2016 election would be "a big ugly lie."[43] This claim, without any substantiation, went against evidence from scholars and neutral news sources that there is remarkably little election fraud in the U.S.

At the third debate, Trump was repeatedly asked by moderator Chris Wallace to affirmatively state that he would abide by the election results. "I will tell you at the time ... I will keep you in suspense," Trump answered. No presidential candidate has ever done that before. Clinton retorted that her opponent's answer was "horrifying."[44]

In the closest of presidential contests, the losers had quietly accepted defeat in public. In 1960, Richard Nixon lost the presidency by a whisker, amid credible charges that votes in Illinois (particularly Chicago) were suspiciously diverted to his opponent John F. Kennedy. Nixon complained privately, but even if Illinois (with its twenty-seven electoral votes) were removed, he still would have lost. Nixon accepted defeat and there was a relatively smooth transition to the new president. In 2000, after prolonged, contentious recount of votes in Florida,

16 Chapter 1: The Election of 2016

which George W. Bush won by just 537 votes, and a controversial U.S. Supreme Court decision to halt a recount, losing presidential candidate Al Gore graciously accepted the bitter news that, despite winning the nationwide popular vote, he had lost in the Electoral College. Of course, the loudest cause for complaint in the aftermath of the 2016 election could have come from Hillary Clinton who won the popular vote by nearly 2.9 million votes. But even after the election, Trump, not content to savor his Electoral College victory, ungraciously claimed— again with no substantiation whatsoever—that "millions" of votes had been fraudulently cast (and presumably to the benefit of Clinton).

If there were any "rigging," it most likely came in the form of state-enacted voter suppression laws, targeting minority voters, those most likely to vote for Democratic candidates. In 2013, the U.S. Supreme Court, in *Shelby County v. Holder*, ruled that the enforcement provision, Section 4, of the 1965 Voting Rights Act was unconstitutional.[45] The *Shelby County* decision stated that Justice Department preclearance of electoral laws was no longer needed, and that new rules should be adopted by Congress (and Congress failed to act).

By 2014, a total of thirty-one states had enacted online voter registration, and according to the Brennan Center on Social Justice at New York University, sixteen states had passed laws to improve access to the voting process. At the same time, twenty-two states, mostly with legislatures controlled by Republicans, enacted restrictive laws, supposedly to either save money or to clamp down on alleged voter fraud. However, academic studies and non-partisan reports have found that there is very little voter fraud.

Perhaps the most evident voter suppression came from states like North Carolina. Reporter Jeffrey Toobin noted that the North Carolina Republican Party had sent out a press release "boasting about how its efforts drove down African-American turnout."[46] The Fourth Circuit Court of Appeals in 2016 struck down the North Carolina law, stating that the law "impose[d] cures for problems [voter fraud] that did not exist," and that the law targeted African-Americans "with almost surgical precision."[47] Judge Diana Gribbon Motz declared that the state legislature offered "only meager justifications" for the restrictive law, and the Court of Appeals found it unconstitutional. A week earlier, a federal court in Texas found that the new Texas state voter ID law discriminated against African-Americans and Latinos. In 2014, a voting law in Wisconsin was similarly rejected. A federal court noted that some 300,000 registered voters lacked the identification forms that were now required to cast ballots. In Milwaukee County, home to many African-American voters, some 60,000 fewer persons voted in 2016 in comparison to 2012. In 2016, Hillary Clinton received 43,000 fewer votes than Obama in Milwaukee—nearly double the vote margin that Trump won the state.[48]

The Complicity and Collapse of the Media

> This is the ultimate reality show. It's the presidency of the United States.
>
> Trump consultant Paul Manafort (May 2016)[49]

> This isn't reality TV. It's reality.
>
> Former New York mayor Michael Bloomberg[50]

In 1993, media scholar Thomas E. Patterson wrote a trenchant analysis of the media's coverage of presidential elections.[51] He criticized the press for focusing too much on the game (who's up, who's down in the polls, who's ahead in Iowa, and so forth), reporting on trivial matters rather than policy substance, and in general being too critical and cynical in their reporting. Patterson's book was written right after the Bush–Clinton election campaign of 1992, when popular trust of the media was much higher than today, before the online revolution with the proliferation of alternative news sites and fake news.

Confidence in the media was at an all-time high in 1976, in the wake of the Watergate scandal and the Vietnam War, when 72 percent of American adults surveyed by the Gallup organization held a favorable view. But that figure has eroded since. Just half of adults surveyed said they trusted the mainstream media in 2004, and it declined to the lowest level in the history of Gallup polling, at just 32 percent in 2016. Younger adults and Republicans, particularly, have the greatest level of doubt about the press.[52]

Bashing the media, especially the mainstream media (or as vice presidential candidate Sarah Palin called it, the "lamestream media") can be a useful tool, particularly with audiences that feel abandoned by elite institutions. George Wallace used the press as a convenient foil, so did Ross Perot. The thin-skinned Perot, running for president in 1992, lashed out at the press: "If you can dish it out, you should be able to take it." Every time he had a fight with the press, Thomas Patterson noted, the switchboard in Perot's Dallas headquarters would light up with people wanting to volunteer for his campaign.[53]

Donald Trump would take news bashing to a whole new level, almost an art form.

During this election, Trump routinely vilified the press, calling them out at rallies, confining them to designated fenced-in pens, banning reporters and news organizations, all to the delight of his audiences. After the second presidential debate, in a rally in Miami Beach, Trump blasted the media and the establishment:

> This is reality. You know it, they know it, and pretty much the whole world knows it. The establishment and their media neighbors wield control over this nation through means that are very well known. Anyone who challenges their control is deemed a sexist, rapist, xenophobe, and morally deformed. They will attack you. They will slander you. They will seek to

18 Chapter 1: The Election of 2016

> destroy your career and your family. They will seek to destroy everything about you, including your reputation. They will lie, lie, lie, and then again they will do worse than that.[54]

But Trump benefitted immensely from the free publicity he was getting, especially on cable television. The more provocative and outrageous he was, the more television grabbed on to him, and made him the lead story. *The Atlantic's* media tracker, showed, as of October 20, 2016, that Donald Trump dominated free media with 1.1 million media mentions, compared to Clinton (567,617), Gary Johnson (4,531), and Jill Stein (1,648).[55] During the primaries, Trump received 68 percent of the media coverage, while Rand Paul, Mike Huckabee, Scott Walker, Lindsey Graham, Rick Santorum, Bobby Jindal, and Rick Perry each received less than 1 percent of the coverage.[56]

CBS chief Les Moonves, at a business conference in early 2016, called the race for president a "circus," full of "bomb throwing," which he hoped would continue. "It may not be good for America, but it's damn good for CBS," he said of the presidential race.[57]

And best of all were the antics and outrages of Donald Trump. Print journalist Nicholas Kristof decried the media's response when

> some in cable TV cover Trump endlessly without sufficiently fact-checking his statements or noting how extreme his positions are, because he is great for ratings and makes money for media companies, we are again failing the country. We are normalizing lies and extremism.[58]

For a first-hand account of Trump's treatment of the press, see Chapter 9, written by the CBS chief White House correspondent, Major Garrett. Other presidential aspirants have battled with the press, but no modern candidate has been so open, confrontational, and successful at de-legitimizing the role of the press while at the same time dominating it.

Twitter and Social Media Come Into Their Own

Another major difference in this campaign has been the impact of Twitter, especially as masterfully deployed by Trump. As seen in Chapter 6 on the digital battle (Suzanne Zurn) and Chapter 8 on the message war (Michael Cornfield and Michael D. Cohen), Donald Trump, through his incessant Twitter messages, focused the spotlight on himself and dominated the news. It was his platform to insult, berate, and occasionally flatter his opponents, slam the news media, President Obama, and even the process of the election itself.

Twitter, which played barely any role in the 2008 election (having been invented just two years earlier)[59] and played a subordinate role in 2012, emerged as the key online platform for the Trump campaign, and copied to varying

Chapter 1: The Election of 2016 **19**

degrees of success by his primary opponents, and by Sanders and Clinton. Trump, author of many of the thousands of tweets, captured the attention of the press and the public, and ended up with millions of followers who could receive messages directly from the candidate himself, rather than through the filter of the media. It was brilliant, and it was calculated.

Just what is acceptable to discuss in public? Years ago, analyst Joseph P. Overton coined the phrase the "Overton Window," to describe what the mainstream media and elites would consider acceptable for public discussion. For decades, many subjects were considered off-limits, such as giving full voice to racist or sexist comments. But as journalist Philip Elmer-DeWitt observed, "Donald Trump, having emasculated the GOP, and broken the Overton Window, says the unthinkable every day of the week about all sorts of things ... and it only seems to endear him further with his supporters."[60] Or as conservative writer David French observed, "On key issues, he didn't just move the Overton Window, he smashed it, scattered the shards, and rolled over them with a steamroller."[61]

Media's Failure to Cover Issues

The 2016 presidential election was not simply name-calling and institutional bashing. There was plenty of posturing about public policy. Some of it was in the rawest and easily understood sense: Trump's call for a wall that Mexico would build, his proclamation that Muslims should be banned, or that once he's in office, how he would bomb ISIS to oblivion. Clinton certainly had her policy focus, but much of it was wrapped in the wonkiness of her campaign website.[62] There were plenty of pressing issues that should have been covered, not just by the candidates and their campaign organizations, but in the news media. But here, according to the research conducted by Andrew Tyndall, is where the old reliable three major networks—ABC, NBC, CBS—failed miserably. "No trade, no healthcare, no climate change, no drugs, no poverty, no guns, no infrastructure, no deficits," wrote Tyndall. By October 25, two weeks before Election Day, Tyndall had tallied just thirty-two minutes of issue coverage by the three networks for the entire campaign, with twenty-four of those minutes taken up by terrorism or the Middle East. "To the extent that these [other] issues have been mentioned, it has been on the candidates' terms, not on the networks' initiative."[63] In past presidential cycles, the three major networks had devoted far more time to issues: 210 minutes in 1992, 203 in 2004, and 220 in 2008, but just over a half-hour total in 2016.[64]

"Post-Truth," Lies, and Fake News—"U Decide"

Recently, Oxford Dictionaries chose "post-truth" as its word of the year. To the dictionary writers, "post-truth" is defined as "relating to or denoting circumstances

20 Chapter 1: The Election of 2016

in which objective facts are less influential in shaping public opinion than appeals to emotion and personal belief."[65]

For generations, citizens got their news from fairly limited sources: the local newspaper, radio, or television station. At the national level, people listened to Walter Cronkite, Chet Huntley and David Brinkley, or Frank Reynolds. The news was generally considered to be reliable, factual, relatively free of overt biases and partisan commentary.[66] News coverage in the 1950s–1970s was certainly a far cry from the raucous, often high-partisan news that came out of newspapers during the nineteenth and early twentieth centuries.

The Walter Cronkite era ended before the proliferation of cable television and talk radio, before highly partisan radio and television personalities, almost all on the conservative side, before online communication, blogs, and Twitter, before the wild west of communications that was so heavily exploited during this election.

Traditional news sources, particularly local and national newspapers, and magazines no longer attract the attention of voters seeking information about candidates and issues. For millennials (age 18–29), social media is the most cited vehicle (35 percent) for learning about the 2016 presidential politics, while traditional national newspapers (1 percent) are barely mentioned. For adults thirty years old and up, the dominant news source is cable television (between 21 and 43 percent), while social media is far lower (between 1 percent for the oldest Americans and 15 percent for those closest to thirty); again, national newspapers rank very low (at most 5 percent for the oldest grouping). For all age groups, late night comedians are turned to more often (3 percent of the time) than national newspapers (2 percent).[67]

Information about politics, candidates, and policies has become far more democratized, flowing from a bewildering array of online sites, some legitimate news sources, others nothing more than prank sites and purveyors of disinformation. As journalist Jonathan Mahler has written, "the democratization of the flow of information [has become] the democratization of the flow of disinformation."[68]

Writing nearly a decade before this election, cultural critic Susan Jacoby took an even more jaundiced view:

> America is now ill with a powerful mutant strain of intertwined ignorance, anti-rationalism, and anti-intellectualism … This condition is aggressively promoted by everyone, from politicians to media executives, whose livelihood depends on a public that derives its opinions from sound bites and blogs, and it is passively accepted by a public in thrall to the serpent promising effortless enjoyment from the fruit of the tree of infotainment.[69]

The 2016 election was replete with disinformation and fake news. But there is nothing new about fake news. As journalist Jacob Soll noted, fake news "has been around since news became a concept 500 years ago with the invention of the

Chapter 1: The Election of 2016 **21**

printing press—a lot longer, in fact, than verified 'objective' news, which emerged in force a little more than a century ago."[70] Indeed, fake and pseudo news, dare we even say outright lies, have swirled around presidential elections throughout American history. In recent times, it has been more prevalent because of the explosion of online, free-for-all information, rumor, and allegation spread virally. In 2008, for example, candidate Barack Obama was accused of being a Muslim, palling around with terrorists, not earning his law degree from Harvard, and the one that stuck the most, not being born in the United States (something Trump pushed in 2012, as well). None of these statements was true, but it didn't matter: they would circulate through viral emails, blog sites, and a new online platform, Twitter. Mitt Romney, exasperated by news organizations checking up on what he said, put it this way in 2012: "We're not going to let our campaign be dictated by fact-checkers."[71]

The 2016 election saw an enormous increase in the amount and traffic in lies, conspiracies, and warnings of imminent danger. We learned in July 2016 that the Pope had endorsed Donald Trump. Well, not really. The Pope did not endorse Donald Trump, but the bulletin from WTOE News 5 (a fantasy fake website masquerading as a television station) sounded pretty convincing to fool some voters:

> News outlets around the world are reporting on the news that Pope Francis has made the unprecedented decision to endorse a U.S. presidential candidate. His statement in support of Donald Trump was released from the Vatican this evening: "I have been hesitant to offer any support for either candidate in the presidential election, but I now feel that not to voice my concern would be a dereliction of my duty as the Holy See."[72]

It wasn't only news from the Pope. Other rumors circulated. For example, Obama immigration officials were letting undocumented immigrants "pour" into the U.S., and the media wasn't reporting it (thus part of the conspiracy). Debate organizers had rigged the system, and the moderators were all working for Clinton. The FBI, despite James Comey's last-minute actions, had failed to thoroughly investigate Clinton. Election officials should monitor "certain areas" (that is, inner cities) where "bad things happen" because of potential voter fraud. International bankers were secretly meeting with Clinton "to plot the destruction of U.S. sovereignty." And the news media were hyping stories about women who accused Trump of sexual harassment.[73]

All this fed into the narrative of a corrupt, secretive Washington, with Hillary Clinton as the poster-child of an elite, self-serving system. Who knows how many people were gullible enough to believe these and many other charges, but surely many did.

One individual who took fake news to heart was a twenty-eight-year-old man from Salisbury, North Carolina, who was determined to "self-investigate" an

22 Chapter 1: The Election of 2016

online conspiracy theory that Clinton and her senior aide, John Podesta, were involved in a child abuse ring, that was centered at a pizzeria on Connecticut Avenue in Washington, D.C. Armed with a rifle, he came to the pizza place, fired at least once, scattering frightened customers. He went to the back of the restaurant, futilely looking for the tunnels where the children were supposedly hidden. He was finally arrested. For three weeks earlier, the neighborhood small businesses had been bombarded with social media threats. Menacing messages appeared on Instagram, with hundreds of death threats, coming from Twitter, Facebook, and other online forums. There were dozens of fake articles, and the pizza store owner at one point counted five #pizzagate Twitter posts per minute. Employees were threatened, images of their children were pilfered, and friends on Facebook accounts were likewise targeted.[74] All this because of a totally fabricated story, eagerly pushed by anonymous voices, sent throughout the world, and believed by some.

Most of the fake news stories were pushed by anonymous readers, just stirring up reaction. But one such online user, ready to pass the story on to eager readers was Lt. Gen. Michael T. Flynn, Trump's key military advisor, who days before the election retweeted a fake news story that Clinton and her advisors were involved in pedophilia, money laundering, perjury, and other felonies. "U decide," said Flynn in his tweet giving at least tacit permission for the lies and falsehoods to continue.[75] The *New York Times* described Flynn as having a "well-established penchant for pushing conspiracy theories about Islamic law spreading in the West and the attack on the American diplomatic compound in Benghazi, Libya."[76]

Fake news became a gold mine for some teenagers in Veles, Macedonia, a rust-belt, out of the way town, where nearly a quarter of its citizens are unemployed. Investigations by Buzzfeed and *The Guardian* traced more than a hundred pro-Trump fake news domain sites to this small town. Many of the sites sounded halfway legitimate: WorldPoliticus.com, TrumpVision365.com, USConservativeToday.com. Enterprising teenagers like Dimitri posted hundreds of fake stories aimed at undermining Clinton, and promoting Trump. The teenager claimed that he was able to earn about $60,000 in online ad revenue, and that he was not alone, estimating that perhaps 300 other Veles people were also cashing in. One story on ConservativeState.com claimed "Hillary Clinton in 2013: 'I Would Like to See People Like Donald Trump Run for Office; They're Honest and Can't Be Bought.'" In a week, that fake news story generated over 480,000 shares on Facebook.[77]

In San Francisco, a two-person operation called Liberty Writers News generated between $10,000 and $40,000 a month from ads that ran on the bottom of news sites. The key was to write "clickbaity" headlines—headlines so intriguing that viewers would almost automatically want to click on the story—and, of course, then generate revenue for the firm. Liberty Writers News estimated that 95 percent of its traffic comes from Facebook. Some of their stories would end with "***Share this right now! Let's beat the liberal media to it. Share, share, share it all over Facebook."[78]

We have not yet in our presidential elections reached the level of China's 50 Cent Party, where hundreds of thousands of individuals (mostly low-level government workers) are paid to post government-approved comments, cheerleading government actions, and distracting from other less pleasant issues that might come to the surface. In China, about 448 million such comments are generated each year. Social scientists Gary King, Jennifer Pan, and Margaret E. Roberts, who conducted the first systematic analysis of the 50 Cent Party, wrote that "the strategic objective of the regime is to distract and redirect public attention from discussions or events with collective action potential."[79]

About 1.8 billion people log on to Facebook every month; billions more check out Weibo, Instagram, WeChat, WhatsApp, Twitter, and other popular social media sites. All become platforms for political information, of whatever degree of truthfulness or falsehood. Right after the presidential election, Google and Facebook announced that they would change their advertising policies to prohibit sites that peddle fake news from gaining advertising revenue. A worthwhile gesture, admits technology analyst Farhad Manjoo, "even if it comes too late."[80]

Russian Hacking of Emails

Also never seen before in U.S. presidential elections: the overt influence of a foreign power, Russia, trying to meddle in the presidential election. A month after the election concluded, the Central Intelligence Agency briefed members of the U.S. Senate, stating that Russia had intervened in the presidential election to help Trump win, rather than an attempt, as earlier believed, to only undermine confidence in the U.S. electoral process. The CIA was able to identify individuals connected with the Russian government who provided WikiLeaks with thousands of hacked emails from the Democratic National Committee. Trump dismissed the allegations, telling *Time* magazine "I don't believe [Russia] interfered" in the election, and that the hacking "could be Russia. And it could be China. And it could be some guy in his home in New Jersey."[81]

The FBI and Homeland Security released their report[82] detailing how the Russian government had used cyber-espionage to influence the U.S. presidential election. Republican lawmakers faced the quandary of whether to investigate these serious allegations or sit on their hands, and believe Trump. Breitbart.com (and Trump ally) was quick to throw doubts on the alleged Russian spying in mid-December 2016 with an article that gave ten reasons why the Russian emails were actually "fake news" conjured up by left-wingers.[83]

It is impossible to tell how much impact the Russian leaks of Democratic Party and Hillary Clinton's senior advisors' emails had on the overall election. But it adds just one more dynamic in a very weird election year. At his first news

24 Chapter 1: The Election of 2016

conference just before his inauguration, Trump conceded that Russia had hacked, but that it had nothing to do with the outcome of the election, and that any allegations that Russia had incriminating information on him was simply "fake news."[84]

Supporting Donald Trump

Journalist Jim Tankersley, in explaining how Trump won the election, encapsulated the problems of working-class white voters:

> For the past forty years, America's economy has raked blue-collar men over the coals. It whittled their paychecks. It devalued the type of work they did best. It shuttered factories and mines and shops in their communities. New industries sprouted in cities where they didn't live, powered by workers with college degrees they didn't hold.[85]

Many Americans were angry, disillusioned, and fed up with what they considered a corrupt class of professional politicians, an ineffective national government, untrustworthy elite institutions, and inattention to their needs and concerns.

They were particularly upset with the two national parties; for many both the Democratic Party and the Republican Party had turned their backs on them. This wasn't just coming out of the blue. Years ago, Democratic pollster Stanley Greenberg warned his party that a bellwether region, Macomb County, Michigan, once a reliably blue-collar Democratic area, was quickly becoming Reagan territory. Voters complained that the Democratic Party had abandoned working-class whites in favor of minorities, feminists, and the poor.[86]

For years, political scientists and social commentators have identified the frustrations and disappointments of white, middle-class American voters. Social scientist Susan J. Tolchin, writing in 1992, wrote in *The Angry American* about the rise of militia groups, the Clinton White House scandals, and voter rage.[87] Journalist and opinion writer E.J. Dionne Jr. captured the sense of outrage and frustration in his 1992 book, *Why Americans Hate Politics*.[88]

More recently, journalist George Packer wrote about the fallout of the 2008 economic collapse in a book aptly titled *The Unwinding*. Journalist Thomas Frank looked at his home state of Kansas, wondering why it turned so conservative, seemingly against its own self-interest in *What's the Matter with Kansas: How Conservatives Won the Heart of America*, and his more recent *Listen, Liberal: Or, Whatever Happened to the Party of the People?* Social scientist Katherine J. Cramer closely observed the attitudes and frustrations of rural Wisconsin voters in *The Politics of Resentment*. For Cramer, the divides in Wisconsin "are not just about politics but who we are as a people."[89] Sociologist Arlie Russell Hochschild wrote poignantly about the Tea Party and Donald Trump supporters in *Strangers in Their Own Land: Anger and Mourning on the American Right* and social scientists

Theda Skopcol and Vanessa Williamson looked at Republican dissatisfaction in *The Tea Party and the Remaking of Republican Conservatism*. J.D. Vance graphically describes the deterioration of middle-class families in *Hillbilly Elegy*, and economist Nicholas Eberstadt chronicles what he terms an "invisible crisis" of *Men Without Work*.[90]

For generations, it was the American Dream that children would do better than their parents: they would be better educated, healthier, able to own their own homes, and have better jobs. But for many, this dream has been elusive. A team of economists, led by Raj Chetty, published the "Equality of Opportunity Project," which graphically showed that for persons born in recent decades, the American Dream has appeared to be quite fragile.[91] The American Dream was a reality for those born in 1940, where 91.5 percent of children would be earning more than their parents. By 1950, that percentage had fallen to 78.5, fallen again to 62.3 percent in for persons born in 1960, and to just over 50 percent for those born in 1980.

> Children's prospects of achieving the "American Dream" of earning more than their parents have fallen from 90 percent to 50 percent over the past half century. This decline had occurred throughout the parental income distribution, for children from both low and high income families ...[92]

Its impact has been most profound in the reality and in the perceptions of middle-class white voters. In many rural areas of middle-class America, there has been an extraordinary increase in drug addiction, alcohol abuse, and suicides. And it was in these rural counties that Trump did better than Romney four years earlier, according to a study by sociologist Shannon M. Monnat.[93]

Many voters were angry, but they were not ideologues. Their anger doesn't come from a deep-seated revulsion against well-defined conservative or libertarian principles. As political scientists John Sides and Michael Tesler observed, one of the keys to understanding Trump's appeal is that most Americans are not ideologues.[94] They argue that this has been long known about voters, going back to the work of Philip Converse fifty years ago.[95] And certainly neither was Trump, who was all over the map in his statements—some deeply conservative, some liberal, and many others non-ideological. Journalists, commentators, and many critics took Trump at his words, but then dismissed them as foolhardy or off-the-wall. But in a prescient observation, journalist Salena Zito wrote that when Trump makes outlandish claims, "the press takes him literally, but not seriously; his supporters take him seriously, but not literally."[96]

The Arizona Republic, a rock-ribbed conservative newspaper, refused to endorse Trump, endorsing Clinton instead. His sin: he was not a true conservative.

> Since *The Arizona Republic* began publication in 1890, we have never endorsed a Democrat over a Republican for president. Never. This reflects

26 Chapter 1: The Election of 2016

> a deep philosophical appreciation for conservative ideals and Republican principles. This year is different. The 2016 Republican candidate is not conservative and he is not qualified.[97]

But the lack of consistent conservative principles did not phase Trump's fervent followers.

Trump attracted many from the Alt-Right and brought on board Stephen Bannon, head of the website Breitbart.com. Bannon in July 2016 boasted that Breitbart was the "platform for the alt-right."[98] As Trump besmirched minority groups, bullying individuals and insulting causes, and proudly stood up against "political correctness," many saw, finally, a candidate not afraid to take on the political establishment and the dominant culture. Finally, many supporters told the press, someone who says what we've been uttering under our breath all these years. Trump was crashing through that Overton Window, and many were loving it. For some, it was the opportunity to let loose their anger. The Southern Poverty Law Center (SPLC), which tracks hate crimes, noted that the election was producing an "alarming level of fear and anxiety among children of color and inflaming racial and ethnic tensions in the classroom." (On the day after the election, the SPLC collected 437 separate reports of hateful intimidation and harassment, mostly targeted at African-Americans and immigrants.)[99]

It is never wise to besmirch a whole swath of voters, especially if they hold a grudge against you in the first place. Hillary Clinton inartfully characterized Trump supporters as a "basket of deplorables." "To just be grossly generalistic, you can put half of Trump supporters into what I call the basket of deplorables," Clinton said. "Right? Racist, sexist, homophobic, xenophobic, Islamaphobic, you name it." She added: "And unfortunately, there are people like that and he has lifted them up. He has given voice to their websites that used to only have 11,000 people, now have 11 million. He tweets and retweets offensive, hateful, mean-spirited rhetoric."

But in polls conducted right afterwards, some two-thirds of respondents rejected Clinton's characterization. She was forced to back down, try to explain what she meant, but the damage was done.[100]

Political scientists John Hibbing and Elizabeth Theiss-Morse argue that it isn't just Trump's blatant appeals to "populism, nativism, ethno-centrists, anti-intellectuals and authoritarians" and angry and disaffected non-college educated white males. They argue that another element needs to be considered. Trump appeals to many citizens who "feel dismissive" of core elements of democratic governance, like "deliberation, compromise, and decision-making by elected accountable officials."[101] In a book written fifteen years ago, *Stealth Democracy*, Hibbing and Theiss-Morse found that many Americans thought democracy should be run as a "business," not relying on debate and compromise. They called such Americans "stealth democrats," persons who had only "the loosest of commitments to core features of democratic governance."[102] They also found

Chapter 1: The Election of 2016 **27**

that during the 2016 election, some 40 percent of Republicans (16 percent of Democrats) were "stealth democrats," and favored a Trump approach to democratic governance.

So for some, Trump represented a business-like approach, a hard-headed, tough negotiator, someone who could get things done. Ross Perot, in the 1992 presidential campaign, presented the same no-nonsense business approach toughness, when he promised (in an analogy of an auto mechanic) to lift the hood, look inside, and get things fixed. For more on the appeal of Donald Trump, see Chapter 4 by Mark S. Mellman.

The Opportunistic Genius of Donald Trump

We have to hand it to Donald Trump. He was able to hack through the established political order, taking on his own party, insulting and demeaning its candidates, showing his disgust for the party's inability to bring about reform, characterizing it as corrupt and content with its own power. He was the candidate without any prior public service experience, a glaring shortcoming for some, but he spun that into a positive. When criticized, he fought back, bluntly and incessantly on Twitter and through his rallies. He encouraged outrage, he belittled the political class, the media, and Wall Street. While he attacked the media, he benefitted enormously from the free publicity television (especially cable TV) gave him. He broke through the filter of television and newspapers by going directly to his vast audience of Twitter supporters.

Big-time Republican funders shunned him, conservative columnists and news outlets excoriated him, political consultants and former campaign workers tried to mount Never Trump movements against him, elected Republicans called for him to step down. None of this mattered: Trump prevailed. Or perhaps all of it mattered: it showed Trump to be the tough outsider, unafraid to take on the political, financial, and media establishment in favor of the little guy. The more Washingtonians and Wall Streeters were outraged, the more middle America loved him.

He was the least liked presidential candidate in modern history; he was considered far less qualified, by his experience and especially by his temperament, than Hillary Clinton. He said things that would easily destroy any other candidate; he behaved in ways that no other candidate could possibly survive. But he certainly could sell himself. He was able to woo voters with his emphatic, plain-spoken assurances. He was the greatest, he would fix the terrible problems on the first day in office, he knew more than the general and intelligence professionals, he would be the "greatest jobs president God has ever created," and he would Make America Great Again.

Trump's huckersterism had a long history. In his book *The Art of the Deal* (written by Tony Schwartz) Trump bragged:

28 Chapter 1: The Election of 2016

> I play to people's fantasies. People may not always think big themselves, but they can still get very excited by those who do. That's why a little hyperbole never hurts. People want to believe that something is the biggest and the greatest and the most spectacular. I call it truthful hyperbole.[103]

Enough people—46.0 percent of the voting public—pulled the lever for Trump, and as luck and strategy would have it, it was just enough for victory.

Forecasting the Winner

In 1948, when President Harry Truman faced a seemingly insurmountable challenge from New York governor Thomas Dewey, the leading pollster of the day stopped measuring public opinion well before Election Day. Eight weeks before the election, Elmo Roper, the most accurate pollster in recent presidential cycles, declared that he would no longer publish polls.

> Thomas E. Dewey is almost as good as elected. That being so, I can think of nothing duller or more intellectually barren than acting like a sports announcer who feels he must pretend he is witnessing a neck and neck race.

Roper, and his colleagues, George Gallup, and Archibald Crossley, were way off the mark, and had plenty of egg on their faces as Truman pulled an upset victory.[104]

Since then, each cycle has brought out pundits, pollsters, and academics with their predictions in the presidential sweepstakes—some accurate, some way off the mark. This election is no different. It probably has had more pundits—reporters, political consultants, activists—putting their two cents in nearly non-stop on CNN, Fox, and other television networks than at any other time.

Since 1996, political scientists routinely have engaged in the practice of forecasting the winner. The political science journal *PS: Political Science and Politics*, and its editor, professor James E. Campbell, dedicated an entire journal number to the forecasting of this election. The political scientists looked into statistical data from past elections, noting how the fundamentals have predicted voters' choices. In a nutshell, these are several of the models and how they predicted the election. A *Third Party-Term* election, where one party (in this case, the Democrats) is seeking a third term and finds it historically very difficult to achieve. The 2016 outlook: "Close Race." A *Polarized Party* election, which means that the parties have hardened lines and reduced the volatility of the electorate. The 2016 outlook: "Close Race." A *Sluggish Economic Growth* scenario gives the outlook: "Tilt to Republicans." A *Pre-Campaign Public Opinion* model suggests that when the public's mood is sour, then unhappy voters will reject the party in power; the outlook: "Favors Republicans." When the focus is on *July*

Chapter 1: The Election of 2016 **29**

Presidential Approval Ratings, the outlook is for a "Close Race." And when looking at *Pre-Convention Preference Polls*, the outlook is a "Tilt to Democrats."[105] One model, the *Primary Model*, forecasted an 87 percent probability that Trump would beat Clinton.[106] Other political and social scientists have made predictions, and most are understandably tentative, often giving us nothing more than the cautious, unsatisfying, and usually accurate "too close to call" as an answer.[107]

Perhaps the most lucid prediction came not from an academic but from activist and filmmaker Michael Moore, who grew up in and knows the industrial Midwest blue-collar heartland. Writing in July 2016, Moore predicted that Trump would focus on "four blue states in the rustbelt of the upper Great Lakes"—Ohio, Michigan, Pennsylvania, and Wisconsin. Each one of those states had elected Republican governors in recent cycles, and Trump's appeal resonated with white blue-collar workers. "From Green Bay to Pittsburgh, this, my friends, is the middle of England," Moore wrote,

> broken, depressed, struggling, the smokestacks strewn across the countryside with the carcass of what we use to call the Middle Class. Angry, embittered working (and nonworking) people who were lied to by the trickle-down of Reagan and abandoned by Democrats who still try to talk a good line but are really just looking forward to rub one out with a lobbyist from Goldman Sachs who'll write them a nice big check before leaving the room. What happened in the UK with Brexit is going to happen here.

He characterized Trump as a "human Molotov cocktail," and that's why, "every beaten down, nameless forgotten working stiff who used to be part of what was called the middle class loves Trump."[108]

Conclusion

In 2004, journalist Bill Bishop wrote *The Big Sort*, explaining how many Americans, over the past quarter century, had moved into places compatible to their political beliefs, interacted with like-minded people, and read books and online postings that reinforced their view of the world. Such separation and polarization began showing up in election results. "In 1974, less than a quarter of Americans lived in places where the presidential election was a landslide. By 2004, nearly half of all voters lived in landslide counties."[109]

In 2016, the big sort was especially pronounced, particularly in the rural–urban divide, with all the social and economic variables that they entailed. Trump overwhelmingly captured rural areas, with many rural counties and small towns throughout America voting for Trump by 75 percent or more. Trump gained more rural votes than Romney did in 2012. In those three crucial states, Trump captured the rural and small town vote: Michigan (67–38 percent), Pennsylvania (71–26 percent), and Wisconsin (63–34 percent). Rural America represents about

30   Chapter 1: The Election of 2016

17 percent of the electorate, but crucially, Trump was able to capture these voters by a three-to-one margin.[110]

In 2008, Democratic pollster Stanley Greenberg felt some relief knowing that the voters in Macomb County, Michigan, who had turned away from the Democratic Party during the Reagan years, were coming back home. In 2008, Barack Obama had defeated John McCain in Macomb County, just as Obama had done in Iowa, Ohio, Pennsylvania, Wisconsin, and other sections of the heartland.[111] But this time around, like so much of once blue-collar white America, Macomb County went solidly for Donald Trump. It turned out to be a revolt of the vast white middle class, whose numbers were so important in the Midwest battleground states.

As Nicholas Confessore and Nate Cohen of the *New York Times* noted, the day after Election Day "you could walk from the Vermont border through Appalachian coal country to the outskirts of St. Louis without crossing a county Mr. Trump did not win decisively."[112]

Clinton was strongest in big cities, in the new economy regions, in the culturally diverse, better educated regions of the country, areas with concentrations of minority voters. She was especially strong on the East Coast and West Coast, especially in the big cities of Boston, New York, Philadelphia, Washington, D.C., Miami, Los Angeles, San Francisco, and Seattle, as well as Chicago, Denver, and Detroit.

But in the crucial Philadelphia suburbs, Clinton could not come up with decisive margins, she could not improve upon Obama's showing in Hispanic sectors of Miami, nor could she build upon Obama's African-American support in big cities throughout the country. Altogether, there was no great surge of Hispanic voters who would be so enraged at Trump's charges and rhetoric that they would make the difference.

As noted in Chapter 11 on Republican strategy during the General Election phase (Katie Packer) and the corresponding Chapter 12 on Democratic strategy (Maria Cardona) other imponderables entered the picture—they always do in elections so maddeningly close. Was it James Comey's last-minute letters that did in Clinton? Was it the final push by the Republican Party to shore up the upper Midwestern that did the trick? Was it the failure of the Democratic strategists to not see the dangers of a crumbling Midwest during the last week, and instead try to extend their reach to Arizona, Georgia and other places? For Democrats, one thing is certain, the long knives will be out, and the weeping will not stop.

Jill Stein, Meet Ralph Nader

In 2000, Al Gore lost Florida by a margin of 537 votes; third party activist Ralph Nader pulled in 97,421 votes. Democrats long charged that if Nader had stayed away, the solid majority of his Florida supporters would have pulled the lever for

Gore rather than George W. Bush. As Florida went, so did the Electoral College, with Bush gaining 271 electoral votes, one more than needed.

As Appendix E shows, there were several states where third party candidates could have made the difference in the outcome. We don't have the data, and don't know for sure what such third party voters would have done. Would Gary Johnson voters have been more inclined to vote for Trump if Johnson were not on the ballot? Would Jill Stein voters have favored Clinton if Stein were not on the ballot? Perhaps many third party voters wouldn't have voted at all. But it is tantalizing to speculate. In Arizona, Johnson (with 2.1 percent of the vote) had more votes than the difference between winner Trump and Clinton. In Colorado, Johnson (5.2 percent) and Stein (1.4) had more votes than the difference between winner Clinton and Trump. Likewise, in Florida, Johnson (2.2 percent) would have made the difference; so, too, would Johnson (5.1 percent) and Stein (1.9 percent) in Maine, and Nevada, with Johnson (3.3 percent) and other third party candidates (3.3 percent). In Minnesota, Johnson (3.8 percent) and Evan McMullin (1.8 percent) made the difference.

The heartbreak for the Clinton campaign had to come in the three crucial Midwest states: Wisconsin, Michigan, and Pennsylvania. In Wisconsin, Clinton lost by 22,748 votes; *fourth* place finisher Jill Stein had 31,072 votes. In Michigan, Clinton lost by 10,704 votes; *fourth* place finisher Stein collected 51,463 votes. In Pennsylvania, Clinton lost by 44,292 votes; Stein, again in *fourth* place, gained 49,941 votes. Stein, the progressive, Green Party candidate, surely cost Clinton dearly in these states, playing no more than the spoiler.

Hillary Clinton, Meet Al Gore

Like Al Gore in 2000, Hillary Clinton won the popular vote but lost in the Electoral College. Gore won by some 540,000 votes; Clinton won by nearly 2.9 million. Clinton's popular vote was 2.1 percent more than Trump's. In presidential history, only two losing candidates had received a greater percentage of the popular vote than Clinton: Andrew Jackson's 10 percent more than John Quincy Adams (1824) and Samuel Tilden's 3 percent more than Rutherford B. Hayes (1876).[113]

The battleground states, indeed, lived up to their names. And here is where Trump was able to squeak out his victory, particularly in the crucial Midwest. Analyst Nate Cohen reminds us that demography was on Trump's side: "[M]ost of the traditional battleground states are much whiter, less educated and particularly less Hispanic than the rest of the country."[114] Trump set a record in American presidential history by winning seventy-one electoral votes in states that were won by 1.5 percent or less; by contrast, in 2012, just twenty-nine electoral votes were won in these very close contests.

The Electoral College, with its winner-take-all format (except for Nebraska and Maine) amplifies the spread between a winner and loser, often making very

32 Chapter 1: The Election of 2016

close contests appear not so close at all. It is an antiquated, cumbersome method of indirectly electing a president, which may have made some sense in the late eighteenth century, but little sense today. There are many reasons why the Electoral College system should be scrapped, but it would be almost as impossible as asking Wyoming or Delaware to relinquish their equal Senate voting status with populous states like Florida or California. According to the National Archives and Records Administration, there have been more than 700 attempts, all unsuccessful, in Congress to change or abolish the Electoral College, more attempts than any other topic of legislation.[115]

But disparities in the dual system of tallying the score—the plainly evident popular vote and the less evident, but final word, in the Electoral College—has brought about uncertainty, distrust, and disappointment twice in the past five presidential elections. With little hope for an abolishment of the Electoral College system, and only a faint-hearted chance of alternative proposals,[116] perhaps the best we can hope for is an unambiguous win in the popular vote with an equally unambiguous win in the Electoral College.

Game Change, but Not in the House and Senate

So much of the argument for the Trump campaign was to kick the rascals out, to "drain the swamp" of Washington, and a plague on both Democrat and Republican career politicians. If this were simply an anti-Washington cry from the electorate, then hundreds of elected officials, both Democrats and Republicans, should have been quaking in their boots. Democrats were especially hungry to regain the majority in the Senate, and with vulnerable Republican incumbents like Richard M. Burr (North Carolina), Ron Johnson (Wisconsin), Rob Portman (Ohio), John McCain (Arizona), Roy Blunt (Missouri), and Patrick Toomey (Pennsylvania), their chances looked promising. In the end, however, just two Republican incumbents were defeated, Mark S. Kirk (Illinois) and in a very tight race, Kelly Ayotte (New Hampshire).[117] In the House of Representatives, Democrats made modest gains, winning back just five seats from Republicans. In the end, hundreds of millions of dollars were poured into House and Senate contests, with nearly all incumbents emerging victorious. So much for the anti-Washington rhetoric.

There was one final point of departure in this extraordinary presidential election. Every time a candidate and political party loses, loyalists are upset, disappointed that their presidential team did not prevail. That's simply the nature of politics. But what sets 2016 apart are the raw feelings of fear and disappointment: Hispanics fearful of mass deportations, Muslims afraid of retaliations and stoked-up resentments, women afraid that services such as those provided by Planned Parenthood and others will be discontinued, persons of all stripes fearful that hate crimes will soar, and, under the guise of rejecting political correctness, our world will be coarser, and that ideologically and culturally divisions will be exacerbated.

Chapter 1: The Election of 2016 **33**

Longtime Washington participants and those who watch from the outside worry that the norms of political civility will be further strained and that we will enter an Orwellian world where truth doesn't matter, longstanding administrative and governing protocols no longer apply, where the legitimate press will be subsumed by outright lies, hyperbole, and sensationalism, and where our longstanding international rivals now somehow become our new buddies and our closest, reliable partners will be derided and dismissed.

Notes

1 CNN and official sources cited therein, www.cnn.com/2016/11/11/politics/popular-vote-turnout-2016/ (accessed December 2, 2016).
2 Those states (and electoral votes): California (55); Connecticut (7), District of Columbia (3); Delaware (3); Hawaii (4); Illinois (20); Maine (4); Maryland (10); Massachusetts (11); Michigan (16); Minnesota (10); New Jersey (14); New York (29); Oregon (7); Pennsylvania (20); Rhode Island (4); Vermont (3); Washington (12); and Wisconsin (10). National Archives and Records Administration, U.S. Electoral College, "Historical Election Results," [n.d.]; www.archives.gov/federal-register/electoral-college/index.html (accessed October 7, 2016).
3 Those states (and electoral votes): Alabama (9); Alaska (3); Kansas (6); Idaho (4); Mississippi (6); Nebraska (5); North Dakota (3); Oklahoma (7); Texas (38); Utah (6); and Wyoming (3).
4 "The Parties on the Eve of the 2016 Election: Two Coalitions Moving Further Apart," Pew Research Center, September 16, 2016, http://pewrsr.ch/2coxNzZ (accessed October 23, 2016); cited in and elaborated upon by Dan Balz, "As Trump Delivers His Gettysburg Address, Republicans Prepare for a Civil War," *Washington Post*, October 23, 2016, www.washingtonpost.com/politics/as-trump-delivers-his-gettysburg-address-republicans-prepare-for-a-civil-war/2016/10/22/6d2c5d64-987e-11e6-bc79-af1cd3d2984b_story.html?utm_term=.d1ee21d467a7 (accessed December 2, 2016).
5 See Nicole Narea and Alex Shepard, "The Democrats' Biggest Disaster," *New Republic*, November 22, 2016, https://newrepublic.com/article/138897/democrats-biggest-disaster (accessed December 23, 2016).
6 Larry J. Sabato, "Why Parties Should Hope They Lose the White House," *Politico*, December 1, 2014, www.politico.com/magazine/story/2014/12/presidents-bad-for-their-parties-113241#ixzz3Pqkfx2ja (accessed January 2, 2017). The data in this study were provided by Geoffrey Skelley. The analysis also considers "Kennedy–Johnson" and "Nixon–Ford" part of the eight-year presidencies.
7 Aaron Blake, "A Record Number of Americans Now Dislike Hillary Clinton," *Washington Post*, August 31, 2016, www.washingtonpost.com/news/the-fix/wp/2016/08/31/a-record-number-of-americans-now-dislike-hillary-clinton/?utm_term=.889a3fe5b9bd (accessed December 2, 2016).
8 Philip Bump, "Barack Obama Is Now Viewed More Positively Than Ronald Reagan Was in 1988," *Washington Post*, November 7, 2016, www.washingtonpost.com/news/the-fix/wp/2016/11/07/barack-obama-is-now-viewed-more-positively-

34 Chapter 1: The Election of 2016

than-ronald-reagan-was-in-1988/?utm_term=.4224f4963f9f (accessed December 6, 2016).

9 Jonathan Rauch, "How American Politics Went Insane," *The Atlantic*, July/August 2016, www.theatlantic.com/magazine/archive/2016/07/how-american-politics-went-insane/485570/ (accessed December 5, 2016).

10 On the history of political consultants in presidential elections, see Dennis W. Johnson, *Democracy for Hire: A History of American Political Consulting* (New York: Oxford University Press, 2017). See also, Adam Sheingate, *Building a Business of Politics* (New York: Oxford University Press, 2016).

11 Joshua Green, "This Man is the Most Dangerous Political Operative in America," *Bloomberg Businessweek*, October 8, 2015, www.bloomberg.com/politics/graphics/2015-steve-bannon/ (accessed October 3, 2016).

12 For example, Sarah Ellison, "How Jared Kushner Became Donald Trump's Mini-Me," *Vanity Fair*, July 7, 2016, www.vanityfair.com/news/2016/07/jared-kushner-donald-trump-mini-me (accessed January 7, 2017).

13 Philip Bump, "Donald Trump's Campaign Has Spent More on Hats Than Polling," *Washington Post*, October 26, 2016, www.washingtonpost.com/news/the-fix/wp/2016/10/25/donald-trumps-campaign-has-spent-more-on-hats-than-on-polling/?utm_term=.4fe0faf75b9b (accessed December 3, 2016). From FEC data, June 2015 through September 2016.

14 *Citizens United v. Federal Election Commission*, 558 U.S. 310 (2010), www.supremecourt.gov/opinions/09pdf/08-205.pdf; *SpeechNow.org v. Federal Election Commission*, U.S. District Court, District of Columbia (2010), http://fec.gov/law/litigation/speechnow.shtml; *McCutcheon et al. v. Federal Election Commission*, 572 U.S. ___ (2014), www.supremecourt.gov/opinions/13pdf/12-536_elpf.pdf (all accessed December 7, 2016).

15 Daniel Fisher, "Inside the Koch Empire: How the Brothers Plan to Reshape America," *Forbes*, December 5, 2012, www.forbes.com/sites/danielfisher/2012/12/05/inside-the-koch-empire-how-the-brothers-plan-to-reshape-america/#3c71e84930ac (accessed December 2, 2016); on the rise of the Koch Empire, see Daniel Schulman, *Sons of Wichita: How the Koch Brothers Became America's Most Powerful and Private Dynasty* (New York: Grand Central Publishing, 2015).

16 Center for Responsive Politics, Opensecrets.org website, www.opensecrets.org/outsidespending/donor_detail.php?cycle=2016&id=U0000000310&type=I&super=N&name=Adelson%2C+Sheldon+G.+%26+Miriam+O (accessed December 5, 2016). Leading the pack of individual donors was Thomas F. Steyer, who gave more than $86 million, chiefly through his Super PAC, NextGen Climate Action, supporting Democratic candidates.

17 Nicholas Confessore, Sara Cohen, and Karen Yourish, "The Families Funding the 2016 Presidential Election," *New York Times*, October 10, 2015, www.nytimes.com/interactive/2015/10/11/us/politics/2016-presidential-election-super-pac-donors.html (accessed December 6, 2016).

18 See Molly Ball, "'There's Nothing Better than a Scared, Rich Candidate: How Political Consulting Works—Or Doesn't," *The Atlantic*, October 2016, 54–63, www.theatlantic.com/magazine/archive/2016/10/theres-nothing-better-than-a-

Chapter 1: The Election of 2016 **35**

scared-rich-candidate/497522/ (accessed December 4, 2017). Data based on reports from Federal Election Commission and Center for Responsive Politics.

19 Nicholas Confessore and Karen Yourish, "$2 Billion Worth of Free Media for Trump," *New York Times*, March 15, 2016, www.nytimes.com/2016/03/16/upshot/measuring-donald-trumps-mammoth-advantage-in-free-media.html?_r=0 (accessed December 5, 2016).

20 Citizens for Responsive Politics, "Bernie Sanders," www.opensecrets.org/pres16/donordemcid?id=N00000528 (accessed December 5, 2016).

21 In 1984, New York representative Geraldine Ferraro was the Democratic candidate for vice president; in 2008, Alaska governor Sarah H. Palin was the Republican candidate for vice president.

22 "Female World Leaders Currently in Power," [n.d.], www.jjmcullough.com (accessed October 2, 2016); data from www.rulers.org and www.worldstatesmen. org. Past leaders have included Benazir Bhutto (Pakistan, 1998–1990, 1993–1996), Corazon Aquino (Philippines, 1986–1992), Margaret Thatcher (United Kingdom, 1979–1990), Indira Gandhi (India, 1966–1974, 1980–1984); and Golda Meier (Israel, 1969–1974).

23 Obama quoted in David Remnick, "Obama Reckons With a Trump Presidency, Inside a Stunned White House, the President Considers His Legacy and America's Future," *The New Yorker*, November 26, 2016, www.newyorker.com/magazine/2016/11/28/obama-reckons-with-a-trump-presidency (accessed December 12, 2016).

24 Jasmine Lee and Kevin Quealy, "The 281 People, Places, and Things Donald Trump Has Insulted on Twitter: A Complete List," *New York Times*, updated October 23, 2016, http://nyti.ms/23wGzj1 (accessed October 24, 2016).

25 Clip from third debate, posted October 19, 2016, YouTube, www.youtube.com/watch?v=9B7KPRo30y4 (accessed December 2, 2016).

26 Jeffrey M. Jones, "Clinton Most Admired Woman for Record 20th Time," Gallup Poll, December 28, 2015 (www.gallup.com/poll/187922/clinton-admired-woman-record-20th-time.aspx?utm_source=genericbutton&utm_medium=organic&utm_campaign=sharing (accessed September 14, 2016).

27 See Mark Mellman, "Of Emails and Image," *The Hill*, December 6, 2016, http://thehill.com/opinion/opinion/309108-mellman-of-emails-and-image (accessed December 8, 2016).

28 George Will, "Donald Trump is the GOP's Chemotherapy," *Washington Post*, October 10, 2016.

29 Ibid.

30 Charles Krauthammer, "It's Not the 'Locker Room' Talk. It's the 'Lock Her Up' Talk," *Washington Post*, October 14, 2016, www.washingtonpost.com/opinions/its-not-the-locker-room-talk-its-the-lock-her-up-talk/2016/10/13/9dd5fbea-9172-11e6-9c85-ac42097b8cc0_story.html?utm_term=.9ce29cf54a55 (accessed December 4, 2016).

31 Robert Draper, "How Donald Trump Set Off a Civil War Within the Right Wing Media," *New York Times*, September 29, 2016, www.nytimes.com/2016/10/02/magazine/how-donald-trump-set-off-a-civil-war-within-the-right-wing-media.html?_r=0 (accessed December 4, 2016).

36 Chapter 1: The Election of 2016

32 Transcript of Romney speech, *Deseret News*, March 3, 2016, www.deseret news.com/article/865649168/Romney-Trump-is-a-phony-a-fraud.html (accessed December 5, 2016).

33 "Statement by Former Ambassadors and Senior State Department Officials," September 21, 2016, linked to report by Karen DeYoung, "75 Retired Senior Diplomats Sign Letter Opposing Trump for President," *Washington Post*, September 22, 2016, www.washingtonpost.com/world/national-security/75-retired-senior-diplomats-sign-letter-opposing-trump-for-president/2016/09/21/5c5dff10-8046-11e6-b002-307601806392_story.html?utm_term=.a1faf786128c (accessed December 5, 2016). Earlier in September, eighty-eight retired generals and admirals signed a letter in support of Donald Trump, and "his commitment to rebuild our military, to secure our borders, to defeat our Islamic supremacist adversaries and restore law and order domestically," "Open Letter from Military Leaders," https://assets.donaldjtrump.com/MILITARY_LETTER.pdf (accessed September 22, 2016).

34 "The Case for Hillary Clinton—And Against Donald Trump," *The Atlantic*, November 2016, 12–13, www.theatlantic.com/magazine/archive/2016/11/the-case-for-hillary-clinton-and-against-donald-trump/501161/ (accessed December 7, 2016).

35 "We Recommend Hillary Clinton for President," *Dallas Morning News*, September 7, 2016, www.dallasnews.com/opinion/editorials/2016/09/07/recommend-hillary-clinton-us-president; "It Has to be Hillary Clinton for President," *Cincinnati Enquirer*, September 23, 2016, http://cin.ci/2d65xUr (accessed October 25, 2016).

36 Michelle Obama remarks, October 12, 2016, YouTube, https://youtu.be/JtBR_JE02rc (accessed October 14, 2016).

37 In 1960, Democrats used Eisenhower's own words to cast doubt on Nixon's abilities. At a news conference, Eisenhower was asked what major ideas Nixon had contributed during Ike's presidency. The glib and damning answer from Eisenhower was, "If you give me a week I might think of one. I don't remember." This became the centerpiece of an ad against Nixon, called "Nixon's Experience?" As a rebuttal, the Republicans produced an ad featuring Eisenhower explaining that Nixon was the best qualified candidate to follow him to the White House. See Johnson, *Democracy for Hire*, 78–79.

38 Steven V. Roberts, "Reagan Endorses Bush as Successor," *New York Times*, May 12, 1988, www.nytimes.com/1988/05/12/us/reagan-endorses-bush-as-successor.html (accessed December 5, 2016).

39 As Melissa Henneberger and Don Van Atta, Jr. wrote,

> Mr. Gore won't pick up the phone. He doesn't call, and Mr. Clinton doesn't know why … Mr. Clinton is both hurt by the personal rebuff and bewildered as to why his political heir won't come to him for advice he is itching to give.

Henneberger and Van Atta, Jr., "Once Close to Clinton, Gore Keeps a Distance," *New York Times*, October 20, 2000, www.nytimes.com/2000/10/20/us/once-close-to-clinton-gore-keeps-a-distance.html (accessed December 5, 2016).

40 Michael D. Shear and Michael Abramowitz, "Bush and McCain Stress Their Unity, and So Do Democrats," *Washington Post*, March 6, 2008, www.washingtonpost.com/wp-dyn/content/article/2008/03/05/AR2008030503067.html (accessed December 4, 2016).

Chapter 1: The Election of 2016 **37**

41 Domenico Montanaro, "Why President Obama Campaigning for Clinton is Historic," *NPR*, July 5, 2016, www.npr.org/2016/07/05/484817706/looking-back-at-a-century-of-presidents-not-campaigning-for-their-successor (accessed December 5, 2016).

42 Excerpts from President Obama's speech at Democratic National Convention, July 27, 2016, on YouTube, www.youtube.com/watch?v=7w5x0NiUtOg (accessed December 5, 2016).

43 Jonathan Martin, "Donald Trump's Heated Barrage Has Little Precedent," *New York Times*, October 15, 2016, www.nytimes.com/2016/10/15/us/politics/trump-speech-highlights.html?_r=0 (accessed December 24, 2016).

44 See, for example, Karen Tumulty and Philip Rucker, "At Third Debate, Trump Won't Commit to Election Results if He Loses," *Washington Post*, October 19, 2016, www.washingtonpost.com/politics/trump-wont-commit-to-accepting-election-results-if-he-loses/2016/10/19/9c9672e6-9609-11e6-bc79-af1cd3d2984b_story.html?utm_term=.362c7a705a3c (accessed December 23, 2016).

45 570 U.S. ___ (2013); online version, www.supremecourt.gov/opinions/12pdf/12-96_6k47.pdf (accessed December 5, 2016).

46 Jeffrey Toobin, "The Real Voting Scandal of 2016," *The New Yorker*, December 12, 2016.

47 *North Carolina State Conference of the NAACP et al. v. McCrory et al.*, opinion written by Judge Diana Gribbon Motz, http://pdfserver.amlaw.com/nlj/7-29-16%20 4th%20Circuit%20NAACP%20v%20NC.pdf (accessed December 5, 2016).

48 Toobin, "The Real Voting Scandal of 2016."

49 Tim Hains, "Paul Manafort on the Election: 'This is the Ultimate Reality Show'," *RealClear Politics*, May 12, 2016, www.realclearpolitics.com/video/2016/05/12/paul_manafort_on_the_election_this_is_the_ultimate_reality_show.html (accessed December 4, 2016).

50 Josh Dawsey, "Michael Bloomberg Calls Donald Trump a 'Dangerous Demagogue'," *Wall Street Journal*, July 27, 2016, www.wsj.com/articles/michael-bloomberg-to-woo-independents-in-convention-address-1469647760 (accessed January 2, 2017).

51 Thomas E. Patterson, *Out of Order* (New York: Vintage, 1994), 27.

52 Art Swift, "American's Trust in Mass Media Sinks to a New Low," Gallup, September 14, 2016, www.gallup.com/poll/195542/americans-trust-mass-media-sinks-new-low.aspx (accessed December 4, 2016).

53 Patterson, *Out of Order*, 27.

54 Trump quoted in John Cassidy, "The Election May Be Over, but Trump's Blowup Is Just Starting," *The New Yorker*, October 13, 2016.

55 Kalev H. Leetaru, "The 2016 Candidates Who Are Making the Headlines," *The Atlantic*, August 28, 2015, www.theatlantic.com/politics/archive/2015/08/graphic-whos-the-most-popular-candidate-mentioned-on-television/402451/ (accessed October 23, 2016). Analysis covered Aljazeera America, Bloomberg, CNBC, CNN, Comedy Central, Fox Business, Fox News, LinkTV, MSNBC and a set of affiliates across the country. Data came from GDELT (Global Database of Events, Language, and Tone), which captures data from throughout the world, and its co-creator was Kalev Leetaru. GDELT describes itself as

38 Chapter 1: The Election of 2016

> an initiative to construct a catalog of human societal-scale behavior and beliefs across all countries of the world, connecting every person, organization, location, count, theme, news source, and event across the planet into a single massive network that captures what's happening around the world, what its context is and who's involved, and how the world is feeling about it, every single day.

56 "2016 Television Campaign Tracker," http://television.gdeltproject.org/cgi-bin/iatv_campaign2016/iatv_campaign2016 (accessed October 23, 2016).

57 Paul Bond, "Leslie Moonves on Donald Trump: 'It May Not Be Good for America, but It's Damn Good for CBS," *The Hollywood Reporter*, February 29, 2016, www.hollywoodreporter.com/news/leslie-moonves-donald-trump-may-871464 (accessed January 2, 2017).

58 Nicholas Kristoff, "How to Cover a Charlatan Like Trump," *New York Times*, September 25, 2016, www.nytimes.com/2016/09/25/opinion/sunday/how-to-cover-a-charlatan-like-trump.html (accessed October 2, 2016).

59 On the history of the creation of Twitter, see Nicholas Carlson, "The Real History of Twitter," *Business Insider*, April 13, 2011, www.businessinsider.com/how-twitter-was-founded-2011-4 (accessed December 4, 2016).

60 Philip Elmer-DeWitt, "Trump, Apple, and the Overton Window," *Fortune*, May 7, 2016, http://fortune.com/2016/03/07/trump-apple-overton-window/ (accessed January 3, 2017).

61 David French, "For Good and Ill, Donald Trump Has Brought Discussion of Political Impossibilities into the Open," *National Review*, December 8, 2015, www.nationalreview.com/article/428200/donald-trump-overton-window-american-political-debate (accessed January 2, 2017).

62 Hillary Clinton for America, www.hillaryclinton.com/ (accessed November 2, 2016).

63 Tyndall Report, www.tyndallreport.com, accessed December 23, 2016. The Tyndall Report monitors the three nightly network broadcasts, *ABC World News* with David Muir, *CBS Evening News* with Scott Pelley, and *NBC Nightly News* with Lester Holt. See, also, Nicholas Kristof, "Lessons From the Media's Failure in Its Year With Trump," *New York Times*, December 31, 2016, www.nytimes.com/2016/12/31/opinion/sunday/lessons-from-the-medias-failures-in-its-year-with-trump.html?emc=eta1 (accessed January 2, 2016).

64 Ibid.

65 "Word of the Year 2016," Oxford Dictionaries, November 8, 2016, https://en.oxforddictionaries.com/word-of-the-year/word-of-the-year-2016 (accessed December 5, 2016).

66 See, for example, Herbert J. Gans, *Deciding What's News: A Study of CBS News, NBC Nightly News, Newsweek, and Time*, Twenty-fifth Anniversary edition (Evanston, IL: Northwestern University Press, 2004).

67 Jeffrey Gottfried, Michael Barthel, Elisa Shearer, and Amy Mitchell, "The 2016 Presidential Campaign—A News Event That's Hard to Miss," *Pew Research Center*, February 4, 2016, www.journalism.org/2016/02/04/the-2016-presidential-campaign-a-news-event-thats-hard-to-miss/ (accessed January 16, 2017).

68 Jonathan Mahler, "The Problem with 'Self-Investigation' in a Post-Truth Era," *New York Times*, December 27, 2016, www.nytimes.com/2016/12/27/magazine/

Chapter 1: The Election of 2016 **39**

the-problem-with-self-investigation-in-a-post-truth-era.html (accessed December 28, 2016).

69 Susan Jacoby, *The Age of American Unreason* (New York: Vintage, 2009), xi.

70 Jacob Soll, "The Long and Brutal History of Fake News," *Politico*, December 18, 2016, www.politico.com/magazine/story/2016/12/fake-news-history-long-violent-214535 (accessed January 3, 2017).

71 Jackie Calmes, "Obama Team Sharpens Attacks on Rival's Character," *New York Times*, August 30, 2012, www.nytimes.com/2012/08/31/us/politics/obama-moves-to-speak-on-romneys-character.html (accessed December 8, 2016).

72 Dan Evon, "Nope Francis," www.snopes.com (accessed December 5, 2016). Snopes is a website that tracks down online rumors.

73 Greg Sargent, "REVEALED: The Vast International Conspiracy to Stop Trump, in One Chart," *Washington Post*, October 18, 2016, www.washingtonpost.com/blogs/plum-line/wp/2016/10/17/revealed-the-vast-international-conspiracy-to-stop-trump-in-one-chart/?utm_term=.cbc38bcbd405 (December 1, 2016).

74 Faiz Siddiqui and Susan Svrluga, "N.C. Man Told Police He Went to D.C. Pizzeria With Gun to Investigate Conspiracy Theory," *Washington Post*, December 5, 2016, www.washingtonpost.com/news/local/wp/2016/12/04/d-c-police-respond-to-report-of-a-man-with-a-gun-at-comet-ping-pong-restaurant/?utm_term=.3901caa117dd; Eric Lipton, "Man Motivated by 'Pizzagate' Conspiracy Theory Arrested in Washington Gunfire," *New York Times*, December 5, 2016, www.nytimes.com/2016/12/05/us/pizzagate-comet-ping-pong-edgar-maddison-welch.html; Cecilia Kang, "Fake News Onslaught Targets Pizzeria as Nest of Child-Trafficking," *New York Times*, November 21, 2016, www.nytimes.com/2016/11/21/technology/fact-check-this-pizzeria-is-not-a-child-trafficking-site.html (all accessed December 6, 2016).

75 Matthew Rosenberg, "Trump Adviser Has Pushed Clinton Conspiracies," *New York Times*, December 5, 2016, www.nytimes.com/2016/12/05/us/politics/-michael-flynn-trump-fake-news-clinton.html?_r=0 (accessed December 8, 2016).

76 Rosenberg, "Trump Adviser Has Pushed Clinton Conspiracies."

77 Craig Silverman and Lawrence Alexander, "How Teens in the Balkans are Duping Trump Supporters with Fake News," BuzzfeedNews, November 3, 2016, www.buzzfeed.com/craigsilverman/how-macedonia-became-a-global-hub-for-trump-misinfo?utm_term=.cdNAPXArW#.dhmkvnk9d; "How Facebook Powers Money Machines for Obscure Political 'News' Sites," *The Guardian*, August 24, 2016, www.theguardian.com/technology/2016/aug/24/facebook-clickbait-political-news-sites-us-election-trump; Alexander Smith and Vladimir Banic, "Fake News: How a Partying Macedonian Teen Earns Thousands Publishing Lies," NBC News, December 9, 2016, www.nbcnews.com/news/world/fake-news-how-partying-macedonian-teen-earns-thousands-publishing-lies-n692451?utm_source=taboola (all accessed December 12, 2016).

78 "How Facebook Powers Money Machines for Obscure Political 'News' Sites."

79 Gary King, Jennifer Pan, and Margaret E. Roberts, "How the Chinese Government Fabricates Social Media Posts for Strategic Distraction, Not Engaged Argument," August 26, 2016, p. 3, http://gking.harvard.edu/files/gking/files/50c.pdf?m=1463587807 (accessed December 14, 2016). See also, Henry Farrell, "The Chinese

40 Chapter 1: The Election of 2016

Government Fakes Nearly 450 Million Social Media Comments a Year. This Is Why," *Washington Post*, Monkey Cage blog, May 19, 2016, www.washingtonpost. com/news/monkey-cage/wp/2016/05/19/the-chinese-government-fakes-nearly-450-million-social-media-comments-a-year-this-is-why/?utm_term=.68d65d8355b6 (accessed December 14, 2016).

80 Farhad Manjoo, "Social Media's Globe-Shaking Power," *New York Times*, November 16, 2016, https://nytimes.com/2016/11/17/technology/social-medias-globe-shaking-power.html?emc=eta1 (accessed January 13, 2017).

81 Adam Entous, Ellen Nakashima, and Greg Miller, "Secret CIA Assessment Says Russia Was Trying to Help Trump Win White House," *Washington Post*, December 9, 2016, www.washingtonpost.com/world/national-security/obama-orders-review-of-russian-hacking-during-presidential-campaign/2016/12/09/31d6b300-be2a-11e6-94ac-3d324840106c_story.html?utm_term=.b64c7fd9fb26 (accessed January 2, 2017).

82 U.S. Department of Homeland Security and Federal Bureau of Investigation, Joint Analysis Report, "GRZZLY STEPPE—Russian Malicious Cyber Activity," December 29, 2016, https://assets.documentcloud.org/documents/3248231/Report-on-Russian-Hacking.pdf (accessed January 2, 2016). A unclassified report was prepared for distribution on January 6, 2017: *Background to Assessing "Russian Activities and Intentions in Recent U.S. Elections": The Analytic Process and Cyber Incident Attribution*, Office of the Director of National Intelligence, National Intelligence Council, January 6, 2017, https://assets.documentcloud.org/documents/3254237/Russia-Hack-Report.pdf (accessed January 9, 2017). For background on Russia cyberspace hacking in the U.S., see Eric Lipton, Davide E. Sanger, and Scott Shane, "The Perfect Weapon: How Russian Cyberpower Invaded the U.S.," *New York Times*, December 13, 2016, www.nytimes.com/2016/12/13/us/politics/russia-hack-election-dnc.html (accessed December 18, 2016).

83 Joel B. Pollak, "10 Ways the CIA's 'Russia Hacking' Story is Left-Wing 'Fake News'," Breitbart.com, December 12, 2016, www.breitbart.com/big-government/2016/12/12/cia-russian-hacking-story-sham/ (accessed January 2, 2016).

84 "Donald Trump's News Conference: Full Transcript and Video," *New York Times*, January 11, 2017, www.nytimes.com/2017/01/11/us/politics/trump-press-conference-transcript.html?_r=0 (accessed January 13, 2017).

85 Jim Tankersley, "How Trump Won: The Revenge of Working-Class Whites," *Washington Post*, November 9, 2016, www.washingtonpost.com/news/wonk/wp/2016/11/09/how-trump-won-the-revenge-of-working-class-whites/?utm_term=.86a4ea4ae2a9 (accessed December 7, 2016).

86 Stanley B. Greenberg, *Middle Class Dreams: Politics and Power of the New American Majority* (New York: Times Books, 1996).

87 Susan J. Tolchin, *The Angry American: How Voter Rage Is Changing the Nation* (Boulder, CO: Westview Press, 1992).

88 E.J. Dionne, Jr., *Why Americans Hate Politics* (New York: Simon and Schuster, 1992).

89 George Packer, *The Unwinding: An Inner History of the New America* (New York: Farrar, Straus, and Giroux, 2014); Thomas Frank, *What's the Matter with Kansas: How Conservatives Won the Heart of America* (New York: Holt, 2005); Thomas Frank,

Chapter 1: The Election of 2016 **41**

Listen, Liberal: Or, Whatever Happened to the Party of the People? (New York: Metropolitan Books, 2016); Catherine J. Cramer, *The Politics of Resentment: Rural Consciousness in Wisconsin and the Rise of Scott Walker* (Chicago: University of Chicago Press, 2016), 2.

90 Theda Skocpol and Vanessa Williamson, *The Tea Party and the Remaking of Republican Conservatism* (New York: Oxford University Press, 2013); J.D. Vance, *Hillbilly Elegy: A Memory of a Family and Culture in Crisis* (New York: Harper, 2016); Nicholas Eberstadt, *Men Without Work: America's Invisible Crisis* (West Conshohocken, PA: Templeton Press, 2016).

91 "The Fading American Dream," Equality of Opportunity Project, www.equality-of-opportunity.org (accessed December 12, 2016).

92 Ibid. See also, David Leonhardt, "The American Dream, Quantified at Last," *New York Times*, December 8, 2016, www.nytimes.com/2016/12/08/opinion/the-american-dream-quantified-at-last.html (accessed December 17, 2016).

93 Shannon M. Monnat, "Deaths of Despair and Support for Trump in the 2016 Presidential Election," Penn State University, Department of Agricultural Economics, Sociology, and Education, Research Brief 12/04/16, www.aese.psu.edu/directory/smm67/Election16.pdf (accessed December 12, 2016). See also, James Hohmann, "Trump Over Performed the Most in Counties with the Highest Drug, Alcohol and Suicide Mortality," *Washington Post*, December 9, 2016, www.washingtonpost.com/news/powerpost/paloma/daily-202/2016/12/09/daily-202-trump-over-performed-the-most-in-counties-with-the-highest-drug-alcohol-and-suicide-mortality-rates/584a2a59e9b69b7e58e45f2e/?utm_term=.9f4b2446c54a (accessed December 21, 2016).

94 John Sides and Michael Tesler, "How Political Science Helps Explain the Rise of Trump: Most Voters are Not Ideologues," *Washington Post*, Monkey Cage blog, March 2, 2016, www.washingtonpost.com/news/monkey-cage/wp/2016/03/02/how-political-science-helps-explain-the-rise-of-trump-most-voters-arent-ideologues/?tid=a_inl&utm_term=.cfe8f777fc04 (accessed December 2, 2016).

95 Philip E. Converse, "The Nature of Belief Systems in Mass Publics," *Critical Review* 18 (1) (1964), http://dx.doi.org/10.1080/08913810608443650 (accessed January 5, 2017).

96 Salena Zito, "Taking Trump Seriously, Not Literally," *The Atlantic*, September 23, 2016; www.theatlantic.com/politics/archive/2016/09/trump-makes-his-case-in-pittsburgh/501335/ (accessed December 12, 2016).

97 "Endorsement: Hillary Clinton is the Only Choice to Move America Ahead," *Arizona Republic*, October 16, 2016, http://azc.cc/2diKeew (accessed October 25, 2016). The newspaper and its employees were later subject to numerous death threats.

98 Sarah Posner, "How Donald Trump's New Campaign Chief Created an Online Haven for White Nationalists," *Mother Jones*, August 22, 2016, www.motherjones.com/politics/2016/08/stephen-bannon-donald-trump-alt-right-breitbart-news (accessed January 5, 2017).

99 Maureen B. Costello, "The Trump Effect: The Impact of the Presidential Campaign on our Nation's Schools," Southern Poverty Law Center, [n.d.], www.splcenter.org/sites/default/files/splc_the_trump_effect.pdf. "Update: More Than 400

42 Chapter 1: The Election of 2016

Incidents of Hateful Harassment and Intimidation Since Election," Southern Poverty Law Center, November 15, 2016, www.splcenter.org/hatewatch/2016/11/15/update-more-400-incidents-hateful-harassment-and-intimidation-election (both accessed January 4, 2017).

100 Aaron Blake, "Voters Strongly Reject Hillary Clinton's 'Basket of Deplorables' Approach," *Washington Post*, September 26, 2016, www.washingtonpost.com/news/the-fix/wp/2016/09/26/voters-strongly-reject-hillary-clintons-basket-of-deplorables-approach/?utm_term=.c42d3cdcba80 (accessed December 1, 2016).

101 John R. Hibbing and Elizabeth Theiss-Morse, "A Surprising Number of Americans Dislike How Messy Democracy Is. They Like Trump," *Washington Post*, Monkey Cage blog, May 2, 2016, www.washingtonpost.com/news/monkey-cage/wp/2016/05/02/a-surprising-number-of-americans-dislike-how-messy-democracy-is-they-like-trump/?utm_term=.d1857fc5a59d (accessed December 4, 2016). Hibbing and Theiss-Morse wrote a seminal book on public attitudes and governance, *Stealth Democracy: Americans' Beliefs About How American Government Should Work* (Cambridge: Cambridge University Press, 2002).

102 Hibbing and Theiss-Morse, "A Surprising Number of Americans Dislike How Messy Democracy Is."

103 Donald Trump with Tony Schwartz, *Trump: The Art of the Deal* (New York: Random House, 1987), 58.

104 See Johnson, *Democracy for Hire*, 46–47.

105 James E. Campbell, ed., "Forecasting the 2016 American National Elections," *PS* (49) (October 2016), 649–654, doi: 10.1017/S1049096516001591.

106 Helmut Norpoth, "Primary Model Predicts Trump Victory," *PS* 49 (4) (October 2016), 655–658, doi: 10.1017/S1049096516001323.

107 On criticism of this sort of predicting, political philosophy professor Jason Blakely writes "Is Political Science This Year's Election Casualty," *The Atlantic*, November 14, 2016, www.theatlantic.com/education/archive/2016/11/is-political-science-another-election-casualty/507515/; a rejoinder comes from professor of international relations Daniel W. Drezner, "Why Political Science Is Not an Election Casualty," *Washington Post*, November 15, 2016, www.washingtonpost.com/posteverything/wp/2016/11/15/why-political-science-is-not-an-election-casualty/?utm_term=.5d49bdb20a00; historian Allan J. Lichtman, author of *Predicting the Next President: Keys to the White House 2016* (Lanham, MD: Rowman, Littlefield, 2016) has correctly predicted the presidential election during the past thirty years, including this one. See Peter W. Stevenson, "Professor Who Predicted Thirty Years of Presidential Elections Correctly Called a Trump Win in September," *Washington Post*, November 9, 2016, www.washingtonpost.com/news/the-fix/wp/2016/10/28/professor-whos-predicted-30-years-of-presidential-elections-correctly-is-doubling-down-on-a-trump-win/?utm_term=.117a7ff30086 (all accessed January 6, 2017).

108 Michael Moore, "Five Reasons Why Trump Will Win," MichaelMoore.com, July 2016, http://michaelmoore.com/trumpwillwin/ (accessed January 7, 2017); Moore, in a speech at Murphy Theatre, Wilmington, Ohio, October 24, 2016, featured in his movie, "Michael Moore in Trumpland," www.youtube.com/watch?v=YKeYbEOSqYc (accessed January 7, 2017).

Chapter 1: The Election of 2016 **43**

109 Bill Bishop, *The Big Sort: Why the Clustering of Like-Minded America Is Tearing Us Apart* (New York: Mariner Books, 2009), 6.

110 Helena Bottemiller Evich, "Revenge of the Rural Voter," *Politico*, November 13, 2016, www.politico.com/story/2016/11/hillary-clinton-rural-voters-trump-231266 (accessed January 16, 2017).

111 Stanley B. Greenberg, "Goodbye, Reagan Democrats," *New York Times*, November 11, 2008, www.nytimes.com/2008/11/11/opinion/11greenberg.html (accessed January 3, 2017).

112 Nicholas Confessore and Nate Cohen, "Donald Trump's Victory Was Built on a Unique Coalition of White Voters," *New York Times*, November 9, 2016, www.nytimes.com/2016/11/10/us/politics/donald-trump-voters.html (accessed January 4, 2017).

113 David Leip, "Atlas of U.S. Presidential Elections," http://uselectionatlas.org/2016.php (accessed January 3, 2017).

114 Nate Cohen, "Why Trump Had an Edge in the Electoral College," *New York Times*, December 19, 2016, www.nytimes.com/2016/12/19/upshot/why-trump-had-an-edge-in-the-electoral-college.html?emc=eta1 (accessed January 12, 2017).

115 "U.S. Electoral College," National Archives and Records Administration, www.archives.gov/federal-register/electoral-college/faq.html#changes (accessed January 6, 2017).

116 See, for example, the National Popular Vote Interstate Compact, www.nationalpopularvote.com, and FairVote, www.fairvote.org/.

117 Emily Cahn, "Ten Most Vulnerable Senators," *Roll Call*, November 6, 2015, www.rollcall.com/news/home/10-vulnerable-senators-2016 (accessed December 23, 2016).

PART I
The Primaries

2

THE DEMOCRATIC PRIMARIES

Lilly J. Goren

On April 12, 2015, via YouTube video, former Secretary of State Hillary Rodham Clinton announced, for the second time, her candidacy for the Democratic presidential nomination. In January of 2007, Hillary Clinton, the junior senator from New York, entered the race for the Democratic nomination for president with a video announcement on her website.[1] In the 2008 race, "Clinton was already under attack for an attitude of 'inevitability'—the charge being that she imperiously viewed the primary process as a ratifying formality and would not deign to compete for what she felt she was owed."[2] And while she was immediately the frontrunner for the 2008 Democratic nomination, she ultimately lost her bid for that nomination after a long and complicated primary battle to the initially less well known first term senator from Illinois, Barack Obama, who went on to win not only the Democratic nomination but also the general election and to win re-election in 2012. The 2008 Clinton campaign was criticized, internally and externally, for a variety of problems throughout the primary campaign, from listening to the wrong advisors, to spending too much money in the wrong places, and, ultimately, because Clinton was not successful in her bid, there were quite a few critiques of the entirety of the campaign. While not the first female candidate to run for a major party nomination, Senator Clinton was the first to get as close as she did in 2008, and, subsequently, to win the Democratic Party's nomination in 2016 for president.[3]

While Secretary Clinton's achievements in 2016—both in terms of her success in her nomination as the Democratic candidate for president, and in her popular vote total in the general election—are historic, especially for a female candidate, her campaign for the nomination in 2016 was also a clear attempt to not make the same mistakes that had been made during the 2008 campaign for the nomination.[4] Clinton's experience in 2008 and since then, as Secretary of State

48 Part I: The Primaries

in the Obama administration, as a private citizen after she left the administration, and in drawing on analyses of her husband, Bill Clinton's, campaign and electoral success and on the success of Barack Obama in his two bids for the White House, all contributed to the kind of campaign and race she ran for the Democratic nomination. At the same time, there were decidedly unanticipated aspects of the electoral dynamic in 2016 that contributed to the way the race unfolded and how it was consumed by voters and citizens, and covered by the media.

Initially when Clinton ran against Obama and John Edwards, both younger candidates who appealed to younger voters and who, in 2008, maximized use at the time of social media and contemporary technology, Clinton's campaign was seen as older, coming from the "Establishment" wing of the party, appealing to older voters through more traditional communication mechanisms. Clinton's campaign also had more money, early on, to spend on television advertising and traditional media approaches. In 2016, Clinton approached the campaign, on some level, more ready and willing to embrace her age, gender, and grandmother status than she had been eight years earlier.[5] She also had more substantial experience on which to run for president, having served for four years as Secretary of State. Thus, in 2015, when Clinton announced her intentions to run for the Democratic nomination *again*, she came to the campaign with not only the experiences she herself had had running for the nomination in 2008, but she also came with a resume that distinguished her as a candidate with unique and traditionally important preparations for the office, including state-wide elected experience as a senator from New York, executive branch experience as Secretary of State, her time as First Lady of the United States and of Arkansas, and as a member of the staff for the House Committee on the Judiciary during the Watergate proceeding.[6] Clinton had also spent time working as a lawyer in Massachusetts and in Arkansas early in her career, where she specifically worked on children's advocacy issues.

The Hillary Primary: The Beginning

In 2015, Clinton entered the race as the candidate to beat for the Democratic nomination. She had similarly entered the race as the frontrunner in 2008, but in 2015, her campaign attempted to downplay this frontrunner status while still making an effort to "clear the field" for a clean and quick path to the nomination. This hoped-for quick and clear path to the nomination was not to be, but unlike in 2008, Clinton's chief rival was the gray-haired, cantankerous junior senator from Vermont, Bernie Sanders, instead of the sleek, cosmopolitan junior senator from Illinois. Around the same time that Clinton made her well-crafted announcement that she was pursuing the Democratic nomination, Senator Sanders indicated that he, too, was going to pursue the Democratic nomination for president, officially announcing his run in May, 2015. Sanders was not the candidate that the Clinton campaign had necessarily prepared to run against in

Chapter 2: The Democratic Primaries **49**

the primary—it had anticipated that Maryland governor Martin O'Malley would likely be the stiffest competition once Vice President Joe Biden decided not to enter the race. This, too, parallels the 2008 campaign when the Clinton campaign had prepared more extensively to run against North Carolina's former one-term senator and John Kerry's vice presidential running mate, John Edwards, and instead found themselves battling for the nomination against Barack Obama.

In an effort not to relive the nomination defeat of 2008, the Clinton campaign paid attention to Sanders early on, and continued to pay attention to his candidacy as it started to gain ground in the summer and fall of 2015. While Sanders was older than Clinton, at 73 when he entered the race for the nomination, and had held more elected offices for longer periods of time than she had, he came to the race as a political Independent, and as an outsider candidate. Sander's appeal overlapped in significant ways with Obama's appeal within the Democratic primary electorate—hitting on populist themes, drawing bigger and bigger crowds, and raising significant amounts of money from smaller donors. This contrasted with Clinton's campaign, which had a plethora of detailed policy plans on the campaign website from the very beginning, but had a harder time distilling a simple campaign message beyond the slogan "I'm with Her." Ultimately, the Clinton campaign focused on the theme "Stronger Together" which reflected not only Clinton's long-standing commitment to inclusion and to the ideals of the Democratic Party, but also to reflect on her own patriotism, and would come to echo her stump speech and her acceptance speech at the nominating convention.

Getting Ready for the Primaries

Office space was leased in early April of 2015 in Brooklyn, New York, days before Clinton made her formal announcement on YouTube.[7] While candidates do spend much of the pre-primary period in states like Iowa, New Hampshire, and South Carolina, doing a lot of what is known as "retail politics and campaigning," meeting voters in diners, and in the homes of their local supporters, locating the headquarters closer to the Clintons' home in Chappaqua, New York made a lot of sense for Clinton and her team, many of whom had New York connections and roots. Clinton also hoped to maximize on the appeal of having the campaign headquarters in Brooklyn, which is often considered the epicenter of progressive, hipster culture, and to signal to younger voters that Clinton and her campaign were in sync with "Brooklyn sensibilities."

The Clinton campaign also started with a significant advantage—not only had Clinton run for a presidential nomination before, she also had some wealthy and politically engaged supporters—and was able to begin her quest for the 2016 nomination with a myriad of fundraiser events and donors who had either supported her or President Obama in the previous election cycles. Thus, when the first fundraising totals came out after the start of Clinton's campaign, she had

50 Part I: The Primaries

raised over $45 million. The campaign explained that the majority of those donations were made at the $100 mark, or less.[8] This became a point of contention during the Democratic primary in 2015 and 2016, as Senator Sanders, whose campaign themes centered on income inequality and economic fairness, made much out of the small size of most of his donations ($27 is the often-cited average donation to the Sanders campaign). Clinton was hoping, upon her entry into the campaign and with her strong fundraising capacity (at least as anticipated), that she would face a greatly reduced field of challengers and, ultimately, the quick dispatch of those challengers when they couldn't raise sufficient funds to remain in the race and compete in the various "super Tuesdays."

The Competition

Many candidates can start the race with limited resources and make it through a contest or two at the beginning without huge amounts of cash on hand, but the pressures that come with competing in multiple states—setting up field offices, buying airtime, hiring staff, and recruiting volunteers—in various parts of the country all on the same day often leads to candidate departures from the field.[9] Thus the time prior to the initial votes being cast in New Hampshire, or the caucuses in Iowa, is often considered the "invisible primary" and is important in terms of fundraising and campaign capacity. Clinton tried to imitate some of the success that Governor George W. Bush had during the invisible primary in 1999, when he mostly "cleared the field" of competition, save for John McCain's Straight Talk Express, because Bush entered the race with a substantial campaign war chest that kept most other potential contenders from entering the field. This approach has been tried a number of times since 1999/2000, and thus far, most attempts to "clear the field" have not done that—Clinton attempted this in 2007 and again in 2015, but in both cases, she faced insurgent candidates who were able to bring in enough funding to keep them and their campaigns operating throughout the primary season. Clinton faced five declared candidates for the Democratic nomination, although only Sanders made it through to June.

Initially, the field contained Senator Jim Webb, who was a one-term Democratic senator from Virginia, a decorated military veteran, who had served as President Ronald Reagan's Secretary of the Navy in the late 1980s. Webb left the race in the fall of 2015, having participated in one of the Democratic Party debates. Lincoln Chafee also entered the race for a brief period of time, although he had long been a Republican senator from Rhode Island, where he had served as an Independent governor as well, before finally moving into the Democratic Party. Chafee also competed in the early Democratic debate before dropping out of the race. Harvard professor Larry Lessig ran for the Democratic nomination as well, but was not included in the initial debate and dropped out of the race by late October, 2015. Lessig ran on a bit of a unique platform, promising that he

Chapter 2: The Democratic Primaries **51**

would step down from the presidency once his three-pronged platform, known as the *Citizen Equality Act*, was passed by Congress.[10]

Finally, there was Martin O'Malley, who had been a fairly popular progressive Democratic governor of Maryland for two terms. The Clinton campaign had initially assessed O'Malley as the most serious challenger to the nomination, since he came from a governor's office, having previously served as mayor of Baltimore, thus coming to the campaign with substantial elected executive leadership experience. O'Malley also represented a progressive side of the Democratic Party, and did not bring with him some of the foreign policy "baggage" that had been proving difficult for Clinton to overcome, namely her support of the Iraq War through her vote in the Senate, and being subsequently caught up in the issues around the incidents in Benghazi, Libya in 2012 that took the life of U.S. Ambassador Chris Stevens and three other Americans. Clinton has generally held more "hawkish" positions in regard to foreign policy and national security.

Thus, the 2016 Democratic primary race, as it was coming together in 2015, had representatives from different aspects of the Democratic party and the ideological spectrum. Chafee, a former Republican, and Webb, another former Republican, came to the Democratic nomination from somewhat different parts of the political spectrum, although neither Webb nor Chafee could be considered traditional Republicans in the contemporary understanding of the party of Reagan and Gingrich. At the same time, neither of these men fit into the Democratic Party establishment all that comfortably; this was especially the case with Webb, who would echo part of the populist, white working-class message championed by both Republican candidate Donald Trump and Senator Sanders, but could not get much traction for his campaign. Webb's political positions were potentially more out of sync with the Democratic Party's mainstream than Chafee's, but both candidates dropped out of the race by the third week of October, after one of the initial Democratic debates.[11] Chafee's positions, if anything, were in many ways to the left of Clinton, and he was and remains certainly much more of a foreign policy dove than she is, but a lot of the ideological space within the Democratic primary he was campaigning to occupy was already taken by both Sanders and O'Malley. And by October, 2015, Sanders's support had increased substantially, while Chafee continued to seem like a strange fit for the Democratic nomination given his various changes in party affiliation, and, to a degree, his quiet demeanor. The one threat that Clinton and her campaign really hoped to avoid, running in the primary against Vice President Joe Biden, was also put to rest in October, when he formally declared that he would not seek the Democratic nomination 2016.

Biden had been thinking about running for the White House during the invisible primary period, as Clinton, Sanders, O'Malley and others were putting together exploratory campaigns and leasing space for headquarters, and, most importantly, raising money for the campaign and collecting endorsements from elected officials and party activists.[12] Biden had twice before run for the

52 Part I: The Primaries

Democratic nomination for president, in 1987 and again in 2007/2008. And he had run as Obama's vice presidential nominee in 2008, and for re-election as vice president in 2012. Thus, Biden was quite familiar with the requirements and demands of a national campaign. He publically acknowledged considering running again for the 2016 nomination but this was complicated by the recent tragedy of the death of his elder son, Beau Biden, at age 46 from a form of brain cancer. At the same time, Biden also noted a promise he had made to his dying son that he would run for the office.[13] Ultimately, Biden choose not to enter the race. He and Clinton would have generally been fighting against each other, as their political positions within the Democratic party are quite close, and they both had substantial foreign policy experience and, to a degree, approached foreign affairs and international engagement from similar perspectives.

The Debates

Thus, as the invisible primary turned into the visible primary as the campaign shifted into high gear in the early voting and caucus states of Iowa, New Hampshire, Nevada, and South Carolina, the race became smaller on the Democratic side, with Clinton, Sanders, and O'Malley as the main contestants. The Iowa caucus, held on February 1, 2016, was the first opportunity for voters to actually cast ballots or indicate their preferences for the candidates. Prior to the first official caucus, followed soon thereafter by the New Hampshire primary, on February 9, 2016, the candidates had five debates as arranged by the Democratic Party. There was also a town hall debate in between the Iowa caucus and the New Hampshire primary. Voters were able to see the candidates engage with each other in these debates, and to hear them describe their policy positions and approaches.

It was the first debate, in October, that contributed to Webb and Chafee dropping out of the race. There was some commentary that the Democratic Party had purposefully scheduled a number of these early debates for Saturday nights, when they would have fairly small audiences, in order to keep voters from actually seeing the candidates. This critique was made against the Democratic National Committee and its chairwoman, Debbie Wasserman Schultz, who was perceived to be a Clinton loyalist even as she tried to maintain an unbiased approach to the primary and caucus processes. The November and December debates both took place on Saturday nights and had meager television ratings; this was in particular contrast to the Republican debates, which were balancing seventeen candidates over two different rounds of debates. If the GOP field had been smaller during this period, the contrast might not have been as striking, but the apparently hidden nature of the early Democratic debates struck many as an attempt to keep those less well known (O'Malley and Sanders) from greater public exposure and the possibility of increasing their popularity among the Democratic Party electorate. The rest of the Democratic debates took place on

Sunday nights or weeknights as the primaries and caucuses unfolded, and ultimately these later debates became an opportunity to see Clinton and Sanders thoroughly engage each other on their visions for the country and the contrast in their policy positions. The debates, because of the small number of participants, allowed for a bit more substantial policy engagement than did the Republican debates that were going on during the same period.

Clinton, Sanders, and, briefly, O'Malley, defined their positions during these contests. Clinton was attacked by Sanders and O'Malley for her Iraq War vote and her generally more muscular foreign policy positions, as well as some of her national security positions. There were some substantive discussions throughout the debates about ways to improve healthcare policy in the United States, with Sanders staking out a position advocating for a single-payer system as the best way to "fix" Obamacare, and Clinton advocating for cost controls, especially for prescription drugs, and for other mechanisms to "keep and expand" on the basic promise of accessible and affordable healthcare coverage. There was much discussion of the cost of and how best to pay for higher education. There were also disputes about international trade and the various treaties that have opened up more such trade in the United States, specifically NAFTA and the proposed Trans-Pacific Partnership Agreement (TPP).

Throughout the summer and into the fall, there was also the ongoing scandal of Clinton's use of a private email server, stored at her home, that she used when she was Secretary of State. The issue of this server, which was extensively investigated by the FBI and by Congress, came up during the campaign and the debates, and Sanders, in the first debate, suggested that this scandal was a distraction from the "real issues" facing the American people, noting that "the American people are sick and tired about hearing about your damn emails."[14] This became one of the more memorable retorts during all of the debates, and was indicative of the approach that Sanders and Clinton both took towards the debates. Clinton has been known as a skilled debater, and had gone through quite the string of debates during the 2008 race against Obama. Both Clinton and Obama became better debaters and candidates during their long battle for the nomination; and given Clinton's three years out of government from the time she left the administration after Obama's re-election until she officially entered the race for the 2016 nomination, there was much discussion among pundits and Democratic Party operatives that a real challenger during the primaries would better prepare Clinton for a tough general election. Sanders had less experience in nationally televised debates and his initial responses to some questions— especially in terms of foreign policy and national security—needed more substance and refinement.

As the primary season progressed and through more and more debates, both candidates fleshed out policy areas and, in some cases, integrated ideas offered by the other candidate. Clinton, in particular, adopted variations of some of Sander's policy positions, including more substantial minimum wage increases and making

54 Part I: The Primaries

public higher education much more available for low or no cost to students. Clinton pressed Sanders on gun control issues, and both candidates advocated for paid family leave, although they offered different ways to pay for it. Clinton ultimately changed her position on the TPP, which she had had a hand in negotiating during her tenure as Secretary of State. Since both Sanders and Clinton were campaigning to succeed Obama, the tone and tenor of their debate differed markedly from the Republican debates that spent a great deal of time attacking Obama and his policies.

Unlike in the 2008 campaign, Clinton wore the feminist mantle and readily acknowledged her unique position as a female trailblazer—she also dealt with continued commentary on her gender, how she conducted herself, as a woman, and comments about her that were never leveled against her male colleagues. Sanders's sustained critique of Clinton, throughout the primaries, was that she was part of the political establishment, and that her policy proposals were not sufficient to contend with the rising economic inequality in the United States. Clinton's private speeches to Goldman-Sachs, her personal email server, the constant congressional hearing on the Benghazi incident, the Clinton Foundation's connection to wealthy individuals and powerful leaders in other countries were all part of the narrative around Clinton herself, and contributed to her lower approval ratings and the populace's general sense of mistrust in her. Clinton emphasized her connection to Obama during her primary run, while Sanders was more critical of the president. Obama himself remained quite popular with Democratic voters, and Clinton's role in his administration and her connection to him was part of the strategy to continue the Obama coalition during the nomination process. And while this was an asset to Clinton in appealing to Obama voters during the primaries and caucuses, it is more difficult to make a case for a "third term," which is, strategically, what she set herself up to do both in the nominating process and in the general election. This approach—which was more successful in helping Clinton reach the nomination—when combined with the emphasis on Clinton's experience in government and politics, resulted in her characterization as an establishment candidate, not a change candidate, even though her gender was novel and distinct, and would be a change as both the nominee and potential president.

The Primary Itself

The voters finally started to weigh in on the candidates with the first caucus in Iowa, and what they had to say was not necessarily decisive. In fact, Clinton and Sanders essentially tied in Iowa, with 0.3 percent separating the two candidates, and an allocation of twenty-three delegates to Clinton, twenty-one to Sanders.[15] Following the results in Iowa, and a very weak showing there, O'Malley dropped out of the race. This was not necessarily the result that Clinton wanted in Iowa, where she would have liked a more decisive win to kick off the primary season.

Chapter 2: The Democratic Primaries **55**

The results also encouraged Sanders to continue his campaign, since he made such a strong showing against the presumptive Democratic favorite. And since the next event was the New Hampshire primary, neighboring state to Sanders's Vermont, his campaign expected to do well there. It did, with Sanders carrying 60 percent of the vote to Clinton's 38 percent, but because of the proportional allocation of the delegates, Sanders got sixteen delegates, and Clinton got fifteen.[16] Between the essential tie in Iowa and Sanders's strong results in New Hampshire, the Clinton campaign was worried that it was going to relive its nomination loss all over again. The demographics are somewhat similar in these two mostly white, fairly small states; Clinton carried older, often wealthier voters, Sanders appealed to younger voters, economically "downscale" voters, and politically Independent voters.

The next contest was the Nevada caucus on February 20th. The calendar in February, for the Democrats, flipped between caucuses and primaries. The Nevada caucus was the first opportunity for the Democratic candidates to contend with a larger Hispanic population than they had seen in either Iowa or New Hampshire, since 28 percent of the population in Nevada is Hispanic.[17] Nevada is another fairly small state in terms of population—although extensive in landmass—and the vast majority of the population is concentrated in Clark County, which includes Las Vegas. The caucus race was fairly close, with Clinton carrying 52.7 percent of the vote to Sanders's 47.2 percent. Clinton received twenty pledged delegates and Sanders received fifteen.[18] Clinton and Sanders tied in two counties in Nevada (Churchill and Storey counties), not unlike some of the outcomes just a few weeks earlier in the Iowa caucuses. And the demographic breakdown of the race followed the trends that had been seen, at least partially, in the two initial contests: Sanders's strength with younger voters, Clinton's strength with older voters. Clinton carried 76 percent of African-American vote in the caucus, while Sanders outdid her in terms of the Hispanic vote, 53 percent to 45 percent.[19] Sanders did better than most expected him to do in Nevada, but Clinton still carried the state "as a win" and she was well positioned to head into the next contest, in South Carolina.

Clinton's success in South Carolina would start to define her coalition for a great deal of the rest of the primary season, as it would, as well, for Sanders. Clinton amassed thirty-nine delegates from South Carolina, compared to Sanders's fourteen, and carried 73 percent of the vote.[20] The results of the race showed Clinton's strength, in the South, with African-American voters, where she carried 86 percent of that vote compared to Sanders's 14 percent.[21] She also had a strong showing with female voters, carrying 79 percent.[22] As the primaries and caucuses moved into states with more racial diversity than Iowa and New Hampshire, the dynamic of the race between Sanders and Clinton evolved and reflected those distinctions within the Democratic coalition. Younger voters supported Sanders in South Carolina, as they had in the other early states. Older white and African-American voters supported Clinton. Bill Clinton had been

56 Part I: The Primaries

popular throughout the South during his two terms in the White House, and while his legacy is complicated on a number of levels, rank and file Democrats in southern states were supportive of Hillary Clinton's candidacy in 2016. Many, especially among African-American Democrats, saw her as a continuation of the legacy of Barack Obama; these voters were more familiar with Clinton, who she was, and what she had been through (from her time as First Lady in Arkansas and of the United States to Bill Clinton's infidelities to her campaign for the nomination in 2008), and she campaigned in the South in venues that connected to these voters. Clinton visited churches and Historic Black Colleges; she was often accompanied by African-American elected officials like congressman James Clyburn (D-SC), or faith leaders.[23] This was Clinton's approach in South Carolina and ultimately would be her approach across the South. In terms of votes and delegates, the South was the backbone of Clinton's strategic strength on her path towards winning the nomination. Her substantial success in the early South Carolina primary also provided her with another much-needed win, after the closeness of Iowa and Sanders's win in New Hampshire. This primary, like in the Nevada caucus, also indicated some of the strategic problems facing the Sanders campaign—the fairly unified African-American support would be a potential threat to Sanders's winning the nomination. African-Americans are some of the most loyal and consistent Democratic voters, and they make up large voting blocs in quite a few states. It is strategically compromising and tactically impossible to win the Democratic nomination without at least substantial support from African-Americans. This became more clear as Sanders and Clinton battled for votes in South Carolina, and after her decisive win there. But South Carolina continued to highlight Sanders's appeal to other blocs of voters, specifically younger voters and white male voters. Younger voters were particularly important to the Obama coalition and it would be quite difficult for Clinton to win the general election if these Sanders supporters stayed home or turned towards a different candidate.

Super Tuesdays and the Contours of the Rest of the Nominating Season

After these four early states, the next test of any campaign is whether they can fight for votes on multiple fronts in different parts of the country simultaneously. (See Appendix D for the Democratic primary and caucus results.) This requires organizational capacity and lots of money. Heading into March, both Clinton and Sanders refocused their efforts as various Super Tuesdays loomed on the horizon. Even before the voting started, the delegate totals coming out of February were not in Sanders' favor, "[b]ut the often overlooked delegate count in the Democratic primary shows Mr. Sanders slipping significantly behind Hillary Clinton in the race for the nomination, and the odds of his overtaking her growing increasingly remote."[24] The March 1st "Super Tuesday" included strongholds for both Sanders and Clinton, with Clinton sweeping through the

Chapter 2: The Democratic Primaries **57**

South, including Alabama, Arkansas (her husband's home state and the state where she had been First Lady as well), Georgia, Tennessee, Texas, and Virginia. Sanders shut Clinton out completely in Vermont, he also carried Minnesota, Colorado, and Oklahoma, although he lost Massachusetts to Clinton by less than 2 percent.[25] Because of the proportional allocation of the delegates based on the population size of the states, and the size of Clinton's margins in larger states like Texas and Georgia, she came out of this initial Super Tuesday with a lead of 602 pledged delegates to Sanders's 413.[26] This multi-state contest showed both candidates' strengths and weaknesses. Clinton continued to do very well among the African-American populations in southern states; she continued to do well with older voters. Sanders continued his strong appeal in states that are generally whiter (Minnesota, Oklahoma, Colorado), and with millennial voters, "she lost among millennials in every state as that demographic continues to support Sanders in large numbers."[27] This became the general narrative of the race as the Democratic primary continued. Sanders and Clinton both sought to appeal to Hispanic voters, but Clinton did particularly well with Hispanic voters in Texas on Super Tuesday.

March was dominated by a number of variations on Super Tuesday, with many states voting on multiple Tuesdays, and sometimes Saturdays. Sanders won Kansas and Nebraska on Saturday, March 5th, Clinton continued to show her strength in the South, carrying Louisiana on the same day. Clinton and Sanders competed the next Tuesday in Mississippi and Michigan, and the polls had initially indicated that Clinton would carry both states on March 8th. Since the summer months, Clinton had seen a sizeable lead in Michigan, and while she led Sanders in the African-American vote there, his support among African-American voters was stronger in Michigan than it had been in many of the southern states. Interestingly—especially given the polling and outcomes in the general election for the Midwestern states of Michigan, Pennsylvania, and Wisconsin—Clinton narrowly lost Michigan to Sanders, while carrying Mississippi. The South continued to be the part of the country where Clinton performed the best against Sanders. Sanders had campaigned hard on Michigan, on issues around trade, jobs, NAFTA, and the TPP, and Trump was making a similar case on the other side of the political aisle at the same time. Because there were fewer other contests going on, the voters in Michigan saw a lot of the candidates themselves, their surrogates, and many advertisements. Given some of the overlap between populist messages from Sanders and Trump, and some of the continued economic weakness in Michigan itself, these issues had particular salience for Michigan voters. This argument, which Clinton at times had some difficulties responding to gave Sanders an unexpected win in mid-March as both campaigns geared up for another "Super Tuesday" contest.[28]

The March 15th primary featured voting in Illinois, Ohio, Missouri, North Carolina, and Florida. Clinton carried the day in all five states, but some of the contests were extremely close, especially in Illinois (Clinton's original home state,

58 Part I: The Primaries

where she was born) and in Missouri, where she carried each contest by only one percentage point.[29] She showed stronger results in Ohio, North Carolina, and Florida. Thus, while Clinton continued to accumulate pledged delegates (and super delegates) and newspaper endorsements, there was a constant discussion in the media (and among political operatives) that she was a weaker or more vulnerable candidate than her frontrunner status might indicate because the Sanders insurgency was able to best her in a number of rustbelt states and had narrowed the size of her wins in a number of other states. This critique goes to the heart of the difficulty of coming into a race as the frontrunner or inevitable candidate, since any electoral "weakness" comes across as more pronounced or damaging, undermining the strength of the candidate if he or she cannot quickly and handily dispatch any insurgent or challenger. And given the results in 2008, this critique was harder for Clinton to ignore or casually dismiss in 2016. At the same time, there were gendered aspects to this critique of Clinton, similar to many of the attacks she had faced during the 2008 primary, when she was weekly called upon to get out of the race because she was standing in the way of Barack Obama's success, or in 2016, because she was standing in the way of Bernie Sanders's success.[30] Rebecca Traister, in *Big Girls Don't Cry: The Election that Changed Everything for American Women*, outlines many of these same calls for Clinton's exit from the nomination fight, noting that this fueled Clinton's fighter persona, and often made the male media commentators look "like heavies."[31] But the "Bernie-Bro" phenomenon, which had a lot of traction on Twitter and other social media outlets, was generally seen as a "Sanders backer who aggressively and condescendingly attacks Clinton and her supporters online on social media, often in a way that's perceived to have a gendered inclination."[32]

Responding to the Sanders's Insurgency

Throughout the pre-primary period and into the primary season, the Clinton campaign took Sanders and his groundswell of support seriously, more seriously than they had taken the Obama candidacy eight years earlier. Clinton and Sanders had some fairly substantive debates about their policy differences and they came to adopt aspects of each other's proposals. Clinton ran a meaningful campaign against Sanders, investing time, money, and support to take on Sanders, and to direct the campaign against him throughout the primaries. While Clinton gained an early lead in elected delegates, and amassed endorsements from quite a few Democratic officials (some of whom were also super delegates) and from newspapers and other forms of media, she continued to engage Sanders and his supporters as she campaigned throughout the primaries. As her lead continued, expanding and shrinking with the outcome of various contests, she also started to direct her attacks at the Republicans, as their field shrank and as Donald Trump became the most likely nominee of the Party. In the aftermath of her loss to Obama in 2008, much commentary was directed at the campaign's inability to

Chapter 2: The Democratic Primaries **59**

switch gears and pay attention to the Obama campaign and its strategic success as the primary season wore on. The 2016 Clinton campaign did not want to be caught "flatfooted" again, re-evaluating the field and directing attention to the Sanders's insurgency. All of this is, again, connected to Clinton's position in both 2008 and in 2016 as the frontrunner for the Democratic nomination.

As the spring campaign season wore on, Clinton divided her focus in two different directions: at accruing sufficient elected delegates to clinch the Democratic nomination, and thus she competed fully in all the Democratic primaries and caucuses, and also at starting to lay the groundwork for the general election in attacking Donald Trump as the GOP nominee. Because of Sanders's populist appeal on the Left, within the Democratic Party and in the nominating contests, Clinton found herself in a situation where she was fending off populist attacks from both the Left, in the Sanders campaign, and from the Right, as Trump continued his populist insurgency through the Republican primaries. Trump was omnipresent during the primary season, and thus all other candidates, Democrats and Republicans, had to fight for media attention of any kind. While Clinton was battling Sanders, she was also battling the ubiquity of Donald Trump as a candidate, as a media fascination and ratings generator, and as potential general election foe. It cannot be overstated how much the Republican primary, the GOP debates, and the media attention on Trump overshadowed all other political developments during the 2015 fall and into the spring. While Sanders and Clinton shared the debate stage throughout the spring, and as they each fought for votes in the primaries, neither candidate could garner the same kind of attention that Trump received, constantly and unendingly.

The primaries in the last weeks of March and into April were among Sanders's strongest showings throughout the season. He carried Idaho and Utah on March 22nd, while Clinton won the Arizona primary. Sanders then went on to carry Alaska, Hawaii, and Washington State four days later on March 26th, concluding his streak with another Midwestern win, in Wisconsin on April 5th.[33] While Sanders demonstrated his continued strength in smaller (by population), whiter states, both candidates continued to increase their delegate totals because of the proportional allocation of the pledged delegates. Sanders also won the Wyoming vote on April 9th. A week later Clinton carried her adopted home state of New York, with 58 percent of the vote on April 19th. (This is also the state where Bernie Sanders was born and grew up.) The next "Super Tuesday," April 26th, with voting in five mid-Atlantic/Eastern seaboard states, gave Clinton another big cache of delegates when she carried Connecticut, Maryland, Delaware, and Pennsylvania, losing only Rhode Island to Sanders. Thus, Clinton had carved out large swathes of the East Coast, with wins in the South, the mid-Atlantic, and parts of New England. While she lost some Midwestern states to Sanders, she carried others. She generally did well in larger states, often states with more diverse populations, and she shaped her own coalition within the Democratic Party as she collected votes, pledged and super delegates during the nomination fight.

60 Part I: The Primaries

Sanders carried Indiana and West Virginia over the next two weeks, while Clinton picked up a small win on Guam. The following week, on May 17th, Sanders and Clinton once again split wins, with Clinton carrying Kentucky by less than a percentage point, and Sanders besting her by 12 percent in Oregon.[34] On June 5th, Clinton won the Puerto Rican Democratic primary and headed into the final multi-state battle on June 7th with a substantial delegate lead. In fact, the night before this last multi-state contest, the Associated Press announced that Clinton had secured enough pledged and super delegates (from their constant canvassing of the super delegates) to "clinch" the Democratic nomination.[35] The next day, Clinton carried California, New Jersey, New Mexico, and South Dakota. Sanders did quite well in North Dakota and also carried Montana.[36] Following the June 7th contests, Senator Sanders contacted the White House and asked for a meeting with President Obama. Obama and Sanders met two days later, on June 9th, and Sanders followed that meeting with a meeting on Capitol Hill with Senate Minority Leader Harry Reid. Obama and Biden had stayed on the sidelines of the Democratic contest throughout, and Obama had directed any attention in the primary contests towards comments and critiques of Donald Trump, especially as Trump became the most likely GOP nominee. But on June 9th, after the White House meeting with Sanders, first Obama congratulated Clinton for "securing the delegates necessary to clinch the Democratic nomination for president"[37] and then he formally endorsed Clinton in a well-produced video that could easily be used as a campaign ad. On the same day, Vice President Biden and Senator Elizabeth Warren of Massachusetts also came out, separately, and endorsed Clinton in her quest for the Democratic nomination.[38] There was still one primary to go, in Washington, D.C., the following Tuesday, June 14th; Clinton and Sanders both competed in that primary, which Clinton won handily.

Conclusion

Clinton ultimately amassed 2,205 pledged delegates from the primaries and caucuses; Sanders's total of pledged delegates was 1,846. Out of the 4,763 delegates 2,383 were necessary, in 2016, to secure the Democratic nomination for president, and while Clinton finished the nominating season with fewer than the sufficient number of pledged delegates to win the nomination, she did have quite a few super delegates who had indicated that they would support her, especially if she ultimately maintained her delegate and vote lead over Sanders. Thus, another 609 super delegates supported Clinton, bringing her total of delegates heading to the Democratic convention in Philadelphia to 2,814.[39]

Clinton's campaign out-fundraised Sanders's campaign, but they did not outspend him, at least via the campaigns. Sanders raised $229 million, Clinton raised $238 million.[40] Sanders's campaign spent $219 million during the primaries, and Clinton's campaign spent $195 million during the nominating campaign. Clinton's Super PAC (Priorities USA Action) raised another $96 million, and

Chapter 2: The Democratic Primaries **61**

increased spending on behalf of Clinton after Sander's strong showing in the New Hampshire primary.[41] The PAC spent money on ads in a number of states, and on GOTV efforts directed towards African-Americans and Hispanics in February and March, but after Clinton's strong showing in the March 15th group of primaries, the PAC substantially reduced its spending on Clinton's behalf, instead saving up the resources for the general election.[42]

In the end, Clinton won the Democratic nomination by securing 16.8 million votes during the nomination contest, compared with Sanders's total of 13.2 million. As election analyst Nate Silver noted, Clinton had a lead of "191 delegates [after Super Tuesday on March 1] and it never dropped below 187 pledged delegates the rest of the way."[43] Clinton's general strategy, as noted throughout, was to appeal to the broad Democratic coalition, including making pitches to women, African-Americans, Hispanic Americans, and both white- and blue-collar workers. The Sanders campaign sustained its appeal to millennial voters throughout the primary contest and made inroads among white blue-collar workers and political independents. Clinton's capacity to dominate the southern states, the larger and often most diverse states, and a sizeable chunk of the rustbelt states made her campaign more formidable, and ultimately, more successful in the 2016 Democratic nominating contest.

Notes

1 Dan Balz, "Hillary Clinton Opens Presidential Bid," *Washington Post*, Sunday, January 21, 2007, www.washingtonpost.com/wpdyn/content/article/2007/01/20/AR2007012000426.html (accessed December 5, 2016).

2 Joshua Green, "The Front-Runner's Fall," *The Atlantic*, September 2008, www.theatlantic.com/magazine/archive/2008/09/the-front-runner-s-fall/306944/ (accessed December 5, 2016).

3 Nichola D. Gutgold does a great job presenting and quickly analyzing some of the more prominent women who have run for the presidency, including Margaret Chase Smith (1964), Shirley Chisholm (1972), Pat Schroeder (1988), Elizabeth "Liddy" Dole (1999), Carol Moseley Braun (2004), and twenty-one others who ran between 1964 and 2004. She also notes that none of them started the race nor held the position of "frontrunner." Nichola D. Gutgold, *Almost Madam President: Why Hillary Clinton "Won" in 2008* (Lanham, MD: Lexington Books, 2009), 5.

4 Keith Brekhus, "Hillary Clinton Seizes the Upper Hand Before Voting Starts With Super Delegate Pledges," *PoliticusUSA.com*, August 29, 2015, www.politicususa.com/2015/08/29/hillary-clinton-moves-lock-nomination-voting-starts-super-delegate-pledges.html (accessed December 6, 2016).

5 She wasn't a grandmother yet, either, in 2008.

6 In many ways, Hillary Clinton came into the 2016 election cycle as the most prepared individual to "run for president again" since Richard Nixon in 1968. In fact, Clinton was more successful in her time since she lost to Obama in the 2008 primary than was Nixon, after he lost to John F. Kennedy in the general election in 1960. While Nixon

62 Part I: The Primaries

had served as vice president during the Eisenhower Administration, he spent the eight years in between his presidential runs far less successfully than Clinton, since he lost his 1962 bid for the California governor's office, and was saddled with a reputation for being a "loser." Clinton's decision to serve in the Obama Cabinet, especially in the position of Secretary of State, an iconic, visible, and important office both domestically and internationally, erased any sense that she was a loser, since she was willing to serve in her former rival's cabinet and to work collaboratively with the man who had defeated her in the primary. For some potential insight into Clinton's decision to serve in the Obama White House, see the somewhat dramatic epilogue in John Heilemann and Mark Halperin, *Game Change: Obama and the Clintons, McCain and Palin, and the Race of a Lifetime* (New York: HarperCollins, 2010), 429–436.

7 Alex Seitz-Wald, "Hillary Clinton Campaign Headquarters to be Based in Brooklyn," *MSNBC*, April 3, 2015, www.msnbc.com/msnbc/hillary-clinton-campaign-office-brooklyn (accessed December 9, 2016).

8 Dan Merica, "Hillary Clinton Raised Over $45 Million in Primary Money, Aide Says," *CNN*, July 1, 2015, www.cnn.com/2015/07/01/politics/hillary-clinton-fundraising-45-million-in-primary-money/ (accessed December 12, 2016).

9 Arthur Paulson, "The 'Invisible Primary' Becomes Visible," in William Crotty, ed., *Winning the Presidency, 2008* (New York: Paradigm Publishers/Routledge, 2009), 93.

10 The *Citizen Equality Act* included three main planks: public funding for all campaigns, an end to gerrymandered districts, and clear and distinct protections of voting rights, including making Election Day a holiday. See Larry Lessig for President 2016 website, https://lessig2016.us/the-plan/ (accessed December 4, 2016).

11 Nick Gass and Daniel Strauss, "Jim Webb Drops Out of Democratic Race," *Politico. com*, October 20, 2015, www.politico.com/story/2015/10/webb-dropping-out-214952 (accessed December 15, 2016); Dan Merica and Tom LoBianco, "Lincoln Chafee Drops Out of Democratic Primary Race," *CNN*, October 23, 2015, www.cnn.com/2015/10/23/politics/lincoln-chafee-2016-election-dnc-meeting/ (accessed December 15, 2016).

12 See Marty Cohen, David Karol, Hans Noel, and John Zaller, *The Party Decides: Presidential Nominations Before and After Reform* (Chicago, IL: University of Chicago Press, 2008), for a more extensive and expansive discussion of the invisible primary and the process of "clearing the field."

13 Edward-Isaac Dovere, "Biden Himself Leaked Word of His Son's Dying Wish. The Vice President is Mourning. He's Also Calculating," *Politico*, October 6, 2015, www.politico.com/story/2015/10/joe-biden-beau-2016-214459 (accessed December 13, 2016).

14 Ben Jacobs and Sabrina Siddiqui, "Bernie Sanders: 'Enough of the Emails—Let's Talk About the Real Issues Facing the American People'," *The Guardian*, October 13, 2015, www.theguardian.com/us-news/2015/oct/13/bernie-sanders-hillary-clinton-damn-email-server (accessed December 16, 2016).

15 "Results from the 2016 Iowa Caucus," *Wall Street Journal*, February 1, 2016, http://graphics.wsj.com/elections/2016/iowa-caucus-results/ (accessed December 12, 2016).

16 "New Hampshire Primary Results," *NBC News*, February 10, 2016, www.nbcnews.com/politics/2016-election/primaries/NH (accessed December 15, 2016).

Chapter 2: The Democratic Primaries **63**

17 Pew Research Center, Hispanic Trends, *Demographic Profile of Hispanics in Nevada, 2014* [n.d.], www.pewhispanic.org/states/state/nv/ (accessed December 14, 2016).

18 "Primary Results: Nevada," *CNN*, February 21, 2016, www.cnn.com/election/primaries/states/nv/Dem (accessed December 14, 2016).

19 "Primary Results: Nevada," *NBC News*, February 21, 2016, www.nbcnews.com/politics/2016-election/primaries/NV (accessed December 14, 2016).

20 Lili Mihalik, Anthony Pesce, and Ben Welsh, "Results from the 2016 South Carolina Primary," *Los Angeles Times*, February 27, 2016, http://graphics.latimes.com/election-2016-south-carolina-results/ (accessed December 15, 2016).

21 "South Carolina Primary Results," *NBC News*, February 28, 2016, www.nbcnews.com/politics/2016-election/primaries/SC (accessed December 15, 2016).

22 Ibid.

23 Hannah Fraser-Chanpong, "Who Supported Hillary Clinton in South Carolina," *CBS News*, February 27, 2016, www.cbsnews.com/news/who-supported-hillary-clinton-in-south-carolina/ (accessed December 15, 2016).

24 Patrick Healy, "Delegate Count Leaving Bernie Sanders with Steep Climb," *New York Times*, February 21, 2016, www.nytimes.com/2016/02/22/us/politics/delegate-count-leaving-bernie-sanders-with-steep-climb.html?_r=0 (accessed December 15, 2016).

25 "Massachusetts Democratic Primary," *Boston Globe*, March 1, 2016, https://apps.bostonglobe.com/election-results/2016/primary/democratic/massachusetts/ (accessed December 17, 2016).

26 "The Race to the Democratic Nomination," *Washington Post*, www.washingtonpost.com/graphics/politics/2016-election/primaries/delegate-tracker/democratic/ (accessed December 17, 2016).

27 "Seven Takeaways from the Democratic Exit Polls," *CBS News*, March 2, 2016, www.cbsnews.com/news/super-tuesday-2016-seven-takeaways-from-the-democratic-exit-polls/ (accessed December 17, 2016).

28 Danielle Kurtzleben, "Tuesday's Elections: 3 Trump Wins, Plus a Big Surprise From Sanders," *NPR*, March 8, 2016, www.npr.org/2016/03/08/469717046/michigan-mississippi-idaho-hawaii-primary-results (accessed December 17, 2016).

29 "March 15 Primary Results," *Wall Street Journal*, March 15, 2016, http://graphics.wsj.com/elections/2016/march-15/ (accessed December 18, 2016).

30 The nomination race itself was much closer in 2008 between Obama and Clinton than it was between Sanders and Clinton in 2016. Clinton and Obama traded delegate leads more than once in 2008, but Clinton stayed ahead of Sanders throughout the nomination battle from the point of the Nevada caucuses on. And those leads excluded super delegates.

31 Rebecca Traister, *Big Girls Don't Cry: The Election that Changed Everything for American Women* (New York: Free Press, 2010), 179.

32 Maxwell Tani, "Bernie Sanders Addresses 'Bernie Bro' Phenomenon: 'We Don't Want That Crap'," *Business Insider*, February 7, 2016, www.businessinsider.com/bernie-sanders-bernie-bros-2016-2 (accessed December 18, 2016).

33 Randy Yeip and Stuart A. Thomson, "Tracking the Delegate Counts," *Wall Street Journal*, July 24, 2016, http://graphics.wsj.com/elections/2016/delegates/ (accessed December 18, 2016).

64 Part I: The Primaries

34 "Primary Election Results: Oregon," *New York Times*, May 18, 2016, www.nytimes. com/elections/2016/results/primaries/oregon (accessed December 18, 2016).

35 Philip Bump, "Hillary Clinton Just Clinched the Democratic Nomination. Here's the Math Behind It," *Washington Post*, June 6, 2016, www.washingtonpost.com/news/ the-fix/wp/2016/06/06/make-no-mistake-hillary-clinton-will-clinch-the-democratic-nomination-on-tuesday/?utm_term=.70c2a14cec5f (accessed December 18, 2016).

36 "Primary Election Results: North Dakota," *New York Times*, September 29, 2016, www.nytimes.com/elections/2016/results/primaries/north-dakota (accessed December 15, 2016).

37 Edward-Isaac Dovere, "Obama to Meet With Sanders on Thursday," *Politico*, June 8, 2016, www.politico.com/story/2016/06/obama-sanders-meeting-224045 (accessed December 18, 2016).

38 Eric Bradner, "President Barack Obama Endorses Hillary Clinton in Video," *CNN*, June 9, 2016, www.cnn.com/2016/06/09/politics/president-barack-obama-endorses-hillary-clinton-in-video/ (accessed December 18, 2016).

39 Yeip and Thomson, "Tracking the Delegate Counts."

40 "Which Presidential Candidates Are Winning the Money Race," *New York Times*, June 22, 2016, www.nytimes.com/interactive/2016/us/elections/election-2016-campaign-money-race.html (accessed December 18, 2016).

41 Ibid.

42 Gabriel Debenedetti, "Clinton Super PAC Won't Spend More on Primary," *Politico*, March 16, 2016, www.politico.com/story/2016/03/hillary-clinton-primary-super-pac-220897 (accessed December 17, 2016).

43 Nate Silver, "Was The Democratic Primary a Close Call or a Landslide? Why It's Easy to Underestimate Both Clinton's and Sanders's Accomplishments," *FiveThirtyEight. com*, July 27, 2016, http://fivethirtyeight.com/features/was-the-democratic-primary-a-close-call-or-a-landslide (accessed December 17, 2016).

3

THE REPUBLICAN PRIMARIES

Wayne P. Steger

The 2016 Republican presidential nomination surprised all but a few observers. The nominee, Donald Trump, ran an unorthodox campaign that resembled a concert tour more than a presidential nomination campaign. He did not build an extensive campaign organization or spend much money on ads, opting instead to communicate with prospective voters through social media and exposure on digital and TV news. He belittled his Republican rivals and other officials. He spoke with near disregard for facts and fomented racial, gender, and nationalist prejudices. His policy ideas departed from long-established party positions on trade, social welfare, same-sex marriage, and more. Numerous party and elected officials opposed his nomination. Some observers called his nomination a hostile takeover of the party.[1] This chapter looks at the process and conditions that made his nomination possible and even predictable, despite rhetoric and actions that would have sunk candidates in previous elections.[2]

Although unlikely, the contemporary nomination process makes possible the selection of a candidate whose policy positions deviate from established political party principles. Since 1972, both political parties have empowered party voters to express their preferences in caucuses and primaries. This process opened the door for outsider candidates to compete for the nomination.[3] Outsider candidates usually do not win, but the conditions were ripe for such an occurrence in 2016. First, there was no early favorite in the race which contributed to a large field of candidates since more potential candidates thought they could win in these circumstances.[4] Second, the Republican Party is deeply divided and a substantial portion of the party's nomination voters were angry with the party's national leaders. This anti-establishment sentiment benefitted an "outsider" candidate. While several candidates, including Chris Christie and Ted Cruz, sought to become the "outsider" candidate who would take on the establishment, Donald

66 Part I: The Primaries

Trump succeeded in attracting more attention than other candidates, knocking down rivals, and drawing support from across the factions of the Republican Party. He slowly gained momentum as other candidates withdrew from the race. Republican Party elites were unable to stop Trump. They were divided about an alternative to Trump, they faced an angry electorate, and they had attacked the "liberal media" for so long that serious criticisms of Donald Trump were ignored or discounted by many Republican voters.

Rules for Selecting the Nominee—A Process with a Window of Opportunity

Presidential nominations are national party decisions that require coordination among party leaders, activists, and groups across the country. Political parties are complex institutions with numerous organizations and officials at the federal, state, and local levels along with intertwining networks of aligned groups, think-tanks, consultants, donors, activists, and party identifiers. Nominating a presidential candidate requires these various elements of a party to work together to select a candidate. Since 1830, the national political party conventions have provided the formal mechanism for coordinating the selection of a presidential nominee. Historically, presidential candidates were selected at the conventions by delegates who were controlled by party bosses who negotiated and bargained in proverbial smoke-filled rooms.[5] Party bosses' control over presidential nominations slowly eroded during the twentieth century until the process changed dramatically during the early 1970s.[6] Since then, most convention delegates have been selected in state primary elections and caucuses open to rank-and-file party voters.[7] Control over the nomination effectively shifted from party leaders to voters in the caucus and primary elections that determine how many delegates each candidate will have at the national convention.[8] Party elites—elected and party officials, groups, donors, and activists—however, have some potential to skew the playing field in favor of their preferred candidate (see below).[9] In most years, caucus and primary voters have followed the lead of party elites and have selected a candidate who advocates for long-standing policy positions. Party voters exercise a more independent voice when party insiders fail to unify in support of a candidate and there are more viable candidates to choose among.[10] Thus the process usually favors the candidate preferred by party insiders, but since caucus and primary voters make the ultimate decisions, there is a window of opportunity for candidates who are less aligned with party positions. As a result, nominations are a mechanism by which political party coalitions and ideologies evolve.[11]

The Candidate Field: "Who Runs" Matters

The outcome of a presidential nomination campaign depends a lot on the candidates who enter the race. Every candidate brings a unique package of

Chapter 3: The Republican Primaries **67**

personal characteristics, experiences, policy positions, and ideological image to a campaign. While all candidates think that they have the right stuff to be president, their self-image and policy vision may not be shared by the constituencies of their party. Some candidates have broader appeal among the different constituencies and groups that make up the political parties, while other candidates' appeal is limited to a narrow subset of the party membership.[12]

Most politicians who consider running for the presidency are ambitious and opportunistic.[13] They calculate their chances of winning and they run when they believe they have a good chance and because running is costly, they tend to stay out of the race if they think their chances are small. The most important factor in this calculus is who else is running and how much appeal these rivals have with various party constituencies.[14] In particular, senators and governors tend to be dissuaded from running when there is a popular candidate in the race. The effect is self-reinforcing. If a popular candidate enters the race, other prospective candidates decide not to run and the front-runner faces weaker opponents. This happened on the Democratic side, where Hillary Clinton looked almost unbeatable in 2013 and 2014.

If there is no early favorite, then more candidates decide to run and the race is more competitive. This happened in the Republican race. None of the potential candidates polled better than 18–20 percent in national polls of Republican identifiers in 2013 and 2014.[15] There was no candidate strong enough to deter other Republicans from entering the 2016 Republican nomination race. This contributed to the largest candidate field in the modern era.

Most of the candidates appeared to be strong contenders although each had limitations as well. Senators Ted Cruz, Marco Rubio, and Rand Paul all could claim a base of support. Marco Rubio was a young, appealing senator who had in his short Senate career established himself as a rising star. As a Cuban-American, Rubio could appeal to Latino voters who were a growing segment of the voting population and whose movement to the Democratic Party had been identified as a major factor in Mitt Romney's defeat in 2012. Rubio's co-sponsorship of a compromise bill on immigration in 2013, however, did not sit well with Republicans opposed to "amnesty" for undocumented immigrants. Cruz, whose father was from Cuba, had established himself as a strong social conservative and as a leader of the Tea Party faction of the party when he advocated shutting down government operations to force President Obama to cut federal spending. Cruz, however, was widely disliked by party insiders. Senator Lindsey Graham joked, "If you killed Ted Cruz on the floor of the Senate, and the trial was in the Senate, nobody would convict you."[16] Rand Paul was the early favorite of libertarians—a minor faction of the Republican Party. Paul's libertarianism and isolationist foreign policy views, however, did not play well with the majority of Republicans who are socially conservative and prefer strong, even hawkish national security positions. A respected foreign policy expert, Lindsey Graham also ran but he was considered a long-shot and he withdrew from the race before the primaries.

68 Part I: The Primaries

Former senator Rick Santorum ran again after showing some strength among social conservatives in the 2012 presidential nomination campaign. Santorum faced lower odds against a stronger field of candidates in 2016.

Governors John Kasich, Scott Walker, Chris Christie, and Bobby Jindal also entered the race. Kasich was nationally prominent in the U.S. House during budget battles between Republicans and President Clinton in the 1990s, but he lost favor among conservatives for supporting the expansion of Medicare and the Affordable Care Act as governor. Christie had established a reputation as a tough, "tell it like it is" politician, but he was saddled with a scandal from his gubernatorial reelection campaign and he had cooperated with President Obama in the aftermath of Hurricane Sandy in 2012. Walker was known as a social conservative who cut taxes and spending and had weakened public employee unions in Wisconsin. Walker, however, spent too much money early and he had trouble raising money once other candidates were in the race. Jindal also had cut taxes and spending as governor, but he was seen as a lackluster speaker and Louisiana was in a budgetary crisis. Walker and Jindal dropped out of the race before the primaries began.

Four former governors, who have fewer constraints in running, also entered the race. Foremost among them was Jeb Bush, brother of President George W. Bush and son of President George H.W. Bush. With name recognition, a massive fundraising network, the ability to appeal to Latino voters, and a conservative record as governor of Florida, Bush was considered the early favorite of party insiders.[17] Bush, however, was not trusted by many conservative party activists because of his support for Common Core Education standards and immigration reform. Bush's family name also was in disrepute—his father was blamed for tax hikes in 1990 and his brother was blamed for the Iraq War and growing budget deficits. The other former governors, Rick Perry, Mike Huckabee, Jim Gilmore, and George Pataki were considered to have low chances of winning the nomination in a race with so many stronger rivals. Perry and Pataki withdrew before the primaries began.

Three candidates without governing experience sought the nomination. Carly Fiorina was a former CEO of Hewlett-Packard who might have an advantage among Republican women. She had, however, lost in her only campaign against California Senator Barbara Boxer in 2010. Dr. Ben Carson had a compelling life story. Born into poverty and raised by a single mother in Detroit, Carson beat the odds to become a famous neurosurgeon. Carson, however, was inexperienced in politics and his lack of knowledge of policy repeatedly hurt him given that his intellect was supposed to be one of his strengths. Donald Trump was a celebrity and a billionaire who had gained popularity with some Republicans by repeatedly claiming that Barack Obama was not a citizen (despite evidence to the contrary). His wealth meant that he could outspend any of his opponents. Indeed, one of his initial strategically successful actions as a candidate was to imply that he would run as an independent candidate if he was treated unfairly by Republican Party

Chapter 3: The Republican Primaries **69**

insiders or other candidates. This threat effectively limited attacks on Trump during the invisible primary because an independent candidacy would ensure a Republican defeat in the general election. Still, Trump was widely discounted as a serious candidate given his inexperience, controversial statements, and his checkered past with three bankruptcies, history of womanizing, and discriminatory practices as a landlord in New York.

There was a lot of uncertainty about which candidate would emerge as the front-runner.

The Party Context: Divisions over Policies and Hostility Toward "The Establishment"

The state of the Republican Party coalition also affected the race. The Republican Party, at the national level, is deeply divided.[18] While factional conflict in political parties is commonplace, party leaders have been unable to mediate and moderate these conflicts.[19] Intraparty divisions make it hard for a given candidate to satisfy all of the factions.

Recent Republican presidential nominations have exhibited four factions with differing preferences for candidates and policy—a declining faction of moderates, a large faction of somewhat conservatives, and very conservatives (who divide into religious and secular branches).[20] Another cleavage that exists that crosses these preferential groupings is the split between the Tea Party movement and "establishment" Republicans.[21] The Tea Party movement, which began after the 2008 bailout of large banks and the election of Barack Obama, challenged "establishment" Republicans who held moderate positions or compromised with Barack Obama. The Tea Party movement pushed Republican candidates and elected officials to adopt more conservative policy positions.[22] By 2016, the Tea Party movement had faded as an organized political force, but the underlying sentiments remained in the form of strong anti–establishment attitudes. A Pew Research Center survey found that 42 percent of politically engaged Republicans were "angry with government."[23] In the same survey, 89 percent of Republican identifiers and leaners responded that they "can seldom, if ever, trust the federal government," and 75 percent agreed that government needs "major reform."

These attitudes made it tough to be an "establishment candidate" like Jeb Bush who was the candidate most associated with the establishment. Other candidates sought, to varying degrees, to establish themselves with one or more of the preferential groupings or with the anti-establishment Republicans. John Kasich was viewed favorably by moderates, but there are too few of them to win a nomination. Chris Christie and Rand Paul sought the support of secular conservatives, while Ben Carson and Ted Cruz sought support from religious conservatives. Marco Rubio offered himself as a candidate with crossover appeal to somewhat and very conservative Republicans. Of the governors and senators,

70 Part I: The Primaries

Ted Cruz most directly courted the support of Tea Party Republicans. No candidate, however, was more effective in attracting support from Republicans who wanted an anti-establishment candidate.

Trump's approach differed from the other candidates. Trump positioned himself as the champion of the conservative populists whose sentiments roughly corresponded to the Tea Party movement. Populism has a lot of different meanings and uses, but the common thread is anti-elite or anti-establishment sentiment.[24] Trump's right-wing populism fused economic nationalism, cultural exclusivity, and anti-establishment rhetoric accusing both political parties of abandoning white working class Americans. He deviated from long-standing Republican positions by expressing support for Social Security and Medicare benefits and gay marriage, while vigorously attacking free trade agreements and promising to bring mining and manufacturing jobs back to America. He proposed building a wall along the Mexican border, deporting illegal immigrants, and banning Muslim immigrants. He repeatedly attacked other Republicans for their relationships with Wall Street. While Trump also adopted conservative positions like advocating deregulation and lower taxes, various commentators likened Trump's campaign to a hostile takeover of the Republican Party.[25]

The Invisible Primary—An Informal Stage of the Nomination Process

While caucus and primary voters cast the ballots that determine which candidate will have a majority of delegates at the convention, these voters may not have as much choice as it appears.[26] Many of the candidates do not have a realistic chance of winning. A lot depends on how the race unfolds during the invisible primary—the phase of the campaign occurring a year or two before the voting begins in the Iowa Caucus. Candidates try to establish themselves as serious contenders by getting commitments of support by party and elected officials, interest group leaders, and donors. They raise money to support a professional campaign organization and pay for campaign ads. They hold events and try to attract media coverage to build their popular support. The candidates with the best chance of winning are those who gain the most support of party insiders and group leaders, raise the most money, attract the most media coverage, and attract more support in national public opinion polls.

During the invisible primary phase of the campaign, party insiders and aligned groups can influence the selection of presidential nominees *if* they work together to promote a candidate.[27] Collusion by party insiders can create an uneven playing field that gives their preferred candidate an easier path to the nomination.[28] Party insiders can help a candidate by visibly signaling their support and talking up a candidate in the media and with group leaders, campaign donors, and party activists.[29] But party insiders' influence on the nomination is conditional on the participation and unity of party insiders in supporting a candidate before the

Chapter 3: The Republican Primaries **71**

voting begins. Party insiders' influence decreases dramatically if these elites refrain from public support of any of the candidates or if they divide their support among the candidates.[30]

In the year leading up to the 2016 primaries, Republican elites mainly sat on the sidelines waiting for a candidate to emerge. About two-thirds of Republican elite elected officials refrained from endorsing any candidate during the invisible primary. Those that did make an endorsement divided their support between Jeb Bush (27 percent), Marco Rubio (23 percent), Ted Cruz (16 percent), and other candidates.[31] The candidate with the most party elite support, former Jeb Bush, received endorsements of fewer than 10 percent of the Republican elites who could have made an endorsement; and almost all of his support came from officials from his home state of Florida. When insiders divide their support or remain uncommitted, caucus and primary voters become relatively empowered because they select among a larger number of viable candidates and they have less guidance about which candidates would be better. That raises the importance of candidate appeal, media coverage, campaign spending, and campaign momentum during the caucuses and primaries.[32]

Several candidates— Bush, Cruz, Rubio, Perry, Kasich, and Carson—raised substantial sums of money. Several others— Santorum, Jindal, Pataki, Graham, and Gilmore—raised so little money that they could not contend for the nomination. The biggest fundraiser was Jeb Bush, who had the support of many big Republican donors. Between his campaign fund and his Super PAC, Right To Rise USA, Bush raised almost $150 million during the invisible primary.[33] While popular with big Republican donors, Bush had a much harder time attracting support among grass-roots Republicans and he was in fifth place in national polls at the end of the invisible primary. While Trump did not raise much money during the invisible primary, his wealth made him a serious candidate.

Instead of raising money to build a campaign organization or pay for television ads, Trump relied on social media and exposure on digital and television news media. Trump gained massive exposure on social media and digital and television news media—more so than his support in national polls would have predicted.[34] Trump received 34 percent of all news coverage devoted to the top six candidates on eight national news outlets, compared to Bush (18 percent), Rubio (14 percent), Carson (14 percent), Cruz (13 percent), and Kasich (7 percent).[35] Trump's coverage also was more positive in tone.[36] Other candidates received less coverage that was more critical than Trump's coverage. This period of extensive, favorable media coverage parallels Trump's rise in national polls in the fall of 2015, although it is hard to say whether Trump's rise in the polls contributed to the media covering him favorably or that the favorable coverage contributed to his rising popularity.

There was no clear front-runner in polls during the invisible primary. Nine different candidates led in various national polls from 2013 through the end of

72 Part I: The Primaries

2015.[37] Rubio, Christie, Paul, and Huckabee all led at some point in 2013 and 2014, but usually with only around 15–16 percent in national polls. Bush periodically surfaced as the front-runner but rarely with more than 20 percent in national polls. A few polls at different times showed Rand Paul in the lead, always with less than 15 percent. Walker emerged briefly in the early spring of 2015 to lead the race. Ben Carson occasionally rose to the top of the polls and his campaign peaked in November of 2015 when he hit 27 percent in one national poll. But, the most consistent leader in national polls was Donald Trump after he entered the race in mid-June of 2015. Trump emerged as the front-runner in national polls in July of 2015 and increased his lead to 36 percent in national polls by January 30, 2016—the day before voting began in the Iowa Caucus. While ahead in the polls, his lead was below the threshold at which the pre-primary leader has gone on to win since the 1970s.[38] Most observers presumed that Trump would fall short of a majority once the voting began.

Thus at the end of the invisible primary, the race remained competitive and there was considerable uncertainty about which candidate would become the nominee.

The Caucuses and Primaries: Winnowing and Momentum

The selection of convention delegates begins with the Iowa Caucus and the New Hampshire Primary. (See Appendix D for a summary of all the Republican primaries and caucuses.) As the first nominating elections, party voters in these states have an outsized role selecting the nominee.[39] Candidates who beat expectations receive more media coverage and campaign contributions and they can continue in the race, potentially gaining momentum.[40] Long-shot candidates who do not finish in the top three candidates in these states usually drop out of the race because their media coverage worsens and they lack the funds to continue in the race. Despite never leading in any national polls, Ted Cruz won the Iowa Caucus with 27.6 percent of the vote, besting Trump (24.3 percent) and Rubio (23.1 percent). The other candidates received less than 10 percent of the Iowa Caucus vote. Cruz did well among conservatives, born-again Christians, and voters saying the most important candidate quality was "someone who shares my values."[41] Rubio had his strongest showing among "somewhat conservatives," college graduates, and voters saying the most important candidate quality was "someone who can win." Trump did the best in Iowa among self-identified moderates, voters who had not attended college, first-time voters, and voters saying the most important candidate quality was someone who "tells it like it is" and who "can bring change." Notably, 45 percent of the voters in the Iowa Caucus were participating in that election for the first time. These new voters typically were Republicans who have voted for the party in general elections but they participated in the nominating election for the first time.[42] Huckabee, Santorum, and Paul all withdrew from the race after the Iowa Caucus.

Chapter 3: The Republican Primaries **73**

Trump rebounded in the New Hampshire primary with 35.3 percent of the vote, winning a plurality of the vote across all age, income, educational, and ideological groups of voters. Kasich came in a distant second with 15.8 percent of the vote. Cruz's third place finish (11.7 percent) dulled his momentum although he was not expected to do as well in the secular Northeastern states. Bush won only 11 percent of the vote despite a heavy investment in the state. The futility of his campaign was exemplified at a campaign rally when he had to beg the audience to "please clap."[43] Rubio was surging in New Hampshire until he made a critical mistake in the last debate before the primary. Instead of answering a question about Obama, Rubio offered a robotic soundbite that was the same answer he had given to a different question. His momentum stalled and he finished fifth in the primary with 10.6 percent of the vote. Christie and Fiorina ended their campaigns after the primary. In one week the candidate field was winnowed from a dozen to six candidates.

Trump solidified his status as the front-runner in the South Carolina primary a week later. Trump won 32.5 percent of the vote, while Rubio rebounded to edge out Cruz for second place winning 22.5 percent of the vote to 22.3 percent for Cruz. In a blow to Ted Cruz's campaign prospects, Trump won a plurality of Evangelical Christians who were supposed to be Cruz's core supporters. As in Iowa, Trump did better among non-college graduates while running behind Rubio among college graduates. Cruz won a narrow plurality of very conservative voters while Trump won among somewhat conservative and moderate voters. Bush ended his campaign after he finished with less than 8 percent of the vote.

The next big event in the race was "Super Tuesday" on March 1st when eleven states held primaries. Trump won plurality (but not majority) victories in Alabama, Arkansas, Georgia, Massachusetts, Tennessee, Vermont, and Virginia. By winning in New England and the South Trump demonstrated his appeal across an ideologically diverse set of voters. Cruz won in Alaska, Oklahoma, and his home state of Texas with less than a majority of votes. Rubio won in Minnesota. Across the states, Trump averaged 34.6 percent of the vote, compared to 25.4 percent for Cruz and 23 percent for Rubio. Cruz and Rubio were now competing to be the alternative to Trump, a non-trivial fight because there was a growing "Stop Trump" movement brewing among party elites.

The Stop Trump or #NeverTrump movement emerged in February and spread in March as Trump gained momentum. Conservative columnists like George Will and others argued that Trump did not respect conservative values and beliefs.[44] The long-time conservative magazine, *The National Review*, featured articles criticizing Trump's policy positions and lack of fealty to conservative principles.[45] Republican strategist Karl Rove met with Republican governors to discuss ways to stop Trump.[46] After Super Tuesday, Mitt Romney publically urged Republican voters to reject Trump. Trump's rhetoric was widely criticized as racist, misogynistic, bigoted, xenophobic, and simply vulgar. Elites feared that Trump's rhetoric would cost votes among women and

74 Part I: The Primaries

minorities, whose support was thought to be needed to win the presidency and to hold the U.S. Senate in the general election. The Stop Trump movement, however, did not develop a coherent strategy nor did Republican elites agree on an alternative to Trump.

Despite opposition from party elites, Trump won four states (Hawaii, Kentucky, Louisiana, and Michigan) while Cruz won two states (Idaho and Maine) and Rubio won in Puerto Rico in the middle of March. Trump's lead grew because he won the states with more delegates to the national convention. The race changed on March 15th, when Trump won four of five elections with an average of 40.3 percent of the vote compared to 27.6 percent for Cruz and 10.4 percent for Rubio. Trump narrowly beat Cruz in Missouri and North Carolina, but won big in Florida and Illinois. The Florida primary was critical because Trump beat Rubio in Rubio's home state by 45 percent to 27 percent. Rubio had put all of his remaining resources into winning his home state and lost badly, effectively ending his campaign. John Kasich won his home state of Ohio and replaced Rubio in the competition with Cruz to be the candidate who could stop Trump from getting the nomination. In late March and early April, Cruz won in Utah and in Wisconsin, establishing himself as the only viable alternative to Trump. But it was too little too late.

Trump won with majorities of the vote in the remaining sixteen states. Trump's momentum grew with increasingly large victories in New York and Pennsylvania. Trump's victory in the Indiana primary on May 3rd effectively ended Ted Cruz's campaign. By late May, Republican insiders started to resign themselves to supporting Trump's nomination. Trump's support among grassroots Republicans grew substantially.

Figure 3.1 shows the trajectory of the leading candidates' vote shares in the caucuses and primaries. Trump's trajectory is one of gaining momentum during the caucuses and primaries, withstanding a too-little/too-late challenge from party insiders, and surging through the end of the primary season. Trump gained momentum in the New Hampshire primary through Super Tuesday, before coming down a bit—but still winning more often than not until March 15th in the Florida primary. After that, Trump's momentum was upward through the end of the primaries. Cruz did well in Iowa but lost momentum in New Hampshire and South Carolina before rebounding until his peak in the Utah and Wisconsin elections—too late to stop Trump from gaining a majority of convention delegates. Rubio also gained momentum in Iowa, but his disastrous fifth place finish in New Hampshire limited his prospects. He rebounded somewhat in March but he never regained the momentum he had from Iowa. Kasich finished second in a few of the more liberal states and won big in his home state of Ohio, but he never drew enough support to be a serious contender for the nomination.

While the other candidates sought to become the leading candidate of one of the major factions in the party, exit polls show that Trump drew support from

Chapter 3: The Republican Primaries 75

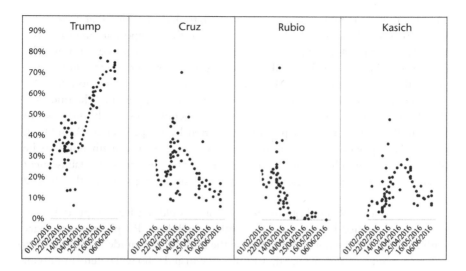

FIGURE 3.1 Caucus and Primary Vote Shares of the Top Four Candidates in the 2016 Republican Caucuses and Primaries

Note: Includes all states, except Colorado and North Dakota; includes primaries in Washington, D.C., Puerto Rico, and Virgin Islands.

across the ideological range of Republican primary and caucus voters. At the state level, Cruz did better in more conservative states like Utah, Idaho, and Oklahoma but ran worse in moderate or liberal states. Rubio and Kasich did better in states with more moderate Republicans, but gained little support among conservatives in the party. Trump won increasingly large shares of the vote across regions and across factions of the party.

While drawing support from across regions and ideological factions of the party, exit polls show that Trump drew the most support from voters who were angry with Washington politicians. Consistent with the Pew Research surveys mentioned earlier, the caucus and primary exit polls showed that 89.6 percent of Republican voters were dissatisfied or angry about the federal government. Trump won almost 53 percent of the votes of voters who described themselves as angry.[47] The extent of anti-establishment sentiment is reflected in the fact that exit polls included a question asking, "Do you feel betrayed by *Republican* politicians in Washington?" [emphasis added]. Over 53 percent of respondents in these polls answered in the affirmative, and Trump won more than 40 percent of these voters—far more than any other candidate.[48]

Although the media paid a lot of attention to the appeal of Trump's positions on immigration, this was the most important issue to only a small percentage of Republican voters. Across the twenty-eight states with exit polls, an average of only 11 percent of voters identified immigration as a major concern. Indeed,

76 Part I: The Primaries

51 percent of the Republican voters in exit polls took the position that immigrants should be given legal status. These voters divided their support among the other candidates, while those supporting deportation strongly favored Trump. The economy and jobs, terrorism, and federal budget deficits were important to more voters than was immigration. Notably, Trump received more support than his rivals among voters identifying these issues as the most important. The one issue that Trump was on the side of the majority of Republicans was his proposal to ban Muslim immigration—a position supported by 69 percent of Republican voters. Trump won strongly among these voters. But, the main point to be gleaned from exit polls is that Trump won mainly because his anti-establishment positions were popular among Republican voters angry with the federal government.

In this context, Republican insiders probably could not have stopped Trump even if they unified behind one of the other candidates. People who are angry with party leaders are not going to follow the cues of party insiders. Party insiders generally want a candidate who they think can win and who will defend important party interests and policy positions.[49] Rank-and-file partisans, in contrast, are often less informed and less wedded to particular policy orthodoxy, which opens the door for a candidate to build a winning nominating coalition that changes what the political party stands for. These voters ultimately make the decisions that select convention delegates. Anger with the government was widespread among Republican voters and this disrupted the normal pattern of an experienced politician winning the nomination.[50]

Conclusion

Presidential nominations are important because the presidential nominee is the foremost spokesperson of a party, the personification of the party image, and the main definer of the ideological vision of a political party. While party insiders and group leaders normally try to coordinate their support for a candidate, party insiders could not unify behind a candidate before or during the caucuses and primaries. Rank-and-file Republican voters had a large field of candidates to select from, and they gravitated to the candidate who most vociferously attacked the Washington establishment. Perhaps more than his policy positions, Trump drew support because a lot of Republican voters were angry and demanded change.

Donald Trump may change the Republican Party coalition because he assembled a winning nominating coalition with a set of policy positions that deviate substantially from Republican policy orthodoxy. Whether Trump's populist coalition prevails as the new direction of the Republican Party will depend a lot on what happens after the election.

Notes

1 Joe Scarborough, "Donald Trump's Hostile Takeover of the Republican Party," *Washington Post*, March 1, 2016, www.washingtonpost.com/blogs/post-partisan/wp/2016/03/01/donald-trumps-hostile-takeover-of-the-republican-party/?utm_term=.ea3e4b2290ef (accessed December 1, 2016).

2 One group of political scientists forecasted that Donald Trump would win the Republican nomination. Andrew J. Dowdle, Randall E. Adkins, Karen Sebold, and Jarred Cuellar, "Forecasting Presidential Nominations in 2016: #WePredictedClinton ANDTrump," *PS: Political Science & Politics*, 49 (October, 2016): 691–695.

3 Nelson W. Polsby, *Consequences of Party Reform* (New York: Oxford University Press, 1983); Jeanne J. Kirkpatrick, *Dismantling the Parties: Reflections on Party Reform and Party Decline* (Washington, D.C.: American Enterprise Institute Press, 1978).

4 Randall E. Adkins, Andrew J. Dowdle, Greg Petrow, and Wayne Steger, "Progressive Ambition, Opportunism, and the Presidency, 1972–2012," paper presented at the annual meeting of the Midwest Political Science Association, 2015, Chicago, IL.

5 Paul T. David, Ralph M. Goldman, and Richard C. Bain, *The Politics of National Party Conventions* (Washington, D.C.: Brookings Institution, 1960).

6 Byron E. Shafer, *Bifurcated Politics: Evolution and Reform of the National Party Convention*, (Cambridge, MA: Harvard University Press, 1988); James W. Ceaser, *Presidential Selection: Theory and Development* (Princeton, NJ: Princeton University Press, 1979).

7 Barbara Norrander, "Nomination Choices: Caucus and Primary Outcomes, 1976–1988," *American Journal of Political Science*, 37 (2) (1993): 343–364.

8 Polsby, *Consequences of Party Reform*.

9 William R. Keech and Donald R. Mathews, *The Party's Choice* (Washington, D.C.: Brookings Institution, 1976); Marty Cohen, David Karol, Hans Noel, and John Zaller, *The Party Decides: Presidential Nominations Before and After Reform* (Chicago, IL: University of Chicago Press, 2008).

10 Wayne Steger, *A Citizen's Guide to Presidential Nominations: The Competition for Leadership* (New York: Routledge, 2015).

11 Stephen Skowronek, *The Politics Presidents Make: Leadership from John Adams to George Bush*, Cambridge, MA: Belknap Press, 1993; Richard Herrera, "The Crosswinds of Change: Sources of Change in the Democratic and Republican Parties," *Political Research Quarterly*, 48 (1995): 291–312; David Karol, *Party Position Change in American Politics: Coalition Management* (New York: Cambridge University Press, 2009).

12 Steven J. Brams, *The Presidential Election Game* (New Haven, CT: Yale University Press, 1978).

13 Lara M. Brown, *Jockeying for the American Presidency: The Political Opportunism of Aspirants* (Amherst, NY: Cambria Press, 2011).

14 Adkins et al., "Progressive Ambition, Opportunism, and the Presidency."

15 Polls were tracked on Pollster.com. http://elections.huffingtonpost.com/pollster/2016-national-gop-primary (accessed July 2, 2016).

16 Catherine Treyz, "Lindsey Graham Jokes About How to Get Away with Murdering Ted Cruz," *CNN*, February 26, 2016, www.cnn.com/2016/02/26/politics/lindsey-graham-ted-cruz-dinner/ (accessed December 2, 2016).

78 Part I: The Primaries

17 Gerald F. Seib, "The Assets and Liabilities of Jeb Bush," *Wall Street Journal*, May 11, 2015, www.wsj.com/articles/the-assets-and-liabilities-of-jeb-bush-1431359095 (accessed December 2, 2016)

18 Geoffrey Kabaservice, *Rule and Ruin: The Downfall of Moderation and the Destruction of the Republican Party* (New York: Oxford University Press, 2014); Marty Cohen, David Karol, Hans Noel, and John Zaller, "Party Versus Faction in the Reformed Presidential Nominating System," *PS: Political Science and Politics*, 49 (4) (2016): 701–708.

19 Hans Noel, "Ideological Factions in the Republican and Democratic Parties," *The ANNALS of the American Academy of Political and Social Science*, 677 (1) (2016): 166–188.

20 Henry Olsen and Dante Scala, *The Four Faces of the Republican Party and the Fight for the 2016 Presidential Nomination* (New York: Palgrave, 2016).

21 Theda Skocpol and Vanessa Williamson, *The Tea Party and the Remaking of Republican Conservatism* (New York: Oxford University Press, 2013).

22 Thomas E. Mann and Norman J. Ornstein, *It's Even Worse Than it Looks: How the American Constitutional System Collided With the New Politics of Extremism* (New York: Basic Books, 2012).

23 Pew Research Center, "Beyond Distrust: How Americans View Their Government," (November 2015), p. 9; see also, "Campaign Exposes Fissures Over Issues, Values and How Life Has Changed in the U.S." (March 2016) and "2016 Campaign: Strong Interest, Widespread Dissatisfaction" (July 2016).

24 Noam Gidron and Bart Bonikowski, "Varieties of Populism: Literature Review and Research Agenda," Weatherhead Center for International Affairs, Working Paper, No. 13-0004 (2013).

25 Ryan Lizza, "Donald Trump's Hostile Takeover of the GOP," *The New Yorker*, January 28, 2016, www.newyorker.com/news/daily-comment/donald-trumps-hostile-takeover-of-the-g-o-p (accessed November 28, 2016).

26 Wayne P. Steger, "Do Primary Voters Draw from a Stacked Deck? Presidential Nominations in an Era of Candidate-Centered Campaigns," *Presidential Studies Quarterly*, 30 (4) (2000): 727–753.

27 Wayne P. Steger, "Two Paradigms of Presidential Nominations," *Presidential Studies Quarterly*, 43 (2) (2013): 377–387.

28 Cohen et al., *The Party Decides*; Kathleen Bawn, Martin Cohen, David Karol, Hans Noel, Seth Masket, and John Zaller, "A Theory of Parties: Groups, Policy Demanders and Nominations in American Politics," *Perspectives on Politics*, 10 (3) (2012): 571–597.

29 Cohen et al. *The Party Decides*, ch. 7.

30 Wayne P. Steger, "Conditional Arbiters: The Limits of Political Party Influence in Presidential Nominations," *PS: Political Science & Politics*, 49 (4) (October, 2016): 709–715.

31 Endorsements were tracked on FiveThirtyEight.com. http://projects.fivethirtyeight.com/2016-endorsement-primary/.

32 Larry Bartels, *Presidential Primaries and the Dynamics of Public Choice* (Princeton, NJ: Princeton University Press, 1988); Audrey A. Haynes, Paul-Henri Gurian, Michael H. Crespin, and Christopher Zorn, "The Calculus of Concession: Media Coverage and

the Dynamics of Winnowing in Presidential Nominations," *Political Research Quarterly*, 64 (4) (2004): 870–883.

33 Center for Responsive Politics, https://www.opensecrets.org/pres16/candidate?id=N00037006 (accessed December 2, 2016).

34 Candidates' share of TV news coverage corresponds closely to their support in national polls. Wayne P. Steger, "A Quarter Century of Network News Coverage of Candidates in Presidential Nomination Campaigns," *Journal of Political Marketing*, 1 (1) (2002): 91–116.

35 Thomas E. Patterson, "Pre-Primary News Coverage of the 2016 Presidential Race: Trump's Rise, Sanders's Emergence, Clinton's Struggle," Shorenstein Center on Media, Politics and Public Policy (2016), http://shorensteincenter.org/wp-content/uploads/2016/06/Pre-Primary-News-Coverage-Trump-Sanders-Clinton-2016.pdf (accessed December 1, 2016).

36 See Thomas Patterson's analysis of news coverage of the candidates at http://scholar.harvard.edu/thomaspatterson/home (accessed December 2, 2016).

37 RealClearPolitics.com, www.realclearpolitics.com/epolls/2016/president/us/2016_republican_presidential_nomination-3823.html (accessed December 4, 2016).

38 William G. Mayer, "Handicapping the 2008 Nomination Races: An Early Winter Prospectus," *The Forum*, 5 (4) (2008): 2.

39 Randall E. Adkins and Andrew J. Dowdle, "How Important Are Iowa and New Hampshire to Winning Post-Reform Presidential Nominations?" *Political Research Quarterly*, 54 (2) (2001): 431–444.

40 Bartels, *Presidential Primaries and the Dynamics of Public Choice*.

41 Exit polls were obtained from CNN, www.cnn.com/election/primaries/polls (accessed December 3, 2016).

42 David Lauter, "The Millions of New Voters Spurred by Donald Trump and Other Campaign Myths, Debunked," *Los Angeles Times*, March 21, 2016, www.latimes.com/politics/la-na-presidential-campaign-myths-20160321-htmlstory.html (accessed December 1, 2016).

43 "'Please Clap': Is This the Most Cringeworthy Moment in the 2016 Campaign?" (February 3, 2016), http://insider.foxnews.com/2016/02/03/please-clap-jeb-bush-pleads-new-hampshire-crowd-saddest-moment-2016-campaign (accessed November 28, 2016).

44 David A. Graham, "Which Republicans Oppose Donald Trump? A Cheat Sheet," *The Atlantic*, November 6, 2016, www.theatlantic.com/politics/archive/2016/11/where-republicans-stand-on-donald-trump-a-cheat-sheet/481449/ (accessed November 28, 2016).

45 Andrew McCarthy, "It's Not My Party," *The National Review*, July 23, 2016, www.nationalreview.com/article/438255/its-not-my-party (November 28, 2016).

46 Alexander Burns, Maggie Haberman, and Jonathan Martin, "Inside the Republican Party's Desperate Mission to Stop Donald Trump," *New York Times*, February 27, 2016, www.nytimes.com/2016/02/28/us/politics/donald-trump-republican-party.html (accessed December 4, 2016).

47 "Republican Exit Polls," *CNN*, www.cnn.com/election/primaries/polls (accessed December 2, 2016).

80 Part I: The Primaries

48 This question was asked in nineteen of the twenty-eight states in which exit polls were conducted.
49 Richard L. Butler, *Claiming the Mantle: How Presidential Nominations Are Won and Lost Before the Votes Are Cast* (Boulder, CO: Westview Press, 2004).
50 Lonna Rae Atkeson and Cherie D. Maestas, "Presidential Primary Turnout: 1972–2016," *PS: Political Science and Politics*, 49 (4) (October, 2016): 755–760.

4

TRUMP'S APPEAL

Mark S. Mellman

How did the most unpopular presidential candidate in history (at least in the history of polling) accede to the highest office in the land? Of course, it matters that our constitutional system honors not the popular vote, which Hillary Clinton won by over 2 points, but rather the Electoral College vote, where Donald Trump prevailed. It helped that Hillary Clinton was the second most unpopular presidential candidate in history, though, not many months prior to the election, she was the best-liked public official in the country.

Turnout, fake news, voter suppression, emails, Russian hacking, letters from the FBI Director and a hundred other things also mattered to the outcome. Everything mattered precisely because the race was so close that if, in three states, a total fewer than fit in the South Williamsport, Pennsylvania stadium that hosts the Little League World Series had changed their vote, Hillary Clinton would have taken the oath of office.

But Donald Trump succeeded in eliciting support from a large minority of Americans, and it's worth understanding why. Some analyses are content with simple demographic answers, of which there are plenty. A post-election survey by my firm, the Mellman Group, found that Trump won and Clinton lost in households dependent on manufacturing for their livelihood.[1] Clinton won non-manufacturing households by 4 points. Had she garnered that margin with the entire electorate, she would almost certainly have been guaranteed an Electoral College victory. Instead, Trump won manufacturing households by 18 points, depriving Clinton of the votes she needed to post an Electoral College victory, particularly in key states like Pennsylvania, Michigan, and Wisconsin.

One could also say the contest was all about partisanship—Clinton won Democrats by 81 points, Trump led by 80 with Republicans, while Independents split mostly down the middle, giving Trump a narrow 4-point advantage.[2] Many

82 Part I: The Primaries

point to Trump's record performance among non-college-educated whites, who gave him a 39-point margin, while, in 2012, Romney had "only" a 25-point lead with this segment.[3]

But *who* does not necessarily tell us *why*, and that is the question this chapter intends to explore in more detail. Trump's showing resulted from a classic "perfect storm"—the confluence of:

a. an underlying structural dynamic that, at worst, put any Republican in striking distance, along with
b. Trump's hitherto rather unique ability to galvanize and unite three distinct strands of American conservatism—all while
c. forging a unique us-versus-them social identity for his followers
d. by election day, an unpopular opponent, and finally
e. Trump's billionaire status.

To eliminate all surprise, but sticking with the classic stricture to "tell them what you are going to tell them, before telling them," I will argue that a number of structural dynamics, including Democrats' search for a third-party term in the White House, along with the (growing, but not fast enough) economy, created an opening for Trump that ultimately helped him succeed, despite being widely disliked.

But there was much more to it than that. In an underappreciated analysis, political scientist Karen Stenner teased out three separate modes of conservative thinking, each based on an aversion—an aversion to government, an aversion to change, and an aversion to difference.[4] Each of these aversions is activated and strengthened when voters perceive threats. Trump sometimes invented, but consistently accentuated those threats, using language, images, and examples other politicians would have been afraid to invoke and then created a unique us-versus-them social identity that melded together these disparate orientations. As with other powerful social identities, the "in-group" is favored and the "out-group" is denigrated.[5]

Added to this potent brew were two other important factors working in Trump's favor—his status as a billionaire businessman and what became a widespread dislike of Hillary Clinton. To some the former meant he would be "unbossed and unbought," while to others it signaled an ability to reinvigorate an underperforming economy.

Before elaborating the arguments and marshaling the evidence, let's look at one additional source of his appeal that mattered a great deal in the primary process that made Trump the GOP nominee.

The Primaries

Most of the factors discussed below apply to Trump's primary supporters as well as to his general election constituency. One element of Trump's appeal, however, was evident mainly within his primary constituency which felt betrayed by a Republican leadership they thought had compromised and equivocated too often and therefore failed to repeal Obamacare, eliminate the deficit, reduce government spending, hold fast to the debt limit, or keep its other promises.

These voters handed control of the entire Congress to the GOP, and yet the policy and platform of the Obama administration had not been dismantled. For many Republican primary voters, that fact was proof positive of an enfeebled leadership—unable, or unwilling, to slay the Democratic dragon.

These voters may not understand "the system," they may not recognize that Senate and House majorities by themselves are not sufficient to undo a president's program, but they were hardly in the mood for excuses. According to a Fox News poll, 62 percent of Republican primary voters felt "betrayed," a strong word indeed, by their party's politicians, while 66 percent believed congressional Republicans failed to do everything they could have to stop Obama's agenda.[6]

These voters backed Trump in large numbers because, by contrast to their feckless leadership, they saw in him a backbone of steel. When criticized for some seemingly "crazy" remark, he did not back down, he doubled down. And, Trump supporters reasoned, someone who doubles down in the face of criticism will not back down in Washington's political battles.

According to a Quinnipiac Poll, Trump was the choice of 66 percent of Florida primary voters who most wanted a "strong leader."[7] A Bloomberg survey of South Carolina GOP primary participants found 51 percent saying Trump was the candidate most likely to "take on the Washington establishment."[8]

Reponses to a question posed in one poll of Republican primary voters summarizes two elements of Trump's appeal: 59 percent of Republican primary voters strongly agreed that "what this country needs is a strong leader to shake things up in Washington."[9] Among this group, focused on leadership and the evils of Washington, 50 percent ranked Trump as their first choice—a level of appeal far greater than any other Republican candidate exerted.

The General Election

In turning to the general election, we first consider underlying structural dynamics.

The Economy and Other Structural Factors

Human beings display a natural inclination to overweight the causal role of people in producing outcomes, while underweighting the role of circumstances. Indeed, this tendency is so pervasive and so powerful that psychologists call it Fundamental Attribution Error.[10] It is no surprise then that political analyses, too, attribute less causal impact to underlying structural dynamics than they deserve.

Economic performance, partisanship, and the length of time a party has held the White House are among the structural fundamentals that help determine the outcome of presidential elections. Analysts vary in the weight they accord to these structural dynamics, individually and collectively, but nearly everyone believes they count for at least something. A cottage industry has arisen among political scientists and economists in developing econometric models employing fundamentals to forecast election outcomes (see Chapter 1 for further discussion).

Some of these econometric exercises employ polls, which can help make the predictions smarter, but sacrifice real understanding of the role played by underlying dynamics. Nine models built by academics rely only on fundamentals and do not include any polling data about the presidential race itself.

On average, before Election Day, these nine predicted a 2-point popular vote victory for Donald Trump. Obviously these models weren't completely accurate in the end, but they reveal an important analytic point. Through the eyes of these models, the stage was set for a Trump victory in the popular vote based solely on the state of the economy (variously measured), the two previous terms during which Democrats had controlled the White House and other measures of partisanship.

The role of economic performance in elections is widely recognized. Figure 4.1, from a pre-election poll we conducted,[11] relates both assessments of individuals' personal economic circumstances and their evaluations of the national economy to their vote choice. As is evident, the correlation is tight, particularly for the nation's economy. While the primacy of the nation's "pocketbook" over the individual's own economic circumstances may surprise political professionals, the academic literature is replete with similar findings.

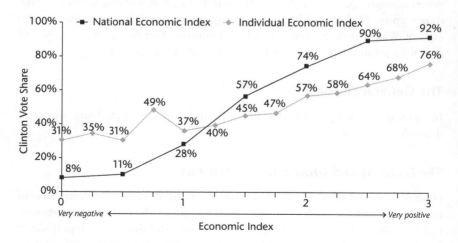

FIGURE 4.1 Clinton Vote Share by National and Individual Economic Indices

A party's tenure in office is another structural factor that bears directly on presidential election outcomes. Americans seem to exhibit a natural proclivity for rotation. Only once since World War II has a party won a third term in the White House, when George H.W. Bush won after two terms of Ronald Reagan.

In fact, the econometric models referenced above find about a 4-point penalty for a candidate seeking a third party-term. Without that penalty, Hillary Clinton could have emerged with a 6-point lead over Trump (the 2 points she got, plus the 4 taken away by running for a third party-term) and would certainly have won the Electoral College and the White House. Trump's failure to capture a plurality of the popular vote suggests he failed to live up to the potential created for him by situational factors over which neither he, nor Clinton, had any influence.

On these accounts, the magnitude of Trump's popular vote requires no explanation: he garnered *less* support than one would have expected, given the fundamentals. None of these circumstances were under Trump's control, but he was not merely a passive beneficiary of structural dynamics—he united and ignited three distinct brands of conservatism.

Conservatism 1—Aversion to Government

The role government should play in society is a traditionally contentious issue between Democrats and Republicans. Indeed, one brand of conservatism takes minimizing government as its leitmotif and central organizing principle, while progressives take as given that government can and should be the engine of reform and progress in society. Since at least Ronald Reagan, Republicans have been the "anti-government party" and have made bashing "big government" a staple centerpiece of their rhetoric.

So, those with a distaste for the federal government have typically made the Republican party their home and GOP candidates their preferred presidents. This year's presidential election was no exception. According to the exit poll, those who believe government was doing "too much" (50 percent of the electorate) gave Trump a 50-point margin, while voters who wanted government to "do more" (45 percent), gave Clinton almost the exact same advantage.

Our own survey[12] asked voters a similar question (with similar results) and included several other items on the role of government. Combining responses to those questions into an index, we found the 48 percent of white voters most hostile to government supported Trump over Clinton by nearly 70 points, while the 46 percent more sympathetic to the federal government preferred Clinton by over 50 points (see Figure 4.2).

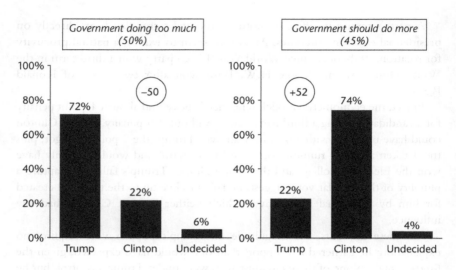

FIGURE 4.2 Presidential Vote by Views on Government

Conservatism 2—Aversion to Change

Classic Burkean conservatism is predicated on respect for tradition and distaste for change. As Edmund Burke wrote, "When ancient opinions and rules of life are taken away, the loss cannot possibly be estimated. From that moment, we have no compass to govern us, nor can we know distinctly to what port to steer."[13] Burke penned these words after the 1789 French Revolution, and, in some ways, 2016 represented the Thermidorian Reaction[14] to America's cultural revolution. Although Donald Trump was pre-eminently a candidate of "change," perhaps the most important word in his slogan was "*again*"—"Make America Great *Again*." Trump was not advocating change to something new and different, but change *back* to something older, traditional, and historical; to "ancient opinions and rules of life," that Democrats had "taken away." He promised a return to an America that he believed once was.

While Trump campaigned as an agent of change, his desire to make America great *again* reflected a sense that the changes already afoot were deleterious and needed to be rolled back. Many voters, particularly Trump supporters, are at best wary of the changes that have swept over America in the last half century or so. That aversion to change was on vivid display and Trump scooped up those voters.

At the level of general Burkean principle, Trump reflects the majority of the American public, 57 percent of whom believe "order and stability" is more important than "progress and reform," which is prioritized by 43 percent. Moreover, these attitudes divide the supporters of each candidate, with those focused on order and stability delivering Trump a 26-point margin, and those attracted to progress and reform selecting Clinton by over 40 points (see Figure 4.3).

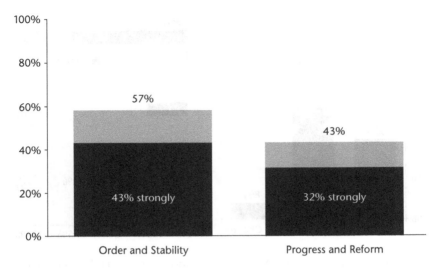

FIGURE 4.3 "Which is More Important to You Personally? 'Order and Stability' or 'Progress and Reform'?"

When people believe treasured values are threatened, they become increasingly committed to them. Right or wrong, fair or unfair (I for one think it's wrong and unfair), many Americans perceive their culture under siege. By 53 percent to 37 percent voters agreed that, "Our country is changing too fast, undermining traditional American values." The majority that found the pace of change too quick, voted for Trump by a 38-point margin, while those who disagreed with this proposition gave Clinton a 63-point advantage.

An even clearer sign of public antipathy to the cultural transformations wrought in this country came in response to a question which asked voters to evaluate the changes in "American culture and way of life" since the 1950s. Recall, as some of our respondents may not have, that the 1950s was before the civil rights era, before LGBT rights, before digital technology, before Medicare, before the advent of nationally broadcast color television, and even before rock and roll as we know it. It was a period when less than 10 percent of Americans had college degrees and only about 40 percent had high school diplomas (see Figure 4.4).

Yet, just 38 percent thought the changes wrought since the 1950s had been for the better, while a solid 55 percent said our culture and way of life mostly changed for the worse. (Eight percent, apparently still playing with hula hoops, listening to monaural record players, and sipping from racially segregated water fountains, were somehow unable to discern much change at all.)

Among the 38 percent of voters who believe America's culture changed for the better over the last fifty years, 74 percent supported Clinton, while among the

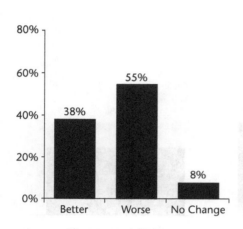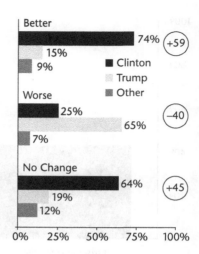

FIGURE 4.4 "Since the 1950s, Do You Think American Culture and Way of Life Has 'Mostly Changed for the Better,' 'Mostly Changed for the Worse,' or 'Not Changed Much at All'?" And Presidential Vote by Views on Cultural Change since the 1950s

55 percent who said it had gotten worse, two-thirds voted Trump. (Nearly two-thirds of the 8 percent who saw little change also supported Clinton).

Again, when these and similar items are indexed, the 37 percent of whites most hostile to the changes gave Trump a vast margin of nearly 75 points. Hostility to change in three different arenas—gender, race, and dispossession or decline—were at the forefront of discussion in this campaign—and in each of these areas, many Americans perceive a threat.

Gender

In 1937, only 33 percent of Americans said they would vote for an otherwise qualified presidential candidate from their party, if the nominee was a woman. By 1958, the number professing willingness to support a woman rose to 54 percent, and to 76 percent by 1978. In 2012, 95 percent told the Gallup Poll they would be willing to vote for a qualified woman. That's not to say all voters would in fact cast their ballots that way, but nearly all Americans realized it was, at least, socially unacceptable to express prejudice against a female candidate. Other studies which attempt to minimize social desirability bias in responses to such questions have produced decidedly mixed results, with some suggesting substantial prejudice against a female presidential candidate and others indicating little or none.

There is no question, though, that gender-based attitudes had a significant impact on support for Trump and Clinton in this election. In our pre-election survey, one of the biggest differentiators between Trump and Clinton voters

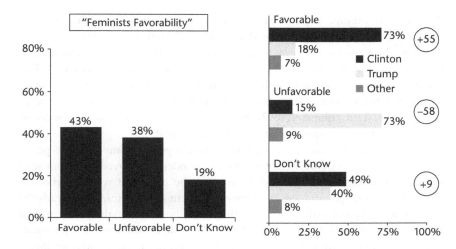

FIGURE 4.5 Views of Feminists, And Presidential Vote by Views of Feminists

came in their responses to the word "feminists." Overall, voters were somewhat divided, with 43 percent holding a favorable opinion of feminists and 38 percent expressing an unfavorable impression. Over three-quarters of those with unfavorable views of feminists voted for Trump, whereas 74 percent of those with favorable opinions supported Clinton (see Figure 4.5). Hostility toward feminists is good evidence of an aversion to some of the changes that have taken place in our country.

Other questions in our survey explored respondents' sexism—their underlying prejudice against women—more directly. For example, overall, Americans divide about evenly on whether "women are too easily offended," with 43 percent saying they are and 46 percent believing they are not. Those who reject the proposition that women take umbrage too easily supported Hillary Clinton by a 56-point margin, while those who agreed, favored Trump by over 50 points. Similarly, among the half who say women complain about discrimination when they lose out to men in fair competition, Trump won by 39 points, while the 32 percent who disagreed gave Clinton a 54-point margin.

Using these and two other related measures in an index reveals that the most sexist 43 percent of the electorate voted for Trump by more than a 50-point margin (71–18 percent), while the less sexist 61 percent of the electorate gave Clinton a nearly 50-point advantage.

Race

It has become commonplace, particularly on the left, to deride Trump supporters as "racists," a term properly loaded with baggage. Fortunately, there are fewer old-style, Jim Crow racists around than there used to be, but those who remain

90 Part I: The Primaries

did warm to Trump. This old racism has at its heart the notion that African-Americans are, and should be treated as, biologically inferior to whites.

Sadly, this view has not been totally eradicated. A PPP poll asked Republican primary voters in South Carolina whether whites were "a superior race." Ten percent agreed outright and another 11 percent weren't sure. Thirty percent of Trump voters took one of these two positions, unwilling to say that whites were not superior. That compared to 24 percent of Rubio voters and 11 percent of Cruz voters, the two runners-up to Trump in this poll.[15]

Another poll question that generated substantial press commentary was posed by *The Economist*/YouGov, asking whether respondents approved or disapproved of "the executive order that freed all slaves in the states that were in rebellion against the federal government."[16] Thirteen percent of Americans and nearly 20 percent of Trump voters disapproved of the order, also known as the Emancipation Proclamation of 1863. Only 5 percent of Rubio's supporters took that position.

As frightening as these results are, it is important not to over-interpret them. First, the question is asked in the midst of a battery of items about the use, and alleged abuse, of executive orders, which could have influenced the answers of some who generally oppose such instruments. Second, as the question makes clear, and some remember from high school history, the Proclamation only freed slaves in the South (not in the Union), which some thought unfair, separate, and apart from their views on slavery. Moreover, while Trump voters are more likely to oppose the Emancipation Proclamation than others, a large majority still favor it.

Questions such as those we've been discussing are rarely asked, though, in part because it is assumed that the vast majority of Americans are beyond this kind of Jim Crow racism, at least when it comes to African-Americans. But whatever the fate of old-style racism, what political psychologists David Sears, John McConaghy, and Donald Kinder defined as symbolic racism, or racial resentment, is abroad in the land and it did affect this election.

This newer, subtler, form of racism reflects negative feelings about blacks as a group. The 36 percent of the electorate that scored highest on symbolic racism gave Trump a margin of over 60 points, while the 38 percent who were lowest on this index supported Clinton by some 55 points.

Dispossession

Trump activated, and was supported by, a revolt of the dispossessed. Anxious to do battle against the changes they believe took away their former status, the dispossessed flocked to Trump, who presented himself as their champion in rolling back the changes that had diminished their standing.

Americans who feel people like them were once politically potent, economically central, and culturally ascendant, but believe they have been increasingly marginalized in each of those areas, came out in large numbers to support Trump.

Half the white electorate believes they are financially worse off than people like them were thirty years ago. They gave Trump a two-to-one margin.

Whites who see themselves as rich or poor, but at least as well off as people like them had been thirty years ago, voted for Clinton by some 13 points—a much bigger difference than the much-discussed gap between college educated and non-college whites. Similarly, 52 percent of whites feel politicians are less concerned with people like them today, than officeholders were thirty years ago. And they gave Trump nearly a 40-point margin. Those whites who perceive no diminution in politicians' focus on people like them gave Clinton a margin of over 20 points.

Trump supporters feel marginalized and dispossessed—pushed out of economic centrality, deprived of their political clout, and forced to accept cultural changes they dislike. Trump defined their plight and gave voice to their anger, eliciting support from those who stood squarely against changes they perceived as threatening them.

Conservatism III—Aversion to Difference

Let's get it out of the way quickly: "aversion to difference" is a phrase Stenner uses to describe the content of the concept widely known as "authoritarianism." That term is also heavily loaded and has been subject to—dare I say it—tortured debate as to its meaning, measurement, and mechanism. This is not the place to relitigate, or even to rehearse those arguments, but it is important to make a few points about the term before delving into its relationship to Donald Trump and Election 2016.

First, authoritarianism, as it has been conceptualized by recent scholars, is a psychological predisposition, not a philosophical absolute or a programmatic agenda. There are not a set of people who are authoritarians and a set of people who are not. Some individuals have greater tendencies toward authoritarianism and some have lesser tendencies. Authoritarianism varies not only across individuals, but across time and situations as well. In some circumstances, authoritarian predispositions lie dormant and are not terribly relevant to political behavior. In other contexts, those tendencies are activated, playing a central political role for those harboring this predisposition.

But the "it" we are describing is an aversion to difference and a preference for unity and sameness, not a concrete platform to which people subscribe. Perhaps most important, despite the intention of the term's originators, it is not another name for "fascism." While authoritarianism has been correlated with various forms of intolerance, it is uncorrelated with a host of behaviors that come to mind when one thinks about fascism. Moreover, we have no idea whether authoritarian psychology was more prevalent in Nazi Germany or Mussolini's Italy, than in Roosevelt's United States or Churchill's United Kingdom.

It is now measured by asking about the relative priority of various child rearing values like independence vs. respect for elders and being curious vs. being

92 Part I: The Primaries

possessed of good manners. To put the matter bluntly, there is obviously a huge distance between preferring a child who has respect for elders and good manners over one who is independent and curious on the one hand, and exterminating 6 million Jews, or even burning down the Reichstag, on the other. Most of those who display authoritarian tendencies are not simply one step away from dropping the Zyklon-B pellets into gas chambers.

All that said, the data do reveal a relationship between aversion to difference and candidate support. The 21 percent of the white electorate with the strongest authoritarian tendencies gave Trump a margin of nearly 50 points, while the 36 percent who are least authoritarian supported Clinton by 30 points.

We noted above that the strength and impact of authoritarian predispositions varies with circumstances. When exhibitions of diversity, difference, and discord seem to overwhelm oneness, sameness, and unity, authoritarian tendencies are activated. When the cultural homogeneity authoritarians crave seems threatened, they react.

By contrast, demonstrations of oneness, sameness, and unity reassure authoritarians, reducing the impact of these predispositions. The reassurance that comes with unity was illustrated by Khzir Khan's moving address to the Democratic National Convention during which he told the story of his heroic son and pulled a copy of the Constitution from his suit pocket. Khan's address highlighted the oneness and sameness of the American people, united in war, and governed by commitment to a shared founding document.

It's no wonder that Trump's attack on the Khans generated almost no support. A *Washington Post*–ABC News poll found a mere 12 percent of Americans approved and 73 percent *dis*approved of the way Trump responded to the Gold Star Family, including 59 percent of Trump supporters.[17]

But immigration, and diversity more broadly, runs directly afoul of authoritarians' desire for oneness and sameness. Many Americans just aren't pleased about immigration. Trump gave voice to their concerns in extreme ways that even other Republicans seemed reluctant to imitate, and he reaped some electoral rewards from it.

In 2015, about 13.5 percent of Americans were immigrants, born in another country as non-U.S. citizens.[18] That may not seem like a lot (it certainly doesn't to me), but it is the largest percentage of immigrants this country has been home to since 1910. Indeed, as recently as 1970, less than 5 percent of Americans were immigrants. So, by historical standards, the immigrant population is relatively large and, since 1970, has increased from about 9.6 million to over 43 million today.

Unfortunately, many Americans do not welcome these developments. Fifty-two percent contend, "Immigrants today are a burden on our country because they take our jobs, housing, and healthcare," while 48 percent take the view that "Immigrants today strengthen our country because of their hard work and talent."

Those who see immigrants making a positive contribution voted for Clinton by over 60 points, while those who perceive immigrants as a burden favored

Trump by more than 50 points. For Americans, immigration is not only a question of resources: a majority perceive it as a cultural threat. Fifty-five percent of voters believe "The number of newcomers from other countries threatens traditional American customs and values," whereas 45 percent maintain that newcomers "strengthen[s] American society" (see Figure 4.6).

Responses to these questions also split the electorate into fairly homogenous groups. Clinton won those who see immigrants as an asset by nearly 70 points, while Trump was victorious among those who see them as a cultural liability, with a nearly 50-point margin.

Indexing these and similar questions produces powerful results. The nearly one-quarter of whites who are the most consistently anti-immigrant gave Trump a margin of over 80 points. The nearly one-third of whites most positive toward immigrants supported Clinton by a nearly 75-point margin. The additional 27 percent who leaned toward an anti-immigrant stance gave Trump a 50-point margin, while those who leaned toward immigrants narrowly supported Clinton, giving her an advantage of just about 8 points.

To be clear, the issues around immigration are not fundamentally focused on policy. Two-thirds to three-quarters of Americans have consistently supported a path to citizenship for undocumented immigrants, while less than 20 percent favor the mass deportations Trump advocated. Rather than policy, the electoral debate centered on perceived threats resulting from immigration—the fear of economic burden and cultural dilution. Democrats tend to welcome immigrants

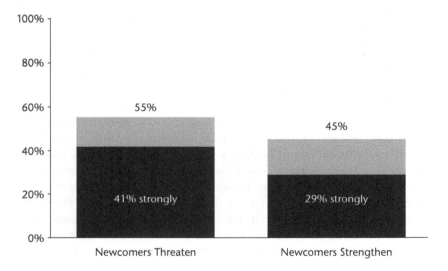

FIGURE 4.6 "Which Statement Comes Closer to Your Own Views – Even if Neither is Exactly Right? 'The Number of Newcomers from Other Countries Threatens Traditional American Customs and Values' or 'The Number of Newcomers from Other Countries Strengthens American Society'"

94 Part I: The Primaries

and celebrate the cultural diversity they bring with them; Republicans focus on the fears and threats.

Social Identity

In uniting these three psychological strands of conservatism, Trump forged a powerful social identity for his supporters by distinguishing an aggrieved "us" from a guilty "them" and offering a clear (albeit completely inaccurate) explanation of why things are the way they are: it's "their" fault—the fault of the Mexicans and Muslims, the African-Americans and the Jews.

Dividing people into groups comes naturally to human beings. Psychologists have been able to produce major features of group effects—favoritism and loyalty to in-groups, along with hostility to out-groups—with great ease, using trivial bases of group identification. Informing people that they were divided based on whether they seemingly under- or over-estimated the number of dots on slides, their favorite modern artist, or even randomly, by the public flip of a coin, all induced significant group effects, including trust, affection, cooperation, and more generous rewards from in-group members, as well as negative responses to out-groups.[19] Such group effects are all the more powerful when the groups appear to have "real" social meaning.

Group identities can be measured in terms of stereotypes. For example, whites who see blacks or Hispanics, or Muslims as lazy, less intelligent and untrustworthy, and see those groups as very different from whites in those respects, have a strong group identity. Our survey inquired in this way about stereotypes of white Americans, African-Americans, Hispanic Americans, and Muslim Americans.

Those with the strongest group identities were much more likely to support Trump. The 47 percent of voters who differentiated most strongly between their group and others gave Trump a 40-point margin, whereas the other half of the sample, those with lower levels of group identification, gave Clinton a lead of similar magnitude. The tendency to be charitable to in-group members helps explain why Donald Trump was forgiven his many trespasses, while Hillary Clinton seems to have been held to a much higher standard. By giving his supporters a powerful identity, which they obviously shared with him, Trump insulated himself from defections. Clinton by contrast evinced little interest in creating a single social identity for her followers, so the tendency to be more forgiving to in-group members operated less strongly among her constituents. This is hardly the only explanation of the differences in the way followers of each candidate treated news of their failings, but it is perhaps one part of the puzzle.

The Role of Economic Dislocation

Many analysts located the roots of authoritarianism and aversion to change in the economic distress of middle-class Americans. It's not really about misogyny or racism or anti-immigrant prejudice, they contend, those were merely seeming symptoms of underlying economic privation. Voters facing economic distress were merely acting out because of their own suffering.

Evidence for this proposition is thin at best. As noted above (and as will be discussed in a bit more detail below) voters' assessments of the national economy were much more highly correlated with vote than perceptions of one's own economic circumstances. Regression analysis demonstrates this is true even after holding other factors constant. Moreover, the statistical analysis also reveals that while there are clear relationships between perceptions of the national economy and the likelihood of harboring authoritarian, sexist, racist, and anti-immigrant views, there is no relationship between personal economic circumstances and the likelihood one expresses those views.

People who think the national economy is failing are more likely than those who are more positive to hew to these conservative dispositions. But poor, hard-pressed people are no more likely to exhibit racist, sexist, or anti-immigrant tendencies than those who feel comfortable about their financial status.

The Billionaire Bounce

While Trump played on negative stereotypes of various groups, his apparent multi-billion dollar net-worth brought with it a number of advantages that stood him in good stead with voters. Of course, it enabled him to spend millions of his own money on a campaign few others were willing to invest in at key points, but beyond that, his financial success carried with it some helpful stereotypes.

Americans are enraged by what they see as rampant corruption in Washington, where they believe votes are bought and sold as often as tourist T-shirts. Last year, 75 percent of Americans told Gallup they believed "corruption is widespread throughout the government,"[20] while a Chapman University survey found government corruption was the single greatest fear of the largest number of Americans.[21]

Some were convinced the real estate tycoon's wealth rendered him "unbossed and unbought," to borrow the words of Shirley Chisholm, the African-American member of Congress who ran for president in 1972. Our work for clients has revealed that voters often believe super-wealthy candidates are less likely to be bought by corruption or bossed by political insiders. That's part of the reason the biggest difference between Clinton and Trump in an early November *Washington Post*–ABC News poll was Trump's 9-point advantage on being able to clean up corruption (Clinton was ahead in this poll by 3 points overall).[22]

Candidates with substantial business portfolios also get the benefit of the doubt from voters when it comes to creating jobs and managing the economy. Almost every time the question was asked in a national poll, Trump came out ahead of Clinton as the candidate better able to deal with these issues. Again, our work has demonstrated that voters assume if candidates have made that much money for themselves, they know how to create jobs and deal with economic matters.

96 Part I: The Primaries

Dislike of Hillary Clinton

Beyond the circumstances and the success Trump enjoyed in forging an us–versus–them social identity among the three sets of conservatives he ignited and united, Trump was advantaged by public dislike of Hillary Clinton (just as he was disadvantaged by the greater number who disliked him).

Some place responsibility for that public distaste at Clinton's feet, while others blame the media or her opponents. Wherever the fault lay, the fact is, not long before the election, Hillary Clinton had been the most popular pubic official in the country. Nevertheless, by Election Day, she had become the second most *un*popular presidential candidate in the history of polling.

One important cause of the deterioration in her image seems to be the widely misinterpreted, and massively over-hyped, email story. During her service as Secretary of State, on average, 64 percent held favorable views of Clinton in Gallup polling, and she left her cabinet position with that same 64 percent favorable, compared to just 31 percent with an unfavorable view.

There is no comparable measure for Donald Trump at the same time, but he seems to have entered public consciousness with a negative image. In April 2011, years before commencing his 2016 campaign, he was already widely disliked—a Fox News poll found just 33 percent expressing favorable views of the reality TV celebrity, while 57 percent were unfavorable.[23] Shortly after he announced his candidacy, an *Washington Post*–ABC Poll put Trump's favorability at a similar 33 percent to 61 percent.[24] On Election Day, the exit polls tell us the numbers barely budged, with 38 percent favorable toward Trump while 60 percent were unfavorable. In short, Trump was consistently disliked by most Americans.

Hillary Clinton's image followed a very different trajectory. As speculation swirled about her potential presidential campaign, she lost some of her cabinet glow, but a year after her departure, and even longer after the Benghazi tragedy, Gallup still found 59 percent with a favorable impression of Clinton and 37 percent unfavorable. Then came the email saga, which began with a March 2, 2015, *New York Times* story.[25]

The impact was substantial. Within a month, her favorables were underwater, with slightly more expressing unfavorable than favorable views. She was never net favorable again. Between late August and October another explosion in negative opinions of Clinton occurred as her favorability ratings deteriorated by a net of 10 points. During this period the email controversy remained a headline story, reaching a zenith at the time of Clinton's two apologies for her handling of the issue, with the press reporting the apologies were offered under protest from the candidate.

In short, before the email story broke, she was about 10 points net favorable. For months after the story emerged, she was just 2 points net unfavorable. By October 2015, she was 12 points net unfavorable. It did get worse: In the wake of the Republican convention she was 18 points net unfavorable. But on Election

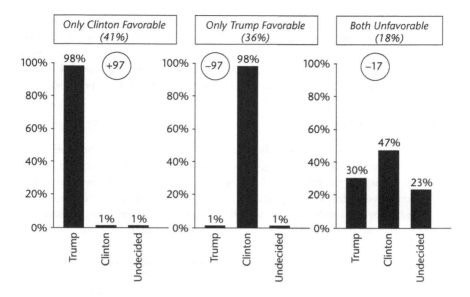

FIGURE 4.7 Presidential Vote by Candidate Favorability

Day, exit polls indicate she was the same 12 points underwater she had been in October 2015—importantly as a result of the email controversy.

Nonetheless, the exit polls revealed that the largest number of voters (41 percent) felt favorably only about Clinton, and not about Trump. A lesser 36 percent had favorable views of Trump alone. As one would expect, nearly all the voters in these two categories (98 percent) opted for the candidate they liked. The race was really decided by the 18 percent who disliked both candidates; they went strongly for Trump, giving him a 17-point margin (47–30 percent) (see Figure 4.7).

Risk Taking

Nonetheless, the vast majority of voters considered Donald Trump in the Oval Office a serious risk. While 52 percent thought Clinton was qualified for the job, only 38 percent said that about Trump. Fifty-five percent believed Clinton had the right temperament to be president, while only 35 percent felt that way about Trump. And while integrity was advertised as Clinton's Achille's heel and only 36 percent thought she was honest and trustworthy, even fewer (33 percent) had the same view of Trump.

In short, for Trump to have a shot at winning, voters had to be willing to take a big risk on him. Voters who thought he was unqualified or unsuited for office had to support him, despite their misgivings. Some did.

Nationally, as well as in Pennsylvania, Michigan, and Wisconsin, one-in-six to one-in-five voters who thought Trump was unqualified, or temperamentally

98 Part I: The Primaries

unsuited, for the presidency cast their ballots for him despite these important reservations. Taking that kind of risk is most likely a function of one of two things. Either voters were so fed up they were willing to take that kind of chance (more likely), or so confident in Clinton's eventual victory that they felt free to cast a protest vote without consequences (less likely, but certainly possible).

What Really Mattered?

To this point we have explored the relationships between Trump support and a variety of attitudes separately. Logistic regression enables us to isolate the impact on vote of each set of attitudes, while holding all the others constant. It is worth considering what fades in importance when all these attitudes are considered together. For example, once all the other viewpoints are considered, authoritarianism, measured in terms of child rearing values, loses significance— both statistically and substantively.

Moreover, as noted above, despite intense media focus on personal economic dislocation as the source of Trump's support, the data offer little evidence for this contention. Perceptions of the national economy were actually important; individuals' own economic problems were not. As decades of research would lead us to expect, partisanship mattered a good deal. Irrespective of any other attitudes or beliefs, Republicans were far more likely to vote for Trump and Democrats far more likely to support Clinton.

However, the most powerful determinant of vote is attitudes toward immigration (see Figure 4.8). Again, this is not a dispute about policy, but something that runs deeper. People who see immigrants as a cultural threat and economic burden gathered around Trump. While this scale is technically different from say the one that measures authoritarianism, it is similar in import. Regardless of what people value in a child, perceiving immigrants as a cultural threat is, in part, about an aversion to difference. The changes wrought by immigration are also of vital import to those who resent the other changes that have swept over this country in recent decades.

Distaste for the changed role of women was also a powerful predictor of support for Trump as was racial resentment. Those who exhibit hostility to blacks or women also rallied to Trump's side during this election. Aversion to change was thus also an important factor.

Conservatives who dislike government were also represented on their own in the statistical analysis. While not nearly as powerful as immigration, those who believe government overreaches were also more likely to support Trump, even after controlling for other attitudes.

So, in some ways this was a normal election where partisanship, the economy, regionalism, and attitudes toward the role of government were all implicated in the outcome. However, in many respects this election was unique. Hostility to difference, to change, and to women, along with antipathy toward immigration,

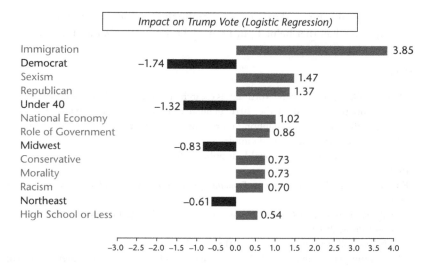

FIGURE 4.8 Strongest Determinants of a Trump Vote among White Voters

all played outsized roles that have not been documented in previous elections. Trump's "skill" gave life and political coherence to these long-simmering grievances.

Conclusion

Accounts like this naturally take on a teleological quality. After reading it, one feels Trump's victory was not only inevitable, but almost over-determined. Nothing could be further from the truth. Trump's win and Clinton's loss were contingent on a wide variety of factors. Indeed, winning the popular vote by over 2 points and losing the Electoral College is a black swan—a low probability, highly consequential event.

When a swing by fewer than 62,000 voters in three states would have changed the outcome, almost everything is important, little is really trivial, and the race could clearly have gone either way. Nevertheless, it wasn't just dumb luck that put history's least popular candidate into the White House. Trump entered a situation that favored the modal Republican candidate over the modal Democrat.

The two candidates faced an electorate that was anxious and angry. Many saw an economy in continuing trouble, a government they believed was overreaching, and a culture and way of life in decline and facing ongoing threats. Some felt they had been displaced from their positions of economic centrality, cultural ascendancy, and political power. In times of anxiety and anger voters seek out threatening news and free themselves (to some extent) from their

100 Part I: The Primaries

previous political habits and moorings, opening them to new choices and greater risk taking.[26] And all that helped put Donald Trump in the White House.

Notes

1 Mellman Group poll, with Northstar Research; national telephone survey of 1,200 voters who participated in the 2016 general election. Interviews were conducted among both landline and cellphone users from November 9 through November 14, 2016, using a registration-based sample.
2 National Election Pool, National Exit poll, 2016.
3 Ibid.
4 Karen Stenner, *The Authoritarian Dynamic* (New York: Cambridge University Press, 2005).
5 Donald R. Kinder and Cindy D. Kam, *Us Against Them* (Chicago, IL: University of Chicago Press, 2010).
6 Fox News poll, September 20–22, 2015.
7 The Quinnipiac University Poll of Florida Republican Primary Voters, February 21–14, 2016.
8 Bloomberg Politics/Selzer and Company Poll of 502 Likely Republican Primary Voters in South Carolina, February 13–16, 2016.
9 Kinder and Kam, *Us Against Them*.
10 L. Ross, "The Intuitive Psychologist and His Shortcomings: Distortions in the Attribution Process," in L. Berkowitz, *Advances in Experimental Social Psychology* (New York: Academic Press, 1977), 173–220.
11 Mellman Group poll, online survey of 5,000 voters, October 2016.
12 Mellman Group poll, national online survey through YouGov.
13 Edmund Burke, *Reflections on the Revolution in France* (Oxford: Oxford University Press, 2009), L.G. Mitchell, editor.
14 The Thermidorian Reaction was a coup d'etat within the French Revolution, ending its most radical phase.
15 Public Policy Polling Survey of 897 likely Republican primary voters and 525 Democratic primary voters, February 14–15, 2016.
16 *The Economist*/YouGov poll, 2000 General Population Respondents, January 15–19, 2016.
17 *Washington Post*–ABC News poll, August 1–4, 2016 of 1,002 U.S. adults.
18 Migration Policy Institute (MPI) tabulation of data from U.S. Census Bureau, 2010–2015, American Community Surveys (ACS), and 1970, 1990, and 2000 Decennial Census.
19 Kinder and Kam, *Us Against Them*.
20 Gallup poll, September 19, 2015.
21 Chapman University Survey of American Fears, October 11, 2016.
22 *Washington Post*–ABC News poll, October 30–November 2, 2016 of 1,768 U.S. adults.
23 Fox News poll, April 25–27, 2011. 911 registered voters nationwide.
24 *Washington Post*–ABC News poll, July 8–12, 2015.

25 Michael S. Schmidt, "Hillary Clinton Used Private Email Account at State Dept., Possibly Breaking Rules," *New York Times*, March 2, 2015, https://www.nytimes.com/2015/03/03/us/politics/hillary-clintons-use-of-private-email-at-state-department-raises-flags.html?_r=0 (accessed December 2, 2016).
26 Bethany Albertson and Shana Kushner Gadarian, *Anxious Politics* (New York: Cambridge University Press, 2015).

PART II

Money and Communication

5

PRESIDENTIAL CANDIDATE FUNDRAISING

An Exception to the Rule?

Anthony Corrado and Tassin Braverman

In a presidential election characterized by unexpected outcomes, the money race was no exception. For the first time in the post-reform era that began with the 1976 election, a candidate who lagged far behind in the chase for campaign dollars in both the primary and general elections won the race for the Oval Office. That candidate, Donald Trump, also became the first primarily self-financed candidate to win a major party nomination. And he did so without the benefit of millions of dollars expended on his behalf by an allied Super PAC established by associates to promote his candidacy, which has become common practice in the unconstrained post-*Citizens United* world of campaign finance.

Donald Trump's unorthodox candidacy defied much of the conventional wisdom regarding money and politics. At a time when fundraising success is considered essential to a presidential candidacy and a sign of a challenger's viability, Trump dismissed the need to engage in traditional fundraising activities throughout most of the campaign, and was consistently outspent by his opponents. While he did agree to participate in party fundraising events during the general election, he did not aggressively solicit campaign dollars, insisting that he did not need to spend as much as other recent nominees to win the race. As a result, his Democratic general election opponent, Hillary Clinton, who did follow the path of other recent nominees and maintained an aggressive fundraising approach from the beginning of the campaign until its final days, enjoyed a substantial financial advantage throughout the general election, outspending Trump in every facet of the campaign. But money did not determine the outcome of the race, highlighting one of the unique aspects of Trump's bid for the Oval Office and raising a fundamental question about the importance of money in the 2016 campaign.

Trump was not the only candidate to pursue an unconventional fundraising strategy. In the Democratic race, Vermont senator Bernie Sanders refused to

106 Part II: Money and Communication

participate in the high-dollar fundraising events typical of a presidential campaign. Sanders made the role of money in politics a cornerstone of his populist message, vehemently denouncing the influence of wealthy special interests in the political system, calling for a reversal of the Supreme Court's decision in *Citizens United*, and warning of the dangers inherent in the unlimited and sometimes undisclosed contributions from millionaires and billionaires to Super PACs and "dark money" groups. Sanders wore his disdain for monied interests as a badge of honor, and his message became a vehicle that empowered an army of small donors, who became the foundation of his unexpectedly competitive campaign.

None of the other candidates pursued strategies as uncommon as those of Trump and Sanders. Instead they followed what has become the common practice in presidential campaigns, incorporating the lessons of the prior election into their strategies and building upon them to maximize the resources that could be spent in support of their candidacies.

The financing of the 2016 election highlighted the diverse financial strategies employed by candidates and the variety of organizational structures that can be used to fund campaigns in the post-*Citizens United* campaign environment. This chapter focuses on the strategies employed by candidates to raise money for their campaigns, since the financial activity of Super PACs and other organizations is discussed elsewhere in this volume (see Chapter 10 on Outside Voices, by Stephen K. Medvic). In doing so, it details the distinctive approaches that were used by the leading contenders in the chase for campaign dollars. It also indicates the limits of money in affecting outcomes, a result that left many observers wondering whether 2016 was an exception that proves the rule or whether there is a need for new thinking on the importance of money in explaining outcomes in presidential elections.

An Overview of Candidate Funding

As in the election of 2012, presidential candidates rejected the public funding option that remains a part of federal law, which would have provided participating candidates with matching funds on small contributions in the primaries and a $96 million grant for the general election in exchange for agreeing to spending limits.[1] The only major party aspirant to accept public funding was Democrat Martin O'Malley, who raised relatively little money and dropped out of the race after the Iowa caucuses. O'Malley qualified for primary public matching funds at a time when his struggling campaign had failed to make payroll and used much of the $1.09 million he received to pay off campaign debts.[2] Jill Stein, the Green Party nominee, also accepted primary matching funds, receiving $456,000 prior to her formal nomination.[3] Furthermore, in 2014 Congress abolished the $18 million convention grant available to political parties to pay for their conventions, which was the only meaningful remnant of the public funding program.[4] This act represented the

Chapter 5: Presidential Candidate Fundraising **107**

final demise of public funding, cementing its irrelevance as a source of money in presidential campaigns.

Presidential candidates thus financed their campaigns through contributions from individuals and political action committees (PACs), which are subject to strict contribution limits. In the 2016 election, an individual was allowed to give $2,700 per election to a candidate for a maximum permissible donation of $5,400, since the primary and general elections are counted separately for purposes of the limit. A PAC is permitted to give $5,000 per election for a maximum permissible donation of $10,000. The law prohibits contributions to candidates from corporations, labor unions, and foreign citizens who do not have legal status as resident aliens. Any contribution of $200 or more, as well as any expenditure of $200 or more, must be disclosed to the Federal Election Commission (FEC), which is responsible for making this information available to the public.

With President Obama completing his second term in office, the presidential race featured open races in both parties for the first time since 2008, and thus was expected to be a costly affair that would place substantial demands on the candidates to raise money. The major party nominees alone spent a total of more than $1 billion in 2008 and again in 2012, with Barack Obama winning the White House after spending $730 million in 2008 and $683 million in 2012.[5] Fundraising professionals estimated that the major party nominees would need to raise even more in 2016, and with the monies raised by Super PACs and other groups included, might result in a race costing $3 billion or more, as compared to total spending of $2.6 billion in 2012.[6]

By Election Day, candidates had raised $1.45 billion, not including any monies spent on their behalf by Super PACs or other political committees. This sum represented a relatively modest increase over the $1.32 billion raised by the candidates in 2012, but was less than the $1.68 billion raised in 2008.[7] The 2016 race thus diverged from the pattern of rising fundraising totals in elections with open contests for the presidency. Most notably, neither Hillary Clinton nor Donald Trump matched the fundraising totals of the 2012 nominees. Clinton raised $564 million, a total well below the $700 million-plus sums that Obama reached in each of his campaigns. Trump raised $328 million, which was less than the amount raised by Republican nominee John McCain in 2008, who was the last candidate to accept general election public funding, and $120 million less than Romney's total in 2012. Given that Clinton and Trump were viewed unfavorably by large percentages of the electorate, making them the two most unpopular nominees in recent memory, it is not surprising that their fundraising lagged behind other recent nominees. Neither stimulated the level of enthusiasm and support generated by Obama in his initial bid for office, and Trump's total was certainly affected by his lack of aggressive fundraising and the sizable, but relatively modest amount ($66 million) that he contributed to his own campaign.

The 2016 election featured very different fields in the competitions for the major party nominations. The Republican race attracted an unusually large

108 Part II: Money and Communication

number of candidates, including many well-established politicians. President Obama's low approval ratings midway through his second term, a growing but sluggish economy, high levels of dissatisfaction with the direction of the nation, deep frustration with the failure of leadership in Washington, and the recognition that the incumbent party is particularly vulnerable in an election year when it is seeking a third consecutive White House term combined to create a political environment favorable to Republican prospects, which encouraged candidates to enter the fray. Many of the aspirants who did so had previously been elected to office and were well known by elite Republican donors.

With so many candidates seeking to recruit financial support, the crowded Republican field produced a competitive chase for dollars. Republican donors divided their giving among the contenders and no candidate reached the $100 million mark Romney achieved during the primaries in 2008 and 2012[8] (see Table 5.1). Indeed, only three candidates breached the $50 million mark: Cruz, who raised $89 million in all and was the last candidate standing against Trump; Carson, whose appeal to conservative grassroots donors allowed him to amass $63 million despite the fact that he was not a serious contender once the primaries began; and Trump, who raised $91 million through the end of May 2016, including $46 million of his own money.[9]

The Democratic race was a different story. Hillary Clinton was widely perceived to be the prohibitive frontrunner even before she declared her candidacy, and few chose to enter the ring with her. Sanders, however, proved to be a formidable opponent. In a manner reminiscent of Obama's rise in the 2008 Democratic primary campaign, Sanders's early fundraising success surprised most political observers and thrust him into the spotlight. Sanders's populist message and progressive platform, which centered on economic inequality and criticism of Wall Street and wealthy special interests, struck a chord with grassroots donors, leading to remarkable success in garnering small contributions. Sanders's small donor fundraising was unparalleled, and enabled him to raise $228 million by the end of the primary campaign, as compared to $274 million for Clinton.[10]

The monies raised by the candidates, however, were not the only source of funding in 2016. Almost all of the contenders had complementary support from one or more Super PACs specifically set up to spend money in their behalf. These committees, established by former staff members, political advisors, consultants, or supporters, could accept unlimited contributions and spend unlimited amounts to assist the candidate of their choice. These committees were prohibited from coordinating their activities with the candidates they supported, but federal regulations allowed some interaction with a candidate, and PAC operatives found a variety of ways to assist candidates or communicate their intentions without directly consulting with the candidates or their campaign staffs.[11]

In 2012, candidate-specific Super PACs constituted an innovation in presidential campaign finance that arose during the course of the primary

Chapter 5: Presidential Candidate Fundraising 109

TABLE 5.1 Presidential Candidates, Receipts and Disbursements, in Millions

Candidate	Receipts	Disbursements
Democrats		
Clinton	563.9	563.0
Sanders	228.2	223.4
O'Malley	5.7	5.6
Lessig	1.0	0.4
Webb	0.8	0.8
Subtotal	799.6	793.2
Republicans		
Trump	328.4	320.6
Cruz	89.5	86.6
Carson	63.3	62.3
Rubio	41.9	45.7
Bush	34.1	34.0
Kasich	18.9	18.7
Paul	12.1	11.9
Fiorina	12.0	11.2
Walker	8.5	8.5
Christie	8.4	8.4
Graham	5.7	5.5
Huckabee	4.3	4.3
Santorum	1.8	1.8
Jindal	1.4	1.4
Perry	1.3	1.6
Pataki	0.5	0.5
Gilmore	0.4	0.4
Subtotal	632.5	623.4
Other		
Johnson	11.6	11.5
Stein	3.5	3.4
McMullin	1.6	1.6
Subtotal	16.7	16.5
Total	1,448.80	1,433.10

Source: Federal Election Commission data through November 28, 2016.

campaign.[12] In 2016, they were widely viewed as an essential component of a campaign; a candidate lacking an allied Super PAC was expected to face a significant financial disadvantage in the nomination race. Consequently, most of the 2016 candidates embraced this model and were supported by at least one Super PAC. In almost every case, these committees were established shortly before a candidate entered the race or relatively soon thereafter. By December

110 Part II: Money and Communication

2015, twenty-one different candidate-specific committees had been established in support of thirteen of the candidates.[13] The two noteworthy exceptions were Sanders and Trump, who benefitted from some support from Super PACs not affiliated with their campaigns during the course of the primaries, but did not encourage the creation of Super PACs to act as a *de facto* extension of their campaigns.[14] In fact, Sanders explicitly condemned Super PACs, and made clear in his statements on the campaign trail that he did not have one and did not want one.

Jeb Bush took the boldest and most controversial approach to Super PAC funding by participating in the formation and fundraising of a Super PAC, Right to Rise, before he declared his candidacy in June 2015.[15] The committee, which Bush described as "tasked with 'exploring a presidential bid'," launched in early January 2015 and mounted an aggressive fundraising effort with Bush serving as the principal fundraiser.[16] By the time he entered the race, Right to Rise had raised $103 million, which primarily came from donors who each gave $100,000 or more.[17] This tactic established Bush as the dominant fundraiser at the start of the race, and donors quickly began to fill his campaign coffers after he declared his candidacy, helping him raise $32 million by the end of 2015, 75 percent of which came from donors who gave the $2,700 maximum.[18] But his hope that spending by the Super PAC would propel him to the nomination was dashed by his lackluster performance on the campaign trail, which failed to attract significant voter support, and his consequent poor showing in the crucial early primaries. Even though the Super PAC financed a massive advertising campaign designed to promote Bush and disparage his leading opponents, its efforts could not convince voters to support a candidate perceived as a representative of the party establishment in a year in which primary voters were frustrated with the status quo and craved change. Indeed, Bush's relatively quick exit from the nomination race in late February was the first indication in 2016 that money may help a candidate be heard, but it alone was not enough to ensure victory.

By the time the Republican primary race was effectively over, Super PACs associated with Republican candidates had raised close to $362 million. On the Democratic side, Priorities USA, the Super PAC supporting Hillary Clinton, had taken in almost $80 million, most of which was held for use in the general election.[19] Yet, despite this support, candidates still needed to raise money for their campaigns, and they took widely divergent paths in doing so.

Candidate Fundraising Strategies

Presidential hopefuls pursued a variety of strategies and tactics in their respective quests for money, which is not unusual. What distinguished candidate fundraising in 2016 were the stark differences among the leading contenders in the strategies they adopted. In large part, the established politicians with fundraising experience followed the playbook that had been used in the past, focusing on the solicitation of maximum contributions or large sums from donors. Political outsiders, including Sanders, employed more innovative approaches, which had been used previously to some extent, but not with such success or in such a way as to make them truly distinctive.

Candidates with established donor bases who are considered likely prospects to win the party nomination typically emphasize the solicitation of large contributions in hope of raising as much money as quickly as possible to establish their viability as contenders. In this regard, the 2016 money race largely followed the patterns of the past. Most of the candidates who successfully raised substantial amounts of money received a sizable share of their funding from donors who contributed $1,000 or more. According to an analysis of FEC records conducted by the non-partisan Campaign Finance Institute, which combined the separate contributions made by an individual donor to determine the aggregate amount contributed by each donor, 41 percent of the money received by candidates during the primaries came from donors who gave at least $1,000, including 25 percent, or $207 million, that came from donors who gave the $2,700 maximum[20] (see Table 5.2). Jeb Bush raised 89 percent of the money he received from individuals from donors who gave at least $1,000, most of which (74 percent) came from donors who gave the legal maximum. John Kasich raised 63 percent of his receipts from individual donors from those who gave $1,000 or more; Marco Rubio, 58 percent; and Ted Cruz, who battled with Trump until the end, 40 percent. Hillary Clinton, however, was by far the best exemplar of this approach, receiving 55 percent of the money she raised from individuals from donors who gave a total of $1,000 or more, including 40 percent, $107 million, from donors who gave the maximum amount. By the end of the primaries, Clinton had recruited more than 40,000 donors who gave the legal limit, which represented more donors of this rank than were recruited by all Republican candidates combined.

Clinton was well positioned to pursue a frontrunner fundraising strategy. She began the race with a well-cultivated base of donors who had supported her over the years. She was a proven fundraiser, having raised $224 million in her unsuccessful race against Obama in 2008. And she was widely perceived to be the candidate most likely to win the nomination in 2016.

Clinton also gained a head start on developing an updated list of supporters as a result of the activities of a Super PAC, Ready for Hillary, which prepared the ground for her 2016 run. Adam Parkhomenko, who had served on the staff of the 2008 campaign, and Allida Black, a history professor at George Washington University, two self-described fans of Clinton, established the PAC in 2013. They hoped that Clinton would run again in 2016 and sought to encourage her to do so. They envisioned a grassroots Super PAC that would focus on building volunteer and donor databases, thereby creating a resource that would allow Clinton to hit the ground running should she decide to run. In accord with this concept, they voluntarily capped donations at $25,000 and emphasized the

TABLE 5.2 Sources of Funds—Individual Donors through June 30, 2016

Candidates	Net Primary Individual Contributions	$200 or less			$201-$999			$1,000-$2,699			$2,700		
		$ Amount (millions)	Percent	# Donors	$ Amount (millions)	Percent	# Donors	$ Amount (millions)	Percent	# Donors	$ Amount (millions)	Percent
Democrats												
Clinton	269.7	63.6	24%	147,895	57.8	21%	30,111	41.0	15%	40,697	107.4	40%
Sanders	226.1	99.7	44%	221,382	86.2	38%	21,699	31.5	14%	3,939	8.6	4%
O'Malley	4.5	0.5	11%	1,547	0.6	14%	734	1.0	22%	889	2.4	54%
Lessig	0.9	0.4	44%	545	0.2	21%	115	0.1	15%	69	0.1	16%
Webb	0.8	0.3	39%	374	0.2	19%	134	0.2	26%	37	0.1	15%
Chafee	0.0	0.0	46%	18	0.0	12%	9	0.0	24%	3	0.0	18%
Dem Subtotal	502.0	164.5	33%	371,761	144.9	29%	52,802	73.8	15%	45,634	118.7	24%
Republican												
Cruz	86.6	25.4	29%	77,953	31.3	36%	11,261	16.1	19%	4,892	18.4	21%
Carson	61.3	30.8	50%	51,939	19.4	32%	6,059	8.2	13%	1,413	3.7	6%
Trump	36.9	23.1	63%	21,103	7.0	19%	2,937	3.5	9%	1,619	3.5	10%
Rubio	39.9	9.9	25%	21,720	8.4	21%	6,880	9.4	24%	6,142	13.6	34%
Bush	32.5	1.7	5%	4,930	2.0	6%	3,841	4.9	15%	9,035	23.9	74%
Kasich	18.5	3.7	20%	7,952	3.0	16%	2,825	3.7	20%	2,972	7.9	43%
Paul	10.7	4.6	43%	7,718	2.9	27%	1,199	1.7	16%	641	1.6	15%
Fiorina	11.7	5.1	44%	7,212	2.8	24%	1,505	2.0	17%	742	2.1	18%
Christie	8.3	0.4	5%	1,251	0.5	6%	1,088	1.5	18%	2,169	6.0	72%
Walker	7.4	2.8	38%	2,994	1.1	15%	885	1.1	15%	1,037	2.4	33%
Graham	3.1	0.2	8%	756	0.3	10%	755	1.1	37%	602	1.8	60%
Huckabee	4.4	1.7	39%	1,775	0.7	16%	577	0.8	19%	383	1.0	23%
Jindal	1.4	0.1	11%	178	0.1	5%	91	0.1	10%	394	1.1	75%
Perry	1.2	0.1	11%	281	0.1	9%	140	0.2	15%	312	0.8	65%
Santorum	1.3	0.3	21%	421	0.2	12%	187	0.3	20%	230	0.6	45%
Pataki	0.5	0.0	5%	107	0.0	7%	80	0.1	23%	119	0.3	62%
Rep Subtotal	325.7	110.2	34%	208,290	79.7	24%	40,310	54.6	17%	32,702	88.8	27%
2016	827.7	274.7	33%	580,051	224.6	27%	93,112	128.4	16%	78,336	207.4	25%

Note: Amounts shown as "0" represent totals less than $100,000.

Source: Based on analysis of FEC data conducted by the Campaign Finance Institute.

Chapter 5: Presidential Candidate Fundraising **113**

development of a website and social media tools to build a community of Clinton supporters who were ready to volunteer in the anticipated campaign.[21] The effort soon attracted the interest and support of a number of Clinton's former campaign advisors and fundraisers, and by 2014 Ready for Hillary had a staff of twenty-six and a highly successful website that raised small symbolic donations of $20.16 and sold branded merchandise that included such images as the "texts from Hillary" meme (a photograph of Clinton working on her phone) created by the PAC that went viral.[22] By the end of 2015, Ready for Hillary had raised $16.4 million, created a pool of more than 135,000 donors, and built an up-to-date email list of 4 million names of Clinton supporters and their communication details.[23] When Clinton officially announced her presidential bid, Ready for Hillary emailed its list six times, encouraging them to sign up with the official campaign. It then turned over its email list and social media platforms to EMILY's List, the well-known women's political organization, which in turn gave access to the list to the Clinton campaign.[24] The PAC then changed its name to Ready PAC to comply with federal regulations prohibiting the use of a candidate's name and began winding down.[25]

Clinton's fundraising strength was evident from the start of her campaign. As soon as she announced her candidacy in April 2015, she embarked on an aggressive fundraising schedule, holding dozens of fundraising events. By the end of June, which marked the end of the quarter for purposes of campaign fundraising reports, she had taken in more than $45 million. This sum set a record for first quarter fundraising, surpassing the previous high water mark of $42 million achieved by Obama in his first quarter of fundraising for his reelection bid in 2011.[26] Moreover, although the campaign noted that nine out of ten donors had given less than $100, 67 percent of this sum came from individuals who contributed the maximum $2,700.[27]

Clinton continued to aggressively raise funds throughout the campaign. She was aided in this effort by "bundlers," volunteer fundraisers who were responsible for gathering checks from friends or associates on behalf of the campaign, either through personal solicitations or by hosting fundraising events or parties. The top bundlers became members of her National Finance Committee, which consisted of individuals who were known as "HillBlazers," with each member responsible for raising at least $100,000. Although federal law only requires registered lobbyists who bundle more than $15,000 to be publicly disclosed, Clinton followed the practice of President Obama and voluntarily disclosed the names of all those who met the $100,000 threshold. By the end of the primaries, Clinton had recruited more than 1,100 of these elite fundraisers, who had collectively raised at least $113 million, which was undoubtedly an underestimate since some of these individuals certainly raised well more than $100,000.[28]

While the HillBlazers were a core component of Clinton's fundraising, she did not overlook smaller contributors. She established a "Hillstarter" program that asked supporters to host fundraising events designed to bring in at least

114 Part II: Money and Communication

$27,000 from smaller donations.[29] The campaign also employed the array of digital means that have become commonplace in presidential campaigns, relying on email solicitations, Facebook, Twitter, and other social media, as well as digital advertising, to solicit small contributions. These methods were used from the start, as the campaign hoped to replicate President Obama's success with small donors. In fact, on the final day of the first quarter of fundraising, the campaign distributed an email asking recipients to "chip in $1" to help reach her goal for grassroots donations, which represented one of the many tactics the campaign used to attract small donors who could be solicited regularly for additional contributions throughout the campaign.[30]

Clinton's small donor fundraising became an important part of her overall funding, but in-person fundraisers remained the core of her fundraising strategy. By the end of 2015, she had raised $113 million, far more than any other candidate in either party, including $19 million from contributions of $200 or less.[31] She raised more than three times as much, $64 million, from donors who gave the legal maximum.[32] She would continue to rely on fundraising events and the recruitment of bundlers throughout the campaign, while building her small donor base. By the end of June 2016, individuals who gave $200 or less in aggregate contributions were responsible for 24 percent of the money she raised from individuals, but 40 percent of her total came from those who gave maximum amount (see Table 5.2).

Small Donors

While Clinton's small donor fundraising was notable, it was dwarfed by Sanders's success. Sanders constructed the most successful small donor fundraising campaign in presidential history, which provided him with the resources needed to mount a serious challenge for the nomination. In all, he raised about $201 million of his $228 million war chest in contributions of $200 or less, receiving donations from more than 2.4 million individuals who collectively gave to his campaign more than 7.6 million times.[33] What is even more remarkable is that he raised $216 million *online*, obviating the need to spend time attending fundraisers and recruiting large donors. In fact, he held only nine in-person fundraising events, a feat thought impossible in the current era of campaign finance, and did not even have a staff member responsible for planning fundraisers featuring the candidate.[34] To put this in perspective, Clinton held more than 350 fundraising events from the time she entered the race through to mid-October 2016, spending time on 200 days attending at least one fundraising event.[35]

Within 24 hours of announcing his candidacy in April 2015, Sanders had received $1 million online.[36] The campaign committed $250,000 to digital advertising and thus launched the fundraising operation that would define Sanders's campaign. Relying on digital advertising, email solicitations, video messaging services like Snapchat, and the campaign's own website, Sanders began

Chapter 5: Presidential Candidate Fundraising **115**

to convert his populist economic message and criticisms of the political influence of millionaires and billionaires into a powerful fundraising engine. Sanders also relied heavily on ActBlue, a decade-old organization that creates fundraising software for Democratic candidates and serves as a portal for linking donors with candidates. ActBlue, which had helped raise $1 billion for candidates as of 2014 through its donation-on-demand technology, helped to build a community of donors for Sanders by facilitating contributions from its existing donor lists, which made it easy for donors who had given to a candidate through ActBlue in the past to make a contribution simply by hitting an icon on a phone or button on their website.[37]

Like Obama in 2007, Sanders emerged as a viable contender for the nomination as a result of his fundraising success in the pre-election year. But the scope of his small donor support greatly exceeded that of Obama's 2008 campaign. By the end of 2015, Sanders had raised $74 million, including more than $52 million from contributions of $200 or less.[38] This sum was almost twice the estimated $40 million that his campaign advisors believed would be necessary to run a credible campaign against Clinton.[39] By the end of September, Sanders had received 1.3 million contributions from 650,000 donors, thus reaching the 1 million contributions mark faster than any previous candidate (Obama did not receive 1 million contributions until February 2008 in his first race and October 2011 in his reelection campaign.).[40] At year-end, he had received 2.3 million contributions, surpassing the previous record of 2.2 million contributions in a pre-election year established by Obama in 2011.[41]

Unlike Obama, Sanders did not also seek out large contributions. He thus became the first major contender for a party nomination to focus exclusively on small donors. He championed his "$27 average contribution," criticized Clinton for her big donor fundraising and accepting money from Wall Street, and urged supporters at every opportunity to join his fight against wealthy interests. His supporters' enthusiastic response and his digital infrastructure allowed him to capitalize on key developments in the campaign and turned election nights into major fundraising events. For example, in the 24 hours after the first Democratic debate in October 2015, Sanders took in $2.5 million;[42] after his narrow defeat in the Iowa caucuses, $3 million;[43] and after his victory in New Hampshire, more than $6 million.[44] Consequently, fueled by an expanding donor base and recurring gifts from supporters, he was able to raise more money than Clinton in January, February, and March, which allowed him to outspend her in a number of crucial primaries. It was not until April, when the race had clearly turned in Clinton's favor after winning five of six primaries in Eastern states including New York, that Sanders's support ebbed and Clinton again assumed the lead in monthly fundraising.

Sanders's campaign evidenced how digital technology enables fundraising strategies and small donor fundraising in particular. His early success provided the resources needed to invest in his digital operations, which proved to be an efficient

116 Part II: Money and Communication

and effective means of raising money. In all, the campaign spent more than $30 million on digital operations, including $15 million on digital advertising, which is much less expensive than broadcast advertising or traditional small donor fundraising tools such as direct mail or telemarketing.[45] These investments produced high rates of return. Sanders raised more than $61 million and acquired more than 3 million email addresses directly through digital ads.[46] His email program accounted for more than $114 million in donations, in large part because emails and donation pages were tailored to the mobile-first audience that made up the core of his base of support.[47] Overall, 43 percent of the donations were made from mobile devices.[48] With easy access to campaign giving and Sanders's victories throughout the primaries that kept his hopes alive, many of his donors made multiple contributions or gave on a recurring basis, leading many of them to eventually give more than the small gift with which they began. The efficacy of Sanders's approach is thus reflected in the final tallies for his campaign, with $99.7 million or 44 percent of his total coming from donors who gave an aggregate amount of $200 or less, and another $86 million or 38 percent from those who gave an aggregate amount of more than $200 but less than $1,000 (see Table 5.2).

Sanders was not the only candidate to energize grassroots donors. Among the Republicans, Ben Carson's conservative message and persona as a non-politician resonated with grassroots supporters, making him the surprising leader in the Republican fundraising race as the election year began. In the first nine months of 2015, Carson raised more than $31 million, placing him at the head of the fundraising race, having received 700,000 contributions from more than 402,000 donors.[49] Of the $54 million he raised by year-end, $32 million came from contributions of less than $200.[50]

Carson, however, relied on more traditional techniques for soliciting small contributions rather than emphasizing online fundraising as Sanders did. While Carson solicited contributions online, he also spent millions of dollars on telemarketing and direct mail in the search for donors. In the third quarter of 2015 alone, he devoted $11 million of his $14 million in spending to fundraising expenses, so his success came at a high cost.[51] In the fourth quarter of 2015, he raised $22 million but spent $27 million, including $21 million that went to vendors involved in his fundraising and prospecting for new donors, a number of which were associated with his chief campaign fundraiser.[52] By year-end, he had already spent $47 million, leaving him with only $6.6 million in cash entering the election year, which restricted his spending on campaign costs outside of fundraising. As his standing fell in the polls and with no strong performances to buoy his fundraising, his funding withered, and by the time the voting began in Iowa, he was no longer a factor in the race. In a candid moment, Carson said on *CNN*, "We had people who didn't really seem to understand finances ... or maybe they did—maybe they were doing it on purpose."[53] Whatever the case, Carson's experience demonstrated the advantages of digital technology over more traditional methods and the greater efficiency of Sanders's approach.

Personal Money

Even though Trump was a member of the donor elite that Sanders pilloried, he too sought to capitalize on the public's disdain for the political status quo and voter concern about the role of money in the political system. But Trump offered a different rationale as to why he would be free of the influence of wealthy donors: He would use his own money to finance his campaign. In announcing his candidacy, Trump noted: "I don't need anybody's money. I am using my own money. I'm not using the lobbyists. I'm not using donors. I don't care. I'm really rich."[54]

Trump was not the first presidential aspirant to rely on personal funding to finance a campaign. Most famously, H. Ross Perot, a Texas businessman who mounted an independent candidacy for presidency under the mantle of his Reform Party in 1992, spent $63 million of his own money in a losing general election effort.[55] In the 1996 and 2000 Republican nomination contests, Malcolm "Steve" Forbes significantly outspent his opponents in the early primaries by putting $38 million and $42 million respectively into his campaigns, but he failed to connect with voters and become a serious challenger for the nomination.[56] Most recently, Mitt Romney gave almost $45 million to his 2008 campaign as part of the $105 million he raised during the primaries, thereby ensuring himself a substantial lead in the primary money race.[57] Romney's largesse established him as a major contender, although it was not enough to win him the nomination.

Trump proved to be an unorthodox candidate in many ways and his approach to campaign finance was one of them. Although it is not unusual for self-funded candidates to claim wealthy donors will not influence them, thereby hoping to make their personal wealth into a political asset, they typically rely on their wealth to take advantage of their ability to outspend their prospective opponents, thereby hoping to establish their viability as candidates. These candidates often need to spend more money since they are not as well known as the more established politicians against whom they compete. Trump, however, was the best-known candidate at the beginning of the Republican race due to his public persona and role as a reality television celebrity, yet with one of the highest unfavorability ratings in the field.[58] While he flaunted his ability to finance a campaign, he did not attempt to use his resources to establish a financial advantage over his opponents, build a conventional fundraising operation, or establish an extensive organization in support of his candidacy. By the end of 2015, Trump had given $12.8 million to his campaign and spent $12.6 million, which was about half of the amounts Bush, Cruz, and Rubio had each spent at that stage of the race, and a quarter of the amount spent by Carson.[59] He lagged well behind in the money race, especially given the fact that other leading contenders had affiliated Super PACs raising millions in support of their candidacies, while Trump had none.

Once the election year began, Trump continued to give money to his campaign, averaging about $6 million per month, which was not enough to

118 Part II: Money and Communication

match the spending of his principal opponents, who held a commanding advantage with respect to both fundraising and conventional electioneering activities. For example, according to an analysis by the Wesleyan Media Project of Kantar Media/CMAG data, as of mid-February 2016, more than 35,000 ads had been aired in support of Bush, more than 32,000 in support of Rubio, and more than 14,000 in support of Cruz. Trump was supported by less than 12,000 ads, which cost an estimated $6.6 million.[60] This basic pattern continued throughout the competitive stage of the primaries. Trump spent substantial sums on advertising, travel, and the large rallies that became a cornerstone of his campaigning, but his opponents spent much more. By early May, with the nomination effectively decided, Trump had spent more than $56 million, including $43.8 million of his own money. His last challenger in the race, Cruz, had spent more than $80 million.[61] In all, with Super PAC spending included, 33,000 ads had been broadcast in support of Trump, as opposed to 59,000 in support of Rubio, 51,000 in support of Cruz, and close to 18,000 ads broadcast against Trump by Super PACs and other organizations that sought to prevent him from winning the nomination.[62]

As Trump's spending totals indicate, he did not rely exclusively on his own money. Even though he repeatedly claimed that he was self-funding his campaign, he also accepted contributions made through his website. Trump did primarily rely on his own money and did not personally solicit contributions. But his website did have two "donate" buttons and many small donors made contributions or at least "contributed" to the campaign by buying hats and other paraphernalia available for purchase from the campaign.[63] Donors began to give early in the campaign; in his first quarter of fundraising, he received $3.9 million from individuals, as compared to $1.9 million that came from his own pocket.[64] They continued to give as the campaign progressed, even though Trump did not use email solicitations to drive contributions or develop an operation to cultivate and build a base of donors. By the time he had in effect secured the nomination in May, he had received $17 million from individual donors, representing about 25 percent of his $65 million in total receipts.[65]

The General Election

Trump thus began the general election in the worst relative financial position of any recent party nominee. At the end of May, he had a paltry $1.3 million in cash, as compared to Clinton's $42 million.[66] He had a staff of about 70 people, as compared to nearly 700 for Clinton.[67] He lacked an organized fundraising operation, while his opponent had already raised more than $200 million in primary funds and was prepared to ask donors to give again in the general election. What's more, Clinton and the Democratic Party had a substantial head start on general election fundraising, even though the race against Sanders continued through the end of the primaries in June.

Chapter 5: Presidential Candidate Fundraising **119**

Clinton had established a joint fundraising committee (JFC) in August 2015 with the Democratic National Committee (DNC) and thirty-two state parties (which would eventually grow to thirty-eight state parties) to begin raising general election money that would be available to the eventual Democratic nominee. While JFCs are a common part of partisan fundraising strategies, no previous JFC had been established so early in the election cycle.[68] The committee allowed donors to give to the candidate, national committee, and state parties by making a single large contribution with the money divided between the candidate, national committee, and state parties, depending on the contribution limit applicable to each. Since party limits are based on annual amounts, donors who gave the maximum amount in 2015 could give again in 2016. Thus, the early start increased the potential receipts of the JFC, which was called the Hillary Victory Fund (HVF).

A JFC was an especially efficient fundraising vehicle in the 2016 election due to the changes in federal law that had occurred since the previous election. In 2014, the U.S. Supreme Court in *McCutcheon* v. *Federal Election Commission* struck down the aggregate limit on the amount an individual was allowed to contribute in federal elections, which at that time restricted a donor to $74,600 in total contributions to parties and PACs, and $48,600 in total contributions to federal candidates.[69] The Court maintained the limits imposed on a candidate committee, a national party committee ($32,400 per year), state party ($10,000 per year), or PAC ($5,000 per year), but freed donors to give these amounts to as many committees as they would like with no aggregate ceiling. Congress amplified the effect of *McCutcheon* as a result of a provision in an omnibus budget bill adopted in December 2014, which dramatically increased the amount an individual could contribute to a national party committee. The new rules, which established limits for different types of party accounts that the law permitted, allowed an individual to give up to $334,000 to a national party committee each year.[70]

HVF allowed Clinton to raise six-figure contributions from supporters, including the $2,700 per election that could be contributed to her campaign. The committee began staging fundraisers in December and by the end of June had already collected $142 million, including more than $33 million that was transferred to Clinton's campaign.[71] HVF became a hub of Clinton's fundraising activity throughout the general election, supplementing her campaign committee's fundraising efforts through various means ranging from large donor events featuring A-list celebrities to small donor programs that expanded her online fundraising efforts. In total, HVF collected $529 million, with $139 million of its proceeds going directly to the Clinton campaign.[72]

Trump and his party did not agree to form a JFC until late May 2016. After wrapping up the Republican nomination, Trump contended that he did not need as much money as a typical candidate because of the publicity he received through news coverage and social media. In the primaries his controversial

120 Part II: Money and Communication

statements, inflammatory tweets, criticisms of the party leadership, and surprising rise in the polls and path to victory had provided him with dominant media coverage, exceeding that of all other Republican contenders combined. One analysis of his media exposure estimated that he had received $4.3 billion of "free" media through television, print, and online sources by the end of July.[73] But Trump reversed course in May, agreeing to participate in fundraising for two JFCs: Trump Victory, which combined Trump's campaign, the Republican National Committee (RNC), and eleven state parties, and Trump Make America Great Again, which was a joint effort of Trump and the RNC.

Like their Democratic counterpart, the Republican JFCs solicited large contributions in amounts up to $449,400, but many traditional Republican big money donors shied away from the effort, unwilling to be associated with Trump's controversial statements and erratic behavior on the campaign trail. While big checks were still an essential part of their revenue, the committees found strength in Trump's grassroots support. By September, Trump and the JFCs had received contributions from 2.1 million donors, and were raising sums that dwarfed the small donor fundraising of either McCain or Romney in previous elections—even though Trump did not issue his first signed email seeking contributions until June 21.[74] Trump's share of these efforts generated substantial sums for his campaign, with Trump Make America Great Again transferring $73.8 million to his campaign and Trump Victory, $12.3 million. In all, Trump Make America Great Again raised $258 million and Trump Victory, $108 million.[75]

Trump gave only $20 million to his general election campaign, bringing his total self-funding for the entire election to $66 million, well below the $100 million he often declared he was going to spend.[76] This donation, along with the money raised by his campaign and Republican JFCs, brought his campaign total to $328 million, including more than $230 million that was raised from July 1 through Election Day. Trump thus depended on the party's efforts and an outpouring of small donor support, rather than his personal wealth in the general election. While he did not match Clinton's post-June total ($289 million), or her overall total of $564 million, he was much more financially competitive than his self-funding suggested, or than was expected at the start of the general election campaign.

Even so, Clinton's financial advantage allowed her to dominate the race as far as conventional campaigning was concerned. Clinton began general election advertising immediately after the final primaries in June, combining with Priorities USA, the Super PAC supporting her, to air $26 million of advertising in that month alone.[77] Trump did not broadcast his first ad until mid-August.[78] By the end of the race, Clinton and her allies led the advertising race by a margin of three-to-one, with the Clinton campaign alone responsible for 282,000 ads as compared to about 85,000 paid for by Trump.[79] Similarly, Clinton held an unprecedented staffing advantage in battleground states. By the beginning of

October, Clinton and her party had employed 5,138 staff in fifteen battleground states, compared to 1,409 staff in sixteen states for Trump and the Republicans.[80] Clinton's fundraising strength provided her with the resources to mount a formidable campaign. This was expected by most political observers, but the final result was not.

Conclusion

Campaign fundraising in 2016 broke new ground, highlighting the efficacy of diverse approaches to the task of raising money. Donald Trump pursued a new route to the presidency by relying on his own wealth at the start and foregoing traditional fundraising tactics. While his own money was a minor share of his general election funding, his approach was still unique: he relied on the efforts of party joint fundraising committees more than any other prior candidate, as well as the support of small donors. No presidential nominee in recent elections had devoted so little effort to fundraising or waited so late in the campaign to actively solicit funds. No candidate had been so critical of his party, yet so dependent on party fundraising, since JFCs ultimately generated a third of his campaign's general election money. And no candidate had been outspent by such substantial margins yet managed to capture the Oval Office.

Trump's victory raised a fundamental question about the importance of money in explaining outcomes. But in this regard, the election sent mixed messages. Clinton's nomination suggested that money still matters, and Sanders's unexpected move from fringe candidate to formidable challenger reflected the success of his fundraising efforts. Indeed, at a time when public attention has largely focused on the role of million dollar donors to Super PACs, Sanders demonstrated the power of small donors and the ability to translate grassroots support into the money needed to finance a competitive campaign. His experience, as well as Trump's, also highlighted the continuing evolution of digital technology and social media as powerful fundraising tools, thus building on the model of Obama. New technology offers an avenue for candidates who lack a traditional donor base or the support of large donors, but the 2016 experience suggests that candidates who appeal to ideological donors, the most progressive or conservative voters who respond to populist messages, are the ones most likely to benefit. His success is certain to be studied by future presidential hopefuls.

Money still matters and commonly accepted approaches to fundraising still work. But money is only a means for a candidate to be heard and to be able to mobilize support. The choice ultimately is in the hands of the voters, and in that regard the election was no exception.

122 Part II: Money and Communication

Notes

1 Under the terms of the federal public funding program, a candidate who meets the eligibility requirements receives a $1-for-$1 public match on the first $250 contributed by an individual. Major party presidential nominees are eligible for a public grant in the general election, which totaled $96 million in 2016, but are limited to that amount of spending and must agree to other regulatory requirements as a condition of accepting the grant.

2 John Fritze, "O'Malley Campaign Secures Public Cash Before Dropping Out," *Baltimore Sun*, February 6, 2016, www.baltimoresun.com/news/maryland/investigations/bs-md-sun-investigates-omalley-money0207-20160206-story.html (accessed December 1, 2016) and FEC, "Federal Election Commission Certifies Federal Matching Funds for O'Malley," press release, April 6, 2016, www.fec.gov/press/press2016/news_releases/20160406release.shtml (accessed December 1, 2016).

3 FEC, "Federal Election Commission Certifies Federal Matching Funds for Jill Stein," press release, August 2, 2016, www.fec.gov/press/press2016/news_releases/20160802_2release.shtml (accessed November 28, 2016).

4 R. Sam Garrett and Shawn Reese, *Funding of Presidential Nominating Conventions: An Overview*, Congressional Research Service Report R43976, May 4, 2016, 8, https://fas.org/sgp/crs/misc/R43976.pdf (accessed November 28, 2016).

5 Amie Parnes and Kevin Cirilli, "The $5 Billion Presidential Campaign?" *The Hill*, January 21, 2015, http://thehill.com/blogs/ballot-box/presidential-races/230318-the-5-billion-campaign (accessed November 29, 2016).

6 Ibid.

7 The fundraising totals included in this paragraph are based on FEC summaries, www.fec.gov/disclosurep/pnational.do (accessed December 1, 2016).

8 Ibid.

9 FEC, "Presidential Pre-Nomination Campaign Receipts Through May 31, 2016," table, June 22, 2016, www.fec.gov/press/summaries/2016/tables/presidential/presreceipts_2016_m6.pdf (accessed December 1, 2016).

10 FEC, "Presidential Pre-Nomination Campaign Receipts Through June 30, 2016," table, July 22, 2016, www.fec.gov/press/summaries/2016/tables/presidential/presreceipts_2016_m7.pdf (accessed December 1, 2016).

11 See Paul Blumenthal, "How Super PACs and Campaigns Are Coordinating in 2016," *Huffington Post*, November 14, 2015, www.huffingtonpost.com/entry/super-pac-coordination_us_56463f85e4b045bf3def0273 (accessed December 1, 2016) and Adam Wollner, "10 Ways Super PACs and Campaigns Coordinate, Even Though They're Not Allowed To," *The Atlantic*, September 27, 2015, www.theatlantic.com/politics/archive/2015/09/10-ways-super-pacs-and-campaigns-coordinate-even-though-theyre-not-allowed-to/436866/ (accessed December 1, 2016).

12 Anthony Corrado, "The Money Race: A New Era of Unlimited Funding?" *Campaigning for President 2012*, ed. Dennis W. Johnson (New York: Routledge, 2013), 67–70.

13 Will Tucker, "$100 Million Floods into Presidential Super PACs in Second Half of 2015," OpenSecrets blog, February 1, 2016, https://www.propublica.org/article/pro-trump-group-blew-by-basic-campaign-finance-laws (accessed December 1, 2016).

Chapter 5: Presidential Candidate Fundraising **123**

14 Nicholas Confessore, "Bernie Sanders Tops His Rivals in Use of Outside Money," *New York Times*, January 28, 2016, www.nytimes.com/2016/01/29/us/politics/bernie-sanders-is-democrats-top-beneficiary-of-outside-spending-like-it-or-not.html?_r=0 (accessed December 1, 2016) and Russ Choma, "Donald Trump Has a Super-PAC Problem," *Mother Jones*, June 20, 2016, www.motherjones.com/politics/2016/05/donald-trump-super-pac-problem (accessed December 1, 2016).

15 Andrew Desiderio, "Jeb Bush's Fundraising Haul: $114 Million," *Real Clear Politics*, July 9, 2015, www.realclearpolitics.com/articles/2015/07/09/jeb_bushs_fundraising_haul_114_million_127314.html (accessed December 3, 2016).

16 Jose DelReal, "Jeb Bush Forms PAC to Explore Presidential Run," *Washington Post*, December 16, 2014, www.washingtonpost.com/news/post-politics/wp/2014/12/16/jeb-bush-forms-pac-to-explore-presidential-run/?utm_term=.0abffc4da2db (accessed December 3, 2016).

17 Desiderio, "Jeb Bush's Fundraising Haul," and Campaign Finance Institute, "Million-Dollar Donors Dominate Presidential Super PAC Giving," press release, June 17, 2016, Table 2, www.cfinst.org/Press/PReleases/16-06-17/Million-Dollar_Donors_Dominate_Presidential_Super_PAC_Giving.aspx (accessed December 4, 2016).

18 Campaign Finance Institute, "Presidential Candidates' Small & Large Donors," press release, February 1, 2016, http://cfinst.org/Press/PReleases/16-02-01/Year_End_Reports_Presidential_Candidates%E2%80%99_Small_and_Large_Dollars.aspx (accessed December 3, 2016).

19 Campaign Finance Institute, "Million-Dollar Donors Dominate."

20 Campaign Finance Institute, "Trump Fundraising Picked Up Steam, But Slow Start Still Leaves Him Well Back," press release, August 18, 2016, www.cfinst.org/Press/PReleases/16-08-18/Presidential_Fundraising_%E2%80%93_Aug_20_Preview_An_Analysis_of_the_Candidates_Parties_and_Joint_Fundraising.aspx (accessed December 2, 2016).

21 Patrick Caldwell, "How Two Hillary Clinton Superfans Became Super-PAC Power Players," *Mother Jones*, February 18, 2014, www.motherjones.com/politics/2014/02/ready-for-hillary-clinton-super-pac (accessed December 4, 2016) and Philip Bump, "Ready for Hillary: The Smartest Political Business in Recent Memory," *Washington Post*, April 6, 2015, www.washingtonpost.com/news/the-fix/wp/2015/04/06/ready-for-hillary-the-smartest-political-business-in-recent-memory/?utm_term=.0fb26868e27c (accessed December 4, 2016).

22 Jaime Fuller, "'Ready for Hillary' Is Spending Money Like Crazy," *Washington Post*, June 13, 2014, www.washingtonpost.com/news/the-fix/wp/2014/06/13/ready-for-hillary-is-already-spending-a-ton-of-dough-on-2016/?utm_term=.44d3055e56d4 (accessed December 4, 2016) and Meaghan Keneally, "'Ready for Hillary' PAC Starts Selling Champagne Glasses, Baby Onesies, and Cell Phone Covers to Raise Funds for the 2016 Campaign," *Washington Post*, March 3, 2014, www.washingtonpost.com/news/the-fix/wp/2014/06/13/ready-for-hillary-is-already-spending-a-ton-of-dough-on-2016/?utm_term=.44d3055e56d4 (accessed December 4, 2016).

23 Dave Levinthal, "Inside Hillary Clinton's Big Money Cavalry," *The Center for Public Integrity*, April 7, 2016, www.publicintegrity.org/2016/04/07/19528/inside-hillary-clintons-big-money-cavalry (accessed December 5, 2016) and Matea Gold, "A Mighty Fundraising Operation Awaits Clinton, as Well as Financial Hurdles," *Washington Post*,

124 Part II: Money and Communication

March 19, 2015, www.washingtonpost.com/politics/a-mighty-fundraising-operation-awaits-clinton-as-well-as-financial-hurdles/2015/03/19/c405a162-cd74-11e4-8a46-b1dc9be5a8ff_story.html?utm_term=.5cbfe81a8bbb (accessed December 4, 2016).

24 Annie Karni, "Clinton Campaign Scores Ready for Hillary Email List," *Politico*, May 30, 2105, www.politico.com/story/2015/05/hillary-clinton-campaign-scores-ready-for-hillary-email-list-118446 (accessed December 5, 2016) and Levinthal, "Inside Hillary Clinton's Big Money Cavalry."

25 Alex Seitz-Wald, "Ready for Hillary No Longer 'Ready for Hillary'," *MSNBC.com*, April 15, 2015, www.msnbc.com/msnbc/ready-hillary-no-longer-ready-hillary (accessed December 5, 2016).

26 Anne Gearan, "Hillary Clinton Raised $45 Million Since April," *Washington Post*, July 1, 2015, www.washingtonpost.com/news/post-politics/wp/2015/07/01/hillary-clinton-raised-45-million-since-april/?utm_term=.7f15ee4d572c (accessed December 5, 2016).

27 Ibid., and Campaign Finance Institute, "Jeb Bush's Big Donor Percentage Sets Record for June 30 Off-year Reports," press release, July 16, 2015, Table 2; www.cfinst.org/Press/PReleases/15-07-16/June_30_Presidential_Fundraising_Reports_Jeb_Bush%E2%80%99s_Big_Donor_Percentage_Sets_Record_for_June_30_off-year_reports.aspx (accessed December 6, 2016).

28 Michael Beckel, "Elite Bundlers Raise More Than $113 Million for Hillary Clinton," *Time*, September 23, 2016, http://time.com/4506275/hillary-clinton-bundlers/ (accessed December 7, 2016).

29 Amanda Becker and Emily Flitter, "Democrat Clinton Raises $45 Million since April U.S. Campaign Launch," *Reuters*, July 1, 2015, www.reuters.com/article/us-usa-clinton-fundraising-idUSKCN0PB59T20150701 (accessed December 8, 2016).

30 Ibid.

31 Total based on the unitemized contributions reported by Hillary For America in its 2015 FEC quarterly fundraising reports.

32 Campaign Finance Institute, "Presidential Candidates' Small & Large Donors."

33 FEC, "2016 Presidential Campaign Finance," www.fec.gov/disclosurep/pnational.do (accessed December 5, 2016) and Bernie 2016, "Sanders Launches Microsite on Historic Fundraising, Outraised Clinton in April," press release, May 20, 2016, www.p2016.org/sanders/sanders050116pr.html (accessed December 5, 2016).

34 Nick Corasaniti, "Bernie Sanders Campaign Showed How to Turn Viral Moments into Money," *New York Times*, June 24, 2016, www.nytimes.com/2016/06/25/us/politics/bernie-sanders-digital-strategy.html (accessed December 4, 2016).

35 Josh Haskell and Liz Kreutz, "Hillary Clinton Has Headlined More Than 350 Fundraisers Since Launching Campaign," *ABC News*, October 25, 2016, http://abcnews.go.com/Politics/hillary-clinton-headlined-350-fundraisers-launching-campaign/story?id=43055539 (accessed December 4, 2016).

36 Corasaniti, "Bernie Sanders Showed How to Turn Viral Moments into Money."

37 Evan Halper, "Bernie Sanders's Campaign Legacy Could Be How He Raises Money from So Many People," *Los Angeles Times*, March 24, 2016, www.latimes.com/nation/politics/la-na-sanders-actblue-20160324-story.html (accessed November 28, 2016).

Chapter 5: Presidential Candidate Fundraising **125**

38 Total based on the unitemized contributions reported by Bernie 2016 in its 2015 FEC quarterly fundraising reports.

39 Matea Gold and John Wagner, "Sanders Nearly Matches Clinton in Fundraising for Third Quarter," *Washington Post*, September 30, 2015, www.washingtonpost.com/politics/heading-into-primaries-sanders-raises-24-million-in-3rd-quarter/2015/09/30/ef061a36-67ac-11e5-8325-a42b5a459b1e_story.html?utm_term=.e320bf3844e8 (accessed November 29, 2016).

40 Ibid.

41 Bernie 2016, "Bernie Sanders Scores Big Win; Breaks Major Fundraising Record," press release, December 20, 2015, https://berniesanders.com/press-release/bernie-sanders-scores-big-win-breaks-major-fundraising-record/ (accessed December 1, 2016).

42 Corasaniti, "Bernie Sanders Campaign Showed How to Turn Viral Moments into Money."

43 John Wagner, "In 24 Hours After Iowa Caucuses, Sanders Donors Pony Up $3 Million, Aides Say," *Washington Post*, February 2, 2016, www.washingtonpost.com/news/post-politics/wp/2016/02/02/in-24-hours-after-iowa-caucuses-sanders-donors-pony-up-3-million-aides-say/?utm_term=.44b11de4e383 (accessed December 1, 2016).

44 John Wagner and Matea Gold, "Sanders Blows Past $6 Million Fundraising Goal for the 24 Hours Following N.H. Win," *Washington Post*, February 10, 2016, www.washingtonpost.com/news/post-politics/wp/2016/02/10/sanders-blows-past-6-million-fundraising-goal-for-the-24-hours-following-n-h-win/?utm_term=.c46f2127a814 (accessed December 3, 2016).

45 Corasaniti, "Bernie Sanders Campaign Showed How to Turn Viral Moments into Money."

46 Ibid.

47 Ibid.

48 Ibid.

49 Jose DelReal, "Ben Carson, Top GOP Fundraiser This Quarter, Sees Huge Grass-Roots Support," *Washington Post*, October 15, 2015, www.washingtonpost.com/news/post-politics/wp/2015/10/15/ben-carson-top-gop-fundraiser-this-quarter-sees-huge-grass-roots-support/?utm_term=.0945d472189b (accessed December 2, 2016).

50 Total based on the unitemized contribution totals reported in the 2015 FEC disclosure reports for Carson America.

51 DelReal, "Ben Carson, Top GOP Fundraiser This Quarter, Sees Huge Grassroots Support."

52 David A. Graham, "Ben Carson's Campaign Is Spending Like Crazy," *The Atlantic*, February 2, 2016, www.washingtonpost.com/news/post-politics/wp/2015/10/15/ben-carson-top-gop-fundraiser-this-quarter-sees-huge-grass-roots-support/?utm_term=.0945d472189b (accessed December 2, 2016).

53 Quoted in David A. Graham, "Does Ben Carson Suspect His Campaign Was a Scam?" *The Atlantic*, February 24, 2016, www.theatlantic.com/politics/archive/2016/02/ben-carson-thinks-maybe-his-campaign-was-a-scam/470715/ (accessed December 3, 2016).

54 "Here's Donald Trump's Presidential Announcement Speech," *Time*, June 16, 2015, http://time.com/3923128/donald-trump-announcement-speech/ (accessed November 3, 2016).

126 Part II: Money and Communication

55 Herbert E. Alexander and Anthony Corrado, *Financing the 1992 Election* (Armonk, NY: M.E. Sharpe, 1995), 130.

56 Wesley Joe and Clyde Wilcox, "Financing the 1996 Presidential Nominations," *Financing the 1996 Election*, ed. John C. Green (Armonk, NY: M.E. Sharpe, 1999), 42–43, and John C. Green and Nathaniel S. Bigelow, "The 2000 Presidential Nominations: The Costs of Innovation," *Financing the 2000 Election*, ed. David B. Magleby (Washington, D.C.: Brookings Institution Press, 2002), 62–63.

57 Anthony Corrado and Molly Corbett, "Rewriting the Playbook on Presidential Campaign Financing," *Campaigning for President 2008*, ed. Dennis W. Johnson (New York: Routledge, 2009), 130–131.

58 Andrew Dugan, "Among Republicans, GOP Candidates Better Known than Liked," *Gallup.com*, July 24, 2015, www.gallup.com/poll/184337/among-republicans-gop-candidates-better-known-liked.aspx?utm_source=Politics&utm_medium=newsfeed&utm_campaign=tiles (accessed November 12, 2016).

59 FEC, "Presidential Pre-Nomination Disbursements through December 31, 2015," www.fec.gov/press/summaries/2016/tables/presidential/PresCand2_2015_12m.pdf (accessed November 12, 2016).

60 Wesleyan Media Project, "Clinton and Sanders Even in Ad War, Cruz and Rubio Gain on Bush in S. Carolina," press release, February 18, 2016, http://mediaproject.wesleyan.edu/releases/update-on-nv-and-sc-contests/ (accessed November 4, 2016).

61 FEC, "Presidential Pre-Nomination Campaign Disbursements April 30, 2016," www.fec.gov/press/summaries/2016/tables/presidential/presdisbursements_2016_m5.pdf (accessed November 2, 2016).

62 Wesleyan Media Project, "Advertising Volume Up 122% Over 2012 Levels; Spending in Presidential Race Over $400 Million," press release, May 12, 2016, http://mediaproject.wesleyan.edu/releases/ad-spending-over-400-million/ (accessed November 24, 2016).

63 Shane Goldmacher, "Hillary Clinton to Begin Collecting General Election Cash," *Politico*, June 3, 2016, www.politico.com/story/2016/06/hillary-clinton-general-election-funds-223853 (accessed November 24, 2016).

64 FEC, "Presidential Pre-Nomination Campaign Receipts through September 30, 2015," www.fec.gov/press/summaries/2016/tables/presidential/presreceipts_2015_q3.pdf (accessed November 24, 2016).

65 FEC, "Presidential Pre-Nomination Campaign Receipts through May 31, 2016," www.fec.gov/press/summaries/2016/tables/presidential/presreceipts_2016_m6.pdf (accessed December 1, 2016).

66 Nicholas Confessore and Rachel Shorey, "Donald Trump Starts Summer Push with Crippling Money Deficit," *New York Times*, June 20, 2016, www.nytimes.com/2016/06/21/us/politics/donald-trump-money-campaign.html?_r=0 (accessed November 12, 2016).

67 Ibid.

68 Matea Gold and Tom Hamburger, "Democratic Party Fundraising Effort Helps Clinton Find New Donors, Too," *Washington Post*, February 20, 2016, www.washingtonpost.com/politics/democratic-party-fundraising-effort-helps-clinton-find-new-donors-too/2016/02/19/b8535cea-d68f-11e5-b195-2e29a4e13425_story.html?utm_term=.5d970c11e624 (accessed November 2, 2016).

Chapter 5: Presidential Candidate Fundraising **127**

69 *McCutcheon* v. *FEC*, 572 U.S. _ (2014); available online at www.supremecourt.gov/opinions/13pdf/12-536_e1pf.pdf (accessed November 2, 2016).

70 R. Sam Garrett, *Increased Campaign Contribution Limits in the FY2015 Omnibus Appropriations Law: Frequently Asked Questions*, Congressional Research Service Report R43825, March 17, 2015.

71 Campaign Finance Institute, "Trump Fundraising Picked Up Steam, But Slow Start Still Leaves Him Well Back," press release, August 18, 2016, Table 14, www.cfinst.org/Press/PReleases/16-08-18/Presidential_Fundraising_%E2%80%93_Aug_20_Preview_An_Analysis_of_the_Candidates_Parties_and_Joint_Fundraising.aspx (accessed December 1, 2016) and FEC, "Presidential Pre-Nomination Campaign Receipts through June 30, 2016."

72 Totals based on an analysis of the Hillary Victory Fund's November 28 FEC disclosure report.

73 Carl Bialik, "Clinton Has Nearly Caught Up to Trump in Media Coverage," *FiveThirtyEight.com*, August 9, 2016, http://fivethirtyeight.com/features/clinton-has-nearly-caught-up-to-trump-in-media-coverage/ (accessed December 1, 2016) and Nicholas Confessore and Karen Yourish, "$2 Billion Worth of Free Media for Donald Trump," *New York Times*, The Upshot blog, March 15, 2016, www.nytimes.com/2016/03/16/upshot/measuring-donald-trumps-mammoth-advantage-in-free-media.html?_r=0 (accessed November 22, 2016).

74 Shane Goldmacher, "Trump Shatters GOP Records with Small Donors," *Politico*, September 19, 2016, www.politico.com/story/2016/09/trump-shatters-gop-records-with-small-donors-228338 (accessed November 23, 2016).

75 Totals based on an analysis of the November 28 FEC disclosure reports filed by these committees.

76 Matea Gold, "No, Donald Trump Has Not Given His Campaign $100 Million, and Other Answers to Your Money Questions," *Washington Post*, October 31, 2016, www.washingtonpost.com/news/post-politics/wp/2016/10/31/no-donald-trump-has-not-given-his-campaign-100-million-and-other-answers-to-your-money-questions/?utm_term=.3deecf023da1 (accessed November 22, 2016).

77 Monica Alba, "Clinton Releases First General Election Ad Against Trump," *NBCNews.com*, June 12, 2016, www.nbcnews.com/politics/2016-election/clinton-releases-first-general-election-ad-against-trump-n590441 (accessed November 23, 2016) and Mark Murray, "Team Clinton Spent $26 M on Battleground Ads in June, Trump Spent $0," *NBCNews.com*, June 28, 2016, www.nbcnews.com/politics/first-read/team-clinton-spent-26m-battleground-ads-june-trump-spent-0-n600611 (accessed November 23, 2016).

78 Nick Gass, "Trump Blasts 'Rigged' Clinton System in First General Election TV Ad," *Politico*, August 19, 2016, www.politico.com/story/2016/08/donald-trump-first-ad-tv-227189 (accessed December 1, 2016).

79 Michael Beckel, "Team Clinton Sponsored 75 Percent of TV Ads in 2016 Presidential Race," Center for Public Integrity, November 8, 2016, www.publicintegrity.org/2016/11/08/20452/team-clinton-sponsored-75-percent-tv-ads-2016-presidential-race (accessed December 6, 2016).

128 Part II: Money and Communication

80 Reid Wilson and Joe Disipio, "Clinton Holds Huge Ground Game Advantage Over Team Trump," *The Hill*, October 22, 2016, http://thehill.com/campaign/302231-clinton-holds-huge-ground-game-advantage-over-team-trump (accessed November 15, 2016).

6
THE DIGITAL BATTLE

Suzanne Zurn

Throughout history candidates have used the latest technology available to reach voters. In recent times, Barack Obama's 2008 campaign is widely credited as forever changing how candidates run for president because of the way he used online tools to communicate and organize. The 2008 election was dubbed the first "Web 2.0 election." That campaign and its successor, the 2012 Obama re-elect, have been studied by many and regarded as "the model" to run a modern digital presidential campaign. In fact, campaigns across the country, and at all levels, have sought to replicate the Obama digital strategy.

In 2016 the Obama model was challenged by a political newcomer who publically dismissed the importance of data and analytics and adopted a fire, ready, aim strategy in its place. The Obama campaigns were unquestionably sophisticated; but their model, even with some enhancements this year and seasoned experts at the wheel, failed.

This was also the first presidential campaign cycle where what was happening in cyberspace dominated the news about the contest. In the analysis of journalist Stephen Dinan, "From the Republican presidential nominee Donald Trump's 3 a.m. Twitter habit to Democratic nominee Hillary Clinton's secret email server and her campaign chairman John Podesta's hacked emails" the public was given "an extraordinary, and sometime troubling look at the inner workings of government and campaigns."[1]

The new digital requirement that emerged from the 2016 cycle is not what was expected. Advances in technology occurred, new platforms emerged, existing channels gained capability, more Americans were online and content creators than ever before, and a greater number of campaign professionals were digitally enabled. These conditions had the potential for a breakout cycle for digital innovation in running for president. The media speculated about this being the

130 Part II: Money and Communication

"Snapchat election" or the "social media election" but these characterizations were too focused on the Obama playbook as the successful digital model. What influenced and mattered to voters in 2016 had changed.

Being a master of the modern digital media culture is a new requirement to run for president. This is perhaps the most enduring lesson cemented by the 2016 campaign that will impact 2020 and beyond. Running for president in 2016 required a personal comfort and adeptness with how the traditional and digital media ecosystem of our multi-channel, always on, highly networked lives worked. Donald Trump shared with the world what was on his mind, without filters, at the moment he thought it. There were typos, controversial images and content. It was real. It was unscripted. It was not filtered or pre-approved. Facts no longer mattered. This approach was a departure from the carefully researched, written, and planned posts of previous cycles and of Hillary Clinton's digital operation. The news media re-published and broadcasted images of Trump's tweets; and voters shared his messages, too, both supporters and opponents each engaging with the content for different reasons but nonetheless spreading it far and wide. Fire, ready, aim is what the modern media culture demanded; Trump understood that and it also represented the personal media broadcasting approach he brought to the campaign.

The Online Audience Grew and Information Sources Shifted

Over the past four years the percent of Americans online has grown slightly from 79.3 percent to 88.5 percent[2] and during that same time the sources they turn to for news and the devices used has changed significantly to a greater reliance on Internet and social media sources. A 2016 Pew Research Center study found that the majority of U.S. adults get news on social media, and 38 percent reported they often get news from digital sources including news websites, apps, or social media sites. More importantly, 65 percent of adults said they turned to digital sources about the presidential election with 44 percent specifically turning to their social media accounts for campaign news. To put the change in context, in 2012 only 36 percent of adults said they used Internet sources for information about the election, and just 17 percent said they regularly turned to social media for campaign news. Likewise, by 2016 unique visits from mobile devices to news websites exceeded visits from desktop devices.[3]

In addition, in a separate study Pew found the role of the campaigns as a direct source of news had grown and the function of their websites as the central hub had evolved. At least two in ten adults learned about the 2016 presidential election directly from the websites, apps, or emails of campaign and issue-based groups. The campaigns still had websites as their online headquarters presence but the study concluded "the role of campaign websites has changed—and in some cases narrowed."[4]

These changes appear to be in response to the growth of social networking sites as a more prominent source of news and an essential destination of modern

Chapter 6: The Digital Battle **131**

TABLE 6.1 How Candidate Websites Changed from 2012 to 2016

Website Feature	2012	2016
Commenting allowed	Yes	No
Sections devoted to unique social and demographic groups	Yes	No
Personal fundraising pages	Yes	No
Average number of new posts per day	6	2.5

Source: Pew Research Center, "Election 2016 Campaign as a Direct Source of News," July 2016.

life. Interestingly, the websites have reduced in scope and in the use of sophisticated personalization tools like those we saw in 2008 with the MyBarackObama portal. Table 6.1 shows the differences in campaign websites from 2012 to 2016.

The analysis appears to show a decline in technology use over the past four years for developing customized experiences and opportunities to engage in a two-way conversation. But in actuality, many of the same capabilities and opportunities to engage continued to exist; they were just on different platforms in 2016. For example, the campaigns deployed custom apps to help keep their most loyal fans engaged using game mechanics and gave them an outlet to demonstrate their commitment by getting involved with the campaign. The Obama and Romney campaigns had mobile apps in 2012, but even Harper Reed, Obama's 2012 chief technology officer, said the app the Clinton team built was "light years different."[5] Despite the more narrowly focused websites, the actual tech stack—the software powering the sites and tracking activity—was more robust than in previous years, and the mobile apps where some of the website functionality moved to, matured. The shift of website capabilities to apps and to social media platforms was a logical progression since this is the first presidential election for a public that is mobile-first oriented.

It is also worth noting the campaigns made adjustments in digitally focused staffing and paid advertising spending in recognition of these shifts to a more mobile, more digital, and greater social ecosystem source of news. Yet total ad spending was still television-dominant (see the next chapter on political advertising) despite the superior targeting and scalability of digital media.

The New Requirement To Run For President

Running for president in 2016 required new personal qualities or skills not necessary in previous cycles and a campaign organization that reflected the changing expectations of the electorate. This cycle revealed the power of socially networked media as a way to strategically communicate. Clinton and Trump differed both in their personal use and experience with social media, and in how their respective campaign and political party organizations planned, staffed, and utilized the full complement of digital organizing strategies, technology, and

132 Part II: Money and Communication

techniques. In a year when the two major party candidates were equally unpopular, mastery of the modern media culture proved to make a difference for the candidate whose campaign (and political party) was considered by most observers to have a significant and insurmountable digital disadvantage. Communications scholar Daniel Kreiss, who closely studied the use of technology and data in the 2012 election, observed in a post-election interview, "We have not had a modern presidential campaign like this before."[6]

The new dynamic of the modern media culture was best explained by veteran journalist Andrea Mitchell in a May 4, 2016 interview with Joel Benenson, Clinton's chief strategist. The two were talking about the general election matchup when Mitchell made an interesting comment that clearly stated what was different about running for president in 2016: "Facts no longer matter. Tweets matter."[7] These six words encapsulate so much about what was different about this cycle. First consider the profoundness of this statement from someone with nearly fifty years of newsroom experience. Mitchell's career covering presidents, those who seek the office, and the domestic and international public policy arena was defined by finding facts and reporting them to the American public. Mitchell's assessment that brief, self-published statements to the American public, regardless of their validity or independent verification, had become more important than facts is extraordinary for two reasons. First, it is a radical transformation from what mattered in the past, and second, for someone of Mitchell's background to make this statement makes it even more poignant.

Trump, running as the outsider to the political system, innately had a better grasp of what "sells," how information moves, and where people engage today. He understood the modern media culture. He and his team were acutely aware of how social media in particular was rocket fuel to advance "truths" that resonated and felt plausible to segments of the population who were seeking answers to explain their own circumstances and desire for change.

The tension between facts versus tweets also played out in the different personal styles of the candidates, and was evident in their very different social media campaigns. Colin Delaney, founder of ePolitics.com, described Trump and Clinton's digital styles as "a contest between brash yahooism and cautious calculation."[8] Zac Moffett, Mitt Romney's digital director on the 2008 campaign, observed that campaign operatives can tell a candidate how to behave, but

> many just aren't natural at it. [Donald Trump] is extremely natural at it. I think that's why [the Clinton Campaign] has so much trouble with Hillary Clinton. ... Even with her on the late shows, it's challenging and I think people see that and don't feel that's authentic.[9]

The stylistic differences in digital campaign operations closely mirrored the personas of each candidate, their biases, priorities, and nature. *Bloomberg Politics*

Chapter 6: The Digital Battle **133**

observed that "Trump uses social media as an extension of his personality. Clinton uses social media as an extension of the campaign."[10] This was also evident in the campaigns' staffing. Clinton preferred a large, corporate model of campaign operations, while Trump's was lean, unorthodox, and unconventional. Clinton had a significantly larger campaign staff, about five times larger than Trump's just one month out from Election Day.[11]

An analysis from the Pew Research Center of the candidates' social media accounts reveals the macro differences in their approaches to online voter engagement. One particular finding from the research on the use of links in social media posts tells us a great deal about the candidates—their biases, priorities, and nature—key indicators of whether a candidate was in sync with the modern media culture. On Facebook and Twitter a best practice is to include links to additional online content with one's post. For political campaigns, links are generally used to provide more information, to help voters get involved, and to provide credibility.

The Pew study showed that Clinton and Trump included links in their posts at a similar rate—about 30 percent. However, the content they linked to revealed a very interesting difference between them. The majority, 78 percent, of Clinton's posts with links pointed to content on her campaign's website— original content created by her campaign team. A Democratic strategist expressed frustration with this strategy in a post-election interview, "If the content is just going back to your own website, where is the case about why I should trust you?" On the other hand, Trump's posts with links pointed to external news media content 80 percent of the time,[12] which filled the void for voters seeking validators, especially to complete the gaps of their identity shaped epistemology.[13] Table 6.2 shows the percentage of Facebook posts with links for the Clinton and Trump campaigns.

TABLE 6.2 Clinton and Trump Links on Facebook and Twitter

Percent of Facebook posts containing links that go to ...

Candidate	Campaign Site	News Media
Donald Trump	none	78
Hillary Clinton	80	15

Percent of Twitter posts containing links that go to ...

Candidate	Campaign Site	News Media
Donald Trump	20	48
Hillary Clinton	60	25

Source: Pew Research Center analysis, posts on Facebook and Twitter, May 11–31, 2016; "Election 2016: Campaigns as a Direct Source of News," Pew Research Center.

134 Part II: Money and Communication

For Clinton, the data highlighted:

- Her personal nature to always be in control of the message was also a core value of her social media operation.
- The campaign sought to be the sole source of news and information to its supporters by creating an echo-chamber loop between platforms.
- The campaign distrusted external sources because they could introduce contradictory ideas.
- A focus on the "internal game" of recruiting supporters, raising money.

For Trump, the data highlighted:

- His personal, ego-focused approach that constantly sought third party validation.
- The campaign's small staff lacked the resources to create original content so it had to rely on content created by others.
- The campaign thought links to niche and large news media sites would give its message and status more credibility.
- A focus on the "external game" of rallies and media appearances.

Trump and Social Media

Trump's personal use of social media is well known. Unlike Clinton, Trump largely ran his Twitter account by himself with two insiders behind the scenes who assisted.[14] "The two most important things for a celebrity on social media are to be authentic and to give your fans what they want," said Justin McConney, Trump's new media strategist and video editor who had worked in the Trump organization before moving over to the campaign.[15] This political neophyte/businessman/reality TV star and his campaign developed a strategy based on what they knew—a keen understanding of how content is consumed today, what engages consumers to tune in, pay attention, and be loyal. Above all, they knew their strength was having the campaign's identity and Trump's as one and the same.

Five months before Trump locked up the nomination, Dan Pfeiffer, Obama's highly regarded former digital and social media expert, said Trump is "way better at the Internet than anyone else in the GOP which is partly why he is winning."[16] Trump's style was to liberally share his views, and no one or thing appeared to be off-limits to his 140-character dispatches. Trump's social media accounts were provocative, braggadocios, confrontational, and self-centered—and extension of his public personality. Their approach was handsomely rewarded with the exposure equivalent of $2 billion in free advertising.[17]

This style of voter engagement had not been seen in presidential campaigning before and supporters loved what they saw in the "unfiltered access to their

Chapter 6: The Digital Battle **135**

candidate's thoughts and emotions."[18] Most candidates in the social media era have maintained virtual online boundaries between their personal and public/ campaign lives, but that would have eliminated Trump's key advantage— beginning the race with a huge social media following and hands-on personal experience using the platforms, especially Twitter. Trump made a personal connection with voters offline and online often with bold and difficult to substantiate claims. "[His] unorthodox approach led to a dramatic share in positive sentiment online across all the key swing states vs. Clinton," according to Aaron Guiterman and Kari Butcher of the Edelman global marketing firm's online analysis of over 24 million online conversations.[19]

Trump is an experienced live-tweeter and that was a powerful credential in 2016. Trump's experience ranged from live-tweeting the 2012 Republican debate to the Oscars, "Celebrity Apprentice," and the Democratic debate in October 2015.[20] Trump knew what worked online because he himself was online.

Even when a Trump tweet was the center of controversy, and there were several times, it served a purpose of dominating the online and offline media ecosystem and keeping his opponents scrambling for attention. No matter how politically incorrect, insensitive, or mean the tweet, nothing seemed to damage his standing with his supporters and some controversial remarks even seemed to boost him with some groups. In fact, the immediate feedback loop of the modern media culture rewarded such activity with the rapid and slippery movement of content across platforms carrying what happened on Twitter, to seeing it reported on cable and network news programs and in the traditional press.

Being "bad" appeared to be "good" for getting his message out, and for Trump this reinforced what he had learned many years ago in his business and personal affairs that "all press is good press." "He is of the mindset that the more his name is dropped, the more a kind of hypnosis, for lack of a better word, there is to the American public," Jim Dowd, chief executive officer of Dowd Ink, who did public relations for Trump from 2004 to 2010, recalled in a recent interview. "He thinks even a negative piece is a positive for him."[21] A data scientist who analyzed more than four million Facebook posts from the two candidates summarized, "With his content and his audience, Donald Trump has found product-market fit on social media."[22]

Clinton and Social Media

Unlike Trump, Clinton was not an avid tweeter or original social media content producer. No stranger to the influence of the 24-hour news cycle, she understood the role of social media in political communications and also sought to manage it as she had always sought to manage the flow of information.

Clinton's social media strategy focused on the "inside game" of marketing her candidacy, organizing supporters, turning people out for events.[23] She was on all

136 Part II: Money and Communication

the major social media platforms with targeted messaging and expertly packaged content for the channel—a quintessential Clintonian tactic to manage information, meet each group where they are, and tell them what they wanted or needed to hear. It was a social full-court press to convince and turn out the coalition Clinton needed to win that she was likeable enough and most qualified for the job.

A key part of the Clinton campaign strategy was to overcome the perception of her being impersonal by showing she's likeable, funny, and approachable. Prior to Clinton's campaign launch in June 2015 communications director Jennifer Palmieri described the campaign's strategy as to "show the person that we know, who is very maternal, very warm and engaging."[24] Jenna Lowenstein, Clinton's then deputy digital director, said the web was a great forum to establish an intimacy with voters[25] which offered a hint into how the campaign planned to learn from its 2008 campaign missteps and to overcome the challenge Andrew Rasiej, founder of the tech non-profit Personal Democracy Media, described as showing Clinton as "engaged, present, listening, involved and understanding the two-way dynamic of the medium."[26]

The plan involved balancing a tightly controlled messaging machine with the need for Clinton's online presence to feel personal, authentic. To implement the plan, the Clinton campaign hired an "A-team" of Democratic tech experts[27] and got to work building what was described as a "production company" by Katie Dowd, Clinton's first digital director. The Clinton digital team consisted of writers, videographers, designers, social media specialists, and motion graphics artists whose focus was creating unique content for the candidate.[28] This Obama playbook approach was both practical and grounded in conventional best practices to shift perceptions.

The Clinton campaign developed creative videos that showed her growing up, as a grandmother, and in other familiar settings to position her as someone that average voters would want to have a cup of coffee with. They also leveraged tongue-in cheek tactics to help re-position Clinton's brand narrative, like Clinton's first Instagram photo of pantsuits with the hashtag #HardChoices, also the title of her book. The campaign developed edgy insider content for her like the "Delete Your Account" tweet to respond to a Trump "Crooked Hillary" tweet about Obama's endorsement of her. In Twitter parlance, "delete your account" roughly translates to "Your tweet or opinion is so bad that you should be immediately disqualified from further participation on the platform."[29] The "Delete Your Account" tweet was one of the most re-tweeted of the cycle. But with all of these excellent social efforts one important voice was missing— Clinton's—and it was noticed.

Clinton's team expertly delivered on all the elements of what previously defined success—creativity, humor, timeliness, and relevancy. The challenge was the operating environment of what was required to run a successful campaign for president was changing at the same time. They knew social media was important, but it turned out to be way more important than Team Clinton could have

Chapter 6: The Digital Battle **137**

imagined at the beginning of the campaign, a Democratic digital media consultant explained in a post-election interview with me. "That is probably the most interesting take away," she explained.

Having the best talent to do social media for Clinton meant there was an authenticity gap that was ever more noticeable by the public who was being driven this cycle by emotion, not issues. Trump's (almost) single-handed social media posting machine "was able to authentically connect with [voters'] emotions, Clinton was not," according to the digital analysis from Edelman's social media intelligence command center of the online conversation around the election.[30] The general predictability and tameness of Clinton's online content matched her control-focused persona which was a barrier to effectively navigating the modern digital media culture which thrives on instant, raw, unfiltered, short form content that reacts to people and situations and thus engages them in knowing who you are (whether that is for better or worse!).

Innovations

In 1965 the founder of Intel, Gordon Moore, made a prediction that became the "gold standard" for our modern digital revolution. Moore was a successful engineer, entrepreneur, and manager and from his experience he reasoned that the "computing world would dramatically increase in power, and decrease in relative cost, at an exponential pace."[31] This was soon dubbed as "Moore's Law." We have seen Moore's Law realized in the past fifty years with rapid innovation in faster, smaller, and less costly computing technology. For the political technology of the 2016 presidential cycle, rapid innovation was no exception. In fact one leading Republican digital strategist who developed data and targeting models for one of the primary campaigns reflected in a private post-election interview,

> First time in my life I've seen the political class move farther and faster than private industry. We usually lagged in innovation because we couldn't demonstrate the effectiveness immediately and could not afford to waste the money. Now we can test and adjust real fast.[32]

Was 2016 innovative? Insiders pointed to Moore's Law as a way to explain that the innovations this year appear to have come in the form of a better utilization of what we already had. "We had many of the same tools, just better. Like an 8-track tape allows you to listen to music, but iTunes provides more flexibility and cost efficiencies. Both allow you to listen to music, one is just better," explained the Republican digital strategist. Zac Moffet also saw the impact of Moore's Law on the campaign, "In 2016 suddenly digital is now more cost efficient and scalable than mail and phones combined."[33] Alan Rosenblatt, a digital communications strategist and professor, explained it another way in a

138 Part II: Money and Communication

post-election interview: the 2016 campaign was a "communications revolution, not a tech revolution."[34]

Thanks to these improvements, costs and implementation times went down and computing power went up. This opened the door to amassing greater amounts of data and the capacity to more quickly build models that learned from the data sets. "This was no small thing," a digital consultant described to me, "because never before could we do it this fast on a large scale."[35]

Related improvements also occurred in the online advertising technology campaigns used to reach voters. "The goal is to deliver the right message to the right user on the right screen at the right time," wrote digital journalist Dan Patterson, "and to convert that user to become a donor, voter, and brand evangelist."[36] Companies built platforms to crunch audience data and apply machine learning to automate actions like email sends and ad buying across the variety of screen types. So-called "big-data" was not new in 2016 but it had come a long way since 2012 and was used to power integrated ad targeting and buying. Pete Sheridan, chief technology officers of Targeted Victory, a political technology company that has developed such platforms, said,

> Heading into the [2012] election the Romney campaign had a handful of national audiences. This year while we were working with the Cruz campaign, they were targeting over 160 audiences in Iowa alone. This impacts every level of the stack, from integration to execution to [data] reporting.[37]

Another example of technology improving digital advertising capabilities was in the number of variations the campaigns could deploy to custom audiences. Custom ad targeting was not new, but the scale on which it was done in 2016 pushed the limits of what was previously possible. The most extreme reported case of this technique came from the Trump campaign and RNC. On one day in August they flooded Facebook with more than 100,000 ad variations aimed at different targeted audiences. By comparison, on an average day they ran 35,000 to 45,000 Facebook ad iterations. While Facebook as a communications tool for campaigning for president was not new, its sophisticated use as a cash register for the campaigns was unlike 2012. "Facebook was the single most important platform to help grow our fundraising base," Trump campaign digital director Brad Parscale told BuzzFeed News.[38]

"The campaign is very open to testing, very open to trying new things," Gary Coby, RNC director of digital advertising said. Referring to the committee and campaign team as a whole, he added, "We've benefited from Parscale's experience outside of politics, which can be slow to push boundaries."[39]

Since this was the year of mobile first, it is no surprise the campaigns looked to SMS or text messaging to engage with voters. Journalist Nick Corasaniti of the *New York Times* described the new focus on older technology,

The killer app for the 2016 presidential campaign is not an app at all. It is not even new. Texting—that 1990s-vintage technology—has suddenly become a go-to vehicle for presidential campaigns when they need to get a message out as widely and quickly as possible, and with confidence that it will be read.[40]

Once a campaign can get a voter to opt-in to receive text messages, it can expect about 98 percent of those messages to be read—the industry average open rate for text messages.[41] Unlike other contact methods, there's typically nothing between you and your mobile device screen when a text message comes through. "A text message—despite its no-frills, retro essence—is something personal. Something invasive. Something almost guaranteed to be read," Corasaniti concluded.[42]

Teddy Goff, chief digital strategist for the Clinton campaign, described text messaging as their high-tech secret tool. "We've been shocked at how many people are responding favorably to these things," he said. "SMS works great for volunteers fearful of being hung up on or rejected. Texting also is reasonably well-received by voters who often don't want to answer phone calls. It's a technology layer on top of old-fashioned organizing," Goff explained.[43]

In addition, many noted this cycle had more trained political tech talent than in years past to leverage the technological advancements. Digital is constantly evolving, and as Moffet put it, "the level of sophistication, data technology, [and] engineering that is required now is exponentially more difficult than it was ten years ago which adds to the complexity of a campaign."[44] The Democrats have long had a perceived advantage in the talent department, and the Republicans grew their bench this cycle in part due the seventeen-candidate GOP primary field where each campaign had a digital director who now has presidential campaign experience that increases the talent pool for 2020 (and key midterm races). Gerrit Lansing, the RNC's chief digital officer, adds additional context to the perception of a Democrat tech advantage: "There never really was much of a gap. All of the macro levers that go into an election—most are outside the control of digital."[45]

The Clinton campaign hired a Google executive, Stephanie Hannon, to be its chief technology officer ten months before the New Hampshire primary to oversee the development of the campaign technological infrastructure.[46] On the other hand, the Trump campaign ratcheted up its operation only after he clinched the GOP nomination by winning Indiana's primary on May 3, 2016. Time and talent were among the key advantages the Democrats had coming into 2016 and it appeared those strengths would be insurmountable for Trump.

The Trump campaign had to try. Trump's son-in-law, Jared Kushner, engaged help from "Silicon Valley people who are kind of covert Trump fans and experts in digital marketing" and also tapped Brad Parscale, a political novice who had managed digital marketing for some of the Trump businesses and been leading digital operations since the earliest days of the campaign, to lead a project called Project Alamo to take the campaign to the next level with online fundraising,

140 Part II: Money and Communication

modeling, and targeting.[47] Matt Oczkowski, former chief digital officer for Scott Walker for America, and two data science colleagues from Cambridge Analytica joined the Project Alamo effort in mid-June. In a post-election interview Oczkowski described what they walked into, "The campaign didn't have a technology infrastructure, no data infrastructure. We just started to work."[48] Soon the Cambridge team grew to twelve and the firm who had worked on Britain's Brexit-upset campaign found themselves engaged in polling, data science, and digital. To have one firm and such a small number of people working on these functions was different than previous campaigns, and also different from the larger and more siloed Clinton operation.

As a practical matter, the Trump campaign's innovation will be remembered for streamlining the functions of collecting data signals from the electorate—from traditional polling, field data, social media, third party data, and others—by assembling a multi-disciplinary integrated team that could focus on what was necessary and working, and was empowered to act on instincts. Professor Jennifer Stromer-Galley, director for the Center for Computational and Data Sciences at Syracuse University, who has been studying social media since before it was called social media, described it in a post-election interview: "The Trump staff was small and not indoctrinated from prior campaigns, like Clinton's staff was, so they followed their own instincts."[49]

One way to think about this is that the blessing of ample time and plentiful talent turned into an albatross for Team Clinton. They had so much time and talent that it was more difficult to quickly make changes to travel, messaging, and other voter contacts based on a new insight from a model or experiment. Team Trump barely had enough time left in the calendar to focus on what was necessary, and thus was more sensitive to cues of what was working/not working. Oczkowski acknowledged they didn't predict a Trump victory but they did see indications in the final weeks that their likely voter was changing so they made adjustments to their "Optimized Path to Victory Tracker" which prioritized cities for candidate travel and the allocation of resources. "We saw trends that played out weeks before it happened. We realized the likely voter was changing to be more white, more rural and that influenced strategy."[50] The strategy is now all in the data, Stromer-Galley concluded.[51]

Conclusion

The post-mortem on what worked, what didn't, and what it all means will be studied in great detail over the next few years—like the significant volumes written about the Obama digital playbook and the ink devoted to the GOP's so-called 2012 autopsy. Keep in mind that whatever is written about 2016, that when you win, you get to write the history.

As insiders start their retrospectives, there are cracks emerging that challenge the concept the left was far ahead on digital and tech. When I asked the RNC's

Chapter 6: The Digital Battle **141**

chief digital officer if 2016 would be remembered as the year when the Republicans caught up, he replied,

> It's an irrational question, "are we caught up." So much of what we do is not explainable. The depths of this stuff goes beyond what the press is capable of understanding. Ninety percent of the iceberg is under water so the press can't see what we're doing to even know.[52]

Former RNC digital directors also took issue with the question. "It's a farce. The GOP was ahead before Obama," Cyrus Krohn who led the RNC digital efforts in 2007–2009 explained in a post-election interview. What changed though, he said, was a willingness to allocate the kind of budgets needed on technology infrastructure and digital.[53]

Whether the GOP was actually behind is not relevant. Likewise, the Obama playbook has lost its patina as the Holy Grail for modern digital campaigning. The 2016 election taught us that no amount of organization, sophistication of resources, or talent could compensate for a candidate who is not able to master the modern media culture. The candidates mattered and so did their communication skills. But we also must be grounded in knowing that the digital campaign is but a set of tools, powered by increasingly powerful data and technology, that goes into winning the presidency. As professionals evaluate how to win in 2020 and beyond, they would be wise to learn from the following 2016 lessons:

- Data can help inform strategy, but an over-reliance on data will hurt you more than help. Don't dismiss the data if it is not what you expected.
- Run as many experiments and models as is practical and can be acted upon. Computing power is practically limitless now to run millions of permutations, but converting those into actionable communications plans has scalable limits.
- Voters expect authenticity and two-way communication channels.
- Facts no longer matter. Do not get hung up on the details of an issue. Focus on the message voters are hearing and the style of the messenger and develop your own authentic way to engage in the rapid-response communications environment.
- Authenticity beats perfection. Do not sweat typos or a missing period. Speed and reality matter more.
- Build a campaign team that is interdisciplinary and highly collaborative to create the conditions to take fast action on the insights learned from data and analytics.
- Innovation can come from enhanced uses of existing technology. If it works, keep doing it. Mastering the fundamentals of our modern media culture will get you far.

142 Part II: Money and Communication

Notes

1 Stephen Dinan, "Ballot Selfies Take Center Stage as Digital Evolution Remodels Voting, Campaign Styles," *Washington Times*, November 7, 2016, www.washingtontimes.com/news/2016/nov/7/ballot-selfies-take-center-stage-as-digital-evolut/ (accessed December 3, 2016).

2 United States Internet Users, *Internet Live Stats*, www.internetlivestats.com/internet-users/us/ (accessed December 4, 2016).

3 Pew Research Center, "Digital News Audience Fact Sheet," June 2016, www.journalism.org/2016/06/15/digital-news-audience-fact-sheet (accessed December 3, 2016).

4 Pew Research Center, "Election 2016: Campaigns as a Direct Source of News," July 2016, www.journalism.org/2016/07/18/candidates-differ-in-their-use-of-social-media-to-connect-with-the-public/ (accessed December 2, 2016).

5 Issie Lapowsky, "Clinton's App Trouncing Trump's Pretty Much Every Way," *Wired*, September 21, 2016, www.wired.com/2016/09/clintons-app-trouncing-trumps-pretty-much-every-way/ (accessed December 6, 2016).

6 Daniel Kreiss telephone interview with author, November 2016. See Daniel Kreiss, *Prototype Politics: Technology-Intensive Campaigns and the Data of Democracy* (New York: Oxford University Press, 2016).

7 Andrea Mitchell, "Andrea Mitchell Reports," *MSNBC*, 12:20 p.m., May 4, 2016.

8 Colin Delaney, "Trump vs. Clinton Online: A Digital Battle Royale with Long-Term Fallout," *Epolitics.com*, June 9, 2016, www.epolitics.com/2016/06/09/trump-vs-clinton-online-a-digital-battle-royale-with-long-term-fallout/ (accessed December 6, 2016).

9 Zac Moffett, "Campaign 2016," *C-SPAN*, September 23, 2016, http://podcast.c-span.org/podcast/moffa0923.mp3 (accessed December 5, 2016).

10 "Clinton and Trump Have Very Different Strategies for the Final Stretch," *Bloomberg Politics*, October 5, 2016, www.bloomberg.com/graphics/2016-clinton-trump-campaign-strategies/ (accessed December 7, 2016).

11 Alex Seitz-Wald, Did Martinez, and Carrie Dann, "Ground Game: Democrats Started Fall with 5-to-1 Paid Staff Advantage," *NBC News*, October 7, 2016, www.nbcnews.com/politics/2016-election/ground-game-democrats-started-fall-5-1-paid-staff-advantage-n661656 (accessed December 6, 2016).

12 Pew Research Center, "Election 2016: Campaigns as a Direct Source of News," July 2016.

13 Kreiss interview.

14 Erik Sherman, "Two Trump Insiders Behind the Campaign's Social Network Explosion," *Fortune*, March 25, 2016, http://fortune.com/2016/03/25/trump-scavino-mcconney-social-media/ (accessed December 5, 2016).

15 Hannah Jan Parkinson, "Can Donald Trump's Social Media Genius Take Him All the Way to the White House?" *The Guardian*, December 23, 2015, www.theguardian.com/technology/2015/dec/23/donald-trump-social-media-strategy-internet-republican-nomination-president (accessed December 15, 2016).

16 Ibid.

Chapter 6: The Digital Battle **143**

17 L. Gordon Crovitz, "Trump's Big Data Gamble," *Wall Street Journal*, July 24, 2016, www.wsj.com/articles/trumps-big-data-gamble-1469395312 (accessed December 5, 2016).

18 "Clinton and Trump Have Very Different Strategies for the Final Stretch," *Bloomberg Politics*.

19 Aaron Guiterman and Kari Butcher, "A Political Share War," *Edelman Insights & Blogs*, November 16, 2016, www.edelman.com/post/political-share-war/ (accessed December 6, 2016).

20 Parkinson, "Can Donald Trump's Social Media Genius Take Him All the Way to the White House?"

21 Michael Kruse, "Trump and the Dark Art of Bad Publicity," *Politico*, July 21, 2016, www.politico.com/magazine/story/2016/07/donald-trump-2016-convention-melania-trump-speech-dark-art-of-pr-214083 (accessed December 13, 2016).

22 Patrick Martinchek, "What I Discovered About Trump and Clinton From Analyzing 4 Million Facebook Posts," NewCoShift, November 9, 2016, https://shift.newco.co/what-i-discovered-about-trump-and-clinton-from-analyzing-4-million-facebook-posts-922a4381fd2f#.6f1ww2wlx (accessed December 13, 2016).

23 Alan Rosenblatt, "What Did Hillary Clinton Leave on the Social Media Table?" *The Huffington Post*, December 2, 2016, www.huffingtonpost.com/entry/what-did-hillary-clinton-leave-on-the-social-media_us_58419d99e4b04587de5de94d (accessed December 13, 2016).

24 Sam Fizell, "Hillary Clinton Launches a More Personal Campaign," *Time*, June 13, 2015, http://time.com/3920461/hillary-clinton-presidential-campaign-rally/ (accessed December 14, 2016).

25 Sam Fizell, "Hillary Clinton's Team Likes Barack Obama's Style," *Time*, July 17, 2015, http://time.com/3963440/hillary-clintons-digital-team-likes-barack-obamas-style/ (accessed December 13, 2016).

26 Darren Samuelson, "Hillary's Nerd Squad," *Politico*, March 25, 2015, www.politico.com/story/2015/03/hillarys-nerd-squad-116402 (accessed December 1, 2016).

27 Ibid.

28 Ashley Codianni, "Inside Hillary Clinton's Digital Operation," *CNN*, August 25, 2015, www.cnn.com/2015/08/25/politics/hillary-clinton-2016-digital/ (accessed December 2, 2016).

29 Daniel Victor, "Clinton to Trump on Twitter: 'Delete Your Account'," *New York Times*, June 9, 2016, www.nytimes.com/2016/06/10/us/politics/hillary-clinton-to-donald-trump-delete-your-account.html (accessed December 2, 2016).

30 Guiterman and Butcher, "A Political Share War."

31 "50 Years of Moore's Law," *Intel*, www.intel.com/content/www/us/en/silicon-innovations/moores-law-technology.html (accessed December 2, 2016).

32 Anonymous interview with author, November 2016.

33 Zac Moffett, "Campaign 2016," *C-SPAN*, September 23, 2016, http://podcast.c-span.org/podcast/moffa0923.mp3 (accessed December 2, 2016).

34 Alan Rosenblatt interview with author, November 2016.

35 Anonymous interview with author, November 2016.

144 Part II: Money and Communication

36 Dan Patterson, "The Advertising Tech Powering the 2016 Election," *TechRepublic*, October 19, 2016, www.techrepublic.com/article/the-advertising-tech-powering-the-2016-election/ (accessed December 3, 2016).

37 Ibid.

38 Charlie Warzel, "Trump Fundraiser: Facebook Employee Was Our 'MVP'," *BuzzFeed*, November 12, 2016, www.buzzfeed.com/charliewarzel/trump-fundraiser-facebook-employee-was-our-mvp (accessed December 4, 2016).

39 Kate Kaye, "Trump Camp and RNC Say This Facebook Ad Onslaught Was Risky," *AdAge*, September 26, 2016, http://adage.com/article/campaign-trail/trump-camp-rnc-facebook-ad-onslaught-brought-donors/306003/ (accessed December 4, 2016).

40 Nick Corasaniti, "Texting Comes of Age as a Political Messenger," *New York Times*, August 18, 2015, www.nytimes.com/2015/08/19/us/politics/presidential-campaigns-see-texting-as-a-clear-path-to-voters.html?_r=0 (accessed December 2, 2106).

41 Michael Essany, "SMS Marketing Wallops Email with 98% Open Rate and Only 1% Spam," *Mobile Marketing Watch*, August 6, 2014, http://mobilemarketingwatch.com/sms-marketing-wallops-email-with-98-open-rate-and-only-1-spam-43866/ (accessed December 4, 2016).

42 Corasaniti, "Texting Comes of Age as a Political Messenger."

43 Lisa Stiffler, "Hillary Clinton's Top Digital Strategist Talks Trump, Twitter and Tech Tools for Voter Targeting," *Geek Wire*, October 6, 2016, www.geekwire.com/2016/hillary-clintons-top-digital-strategist-talks-trump-twitter-tech-tools-voter-targeting/ (accessed December 4, 2016).

44 Moffett, "Campaign 2016."

45 Gerrit Lansing, phone interview with author, November 2016.

46 Phillip Rucker, "Hillary Clinton Hires Google Executive to be Chief Technology Officer," *Washington Post*, April 8, 2015, www.washingtonpost.com/news/post-politics/wp/2015/04/08/hillary-clinton-hires-google-executive-to-be-chief-technology-officer/ (accessed December 5, 2016).

47 Joshua Green and Sasha Issenberg, "Inside the Trump Bunker with 12 Days to Go," *Bloomberg*, October 27, 2016.

48 Matt Oczkowski interview with author, November 2016.

49 Jennifer Stromer-Galley interview with author, November 2016.

50 Oczkowski interview.

51 Stromer-Galley interview.

52 Lansing interview.

53 Cyrus Krohn interview with author, November 2016.

7

POLITICAL ADVERTISING IN THE 2016 PRESIDENTIAL ELECTION

Peter Fenn

The very real and fundamental question to be answered after this most bizarre of presidential campaigns is this: What *is* political advertising in 2016? Is it traditional television, radio, and print ads? Or is it online advertising, Facebook, Snapchat, and Twitter? Related to that fundamental question are these: What works, what doesn't, and where are we headed?

This certainly isn't your grandmother's advertising any more. This isn't *I Love Lucy* or *Father Knows Best* television, let alone *Happy Days* or even *The Simpsons* or *X-Files*.[1] This isn't the time of three national networks (NBC, CBS, ABC) where you only buy national television ads or even a collection of cable stations competing with those networks or, for that matter, a fledgling Internet that carries news content of interest to a small number of voters. We have come a long way, baby. Even in the last decade, even in the last four years.

When a similar chapter was written for the re-cap of the 2008 presidential campaign, there was a great deal of discussion of "new media"—Internet ads, the use of cell phones, targeting, customizing ads for particular audiences, going viral, and so forth. Facebook was in its infancy and Twitter was barely off the ground. Back then, one could hardly imagine a television celebrity whose trademark line was "You're Fired" on his show *The Apprentice* would some day be tweeting his way to the presidency.

No question, we just witnessed a real sea-change in presidential political advertising. The question is, how did it come about? How will it evolve and change? Will it even last? What is in store for the future of getting out the message and breaking through the clutter?

In this chapter, let's examine what happened to political advertising in 2016, how effective was it, how did it compare to past years, and what might the future hold. More data will be coming out in the coming months on ad spending, the

146 Part II: Money and Communication

influence of particular ads, the impact on turnout, the role of traditional press coverage, and so forth, but we will provide an analysis formed in the immediate aftermath of campaign 2016.

Let's confine this study to advertising in the presidential campaign, and leave aside down ballot races. My many years of experience suggest that there are a whole host of differences in the effect and impact of advertising in down ballot races from the presidential race. When you are dealing with down ballot candidates who are much less known, much less covered by the press, and where voters are much less aware of who they are and where they stand, traditional advertising is more critical in determining the actual outcome of the race. So, for races such as governor, senator, member of Congress, statewide office, and the state legislature, ad campaigns play a larger role in who wins and who loses than in presidential elections, where general election candidates are so heavily covered by the press and where voters' attention is so focused.

The Evolution of Presidential Advertising

For those of us who teach, study, and practice political advertising, the changes have come with lightning speed. We can remember when it would take days, even weeks, to put together and get approval for a political ad. We can remember when every piece of film would have to be shot, developed, edited. There was no such thing as buying "stock footage" online. Heck, there was no such thing as digital; no one conceived of editing on a laptop.

And the delivery of advertising was simple. You had television ads that were confined to broadcast and later cable; radio ads that went to a manageable number of stations; and, if you so chose, newspaper ads that went into print for papers with a defined circulation. That was it, pretty much. Maybe we would have discussions about billboards, planes that flew overhead carrying a banner, direct mail to targeted households. But it was pretty simple and straightforward.

Think about the dawn of television in the mid-twentieth century, as seen in the groundbreaking book *The Spot*. The authors, Edwin Diamond and Stephen Bates, describe how Harry Truman in 1948 spent three months on the road, traveling 31,000 miles, and shaking the hands of some half million people. Just four years later, television had been brought into presidential campaigns. Rosser Reeves of the Ted Bates advertising agency rounded up tourists who were visiting Radio City Music Hall, and filmed them while they asked short, simple questions of Republican candidate Dwight Eisenhower. In a split-screen format, Ike answered each question with a pithy response. Thus was born the fifteen-second television spot, and "Eisenhower Answers America" brought in a new era of political communication.[2]

Over fifty years later the political landscape had changed and television was no longer the stand-alone method to communicate. You could no longer capture two-thirds of America as you did with the show *I Love Lucy* in the 1950s. The

Chapter 7: Political Advertising **147**

top program over the last several years has been *Sunday Night Football* with an audience of just over one in ten Americans. Table 7.1 illustrates the percentage of viewing audience captured by the most popular television shows in each decade. Decade after decade, as television became more competitive, it became harder to capture a large share of the viewing public.

Until the Clinton–Bush campaign of 1992 most political advertising was bought nationally not locally in individual markets. Over the last twenty-five years that has changed. More and more political ads were targeted to specific states and audiences as defined by polling and the Electoral College votes needed to win the presidency. The fact that campaigns could not capture large national audiences with ads anymore (aside from the costly Super Bowl or Academy Awards) clearly diluted their message. In addition, in recent years voters were more likely to be watching the wide range of cable channels and live streaming shows. A further problem for television advertising was the increased use of digital video recorders, like TiVo, which permitted viewers to record their favorite shows and skip commercials. As some of us in the media consulting business like to put it: you pay more, and get less.

We have just completed an election where candidates did not show up in most states for campaign rallies, nor did they buy air time in those markets. Clearly, the Clinton campaign wishes it paid more attention to Wisconsin and Michigan in the closing weeks of this race, both with ads and visits. But no one

TABLE 7.1 Top Television Show, by Percentage of Household Share, 1950s–2010s

Decade	Series	Peak Season Household Share	Debut Season at Nielsen No. 1	End Season at Nielsen No. 1	Total Number of Seasons at No. 1	Network
1950s	*I Love Lucy*	67.3 (1952–1953)	1952–1953	1956–1957	4	CBS
1960s	*Gunsmoke*	43.1 (1957–1958)	1957–1958	1960–1961	5	CBS
1970s	*All in the Family*	34.0 (1971–1972)	1971–1972	1975–1976	5	CBS
1980s	*The Cosby Show*	34.9 (1986–1987)	1985–1986	1989–1990	5	NBC
1990s	*60 Minutes*	28.4 (1979–1980)	1979–1980	1993–1994	5	CBS
2000s	*American Idol*	17.6 (2005–2006)	2003–2004	2010–2011	8	Fox
2010s	*NBC Sunday Night Football*	13.3 (2015–2016)	2011–2012	2015–2016	4	NBC

Source: Nielsen Ratings/Historic/Network Television by Season/1950s–2000.

148 Part II: Money and Communication

is going back to the 1960 campaign when Richard Nixon pledged to visit all fifty states and ended up having to travel to Alaska in the closing days to fulfill his promise.

Effective political communication is very much about targeting, targeting, targeting. Apart from the constant press coverage, how do you reach voters with traditional paid political commercials? Most younger voters do not watch that much regular television programming and, if they do, they DVR the programs and speed through the commercials. Older voters watch more live TV and more news programs. Most careful media buyers pay close attention to their target audiences, what they are watching, and what kinds of ads to create to sway undecided voters and motivate the base to turn out and vote.

Clearly, the data available about voters' interests, intent, background, and viewing habits are extraordinary compared to what was available ten or twenty years ago. This abundance of data gives campaigns new methods for targeting and communicating. From cookies on computers to computerized demographic information to socio-economic data, as they say, we know where you live. Increased efforts are being made to target specific messages to specific people. My guess is that this will expand exponentially.

All the money and metrics in the world won't help most candidates without a strong message. A strong and compelling message that cuts through the clutter is, and will remain, the centerpiece of any campaign, especially for president. "Time for a Change" or some version has worked often since the founding of the Republic; "Morning in America" worked for Reagan in 1984; "Compassionate Conservative" sure worked for Bush in 2000; "Change You Can Believe In" served Obama well in 2008, and, of course, "Make America Great Again" was a rallying cry for Trump this year, as was "Let's Make America Great Again" for Reagan in 1980. These are slogans, of course, but smart campaigns build messages and themes off them that communicate a compelling, concise, and clear reason to vote for their candidate.

Advertising in the 2016 Primary Campaigns

The Republicans

The role of advertising in the 2016 primaries was vastly different than in previous years. In 2012, for example, Mitt Romney overwhelmed and outspent his rivals, particularly former Senator Rick Santorum in the later primaries. In the key states his campaign beat Santorum with a combination of "overwhelming force" on television and mobilizing traditional Republican voters, despite the pull Santorum had with Tea Party conservatives.

The big story of the 2016 Republican primary season was the unexpected rise of Donald Trump without the traditional trappings of a vast organization, large media buys, and a typical campaign structure. He managed to vanquish his

Chapter 7: Political Advertising **149**

opponents by dominating debates, dominating the free media coverage, and dominating attention with outrageous comments and Twitter feeds.

According to an article in *Politico*, Trump foreshadowed his presidential campaign strategy in December 2013 before a gathering of New York political professionals. They had come to sound out a possible run for governor, but Trump had bigger plans.

> He said, "I'm going to walk away with it and win it outright," a long-time New York political consultant recalled. Trump told us, "I'm going to get in and all the polls are going to go crazy. I'm going to suck all the oxygen out of the room. I know how to work the media in a way that they will never take the lights off of me."[3]

As brash and narcissistic as that boast was three years ago, it certainly turned out to be true. *Market Watch* reported that from May 2015 to May 2016 Donald Trump amassed nearly $3 billion in free television advertising by dominating the airwaves with appearances. The firm MediaQuant compared the candidates and found that Trump received four times the amount of free media that Ted Cruz received when he dropped out—$2.8 billion compared to $771 million. During that comparable time frame Hillary Clinton had earned the equivalent of $1.1 billion in free media advertising.[4]

Journalist Jim Rutenberg pointed out that Trump with "his pedigree, his demagoguery and his inscrutable platform…make him a giant story."[5] And that sells newspapers and, more important, online clicks. And that brings in advertising revenue. CNN's President Jeff Zucker admitted to Rutenberg that with Trump and the debates the CNN ratings have increased 170 percent in prime time in 2016. On debate nights CNN charged $200,000 for a thirty-second spot, forty times what it charged on a regular night. As they say, that's real money.

In addition to recognizing that Trump was "making good copy" the news media surely recognized that he improved their bottom line. And that led the news shows to allow Trump to call in for interviews, even the Sunday programs, which nearly always demanded that guests appear in studio. Trump could be in his pajamas at Trump Tower and demand what others could not—instant access and coverage. Thus, the pressure was off Trump to focus his attention on paid television ads. As he told the *New York Times* in September 2015, "I've gotten so much free advertising, it's like nothing I'd have expected. When you look at cable television, a lot of the programs are 100 percent Trump, so why would you need more Trump during the commercial breaks?"[6]

Table 7.2, with data from the Wesleyan Media Project, provides a look at the amount spent on television ads from January 2015 until May 8, 2016 by the candidates and their supporters (like Super PACS). Sanders, Rubio, Bush, and Clinton account for the largest share by far, all over $60 million each. But Donald

150 Part II: Money and Communication

TABLE 7.2 Television Ad Spending by Candidates and Outside Groups During Primaries

Candidate	Spent (in millions)
Bernie Sanders	73.7
Marco Rubio	72.7
Jeb Bush	66.9
Hillary Clinton	62.6
Ted Cruz	37.5
John Kasich	18.9
Donald Trump	18.5
Chris Christie	14.6
Ben Carson	4.3
Bobby Jindal	3.8
Rand Paul	1.7
Lindsey Graham	1.4
Rick Perry	1.1
Mike Huckabee	1.0
Carly Fiorina	0.5

Note: Spending totals are from January 1, 2015 through May 6, 2016.

Source: Data from Kantar Media/CMAG, with analysis by the Wesleyan Media Project.

Trump accounts for only $18.5 million in paid advertising, below even that of Governor John Kasich.

The conclusion that is inescapable throughout the Republican primary fight is that television advertising mattered very little. It may have given Kasich a boost in New Hampshire or helped Cruz in Iowa but, overall, Trump's mastery of the media was what counted. Jeb Bush and his Super PAC spent tens of millions to no avail.

Most of the Republican ads were not terribly memorable, either. They were bio ads, introductory spots, nothing that was as noteworthy as the debates or Trump's tweets. The exception may have been one of Ted Cruz's ads that showed professional men in suits and women in dresses and high heels crossing what was supposed to be the Rio Grande.[7] Cruz was focusing on illegal immigration and making the point that if these types of people were crossing over it would grab voters' attention. The problem with the ad, of course, was that Trump had already captured that issue in his announcement speech at Trump Tower. The Cruz ad was clever, broke through the clutter with the striking visual, but the message was already associated with Trump.

Clearly in terms of the money invested and the impact of particular ads we would be hard pressed to conclude that advertising played much of a role in the outcome of the bulk of the primaries on the Republican side. The narrative of the campaign and the flow were more determined by Trump's "sucking all the oxygen out of the room," as he so aptly put it, than paid advertising.

Chapter 7: Political Advertising **151**

The Democrats

The Democratic primaries told a bit of a different story. The dynamics of that race showed a contest that pitted a virtual unknown, Bernie Sanders, against a very well-known Hillary Clinton. Initial polls showed Clinton with a commanding lead. In June 2015, Clinton led Sanders by 63–12 percent; one year later, at the end of the primaries in June 2016, she led Sanders by 54–38 percent. Sanders had even narrowed the gap in mid-April to 49–42.[8]

Clearly, Bernie Sanders began to exceed expectations early with large rallies, drawing a combination of liberal activists and younger people who were searching for fundamental change. Throughout 2015, Sanders would fill large halls and outdoor venues with 10,000 people and more. This translated into enthusiasm for his candidacy (as opposed to O'Malley who really never got out of the starting block) and a more traditional campaign by frontrunner Hillary Clinton.

It also translated into money, beyond the Sanders's campaign's wildest dreams. All told, Sanders and his groups raised nearly $230 million dollars with over 2.7 million donors, many of whom gave repeatedly over the past year and a half.[9] What that meant was plenty of money for television advertising in primary states. As Table 6.2 indicates, the Sanders's campaign spent the most in the primaries on television—nearly $73 million through May 8, 2016.

Unlike the Republican primary race, money and paid television did make a difference for the Democrats. The combination of the large number of donors, volunteers, and voters for both Clinton and Sanders made for a race that was longer and more drawn out than many had expected. If Sanders had not had the resources to go all the way until June and advertise in so many states, the race would have been over a lot sooner. Debates brought attention to the race and the press coverage certainly mattered but when it became clear that Sanders, unlike O'Malley, wasn't going to fold for lack of funds, it made Clinton's road to the nomination more difficult.

Both the Sanders and Clinton camps created dozens of ads during the primaries, some geared to specific primary states. The most memorable ad for Sanders was undoubtedly "America," a sixty-second spot set to Simon and Garfunkel's song with the memorable lyric "They've all come to look for America."[10] It was an upbeat, uplifting montage of scenes that seemed to appeal to not only liberal, aging baby boomers but young millennials as well. Not only was it aired across the country in key states but it garnered nearly four million views on YouTube. His other ads focused on his populist message of "A Future to Believe In" and "Feel the Bern" which called for reform of Wall Street, taking on the 1 percent and rethinking trade deals.[11]

Hillary Clinton's primary ads focused on her fights for children and families, her values and lessons learned from her mother, Dorothy, and her commitment to those left out in society. She characterized herself as an experienced fighter for working families and someone who would be successful as an effective president

152 Part II: Money and Communication

carrying on the Obama legacy. Her slogan "Fighting for Us" was used for most of the primary season but evolved into her final message of "Stronger Together."

It took Clinton until June to wrap up the nomination, although the signs were clearer much earlier. In the end, she won thirty-four states and Sanders won twenty-three. The Republicans focused on Clinton and rarely went after Sanders during the primary season, continuing to raise her negatives.

The General Election

For 100 consecutive days prior to November 8, the Real Clear Politics poll of averages had Hillary Clinton defeating Donald Trump. The numbers were based on national polling and the popular vote and, in the end, Clinton did win by over 2.8 million votes (2.1 percent). Many could well argue that the polling was not that far off! The trouble, of course, was that Clinton underperformed in thirteen key states that mattered and lost the critical states of Florida, North Carolina, and Pennsylvania, plus Michigan, Ohio, and Wisconsin.

So, as it finally unfolded, what was the role of television advertising in the 2016 presidential campaign? Large expenditures were earmarked for television advertising, particularly by the Clinton campaign. According to the Center for Responsive Politics, Clinton outspent Trump by about two to one in total spending.[12] Final numbers were not available for the television spending but it appears that Clinton probably outspent Trump by a similar margin, if not more, over the course of the campaign, although the Trump campaign and their surrogates were spending more heavily toward the end including buying national ads not just specific states. This may have provided a benefit for Trump in states like Michigan, Wisconsin, and even Minnesota which was, in the end, a very tight race won by Clinton by less than 3 points.

Kantor Media/CMAG provides a number of interesting analyses of television ads. For the entire election cycle, Clinton aired 39 percent of all broadcast ads, with Trump and Sanders airing 12 percent each. Clinton aired 187 unique spots over the course of the entire election season while Trump ran just 40 unique television spots. In the general election, 80 percent of the presidential ads were either negative or contrast ads. Of those negative ads, 60 percent were directed at Trump and only 20 percent directed at Clinton. In terms of issues, jobs led the list with 21 percent of ads mentioning that issue while only 3 percent mentioned Obamacare. Florida led the states with the most expenditures on ads with $110 million in the general election, a quarter of all the money spent, with Ohio coming in with just half that amount.[13]

Many of Clinton's ads used Trump's own words or videos of his appearances to make the argument that he was unfit and lacked the temperament to be President. His sexist statements and attacks against minorities, immigrants, and the disabled played prominently in her ads. Most of Trump's ads referred to Clinton's emails and made ad hoc attacks that she violated the law as well as

Chapter 7: Political Advertising **153**

stressing his message of improving the economy and making America great again.

Despite the money spent and the focus of the advertising both campaigns seem to agree that paid advertising was not a major factor in this election. According to a *Kansas City Star* summary of a post-election conference at the Dole Institute of Politics at the University of Kansas: "Both sides agreed that paid political advertising on television was a nonfactor in the race, making Clinton's financial advantage less significant."[14]

Monday-morning quarterbacks would argue that putting more advertising resources during the last critical days in Wisconsin, Michigan, even Pennsylvania, could have made up the difference for Clinton. But over all, the basic dynamics of the race and the flow of the race were more determined by events, by press coverage, by social media, by the candidates' successes as well as gaffes.

Conclusion

As a headline in *USA Today* puts it: "TV, The Old King of U.S. Politics, Faces Mortality."[15] No one is ready to abandon paid advertising in presidential campaigns, nor should they, but as the article makes clear "digital advertising is beginning to challenge TV's dominance." Some, like the consulting firm Borrell Associates, predict that

> by 2020 TV will have lost almost 14 share points, as digital nips at its heels. For now, though—whatever its expense and however questionable its utility—TV advertising in a close election is like nuclear weapons in the Cold War: No one wants to risk disarming unilaterally.[16]

A 2016 study by the Pew Research Center shows that just 13 percent of adults in 2016 do not use the Internet; in 2000, by contrast, 48 percent did not use the Internet. Furthermore, some 92 percent of adults now use cell phones and 68 percent of adults have smartphones. Tablet computers are now owned by 45 percent of adults.[17] Our media mix is changing and candidates and campaigns are adjusting accordingly.

But no one was able to take advantage of these shifts in communication more than Donald Trump, especially with his use of Twitter and other forms of online communication. As of mid-November 2016 Donald Trump had over 16 million Twitter followers and tweeted over 34,000 times. Hillary Clinton had over 11 million followers and tweeted 9,839 times.[18] Certainly, the bombastic nature of Trump's tweets led to overwhelming coverage by the news media. Much less so for the Clinton tweets that were not nearly as controversial. (For more on the use of Twitter, see the next chapter by Michael Cornfield and Michael D. Cohen.)

Breitbart.com, the website formerly run by Trump strategist, Steve Bannon, claims a strong impact from Trump's social media operations:

154 Part II: Money and Communication

His Facebook page reached more than 21 billion impressions—21,031,446,611 to be exact—from the day Trump launched his campaign until November 22, 2016. There were more than 485 million engagements on his Facebook page during that timeframe, and nearly 50 million 'likes.' … [B]etween June 2015 and November 2016, Trump's Twitter posts have had nearly 9 billion impressions and more than 400 million engagements.[19]

The Trump unconventional campaign was able to achieve much more in "free media" than ever before. No question. The non-politician, the free-wheeling and fact-lacking speeches, the consummate outsider-insider held to a different standard than other elected officials, the businessman with braggadocio, Trump is a unique brand of celebrity at a time of deep disaffection.

Can other candidates in the future command that level of attention? It is hard to imagine. Can other candidates succeed with such a non-conventional approach? Will this style become more in-style? Will American politics be forever changed? All hard to know, but one thing is clear when it comes to traditional campaign advertising: We are moving into the post-television age, and although we aren't there yet, there are more ways to communicate and drive the messages that penetrate. Much more research will be coming out in the months and years ahead but the change we predicted in the 2008 chapter is upon us. If the message of that chapter was the old Bob Dylan song "The Times They Are A-Changin'," the message this year is, clearly, change is here and progressing rapidly. We will no longer be talking about presidential TV ads as the dominant form of political communication in the future.

Notes

1 *I Love Lucy* (CBS) played from 1951 to 1957; *Father Knows Best* (ABC, 1954–1963); *Happy Days* (ABC, 1974–1984); *The Simpsons* (Fox, 1989–present); *X-Files* (Fox, 1993–2016).

2 Edwin Diamond and Stephen Bates, *The Spot: The Rise of Political Advertising on Television*, 3rd ed. (Cambridge, MA: MIT Press, 1992); see also, Dennis W. Johnson, *Democracy for Hire: A History of American Political Consulting* (New York: Oxford University Press, 2017), 64–71.

3 Eli Stokols and Ben Schreckinger, "How Trump Did It," *Politico*, February 1, 2016, www.politico.com/magazine/story/2016/02/how-donald-trump-did-it-213581 (accessed December 1, 2016).

4 Robert Schroeder, "Trump Has Gotten Nearly $3 Billion in 'Free' Advertising," *MarketWatch*, May 6, 2016, www.marketwatch.com/story/trump-has-gotten-nearly-3-billion-in-free-advertising-2016-05-06 (accessed December 2, 2016).

5 Jim Rutenberg, "The Mutual Dependence of Donald Trump and the News Media," *New York Times*, March 21, 2016, www.nytimes.com/2016/03/21/business/media/the-mutual-dependence-of-trump-and-the-news-media.html (accessed December 12, 2016).

Chapter 7: Political Advertising   155

6 Patrick Healy, "Willing to Spend $100 Million, Donald Trump Has So Far Reveled in Free Publicity," *New York Times*, September 18, 2015, www.nytimes.com/2015/09/19/us/politics/donald-trump-republican-nomination.html (accessed December 12, 2016).

7 The video can be seen on YouTube, www.youtube.com/watch?v=3GeElO3JHjQ (accessed December 12, 2016).

8 "National Primary Polls," Fivethirtyeight.com, July 1, 2016, http://projects.five thirtyeight.com/election-2016/national-primary-polls/democratic/ (accessed December 4, 2016).

9 Center for Responsive Politics, 2016 Presidential Candidates, www.opensecrets.org/pres16/candidate.php?id=N00000528 (accessed December 12, 2016); Russell Berman, "Addicted to Making Campaign Contributions?" *The Atlantic*, August 30, 2016, www.theatlantic.com/politics/archive/2016/08/slot-machine-fundraising/497276/ (accessed December 10, 2016).

10 Sanders ad, "America," on YouTube, www.youtube.com/watch?v=2nwRiuh1Cug (accessed December 12, 2016).

11 Sanders ad, "A Future to Believe In," on YouTube, www.youtube.com/watch?v=RFWXJLP69UQ (accessed December 12, 2016); Sanders ad, "Feel the Bern," on YouTube, www.youtube.com/watch?v=1QFg-Kg6bwI (accessed December 12, 2016).

12 Center for Responsive Politics, https://www.opensecrets.org/pres16 (accessed December 12, 2016).

13 "56 Interesting Facts About the 2016 Election," *Cook Political Report*, December 16, 2016, http://cookpolitical.com/story/10201 (accessed December 20, 2016).

14 David Helling, "'Authentic' Trump Prevailed Nov. 8, Campaign Insiders Say in Post-election Conference," *Kansas City Star*, December 9, 2016, www.kansascity.com/news/politics-government/article120060403.html (accessed December 12, 2016).

15 "TV, The Old King of U.S. Politics, Faces Mortality," *USA Today*, December 30, 2015, http://usat.ly/1JhqdUu (accessed December 14, 2016).

16 Ibid.

17 Pew Research Center, "Survey of U.S. Adults." Data include surveys conducted in 2015 and 2016, www.pewresearch.org/fact-tank/2016/09/07/some-americans-dont-use-the-internet-who-are-they/ (accessed December 12, 2016).

18 Social Bakers website, www.socialbakers.com/statistics/twitter/profiles/detail/25073877-realdonaldtrump (accessed December 14, 2016).

19 Matt Boyle, "Under the Hood: How Donald Trump Has Cut Around Corporate Media to Reach Millions Directly Online," Breitbart.com, http://bit.ly/2gjbgr0 (accessed December 12, 2016).

8

#CAMPAIGNS2016

Hashtagged Phrases and the Clinton–Trump Message War

Michael Cornfield and Michael D. Cohen

The hashtags that send tweets spinning and tumbling through public media are a new source of campaign intelligence. Through analysis of the content and metrics associated with hashtagged phrases, we can learn about how well strategically crafted and deployed messages are faring in a political contest: which side's phrases have caught on, with whom, for how long, in what proportions. In this chapter, we demonstrate how a few slogans and sobriquets associated with the Hillary Clinton and Donald Trump campaigns—from #MakeAmericaGreatAgain (or #MAGA) to #StrongerTogether— can be studied fruitfully, yielding usable information about public reactions to the ideas, opinions, emotions, and factions that the phrases brought to life. We also show how the Trump campaign markedly outperformed the Clinton campaign in the battle to frame the presidential race through Twitter.

The Political Magic of a Hashtagged Phrase

Hashtagged phrases, like pennants, buttons, yard signs, and bumper-stickers, seek to build support for a campaign through repeated glanceability. Their placement throughout a physical jurisdiction means to foster the impression (which may or may not be accurate) that a campaign has caught on with the citizenry, since it can be a personal as well as an organizational decision to display them. They often sport branded slogans also seen and spoken at rallies, in advertisements, and on literature. Ideally, these terms touch enough voters in enough ways to make a winning coalition plausible. Eventually, they become pop culture artifacts of a time and place.

But hashtagged phrases also possess digital powers. Even in the shortest message forms, they leave room for individuals to append their own content. (Such

Chapter 8: #Campaigns2016 **157**

individuated content helps with the detection of the automatically manufactured messages known as "bots," about which more ahead.) Digital slogans permit the tracking of audience reactions to them, which collect around messages like beads on a string and strings in a woven fabric. And both the dispatches and reactions, in turn, are comprehensible as data: sortable, searchable, countable, and amenable to mathematical modeling.

To voters who came of age before the 1990s, these properties of personal customization, distributional tracking, and unitization into data can seem like magical attributes. But as anyone who has grown up since then can attest, they are now ordinary features of contemporary life—which makes the relative paucity of hashtag-keyed intelligence as a feature of campaign strategy, as compared with the routine analysis of poll results and news media content, somewhat surprising. Perhaps the lag in social media analytics by campaigns is the result of a hangover dominance of the political management field by older people. (This is less true, to be sure, of digital advertising and field report analytics, the use of which has greatly expanded in campaigns during the last decade and a half.)

As part of the Graduate School of Political Management PEORIA Project,[1] we have been analyzing socially mediated communications about the 2016 presidential contest in terms of rhetorical efforts and audience responses. For this chapter, we rely on data compiled by Crimson Hexagon (CH), a Boston-based social media analytics company which collects and allows us to examine the universe of all publicly available English-language tweets between January 1 and November 8, 2016. Where we cite phrase frequency in this chapter we are referring to all common instances of that phrase where it showed up on Twitter with a pound sign in front of it.

This election campaign has been a particularly good case to study. The long time span gave rise to a superabundance of content and metadata in changing circumstances. The eventual winner became notorious for his tweets. There were approximately 14,000 tweets sent out under Trump's name in our time period; approximately one in nine of those were insults.[2] A programmer who has wisely chosen to remain anonymous has created a searchable database of each Trump tweet since he started in 2009; the current home page at trumptwitterarchive. com features links to the 235 tweets with the word "loser," the 222 with "dumb" or "dummy," and downward through "terrible," "stupid," "weak," and so forth. But it is not all negative: Trump also sought to create a bandwagon effect, using the word "poll" 586 times to crow about his high standings.

We argue here that hashtagged phrases enhance the efforts of campaigners in four basic ways. First, they serve as brand crystallizations which viewers can come to recognize as distinctive rationales for choosing one candidate over others. Second, they supply news media with fresh, importable, and appealing content; media usage expands the reach of the phrase. Third, they provide volunteers inspired by tweet messages (and perhaps also prompted by campaigner asks) with at-hand methods of contribution: viewers can click to share, favor, subscribe,

158 Part II: Money and Communication

donate, join, and even lead others at moments of opinion and vote mobilization. Fourth, the first three functionalities are optimizable through data analytics. Managers can see what's working and devote more resources to them while paring away resources from what's not.

Twitter as a Campaign Venue

Twitter, the home of the hashtag, is famous for its restriction on message length: 140 characters to a tweet. The reason for the tight limit originated with the mobile phone constraint on text messages that split them once they reached 160 characters.[3] The founders of Twitter allotted 20 characters for the username and left the remaining 140 to what the user wants to say. Today, tweets can include links, photos, videos, and mini-polls as well as words. Tweeters may attach up to four photos at a low "cost" of 23 characters, an incentive rationalized by company research which found that photos increase viewership. For no character charge, individuals may also "tag" up to ten persons using the "@username" form of address.[4]

Twitter has become distinctive for what it markets itself to be: a medium people turn to in order to magnify "moments that matter in the world."[5] Moment-magnifying bursts of comments, photos, and links come from event sponsors, supporters, detractors, casual observers, historical witnesses, and bots. A cyclone of tweets constructs a virtual crowd which can solidify over time into a community of interest from which campaigners can elicit support. (By contrast, a "tweet storm" refers to a blog-post length message chopped into tweets, which may or may not attract widespread attention.)

Of course, political capital accrues from gatherings on other social media platforms as well. But Facebook, Snapchat, Google/YouTube and the like afford a broader set of social gratifications than Twitter. Twitter's character limits and rewards are geared to the cultivation of instant reactions, personal takes that mean to define what's happening now. Indeed, "What's happening?" is the default prompt in the box where tweets are to be composed. When sufficient numbers of tweets accumulate around an event or name in the news, it wins the company's designation as a "Trending Topic," a list of which people see when they access the site. (For advertising purposes, each Trend list is customized based on prior behavior and any other personally identifiable information available to the company.) Being labeled a Trend serves to increase the accumulation of tweets and, ideally, enable the shared object of interest to reach the next level of trendiness by crossing over into other media channels, both social and mass.

Twitter has a much smaller user population than Facebook, 317 million to 1.7 billion. But it is more valuable to politics in some ways because its rules and habitual practices are distinctively public, that is, dedicated to the encountering of strangers and discussing of common concerns. Twitter has been built for

Chapter 8: #Campaigns2016 **159**

maximum free expression, and its executives have remained stoutly committed to free speech in the face of bad publicity for facilitating the dissemination of hateful and untrue information.[6] In contrast to other social media, privacy protection comes second, if that. For example, when opening a Twitter account, the default option sets tweets to be seen by anyone, whereas on Facebook and Snapchat that option restricts the content one creates to friends in one's social network. Snapchat, which recently overtook Twitter monthly active users, restricts a user's content from being seen beyond who they have added to their network. Additionally, Twitter does not require people to supply their real names and basic identifying information. Some do. But anonymity protects both dissidents and jokers.

After the 2016 election, Twitter introduced a "mute button" which enabled users to block future notifications of a conversation that offended them. Nothing could be done to eliminate the existing tweets, however. Twitter also suspended some accounts on grounds of harassment. It had done this in July 2016 to *Breitbart* technology editor Milo Yiannopoulous after he barraged actress Leslie Jones with racist tweets and incited others to do the same. Non-celebrities have rarely received similar redress.

Even as Twitter's population growth rate flattened in 2015 and 2016, its political significance soared. Would-be influencers could enter the site, locate a trending topic, and slap on its hashtag to pipe their voice into a public space where people rewarded snappy comments with attention. Twitter has become the back row of the global lecture hall, a whistle ready to blow on acts of observed evil, a universal Zapruder camera that captures tragedy and disaster where conventional news media lack reporters on the scene but are all too ready to incorporate feeds from those who are.

For the fall of 2016 Twitter promoted #debates in collaboration with the Commission on Presidential Debates. To reward its use, Twitter automatically attached a special emoji debate podium to the hashtagged tweet and didn't count it against the 140-character limit. Before the last debate the makers of Excedrin posted "The possibility of a #DebateHeadache is high. Be prepared with Excedrin®." The tweet also included a graphic showing the medicine box and a poll showing that 64 percent of American say avoiding headaches is impossible during a presidential election.

It was a master stroke that monetized recognition of the impact that the previous debates and debate tweets had worked on the minds of the #debates assembly. It illustrated as well how a hashtag can engage people in three directions at once: by topic, by topic talkers, and by topic audience seekers. And since hashtag follower growth is an online phenomenon, the size, roster characteristics, and even the individual names responding could be monitored as a source of intelligence on audience reception to messages and engagement forays.

160 Part II: Money and Communication

Followers and Followings (Including the Press)

The basic metric demonstrating the strength of an account on Twitter is the follower. The more users following an account, the more potential impact it has on the platform. Followers also have followers of their own so any tweet that is read by a follower may then be passed along, multiplying the number of potential people who could see the original tweet.[7] But we do note this as a sign of the power of hashtags. In 2016 Donald Trump's following started (7 million) and ended (17 million) much higher than his competitors.

One of the metrics we watched closely over the campaign season was the follower growth rate. In one of our initial PEORIA releases, we noticed that Trump's account was growing at a much higher rate than his GOP nomination opponents, and ahead of his growth in polls. We also found that after candidates left the presidential race their accounts continued to grow, albeit at a slower pace. For those looking at future campaigns, a following can be a continuously tended asset.

The news media constitute a special subset of followers. They reach people who spend little to no time online and, at the same time, people who spend a lot of their online time engaged with campaigns and regard media coverage as an indication of success or failure. Clinton announced her candidacy with a tweet, and both she and Trump tweeted first word of their vice presidential choices. In this way hashtagged phrases sometimes received additional distribution and significance.

For decades the news media have validated campaign television ads as important by organizing stories about them. They have publicized ad messages even when, perhaps especially when, they have criticized ads as unduly negative and factually suspect. By 2016 the news media were incorporating campaign tweets into their stories, treating tweets as though they were quotes from interviews, which both presidential general campaigns largely denied to the press. Candidate tweeting kept pace with live news media's demand for non-stop fresh content—and online, *all* media outlets are in effect live, including pages and Twitter accounts produced by journalists employed at "legacy media" newspapers and magazines. It will be interesting to see if the press makes a concerted effort to monitor tweets more rigorously in the future, much as they began "ad watch" boxes after the 1988 campaigns.

Bots

An important concern about Twitter metrics is whether users and usages represent individual posting choices or automated programs posing as such. "Twitterbots" (-bot as in robot) consist of software programs that shoot out identical posts. Bots bloat frequency counts and derivative metrics, raising the question of whether they seriously warped our data and analysis. The

Chapter 8: #Campaigns2016 **161**

independent firm TwitterAudit.com estimated that 63 percent of @HillaryClinton and 61 percent of @realDonaldTrump followers were real people.[8] Similarly, scrutiny by an academic research team found considerable but equally distributed bot penetration of the presidential campaign discourse on Twitter.[9] On this basis we conclude that bots did not bias our results to a significant degree. That conclusion cannot be generalized to other political contests and situations.[10]

Hashtagged Phrases in the Clinton–Trump Contest

In order to demonstrate the value of Twitter metrics to political managers, we have extracted data in a manner we believe can be replicated in the actual heat of a campaign (see Table 8.1). We selected prominent hashtagged messages, checked the frequency of their appearances from the start of 2016 through Election Day, and analyzed the rhetorical construction of the top nine results. While our phrase list was neither comprehensive nor systematically generated, as academically sound research would require, we know as any campaign observer would know that our selections were present in a significant amount of discussion on Twitter. Our first research move compared the phrases' appearances over time to see who was winning the message circulation competition on Twitter. As a benchmark, we included the hashtag of the advocacy movement Black Lives Matter. Below are the totals.

Five of the top nine benefited Trump, while three helped Clinton. The phrase #NeverTrump was put forward by Republicans upset with Trump. Trump's main slogan circulated nearly twenty times as often as Clinton's (Stronger Together); as discussed ahead, Clinton's primary campaign slogan (I'm With Her) performed much better, although combining the two still gives Trump a two-to-one advantage.

TABLE 8.1 Top Campaign Hashtags of 2016

Hashtagged Phrase (Trump or Clinton)	Total 1/1/16 to 11/8/16
Make America Great Again/MAGA (Trump)	20,411,337
Black Lives Matter (Benchmark)	11,267,383
I'm With Her (Clinton)	8,843,164
Never Trump (anti-Trump)	6,598,957
Crooked Hillary (Trump)	5,789,682
Stronger Together (Clinton)	1,215,918
Basket of Deplorables (Trump)	1,212,342
Lock Her Up (Trump)	1,091,583
Build The Wall (Trump)	1,079,371
Delete Your Account (Clinton)	875,160

162 Part II: Money and Communication

Gridding Hashtagged Phrases

Next, like many campaign strategists, we sorted hashtagged messages into the four cells of a two-by-two grid. The categories of the grid are:

A. What a candidate says about him/herself. One good Twitter practice inserts the campaign's hashtagged brand message into a tweet thanking an organization or individual for support. A conversational comment enhances the engagement potential by making the tweet seem as though it came from the candidate (which may or may not be the actual case). For example, on October 25 Donald Trump expressed appreciation for the Bay of Pigs Veterans Association's endorsement.

From: Donald J. Trump
@realDonaldTrump

"Truly honored to receive the first ever presidential endorsement from the Bay of Pigs Veterans Association. #MAGA #ImWithYou

Retweets: 19,983 Likes: 49,495
11:27 AM – 25 Oct. 2016 from Miami, FL

Along with the main Trump slogan this tweet featured #ImWithYou, a riposte to one of Clinton's slogans. The better the brand, the more effective the outreach, since the message spreads through the hashtag's topicality as well as the social networks of the campaign and the designated recipient or "honoree."

B. What a candidate says about the opponent. Attack tweets have become the signature weapon of Donald Trump's political arsenal. They affected candidate behavior, election outcomes, and the quality of public discourse. On the same day as the previous example, October 25, when news hit of Affordable Care Act premium increases, Trump linked to a CNN news graphic and sharpened it into a spear thrust at Hillary Clinton via Obamacare:

From: Donald J. Trump
@realDonaldTrump

#Obamacare premiums are about to SKYROCKET --- again.
Crooked H will only make it worse. We will repeal & replace!

Linked with headline from money.cnn.com: "Obamacare premiums to soar 22% on average." "Average monthly premiums for an Obamacare benchmark plan to climb to $296 for 2017, up 22%, according to latest government data."

Retweets: 9,353 Likes: 17,739
7:33 AM – 25 Oct. 2016 from Doral, FL

The attention-getting power of this attack tweet derives from its economy of words and comic-book style usage of typographical accentuators: the all caps, dashes, ampersand, and exclamation point. Surprise, disinformation, the celebrity status of the targets, and a violation of conventional norms of public conduct can be draw factors as well.

C. *What a candidate's opponent says about him/herself.*

D. *What a candidate's opponent says about the candidate.* Turning now to the mirrored cells that complete a grid, this October 21 Clinton tweet explicated its hashtagged slogan with a contrast quote from the candidate.

From: Hillary Clinton
@HillaryClinton

"I want to be every single American's president. ... I believe we can disagree without being disagreeable." -- Hillary #StrongerTogether

Retweets: 663 Likes: 1,636
2:11 PM – 21 Oct. 2016

And this full-fledged attack quoted the candidate during the third debate, using the generic event hashtag to enlarge the viewership (ten times that of the previous example):

From: Hillary Clinton
@HillaryClinton

"Donald thinks belittling women makes him a bigger man.
It just makes him a bully." #DebateNight.

Retweets: 76,475 Likes: 18,367
6:57 PM – 19 Oct. 2016

Message grids help professional campaigners spot holes and duplications in what they say. The underlying assumption is that the more the public conversation is about Trump on Trump *and* Trump on Clinton, the better things are going for Trump in the message wars. Comparing frequency counts for hashtags as sorted through the grid can thus help political managers see how the campaign is faring as it maneuvers to define the contest to its advantage.

A campaign strategy team fills a message grid with respect to its chief competitor. In primaries and multi-party systems this becomes problematic. Other candidates must be excluded or multiple grids constructed and juggled because a three-by-three or larger grid is practically useless. The contents of a

164 Part II: Money and Communication

Trump and Clinton campaign grid might well differ in terms of what each campaign puts into each cell. For this chapter, we have deployed the two-by-two matrix from the perspective of a neutral observer.

Trump on Trump: #MakeAmericaGreatAgain/#MAGA

The ubiquitous campaign slogan of 2016 was "Make America Great Again," a slight but telling revision of Ronald Reagan's 1980 tagline "Let's Make America Great Again." Trump's dropping of the plural subject makes the phrase less of an invitation and more of a promise. It can be read as an omen of authoritarianism by taking the now implicit agent of greatness-making as singular, echoing Trump's declaration "I alone can fix this [country]" in his nomination acceptance speech. Alternately, a reader can impute a plural subject to the phrase, in keeping with how Trump's campaign website attached the words "Together, we will" before the slogan. On such a grammatical distinction, as will be played out in the official actions and public responses of 2017 and beyond, hangs the fate of the American republic.

At times during the campaign Trump claimed to have coined the phrase. That's a stretch, a relatively benign instance of what Trump terms his penchant for "truthful hyperbole." But Trump certainly settled on it early and sought legal exclusivity for its use. Just two weeks after the 2012 election, an attorney working for Trump registered "Make America Great Again" with the United States Patent and Trademark Office as the name for a political action committee.

The theme of restoration was a shrewd choice that proved distinctive and popular in 2016. Where Bernie Sanders proposed revolutionary changes under a banner of economic equality, and Hillary Clinton focused on growing the *status quo* Obama coalition, Donald Trump sought to reunite Reagan's two-time electoral majority, a coalition that notably encompassed the so-called "Reagan Democrats," working class whites shaken by their stalled and arguably sunken economic, social, and psychological status in the nation.

Through November 8, both hashtag versions and the statement "Make America Great Again" surfaced in more than 20.4 million tweets. The brand had been established by the start of the year (a month before the Iowa caucuses) and Twitter users sustained its primacy without a serious challenge. While Trump's negatives would, at times, seriously obstruct his path to victory, no one came close to matching the level of hashtagged approval he received for his positive self-definition. As surprising as the final election outcome was, it attested to the political maxim that the presidency goes to the candidate who best projects optimism—and evidence that Trump filled that role for more people than anyone else in the field was consistently on view to anyone who looked at this social media metric.

Beneath the #MAGA umbrella, Trump declared several ways in which America would recover its greatness during his presidency, including a prominent and extremely controversial proposal to build a wall along the southern border of

Chapter 8: #Campaigns2016 **165**

the country. As much as that idea caught fire among supporters and opponents, #BuildTheWall, #BuildThatWall, and cognate phrases appeared in only 1,079,371 Twitter posts in 2016. That's considerably more often than the slogans of most of Trump's rivals, but only 5 percent of the total for #MAGA. The end out-echoed a means to it by a ratio of twenty to one.

Clinton on Clinton: #ImWithHer and #StrongerTogether

While Trump stuck with his national revival theme, Clinton and her campaign team adopted a series of tentpole slogans. First came "Ready for Hillary," which doubled as the name of the Super PAC fueling pre-announcement campaigning. "Champion of Everyday Americans," a bid to lead the non-rich, appeared as the tagline in her announcement rhetoric. While strategically promising, neither the words nor the acronym COEA show much potential as Twitter material. "Fighting for Us" and "Breaking Down Barriers" had try-outs. Eventually, the Clinton team settled upon "I'm with Her," only to switch to "Stronger Together" as the campaign transitioned from the primary season to the convention and general election. These last two slogans registered in our database as top-ten hashtagged phrases.

"I'm With Her" fostered a sense of allegiance to a candidate on her way toward becoming the first woman president, a feeling that could be activated online. The hashtagged #ImWithHer earned placement in a whopping 8.8 million tweets in 2016 through Election Day. It enjoyed several boom days, including the last primaries on June 7 (109,113 tweets), the night Clinton accepted the nomination on July 28 (192,101 tweets), and during the three debates on September 26 (212,858 tweets), October 9 (128,116 tweets), and October 19 (166,253 posts). The phrase's biggest Twitter boom occurred on Election Day (396,892 tweets). This was well after it had been jettisoned by the Clinton campaign in favor of "Stronger Together."

"Stronger Together" expressed a vision of unity from diversity as a national asset, a variation on "E Pluribus Unum" similar to Jesse Jackson's "Rainbow Coalition" of 1988. As Clinton campaign press secretary Brian Fallon noted, "Stronger Together" evoked the ethos of Clinton's 1996 book *It Takes a Village*.[11] Like Trump's positive slogan, then, Clinton's final counterpart embraced the past. It banked on the changing demographics of the American electorate as the topper.

But "#Stronger Together" did not catch on as much as ""#ImWithHer." The hashtagged phrase netted only 1.2 million tweets in 2016 through Election Day. It failed to make the curve into the top tier; the next highest phrase garnered 5.7 million. #StrongerTogether's largest boom day, during the convention on July 28 (61,420 tweets), scored less than a third of that for "#ImWithHer" the same day. On Election Day, #StrongerTogether appeared in only 40,015 tweets, nearly ten times fewer than #ImWithHer.

166 Part II: Money and Communication

What accounts for this sharp disparity in Twitter user preference? Perhaps "#ImWithHer" had superior appeal because it was a crisp, complete, active sentence while "#StrongerTogether" is an under-specified modifying phrase. Perhaps other aspects of the Clinton campaign, from policy positions and historical references to ad placements and celebrity surrogates, reinforced gender better than diversity as a theme. Whatever the reasons, the inconstancy violated the campaign vocation's well-known adage about the importance of sticking to a single theme. Trump put the emphasis on America. Clinton put it on herself, the 99 percent, women, and an array of social identities.

Trump on Clinton: #CrookedHillary and #LockHerUp

Throughout the campaign Trump displayed a knack for belittling nicknames, a searing form of candidate-on-opponent branding suited to Twitter's rewards for brevity. More than 500 of Trump's 2016 insult tweets as tabulated by *The New York Times* were aimed at Bush, Rubio, Cruz, and Clinton, and he fashioned a nickname for each of them.[12] Name-calling has a long history in American politics. Demeaning monikers for politicians strike people by turns as colorful, humorous, outrageous, satisfying, or inappropriate depending on their tastes and biases. In a May 2016 interview with the *New York Times Magazine* Trump called his aptitude for put-downs "an instinct" and bragged that he didn't do focus groups to land on the right anti-brands for his targets.[13] In numerous primary debates, Trump's barbs clearly got underneath the skins of their targets. Low-Energy Jeb, Liddle Marco, and Lyin' Ted chafed, huffed, countered, ignored, and pivoted, but they failed to turn Trump's spitballing back on him.

Trump turned to Hillary Clinton before clinching the GOP nomination. On April 16, at a raucous rally in Watertown, New York, Trump hit Clinton with the name "Crooked Hillary." The brand advanced the contrast that he was self-funding his candidacy while she took money from lobbyists and special interests in exchange for access to her while serving as Secretary of State. It also alluded to Clinton's controversial decision to operate a private email server while in office, and to the big money she made giving speeches upon leaving public service. Trump tweeted the pejorative the next day, at first without a hashtag. But that changed quickly.[14]

While Trump said many things to denigrate Clinton, he stuck with #CrookedHillary. By the end of the campaign, #CrookedHillary had surfaced in 3.6 million tweets. Its top boom day on Twitter was the day of the terrorist attacks in Nice, France with over 88,000 tweets. After the election Nancy Scola, a journalist who specializes in digital politics stories, reported that the Trump campaign had sought to distribute a Crooked Hillary emoji, with a stick figure of her toting bags of cash, but that Twitter rejected it.[15]

At the Republican National Convention, Trump supporters chanted "Lock Her Up" several times when Clinton's name was uttered. Trump tried to discourage it in his acceptance speech, but subsequently embraced it at rallies and in the last fall debate. #LockHerUp appeared in about 500,000 tweets over the course of the campaign. Its top boom day for the hashtag was on July 28 (close to 70,000 tweets), the day Clinton accepted the Democratic nomination. Some supporters launched other epithets at Clinton including #TrumpThatBitch, which found its way on to T-shirts outside rallies and into about 20,000 tweets with a boom day on October 9, the night of the second presidential debate.

"#LockHerUp" and "TrumpThatBitch" illustrate how invective can go beyond the candidate and campaign when it strikes a chord among a section of the public. There were next to no editorial or strategic restraints to moderate the language online.

Clinton on Trump: #DeleteYourAccount and Missed Opportunities

On the whole, "Crooked Hillary" struck at Trump far more effectively than Low-Energy Jeb, Liddle Marco, and Lyin' Ted. Clinton was persistent, logical, and restrained in manner, a campaign derivative of her career as an attorney. In their debates she provoked Trump into angry retorts that illustrated her accusations about his volatility and vanity. However, the case Clinton made against Trump did not reverberate through Twitter and other media in a hashtagged formulation.

The Clinton campaign did not lack for examples. She demeaned him as "The Donald." She saddled him with the charge of possessing an "unfit temperament" to be president.

Clinton attacked Trump's businesses practices with tweets about making products overseas instead of in the United States, his questionable commitment to diversity in hiring and contracting, and the fact that some of his ventures resulted in investors and, more important, vendors and employees losing money. One available symbol of these business practices that lent itself to a hashtag (and an emoji) flowed from the fact that Trump had used Chinese steel in his buildings. She criticized Trump for derogatory things he said on the campaign trail about veterans, Latinos, and women. She labeled his economic proposals "Trumped-up Trickle-Down." Usually, these attack-tweets closed with a link to a website or an ad reinforcing the message. But, partly because they lacked an umbrella slogan (e.g., "#Unfit"), none of these specific-laden tweets resulted in widespread adoption. Where her self-descriptive quadrant suffered from an excess of slogans, her opponent-descriptive quadrant suffered from a dearth.

Consequently, when moments arose to make hashtag hay out of this grid quadrant's natural content, the potential to coalesce campaign support was dissipated. The #NeverTrump hashtag, which exposed a long-festering intraparty rift within the Republican Party, posed one such opportunity. The hashtag amassed 5.3 million posts in 2016 after a boom debut with more than 275,000 tweets on February 27, the day Jeb Bush suspended his campaign after losing the

168 Part II: Money and Communication

South Carolina primary to Trump. That would have been too soon for Clinton to attempt a siphoning of support, since she was still competing on her left against Sanders. Still, #NeverTrump remained available and popular enough to constitute a digital bridge for disaffected Republicans to cross in the fall had it been frequently paired with a Clinton hashtag.

Another opportunity flared in response to a mid-summer avalanche of #CrookedHillary posts, when Clinton's team dropped the ultimate putdown in Twitterspeak: Delete Your Account. The phrase directs its target to vacate the platform.[16] In 2016 #DeleteYourAccount peaked on the debut day of its use by the Clinton campaign, June 9, with 242,831 posts. Here was a bridge for techies and millennials to cross over, especially those supporting Sanders, who retweeted Clinton. This phrase would accumulate to almost 900,000 posts, although it was used in non-political contexts as well.

Early October brought a scandal that staggered the Trump campaign: #TrumpTapes. It was set up at the end of the first presidential debate, when Clinton revealed that Trump had attacked a former Miss Universe for gaining weight after she won the title. On October 7, two days before the second debate, a 2005 videotape was leaked to the *Washington Post* with audible bits of conversation in which Trump talked about how he forced himself on married women and how fame allowed him to do anything he wanted. The video went viral, made the news, and naturally generated a hashtag boom the day before the debate. As part of the reaction, Canadian writer and social media impresario Kelly Oxford called for women to "tweet me your first assaults ... I'll go first." By Monday afternoon (the day after the second debate), she had received more than 27 million tweets and visits to her page.[17] The hashtag #notokay, coined as part of an advocacy campaign of that name, accompanied many of these statements. But not an #Unfit and nary an #ImWithHer hashtag.

Trump's misogyny resurfaced during the final debate, as he interpolated the comment "Such a nasty woman" during remarks by Clinton. On October 19, the night of the third debate, #NastyWoman appeared in over 240,000 tweets. By the end of the campaign it was close to half a million tweets. The Clinton campaign approved T-shirts and other memorabilia with "Nasty Woman" on it. But again, there were no linked tweets to any discernible degree.

A Gaffe-tag: #BasketOfDeplorables

#NastyWoman is an example of a hybridization we may call a gaffe-tag. It originates in a slip of a candidate's tongue which becomes widely interpreted as a true sentiment that had been heretofore hidden because the candidate knew it would offend voters. Clinton committed a gaffe during a speech to high-dollar donors on September 10, when she said that half of Trump's supporters could be put into a "basket of deplorables" who were "racist, sexist, homophobic, xenophobic, Islamaphobic, you name it."

Clinton and her team quickly recognized the error. She expressed "regret" for using the word "half." Trump, his running mate Mike Pence, and other Republicans seized the phrase, as did many of the labeled. The hashtagged #BasketOfDeplorables spiked immediately, with more than 627,000 tweet appearances in the first twenty-four hours, on the way to 1.2 million posts.

Conclusion

Hashtags empower campaigns to depict, enlarge, and prolong their messages into "trending topics" acknowledged as such by as many as tens of millions of people. Their affirmations, oppositions, ironic takes, and other types of comments propel the meme farther across society and higher on the analyst's chart. In this way, yesterday's bumper sticker turns into today's hub of democratic disputation.

Just how much this focalizing and dispersing process affects voter choices and election outcomes remains murky. But a connection seems likely. A Pew Research survey reported that 20 percent of social media users "have changed their minds about a political issue or about a candidate for office because of something they saw on social media." Four of five (79 percent) agreed that social media help people get involved with issues that matter to them, and three in four (74 percent) agreed that they bring new voices into the discussion.[18] A team of political scientists examining responses from the authoritative American National Election Survey in 2012 (when Twitter was less common in politics) concluded that "online contact … does appear to be able to mobilize certain segments of the electorate, particularly older voters in the United States."[19]

The presidential campaigns of 2016 confirmed the strategic importance of using Twitter well. There can be no gainsaying the competitive advantage of a twenty to one ratio of "#MAGA" over "#StrongerTogether," or two to one with "ImWithHer" added to the total. The same goes for having "#CrookedHillary" run uncountered by a comparable phrase. If there remains campaign value in swapping out primary for general election slogans, it is now the case, and likely to be the case in political contests to come, that the rise of social media levies greater switching costs which should be factored into that decision. Whatever the sharper contrast achieves (assuming the message works) is diminished by splintering the online cynosure.

A string of campaign emails publicized via WikiLeaks documents how the Clinton campaign devoted twelve hours and involved twelve staffers to craft a tweet that went through ten drafts before emerging under the candidate's "-H" signature.[20] Fewer than 5,000 viewers expressed approval for the result: "Every American deserves a fair shot at success. Fast food & child care workers shouldn't have to march in streets for living wages. -H **7:23 PM – 15 Apr. 2015** 2,988 Retweets 4,969 likes." No hashtagged phrase is present. The example attests to the finding of another trio of scholars who concluded that Clinton used Twitter more to pronounce positions than to interact and engage with people.[21]

170 Part II: Money and Communication

The Trump campaign, by contrast, delivered consistent, concise, and sensationalist messages. His tweets were widely regarded as coming from his own voice, for better and worse. He excerpted and commented on tweets directed to him and about him, the hallmark of engagement. His Twitter presence was stronger and more together with his supporters.

It's worth adding a note of tactical praise for the Bernie Sanders campaign, whose small team pioneered the use of Twitter to comment in real time during opposition party debates. As recalled by Sander's chief twitterer, Hector Sigala, Sanders watched the August 6, 2015 Republican debate from a couch in his campaign headquarters and fed comments to Sigala, who posted them with the hashtag #debatewithBernie.[22] Traffic to Sanders's website skyrocketed, and other candidates soon adopted the practice. It was an effective move in a time and place of extreme partisan polarization, where polls show that voter antipathy to the other party's candidate and ideology exceeds attachment to one's own.[23]

It's a common notion that Twitter and social media are communications channels where coarse, siloed, and simplistic statements sow anxiety and frustration. This stereotype reflects an undeniable and self-evident portion of the content to be found in campaign-related tweets. But there is more to be found in the Twitterverse than insults and invective. How else could we explain the Pew survey findings that most people appreciate politics on social media? How else can we encourage community building and hopeful excitement around campaigns?

Hashtagged phrases provide a good window into this discourse venue. Their reception and recirculation help us understand the dialogues of democracy. Strategists should shape poll questions, campaign message tests, and voter turnout models with hashtag results at hand. By 2018 and 2020, Twitter as a business may cede market share to another purveyor of short form messaging; such is the volatile nature of the information technology sector. But this type of communication has demonstrated its worth to the public and to political management. Hashtagging will endure, and campaigns will develop better methods to understand and use it.

Notes

1 For more on the George Washington University Graduate School of Political Management PEORIA (Public Echoes of Rhetoric in America) research project, see https://gspm.gwu.edu/peoria-project.
2 Kevin Quealy, "How to Know What Donald Trump Really Cares About: Look at What He's Insulting," *New York Times*, December 6, 2016, www.nytimes.com/interactive/2016/12/06/upshot/how-to-know-what-donald-trump-really-cares-about-look-at-who-hes-insulting.html?_r=0 (accessed December 13, 2016).

3 David Sarno, "Twitter Creator Jack Dorsey Illuminates the Site's Founding Document," *Los Angeles Times*, February 18, 2009, http://latimesblogs.latimes.com/technology/2009/02/twitter-creator.html (accessed December 13, 2016).

4 *The Twitter Government and Elections Handbook*, 2014 U.S. Edition, 29, 47, 52.

5 Richard Alfonsi, Twitter vice president for Global Online Sales, Targeted Victory Summit, Washington, D.C., August 25, 2016.

6 Charlie Warzel, "'A Honeypot for Assholes': Inside Twitter's 10-Year Failure to Stop Harassment," *BuzzFeed*, August 11, 2016, www.buzzfeed.com/charliewarzel/a-honeypot-for-assholes-inside-twitters-10-year-failure-to-s?utm_term=.pa8ynVERd#.kc2vXbZ2G (accessed December 14, 2016).

7 While Crimson Hexagon provides metrics on both followers and potential followers we do not incorporate that data in this chapter. But we do note this as a sign of the power of hashtags.

8 TwitterAudit.com "takes a random sample of 5,000 Twitter followers for a user and calculates a score for each follower based on the number of tweets, date of the last tweet, and ratio of followers to friends."

9 Bence Kollanyi, Philip N. Howard, and Samuel C. Woolley, "Bots and Automation Over Twitter during the U.S. Election," *Comprop Data Memo* 2016.4, November 17, 2016, www.politicalbots.org (accessed December 14, 2016).

10 Nor are we in position to judge this claim by Clint Watts and Andrew Weisburd, "How Russia Wins an Election," *Politico*, December 13, 2015, about the use of bots as part of Russian interference in the elections, except to note that we agree with the circulation route they mapped from Twitter trend to mainstream media, if not the infected content and their influence independent of above-board messaging by candidates, citizens, and media figures:

> After using hacked information to craft manipulated truths, Russia propagates and amplifies stories using automated bots. Series of accounts programmed to appear as members of the target audience comment, retweet and share breaking conspiracies at a dizzying pace, turning keyword hashtags into Twitter trends. When successful, this artificial volume entices mainstream media outlets to engage on the trending issue, further amplifying the Kremlin's narrative. Even if the false or manipulated truth pushed by Russian bots is later proven false, the firehose of fake or manipulated news often drowns out the mainstream media's efforts to correct the record. The net result is an information world in which Western electorates cannot distinguish fact from fiction, eroding the integrity of democratic institutions and the voters' trust.

11 Tamara Keith, "How 'Stronger Together' Became Clinton's Response to 'Make America Great Again'," *National Public Radio*, August 8, 2016, www.npr.org/2016/08/08/489138602/trump-comment-gives-clinton-a-campaign-slogan-with-layered-meaning (accessed December 13, 2016).

12 Quealy, "How to Know What Donald Trump Really Cares About."

13 Mark Leibovich, "Donald Trump Shares His Opponent-Branding Secrets," *New York Times*, May 9, 2016, www.nytimes.com/2016/05/09/magazine/donald-trump-shares-his-opponent-branding-secrets.html (accessed December 13, 2016).

172 Part II: Money and Communication

14 Sydney Moorhead, "Tweet of the Day: Hillary Clinton Doesn't Care About Donald Trump's #CrookedHillary Tweet," GoKicker.Com, April 17, 2016 (accessed December 14, 2016).

15 Nancy Scola, "Twitter Cut Out of Trump Tech Meeting Over Failed Emoji Deal," *Politico*, December 14, 2016, www.politico.com/story/2016/12/donald-trump-twitter-emoji-crooked-hillary-232647 (accessed December 14, 2016). Sources at the Trump campaign and Twitter denied that the emoji rejection cost Twitter a seat at the well-publicized meeting of the president-elect with digital technology executives, but not that such an emoji had been proposed.

16 For a primer, see the "Delete Your Account" entry at knowyourmeme.com.

17 Jonathan Mahler, "For Many Women, Trump's 'Locker-Room Talk' Brings Memories of Abuse," *The New York Times*, October 10, 2016, www.nytimes.com/2016/10/11/us/politics/sexual-assault-survivor-reaction.html (accessed December 14, 2016).

18 Maeve Duggan and Aaron Smith, "The Political Environment on Social Media," *Pew Research Center Report*, October 25, 2016, www.pewinternet.org/2016/10/25/the-political-environment-on-social-media/ (accessed December 18, 2016).

19 John Aldrich, Rachel K. Gibson, Mara Cantijoch, and Tobias Konitzer, "Getting Out the Vote in the Social Media Era: Are Digital Tools Changing the Extent, Nature and Impact of Party Contacting in elections?" *Party Politics*, February 28, 2015, http://journals.sagepub.com/doi/abs/10.1177/1354068815605304?journalCode=ppqa (accessed December 13, 2016).

20 WikiLeaks.org, at wikileaks.org/podesta-emails/emailid/24510.

21 Ann Crigler, Marion Just, and Whitney Hua, "Populist Disruption: Sanders and Trump Tweets in the 2016 US Presidential Primaries," paper prepared for presentation at the annual meeting of the American Political Science Association, Philadelphia PA, September 2016.

22 Sigala interview with authors, October 19, 2016.

23 For a recent and pertinent summary of the extensive social science literature attesting to this political phenomenon, see Alexander George Theodoritis, "The Hyper-Polarization of America," *ScientificAmerican.com*, November 7, 2016, https://blogs.scientificamerican.com/guest-blog/the-hyper-polarization-of-america/ (accessed December 23, 2016).

9

THE TRUMP EFFECT ON THE PRESS, THE PRESIDENCY, RHETORIC, AND DEMOCRACY

Major Garrett

The press—debated, derided, and dismissed—has always been a component of every presidential campaign, but it may be fairly argued that media involvement in this presidential campaign was never more scrutinized, scandalized, and scapegoated. In that broad sense, it is difficult to over-state the role Donald Trump's public animosity against the media, his flagrant use of misinformation and falsehoods to drive a campaign narrative, and the media's own culpability in contributing to his early rise in the polls affected the presidential campaign.

Trump's victory and his uncharacteristically dismissive attitude about press coverage—from dodging the protective pool of reporters to ignoring press conferences in favor of campaign-style "Thank You" rallies—raise significant questions about the relationship between reporters and the institution of the White House. The Trump campaign may also change the way future presidential candidates view their approach to political reporters and the media in general. Presidential politics is the ultimate proving ground for new strategies and successful ones tend to be replicated or copied. The Trump relationship with the press corps could have profound consequences not only in Washington and in future White House campaigns but more immediately in state capitols and city halls across the country. As with so much regarding Trump, the consequences are uncertain. But the recent past does suggest a brave new world for journalism and the American presidency—a turnstile moment that may decide whether the existing model of accountability, transparency, and scrutiny survive. These issues are uncertain because Trump did more than any other presidential candidate in recent memory to vilify and marginalize journalism and journalists.

For all the complaints reporters repeated and necessarily lodged against Trump—his serial fabrications, his refusal to create a protective news pool with access to him as the GOP nominee, as well as his malevolent stoking of hatred

174 Part II: Money and Communication

toward traveling reporters (which I experienced dozens of times at Trump rallies)—American media corporations must confront two hard truths about the role they played in the rise of Trump.

Blurring the Lines and Celebrity News

One role is subtle and took many years to manifest: the blurring of the lines between news content and advertising, followed more recently by the second role, the comingling of celebrity news and politics and policy coverage. The *Merriam-Webster* dictionary recognized the word "advertorial" in 1946. Advertorials were special sections printed by the newspaper that looked almost identical to news copy but were nevertheless advertisements for the paying sponsor. To meet obligations of professional journalism, the newspaper would typically affix small agate type at the top of the page indicating it was an advertisement and not part of the reporting contained on pages wrapped around the advertorial. Only the most discerning reader could tell the difference. That was the point—the authority of the written word could be commoditized and appear in full public view. That trend gained traction in the 1970s and became a more visible part of newspaper content in the 1980s when I began my career as a journalist. In its more modern incarnation, online news copy has for years now been stacked on top or alongside so-called "native" advertising copy embedded in the visual flow of straight news copy to improve the likelihood unsuspecting readers will click on it and fall into the advertisers' crafty clutches.

As Amar C. Bakshi wrote in 2015:

> Native advertisements online are the latest incarnation of the long-running practice of blurring the lines between paid advertisement and independently created publisher content. This practice benefits advertisers by allowing them to leach credibility from news publications in exchange for payment. However, readers, as both consumers and citizens, lose out in this deal. Readers find it harder to accurately assess product claims and lose faith in the media as a vehicle for democratic discourse.[1]

Whether journalists or the corporations that employ them want to admit it, this blurring of standards and strict separation between news and advertising is one reason Trump was able to assail truth and mock journalism. He created an alternate narrative driven by his own sense of marketing bravado which he sold as more pure and less disguised. This is an inference, of course, but one rooted in more than thirty-two years in professional journalism and sixteen months on the campaign trail attending more than seventy Trump rallies and interviews with hundreds of Trump supporters. For many of his supporters, the most believable and credible political advertising was Trump's nakedly self-congratulatory and boastful statements. It is difficult to separate the trends that brought objective

Chapter 9: The Trump Effect on the Press **175**

news copy and advertising so closely together and a political actor who told voters marketing was its own truth and its commercial success was proof of its political potency.

The news media must also come to grips with the fact that the rise of celebrity coverage in mainstream newspaper and TV journalism worked to Trump's advantage. As someone who built his New York image during the 1980s and 1990s—and thereby created a national launching pad for his network TV career and eventual presidential campaign—Trump understood the rising power of tabloid coverage.

In the 1980s and 1990s, Trump milked the New York tabloid press for attention. The *New York Post*'s "Page Six" was, according to longtime reporter Frank DiGiacomo, a coveted space for the "media-celebrity culture, not only in New York" but increasingly nationwide, and Trump used the tabloids in that era as a "trial run for his presidential campaign." According to DiGiacomo, "he was radiating this almost cartoonish idea of wealth and celebrity status. He honed a very simple, easily disseminated message. … It's not that different from what it is now. I embody success. I'm a winner."[2] Journalist Michael Kruse asked DiGiacomo if he regretted his role in pumping up Trump in the New York tabloids: "I guess maybe I do feel a little guilty," he says. "But I think I probably share that guilt … If I'm going to hell, I'm going to hell with a lot of people."[3]

Trump's New York experience taught him where news was heading—toward tabloid coverage where names, tidbits, and dazzle meant more and sold more than ever. This led to Trump's central insight as he launched his campaign—that the emerging business model for media companies struggling for audience share induce them to choose ratings and web clicks over probity, skepticism, and distance.

Trump and Free Media

In the early months of his campaign, Trump commanded saturated media coverage of the kind no political novice had ever seen before. During the pre-primary season, from July 2 until December 11, 2015 there was only one week—November 7 to 15—when Trump did not receive more television mentions than any of his Republican rivals. In that week in November, Ben Carson out-paced Trump. But for most of the primary season, Trump dominated television coverage, often garnering twice or three times the mentions of his closest GOP competitor.[4]

Cable television coverage and web stories proliferated, each driving more of the other as ratings increased cable appetite for Trump and television visibility made news coverage on mainstream and fringe websites more profitable than any candidate in the modern era. For more on Trump's free media, see Chapter 1 (Dennis W. Johnson) and Chapter 7 on political advertising (Peter Fenn).

176 Part II: Money and Communication

Fake News

This phenomenon eventually led enterprising college students and other young people in Macedonia to create websites with cribbed, invented, and or plagiarized stories on Trump to turn a profit during the general election. Craig Silverman and Lawrence Alexander, in a path-breaking story in BuzzFeed News, exposed the "digital gold rush" of fake news and sensational headlines found in some 140 bogus websites dedicated to U.S. politics. Many of the sites sounded like legitimate news outlets, WorldPoliticus.com, TrumpVision365.com, USConservativeToday. com, DonaldTrumpNews.co, and others.[5] It wasn't about politics in the far off United States, it was solely about the money that the young entrepreneurs could collect from ad clicks, particularly coming from the lucrative Facebook market. They would earn a fraction of a penny every time someone clicked on their news, adding up to millions of clicks and thousands of dollars in their pockets. (See Chapter 1 for further information analysis of fake news.)

That BuzzFeed article, according to *New Yorker* journalist David Remnick, became a late-campaign obsession of Barack Obama and White House political director David Simas. As Remnick wrote:

> The new media ecosystem "means everything is true and nothing is true," Obama told me later. ... The capacity to disseminate misinformation, wild conspiracy theories, to paint the opposition in wildly negative light without any rebuttal—that has accelerated in ways that much more sharply polarize the electorate and make it very difficult to have a common conversation.[6]

Trump may have known little about policy or presidential rhetoric, but he possessed a keen and potent insight into the media landscape—if he fed it, it would come. And the more he fed it, the more it came. And with each feeding the political relevance of his GOP opponents began to atrophy to the point of withering. Governors with huge war chests like Scott Walker of Wisconsin, a conservative darling for his efforts against the teachers' union in Wisconsin, couldn't last three months. Former Florida governor Jeb Bush, with a campaign and supportive Super Pac that spent more than $130 million on his behalf, never finished higher than fourth and collected four delegates. Senator Ted Cruz of Texas survived largely because he tried to ride on Trump's media coattails, buttering him up every step of the way until Trump delivered the same summary media execution visited on his rivals—high-profile lies and dismissive remarks that could not be countered with speeches, superior field organizing, or Super PACs.

The last American political figure credited with revolutionizing the relationship between a candidate and the media is Ronald Reagan. Every successful president after Reagan essentially fine-tuned the model Reagan developed for driving message first through images and reinforcing them through policy and politics. Trump brought another revolution to the relationship—one where the candidate

Chapter 9: The Trump Effect on the Press **177**

dictates the terms by seizing operational control of the media business model—a big difference from Reagan, who co-opted the dominance of network television coverage and major newspaper authority by playing to its inherent bias toward powerful imagery. Reagan could not dictate media coverage but he could shape it. Trump, in ways no modern candidate had before, dictated it because he understood its new commercial imperatives.

Trump: Good News for Media's Bottom Line

It was highly unlikely that Les Moonves, chief executive officer and executive chairman of CBS (and my boss) would ever vote for Trump. Moonves called the Trump campaign a "circus" full of "bomb throwing." But as Paul Bond of the *Hollywood Reporter* wrote, Moonves may not like Trump, but he certainly likes the advertising money that Trump and the rest of the field brings to CBS. "It may not be good for America, but it's damn good for CBS," Moonves said of the presidential race. "Man, who would have expected the ride we're all having right now? ... The money's rolling in and this is fun," he said. Moonves told a Morgan Stanley Technology, Media & Telecom Conference in San Francisco that "I've never seen anything like this, and this going to be a very good year for us. Sorry. It's a terrible thing to say. But, bring it on, Donald. Keep going."[7]

What was true for CBS was true for every other network and media company. And nowhere was that more true than on social media. Trump's use of Twitter and Facebook became, and remain, a crucial fault line in political journalism. As of December 11, 2016, Trump had 16.9 million followers on Facebook and 17.3 million on Twitter (with an additional 4.3 million on Instagram). Trump's dominance on social media and his manipulation of journalism through it is, I would argue, an important dividing line. On one side sits an increasingly distant past where reporters like myself and legions of others received a campaign press released and reported through and around it before producing a story. On the other side sits an unsettling present where Trump tweets are reported with an authority of free-standing truth, with no additional reporting or follow-up questioning. Trump tweets are nothing more than mini press releases, the kind reporters and editors scrutinize before rushing into print or broadcasting. But Trump's command of social media forces news companies—which live in constant fear of losing market share—to report them without any filter or risk losing legitimacy in the crowded and competitive space of Trump coverage, web clicks, and social media echoes. I have experienced this phenomenon first-hand, arguing unsuccessfully against reporting Trump tweets but losing the newsroom argument against those who feared CBS News would be left out of the political conversation that was "trending" or being driven by Trump.

It is in this respect I would argue Reagan and Trump are most alike. Reagan, like Trump, was a student of an evolving media landscape and participated in it as his career and the medium evolved. Both were initially derided for being part

178 Part II: Money and Communication

of that supposedly gauche culture—Reagan's B-movies and Trump's tabloid image. And yet, both saw how the medium of their time could work uniquely to their advantage and exploited that insight more rapidly and more successfully than any of their contemporaries. In this respect, Trump and Reagan are most similar and their approach to media messaging and innovation represent important achievements in presidential politics—ones worthy of further academic assessment and comparison.

Trump Goes After the Press

While Trump was innovative, he also brought something shocking and disturbing to presidential coverage. Trump's campaign routinely banned news organizations from covering public rallies, entirely because Trump operatives objected to something the reporters had written or said. That sentence itself is almost absurd when viewed in the context of modern political coverage.

There was a "blacklist," a list of news organizations, from traditional news sources, online outlets, the largest Spanish-language television broadcaster, and even the *Washington Post*. As Tom Kludt and Brian Stetler wrote for *CNN Money*:

> In some cases, reporters from the offending outlets can still attend Trump campaign rallies as members of the general public, but without the access and privileges that press credentials provide. In other situations, like press conferences, the reporters cannot attend at all.[8]

When the Trump campaign revoked the press credentials of the *Washington Post*, the newspaper's executive editor Martin Baron wrote:

> Donald Trump's decision to revoke the *Washington Post*'s press credentials is nothing less than a repudiation of the role of a free and independent press. When coverage doesn't correspond to what a candidate wants it to be, then a news organization is banished.[9]

Those reporters allowed to cover Trump rallies were prevented from freely mingling with Trump supporters. They were permitted to interact briefly before rallies but otherwise confined to a press pen built around the risers constructed for TV cameras and still photographers. Frequently, reporters were forced to remain in this "pen" long after a rally was over. All of this was to keep reporters from interviewing Trump supporters or covering any protests up close. Enterprising reporters, like myself, worked around these restrictions by meeting supporters and protesters outside of Trump rallies or interviewing them on the rails of the press "pen." Still, the restrictions were without precedent and symbolized Trumpian disdain for political journalism.

Chapter 9: The Trump Effect on the Press **179**

While reporting on Trump, reporters were subject to verbal harassment and abuse. Television reporters, myself included, were taunted with screams during live shots as Trump supporters would shout vulgarities in an effort to distract the correspondent or deposit their anti-media rage on the broadcast. Many reporters told the *Washington Post* in February 2016 that they already felt a sense of menace at Trump rallies.[10] During the homestretch of the campaign, chants of "CNN Sucks" would rain down on the press riser as hundreds and sometimes thousands of Trump supporters would join the chorus. Threats of violence at rallies—via emails and on social media—led several correspondents and the networks that employed them to deploy security personnel. I know more than a few correspondents who did not feel safe at Trump rallies. In the final days of the campaign, as I walked the gauntlet of Trump supporters to the press "pen" I felt a sense of dread—a lurking curiosity if a thrown battery might rain down on my head or an anonymous punch might fly from the edge of the barriers. I have covered presidential campaigns since 1992—all but the 1996 and 2000 cycles on the road—and never felt so uneasy. I would not for a moment compare this anxiety to that experienced by war correspondents. My only point is that politics and the journalism of politics never felt to me like war before. On the Trump campaign it did. It is impossible for me not to wonder uneasily where or when the war footing will end and what it holds in store for political figures, journalists, and the public at large.

Trump stoked this animosity and blind rage by routinely assailing reporters as "dishonest ... horrible ... liars" and worse. Trump mocked fact-checkers and used his Twitter account to undermine reporters and make them targets of his social media acolytes (trolls is too pejorative and judgmental, a level of restraint Trump rarely exhibited). The *New York Times* published a running list of reporters and others to whom Trump directed his Twitter lash. I first appeared on the list January 28, 2016.[11] There was a time when this felt like another form of campaign shtick, a more testosterone-driven version of stock GOP protestations about "liberal media" bias.[12] But Trump was different. His rhetoric matched his actions and stories about his curdled contempt for reporters created a feedback loop among his aggrieved supporters. The more Trump bashed reporters, the more his supporters came to believe him and disbelieve them. Viewed with the perspective of time, it is now clear from my many months on the campaign trail that Trump's mistreatment of and disdain for reporters and journalism was a purposeful strategy to inoculate him from repeated factual errors, misstatements, and intentional lies.

Trump did not, however, operate in a vacuum. The stature of American journalism has been in decline for at least two decades. As the Gallup polling and analytics organization recently reported, national confidence in the mass media "to report the news fully, accurately and fairly" plummeted to the lowest level in the polling organization's history. According to the Gallup survey, only 32 percent of respondent have a great deal or fair amount of trust in the media, down from 50 percent in 2005 and 55 percent in 1999. As Gallup's Art Swift

180 Part II: Money and Communication

noted, Americans' trust and confidence in journalism hit a high point in 1976, following the investigative reporting of the Vietnam War and Watergate. In 1976, some 72 percent of Americans voiced confidence in the press. During this election cycle, however, trust has fallen sharply. Some Republicans argue that Trump is not receiving fair treatment, while other Republicans note Trump's criticism of the press. For Republicans, trust in the press has reached a twenty-year low, plummeting from 32 percent trust in 2015 to just 14 percent in 2016.[13]

Trump sensed this and used his unique blend of celebrity status, tabloid moxie, and raw political talent to turn skepticism about media trustworthiness into a campaign message and a heat shield against his own serial misstatements (something Republicans, even Reagan, tried but failed to accomplish). The Trump campaign raised the most audacious question put before the electorate and political journalists. It was two questions, actually.

Do Facts Exist and If So, Do They Matter?

At a now famous post-election conversation between senior strategists for Trump and Clinton's campaign, Corey Lewandowski, the first of three Trump campaign managers, said something that had the ring of Trumpian satire but was, instead, said in deadly earnest:

> This is the problem with the media. You guys took everything Donald Trump said so literally. The American people didn't. They understood it. They understood that sometimes, when you have a conversation with people, whether it's around the dinner table or at a bar, you're going to say things and sometimes you don't have the facts to back it up.[14]

A Trump surrogate, Scottie Nell Hughes, who appeared on NPR's Diane Rehm radio show amplified Lewandowski's lament over factualism.

> People say facts are facts. They're not really facts. Everybody has a way of interpreting them to be the truth or not true. There's no such thing unfortunately anymore [as] facts. When he says that millions of people illegally voted, he has some facts—amongst him and his supporters—and people believe they have facts to back that up. Those that do not like Mr. Trump, they say those are lies and there's no facts to back it up.[15]

In both formulations, the fault lies not with a political figure and eventual major party nominee spouting falsehoods at an astonishing rate (more on that momentarily) but on the journalists who concluded a politician ought to know fact from fiction as well as the danger of peddling untruths that, as was so often the case with Trump, fed into racial biases or marginalized minorities.[16] According to Lewandowski, reporters were too dense, too obtuse to see Trump's larger

Chapter 9: The Trump Effect on the Press **181**

truths—the ones so evident at a family meal or edge of a barstool. For Neil Hughes, the pursuit of facts is useless because they have disappeared in a miasma of conflicting interpretation. No longer is it true, as John Adams said in 1770, that "facts are stubborn things"[17] or that "everyone" as Daniel Patrick Moynihan once said "is entitled to his own opinion, but not to his own facts."[18] Instead, the stubborn interpretation of Trump supporters was supposed to rule the day and those supporters were entitled to their own facts, or their own interpretation of quasi facts to settle the issue. In this world and only in this world did Trump's mendacity make sense. And Trump did a very great deal to create this world— in part by saturating the landscape with so many lies it was impossible to keep one's footing.

I remember covering my first Trump rally in Birch Run, Michigan on August 11, 2015. At a press conference, carried live on cable TV, I asked Trump if he wanted to tell the voters of Michigan if he had been president would he have approved the two federal bailouts of the U.S. automakers (Bush did the first in 2008 and Obama the second in 2009).

> *Garrett*: Speaking of President Obama, he describes his leadership during the great recession as important and says the stimulus was vital to reviving the American economy, the bailout of Detroit was central to rebuilding the entire economy here. How would you grade his leadership then? Would you have done all the things that he did? And what would you say to Michiganders who wonder what you would have done about Detroit?

> *Trump*: Very fair question. There are two ways of looking at it. You could have let it go and rebuilt itself through the free enterprise system. You could have let it go bankrupt frankly, and rebuilt itself and a lot of people think that's the way it should have happened. I could have done it either way. Either way would have been acceptable. I think you would have ended up ultimately in the same place.[19]

Trump said it wouldn't have mattered either way. I followed up to make sure I understood. It wouldn't have mattered if Detroit-based automakers and auto suppliers received $79.6 billion in federal loans or nothing.[20] Trump agreed. Trump said Detroit would have ended up in the "same place" regardless of federal action. That was the first of many untruths Trump rolled out that afternoon—others touched on trade, immigrant criminals, the deficit, the Affordable Care Act, taxes, and unemployment. There were too many to catalog—too many to unwind on deadline. It was exhausting just to remember them all let alone knock them down one-by-one. That was one of Trump's tricks on the road to an interpretive world of malleable facts—flood the zone so reporters either cannot keep up or give up. Those reporters who did try to keep up were later dismissed as fly-specking nags with nothing better to do (in

182 Part II: Money and Communication

Trumpian parlance "losers."). After that rally, I caught up with Trump and asked him about reaction measured in some polls indicating voters had grown more uncomfortable with him after the first GOP debate.

> *Trump*: Well, I don't think so, I think that actually if you look at Fox and you look at what happened I think that people probably agreed that not only did I win but I won by a large margin. Look at all of the polls, if you look at Drudge, if you look at *Time* magazine, all of the polls have me winning by significant numbers, but those are not the important numbers, the important numbers are the ones that happened after the debate and you see Iowa, you see New Hampshire, you see South Carolina.

> *Garrett*: But that's what I was just asking about—in all those states—voters were less comfortable with you after the debate.

> *Trump*: Well, I haven't seen that, my numbers went up.

> *Garrett*: That's in the Suffolk poll and the New Hampshire poll.

> *Trump*: Well I haven't seen that, my numbers went up. Excuse me, did I win?

> *Garrett*: That's for you to decide.

> *Trump*: Excuse me, if you don't say yes then you're not an honest reporter. Good bye.[21]

That was the Trump I came to know and cover, one who dismissed any data contrary to his interpretation of himself or his own orientation to the facts. Any reporter who disagreed with him or merely pointed to data in conflict with his world view was, *a priori*, dishonest. This created havoc for reporters on the Trump beat and made the life of fact-checkers almost Kafkaesque.

But Trump himself was a fountain of false and misleading statements. Daniel Dale, a writer for the *Toronto Star*, began compiling a daily list of Trump's dishonesty. Dale started publishing a daily list of Trump's false claims in mid September, 2016. As he wrote in *Politico*:

> The fewest inaccuracies I've heard in any day is four. The most is 25 (Twenty-five!) That doesn't include the first two debates, at which I counted 34 and 33 respectively. Over the course of 33 days, I counted a total of 253 (including some that repeat).[22]

The *Washington Post*'s respected fact-checker Glenn Kessler published a list on November 3, just five days before the election, that listed all of Trump's most egregious falsehoods. For the worst statements, Kessler awarded four Pinocchios. "There's never been a presidential candidate like Donald Trump—someone so

Chapter 9: The Trump Effect on the Press **183**

cavalier about the facts and so unwilling to ever admit error, even in the face of overwhelming evidence," wrote Kessler.

> As of November 3, about 64 percent (59 of 92) of our rulings of his statements turned out to be Four Pinocchios, our worst rating. By contrast, most politicians tend to earn Four Pinocchios 10 to 20 percent of the time. (Moreover, most of the remaining ratings for Trump are Three Pinocchios).[23]

The Trump world was a tornado of misinformation, deliberate falsehoods, semi-facts, stereotypes, hype, innuendo, and historical tripe. The simplest facts escaped Trump and audiences that knew better were forced to sit in uncomfortable sympathetic silence as Trump carelessly steam-rolled basic truths.

I remember covering a meeting Trump attended on August 11, 2016 in Orlando, Florida, with evangelical pastors and listened to him describe his intention to eliminate the Johnson amendment—a federal law that prohibits churches from engaging directly in political speech or advocacy. In the span of about five minutes, Trump misstated the years of the Lyndon Johnson presidency and when the amendment was passed and even garbled its underlying motivations. At times Trump's relationship to simple concepts was almost child-like in its clumsiness and indifference. The audience of pastors sat in stunned silence—unsure what to make of Trump's actual interest (if he won't study the history, why would he change the future?). In the end, Trump's intentions won the room, the day, and, eventually, evangelical voters.[24]

This episode is instructive at many levels because it topples basic understanding about rhetoric and reportage. Under ground rules created informally but understood to benefit the public and political discourse, politicians are expected to converse factually about issues they have studied and use that knowledge to inform their judgments so they can be explained to the public with the hopes of persuading it to embrace the politician's point of view. Reporters are assigned to scrutinize the language and history and see if they add up as presented and then check with voters to see if it is persuasive. Trump obliterated every aspect of this model, leaving journalists scorned for checking facts, supporters sometimes perplexed by Trump's true intent, and the historical record so misshapen by falsities and semi-truths the ability to hold Trump accountable to his own words may lack meaning, resonance, or political vitality.

When facts no longer matter and interpretations, forgive me, trump verifiable truths, then propaganda can reign supreme. The power of intellectual or political prerogative triumphs over numbers, science, history, data, and law. That I wish it so or that I believe it so becomes a counter-weight to what is so, what has been so, or what is provably so. Whether they ought to weigh the same has been rendered irrelevant and the consequences for politics, journalism, law, and reason are as profound as at any time since the advent of America's modern media culture

184 Part II: Money and Communication

(the one in which newspapers, radio, and TV competed for market share). George Orwell gave western thought a way to measure rhetoric and the Orwellian critique has never quite lost its ability to sting.[25] But that was because it was applied in isolation, to elevate for stricter scrutiny a particularly appalling manipulation of fact, history, or language. Orwellian was a singular concept about an individual assault on reason. What if the atmosphere is entirely Orwellian? What if assaults on reason are only comparable by degree and thereby become first commonplace then, over time, a kind of immovable, impenetrable reality? That is the essence of the Orwellian nightmare. It would be incautious to predict such a thing. But I can begin to see the rough outlines emerging of a Trump-centric world where even his own words mean nothing, facts are non-existent, and points of view, notions, preferences, and social media "likes" or retweets become flexible, interpretive, and mob-ratified arbiters of fact and fiction.

Hillary Clinton and the Press

But Hillary Clinton's approach to the press created dilemmas of its own. Clinton remained standoffish, just as she had during 2007–2008, a campaign I also covered extensively. It hurt her then, and it hurt her during this election as well. Clinton and her aides walled her off from reporters and when negative news broke they frequently responded by not responding, or by suggesting the revelation was either factually wrong, inconsequential, or just partisan mud-slinging. Clinton did not appear to take the accountability side of journalistic scrutiny seriously. Never was that inclination more evident than when news broke about her home-brewed email server. Clinton waited several days to offer an explanation to reporters. When she did the leaden words of lawyerly ambiguity obscured more than they revealed. Moreover, even the declarations Clinton made that sounded clear cut and definite were, under the weight of evidence later released, provably false. In fact, many things Clinton said in her defense at the March 10, 2015 United Nations press conference turned out to be false.[26]

It was this act of deliberate misleading and misdirection that intensified popular perceptions that Clinton was untrustworthy. This is related to Trump in one significant way. Even when Trump supporters acknowledged he did not tell the truth and frequently recklessly exaggerated, they rationalized that as acceptable alongside what they regarded as Clinton's serialized and more frequent lies about her server and other issues, particularly the terrorist attack in Benghazi, Libya. It is worth noting this dynamic in regard to acceptable standards of misinformation because what is acceptable for one candidate's supporters is rarely if ever deemed acceptable in isolation. Typically it is direct comparison with the major party alternative. Clinton's own rough relationship with the truth not only made it challenging for reporters to separate fact from fiction and revelation from incremental development, it may well have contributed to the political environment where Trump's free-form relationship to facts was allowed to flourish.

Conclusion

This chapter has dealt extensively with the Trump effect on rhetoric and journalism because of the obvious challenges it posed to the previous order. With a Trump presidency, the model of dissembling dishonesty could permeate the bloodstream of American life and significantly change concepts of accountability, transparency, and visibility.

It is always dangerous to suggest something politically unusual is without precedent. As Harry Truman tartly observed, "The only thing new under the sun is the history you don't know."[27] But in my experience and in a lengthy review of presidential politics and journalism in the modern age, it is fair to say there has been nothing like Trump. He is the first novice elected president. He is the first socially media dominant president (not the first socially media aware president). He is the first president to make mockery of the mass media a rhetorical cudgel and the banning of news organizations from public events a rallying cry for supporters and proof of his own political strength. While plenty of presidents and presidential candidates have scorned the free press, none before Trump created the atmosphere of popular animosity and anger visited upon journalists. Trump turned concepts of intimidation into reality. He also uprooted common understandings of facts and agreed-upon foundations for policy debates. All of this, I believe it can be argued, is unique in modern presidential politics and American journalism.

The consequences have only begun to be felt and were largely discounted before Trump won the presidency. Now with the vast powers of that office before him, Trump may find it within his power to further alter the landscape of presidential rhetoric and the public's ability to rely on an independent press to hold that rhetoric up against Trump's previous statements or his campaign promises. The Trump effect on the presidency and American journalism and the First Amendment is potentially historic—a history we not only do not know but cannot know. All we have is the presidential campaign and its disturbingly hostile, fact-free, and mocking residue.

Notes

1 Amar C. Bakshi, "Why and How to Regulate Native Advertising in Online News Publications," *University of Baltimore School of Law Journal of Media Law & Ethics* 4, No. 3/4 (Winter/Spring 20015): 4–46, at 4, http://law.ubalt.edu/academics/publications/medialaw/pdfs_only/Vol.%204%20No.%203-4.pdf (accessed December 2, 2016).

2 Quoted in Michael Kruse, "Tales from the Tabloids," *Politico Magazine* (May/June 2016), www.politico.com/magazine/story/2016/04/tabloids-donald-trump-new-york-post-daily-news-gossip-1980s-1990s-213853 (accessed December 4, 2016).

3 Kruse, "Tales from the Tabloids."

4 Television News Archive, 2016 Campaign Television Tracker, 2015–2016, http://television.gdeltproject.org/cgi-bin/iatv_campaign2016/iatv_campaign2016?filter_

186 Part II: Money and Communication

candidate=&filter_network=NATIONAL&filter_timespan=SINCETRUMP&filter_displayas=PERCENTGOP (accessed December 6, 2016).

5 Craig Silverman and Lawrence Alexander, "How Teens in the Balkans Are Duping Trump Supporters With Fake News," *BuzzFeed News*, November 3, 2016, www.buzzfeed.com/craigsilverman/how-macedonia-became-a-global-hub-for-pro-trump-misinfo?utm_term=.nnW0ADDLk#.avMQg33Zd (accessed December 1, 2016).

6 David Remnick, "Obama Reckons With a Trump Presidency, Inside a Stunned White House, the President Considers His Legacy and America's Future," *The New Yorker*, November 26, 2016, www.newyorker.com/magazine/2016/11/28/obama-reckons-with-a-trump-presidency (accessed December 4, 2016).

7 Paul Bond, "Leslie Moonves on Donald Trump: 'It May Not Be Good For America, But It's Damn Good For CBS'," *The Hollywood Reporter*, February 29, 2016, www.hollywoodreporter.com/news/leslie-moonves-donald-trump-may-871464 (accessed December 8, 2016).

8 Tom Kludt and Brian Stetler, "'The Blacklist': Here Are the Media Outlets Banned by Donald Trump," *CNN Money*, June 14, 2016, http://money.cnn.com/2016/06/14/media/donald-trump-media-blacklist/ (accessed December 8, 2016).

9 Paul Farhi, "Trump Revokes Post Press Credentials, Calling the Paper 'Dishonest' and 'Phony'," *Washington Post*, June 13, 2016, www.washingtonpost.com/lifestyle/style/trump-revokes-post-press-credentials-calling-the-paper-dishonest-and-phony/2016/06/13/f9a61a72-31aa-11e6-95c0-2a6873031302_story.html?utm_term=.1392bb4b9071 (accessed December 12, 2016).

10 Paul Farhi, "Insults, Threats and More Insults: What It's Like Being a Reporter Covering Trump," *Washington Post*, February 4, 2016, www.washingtonpost.com/lifestyle/style/insults-threats-and-more-insults-what-its-like-to-be-a-reporter-covering-trump/2016/02/04/561743a8-c9eb-11e5-ae11-57b6aeab993f_story.html?utm_term=.360965c709a3 (December 13, 2016).

11 Jasmine C. Lee and Kevin Quealy, "Introducing the Upshot's Encyclopedia of Donald Trump's Twitter Insults," *New York Times*, January 28, 2016, www.nytimes.com/2016/01/29/upshot/introducing-the-upshots-encyclopedia-of-donald-trumps-twitter-insults.html (accessed December 12, 2016).

12 James Hohmann, "Bobby Jindal vs. The World, He Says Elites Can't Stand the Idea of an Ivy-League Educated Pure Conservative," *Politico*, February 9, 2015, www.politico.com/story/2015/02/bobby-jindal-115048 (accessed December 10, 2016).

13 Art Swift, "Americans' Trust in Mass Media Sinks to New Low," *Gallup*, September 14, 2016, www.gallup.com/poll/195542/americans-trust-mass-media-sinks-new-low.aspx (accessed December 6, 2016).

14 Aaron Blake, "Corey Lewandowski's Very Odd Explanation of Donald Trump's 'Facts'," *Washington Post*, December 2, 2016, www.washingtonpost.com/news/the-fix/wp/2016/12/02/corey-lewandowskis-very-odd-explanation-of-donald-trumps-facts/?utm_term=.ef476998427a (accessed December 12, 2016).

15 Transcript, "How Journalists Are Re-Thinking Their Role Under a Trump Presidency," *The Diane Rehm Show*, WAMU 88.5 FM, National Public Radio, November 30, 2016, http://thedianerehmshow.org/audio/#/shows/2016-11-30/how-journalists-are-rethinking-their-role-under-a-trump-presidency/114095/@15:36 (accessed December 10, 2016).

Chapter 9: The Trump Effect on the Press **187**

16 Michael D'Antonio, "Is Donald Trump Racist? Here's What the Record Shows," *Fortune*, June 7, 2016, http://fortune.com/2016/06/07/donald-trump-racism-quotes/ (accessed December 10, 2016).

17 John Adams, argument in defense of the soldiers in the Boston Massacre Trials, Boston Massacre Historical Society, December 1770, www.bostonmassacre.net/trial/acct-adams3.htm (accessed December 11, 2016).

18 Steven R. Weisman, "An American Original," *Vanity Fair*, November, 2011, www.vanityfair.com/news/2010/11/moynihan-letters-201011 (accessed December 11, 2016).

19 Transcript, press conference with Donald J. Trump, Birch Run, Michigan, August 11, 2015.

20 Brent Snavely, "Final Tally: Taxpayers Auto Bailout Loss $9.3 Billion," *Detroit Free Press*, December 30, 2014, www.usatoday.com/story/money/cars/2014/12/30/auto-bailout-tarp-gm-chrysler/21061251/ (accessed December 12, 2016).

21 Transcript, Trump interview.

22 Daniel Dale, "Confessions of a Trump Fact-Checker. I Spent 33 Days Fact-Checking 253 Donald Trump Falsehoods. Here's What I Learned," *Politico*, October 19, 2016, www.politico.com/magazine/story/2016/10/one-month-253-trump-untruths-214369 (accessed December 12, 2016).

23 Glenn Kessler, "All of Donald Trump's Four Pinocchio Ratings, in One Place," *Washington Post*, November 3, 2016, www.washingtonpost.com/news/fact-checker/wp/2016/03/22/all-of-donald-trumps-four-pinocchio-ratings-in-one-place/?utm_term=.0b0e052725c1 (accessed December 12, 2016).

24 Sarah Pulliam Bailey, "White Evangelicals Voted Overwhelmingly for Donald Trump, Exit Polls Show," *Washington Post*, November 9, 2016.

25 George Orwell, *Politics and the English Language* (New York: Penguin Modern Classics, 2013, 1945).

26 Chuck Ross, "'Count The Lies' Marks 1-Year Anniversary of Hillary's UN E-mail Speech," *The Daily Caller*, March 10, 2016, http://dailycaller.com/2016/03/10/count-the-clinton-lies-marks-1-year-anniversary-of-hillarys-un-email-speech-video/ (accessed December 12, 2016).

27 Harry Truman quotation from Harry S. Truman Library & Museum, www.trumanlibrary.org/news/hday09.html (accessed December 12, 2016).

PART III

The General Election

10

OUTSIDE VOICES

Super PACs, Parties, and Other Non-Candidate Actors

Stephen K. Medvic

In a typical presidential election, the candidates' campaigns operate in roughly similar ways. The candidates spend roughly the same amount of money and their allies—the parties, interest groups, and Super PACs—serve roughly the same functions for the candidates. Because neither side wants the other to get an advantage, they try to match each other dollar for dollar and move for move.

Of course, the 2016 presidential election was anything but typical. The Republican nominee was an unconventional candidate and he ran an unconventional campaign. The Democratic nominee, although unconventional in terms of gender, was conventional in virtually every other way and ran the sort of campaign one would expect from a conventional candidate. To some extent, the outside groups mirrored the campaigns of the candidates they supported. Republican allied groups were far less active than they had been in the past and they spent less than Democratic groups. The Republican National Committee focused virtually all of its efforts on voter mobilization, which was a change from its typical approach. The Democratic National Committee eschewed television ads to concentrate on turnout, an approach it usually takes.

As if this election were not unusual enough, there was also activity from an outside actor that wasn't formally aligned with either candidate but whose actions certainly seemed intended to help just one of them. That activity, the Russian hacking of Democratic Party computer systems, not only provided Donald Trump with fodder on the campaign trail, it also alarmed many political observers. Just how much damage it did to Clinton is, of course, difficult to determine. But it undoubtedly left a mark on the campaign.

This chapter is intended to describe and analyze the efforts of non-candidate actors in the general election. In doing so, I will highlight the activity of the national parties, interest groups, and Super PACs on either side. I will also briefly

192 Part III: The General Election

consider the actions of Russia as an unaligned non-candidate actor that may well have attempted to influence the outcome of the race. At the end of the chapter, I contemplate the generalizability of the conclusions reached after examining the activity of non-candidate actors in this election. Ultimately, and perhaps paradoxically in the post-*Citizens United* era we're in, the question is—whether outside voices even matter anymore.

Hillary Clinton's Allies

The Democratic Party and Joint Fundraising Committees

Although officially neutral during the nomination phase of the election, revelations in the summer of 2016 suggested that the Democratic National Committee (DNC) may have had a thumb on the scale for Hillary Clinton.[1] Hacked emails released by WikiLeaks showed party officials—including the chair of the DNC, Florida representative Debbie Wasserman Schultz—deriding Clinton's chief rival for the nomination, Bernie Sanders. The controversy forced Wasserman Schultz to resign as DNC chair on the eve of the Democratic National Convention.[2]

Clearly, then, the leadership of the DNC was not upset that Clinton had become the party's nominee and the national committee eagerly played its role in trying to elect Clinton as president. Well before Clinton was the party's nominee, her campaign and the DNC began cooperating to raise money. The DNC and Clinton's campaign ("Hillary for America") announced the formation of a joint fundraising committee in August of 2015.[3] More than thirty state party committees would join the pact shortly thereafter. While all the candidates for the Democratic presidential nomination were offered similar arrangements, only the Clinton campaign fully embraced the option.

Joint fundraising committees (JFCs) are a mechanism through which donors can make large contributions by writing a single check, rather than a number of smaller checks to each of the separate campaign and party committees. Contribution caps for each of those committees remain in place and, in theory, the JFC distributes the money to each of the committees based on those caps. Prior to the 2014 Supreme Court decision in *McCutcheon v. FEC*, however, there was an aggregate limit on how much an individual could give in a two-year cycle to federal candidates, party committees, and political action committees (PACs). That limit in the 2012 election cycle was $117,000. The *McCutcheon* decision ruled the aggregate cap unconstitutional. As a result, the 2016 presidential election cycle was the first in which an individual could give the maximum allowable under the contribution caps for individual candidates, committees, and PACs. For Clinton's JFC, the Hillary Victory Fund, this meant that a single individual could write a check for $356,100 ($2,700 to the Clinton campaign, $33,400 to the DNC, and $10,000 to each of the state party committees) in both 2015 and 2016, or $712,200 for the 2016 cycle.[4]

Chapter 10: Outside Voices **193**

The distribution of funds raised by the Hillary Victory Fund was the source of some controversy during the primaries. The Sanders campaign accused the Clinton JFC of funding Clinton's campaign beyond what the contribution limits allow and media reports suggested that very little of the money raised was being allocated to the state party committees as was required by the agreement.[5] The Clinton campaign and the DNC denied they were short-changing the state parties, but hacked emails made public in July indicated that DNC and Clinton campaign officials had agreed "to withhold information from reporters about the Hillary Victory Fund's allocation formula, working to align their stories about when—or if—the DNC had begun funding coordinated campaign committees with the states."[6]

The coordinated campaign committees are vitally important to the party's candidates. These committees organize volunteers and get-out-the-vote (GOTV) efforts for all of the party's candidates on the ballot in a given state. Presidential candidates want to assist, or at least to have been seen as assisting, down-ballot candidates, particularly those in competitive congressional races. However, their first priority is their own campaign. Thus, when the Hillary Victory Fund sent $2 million in the spring of 2016 to support state coordinated campaign efforts, the eight states receiving funds were presidential battleground states (that also happened to have closely watched U.S. Senate races).[7]

It wasn't only the state party committees that expected more support from the top of the ticket. Congressional Democrats privately expressed their displeasure with "Brooklyn" (the site of the Clinton campaign headquarters) as well. The House and Senate campaign committees felt that the Clinton campaign had not been forthcoming with financial support for congressional candidates and they also objected to Clinton's framing of Trump as so uniquely dangerous that even other Republicans found him unacceptable.[8] Congressional Democrats wanted to tie their opponents to Trump, but Clinton's approach made that more difficult. Clinton's strategy, according to an unnamed House Democratic advisor, was "selfish."[9]

There was a rationale for the Clinton team's message about Trump. Since the Republican Party is part of the mainstream of American politics, they reasoned, making Trump just another Republican would normalize him. Nevertheless, some at the DNC disagreed with that logic. DNC communication director Luis Miranda wrote in an internal email (also released by WikiLeaks) that it was "crazy" not to link Trump to the Republican Party and said it was problematic that the Clinton campaign wanted the DNC "to embrace the 'Republicans fleeing Trump' side, but not hold down ballot GOPers accountable."[10]

After the election, additional tensions between the DNC and the Clinton campaign surfaced as some DNC staffers expressed frustration with Brooklyn. DNC operatives felt "demoralized" and "largely marginalized or altogether neglected for most of the campaign."[11] The DNC was expected to take orders from the Clinton brass, according to staffers, and were to "be seen and not

194 Part III: The General Election

heard."[12] This sort of tension between the candidate's campaign and the national committee is not uncommon in presidential races, and some amount of finger pointing is to be expected following a shocking loss. Still, these accounts of dissention and demoralization suggest that the DNC and the Clinton campaign may not always have been on the same page, despite outward appearances.

Nevertheless, the DNC performed the role it typically performs for its presidential candidates. First and foremost, it helped support the voter mobilization efforts of the Clinton campaign and the various state coordinated campaign organizations. By the end of October, Democrats had over 5,100 paid staffers on the ground in fifteen of the most competitive states.[13]

The DNC recorded GOTV robocalls from President Obama and Vice President Biden, ran phone banks out of the DNC headquarters in Washington, and also launched a seven-figure print, digital, and radio ad buy. This paid media effort targeted primarily communities of color to encourage them to go to the polls. For instance, one radio ad, "Protecting the Progress," featured First Lady Michelle Obama talking about the legacy of her husband and ran on nationally syndicated African-American radio shows.[14] As it had in the past, the DNC largely avoided advertising on television, although it did air a GOTV ad called "Show Up."[15] In fact, the DNC aired just 475 television ads for Clinton between June 8 and October 30. According to the Wesleyan Media Project, this was down from the 7,210 ads the DNC aired on behalf of President Obama during the same period in 2012.[16]

In addition to its voter mobilization efforts, the DNC also engaged in voter protection activity. As Trump escalated his rhetoric about "rigged elections" and called on supporters to monitor voting in "certain areas," the DNC went to court to prevent the Republican National Committee (RNC) from cooperating with the Trump campaign in such efforts. A 1982 consent decree bars the RNC from undertaking "ballot security" measures that might intimidate minority voters.[17] On November 5, a federal judge rejected the DNC's motion to find the RNC in violation of the consent decree, at least prior to Election Day.[18] Still, the move by the DNC put the Republicans on notice that they would be watching closely for any activity that crossed the line into voter intimidation.

Super PAC Allies

Parties are not the only allies of presidential candidates. In the post-*Citizens United* era, Super PACs play a critical supporting role as well. In 2016, the most active Super PAC, on either side of the race, was Priorities USA Action, which spent over $130 million in support of Clinton.[19] The vast majority of this money was spent attacking Trump. However, the group's first foray into the 2016 election came in October of 2015, when it ran an ad defending Clinton in advance of her testimony to the House Select Committee on Benghazi.[20] Several days after that, it launched $1.5 million worth of digital ads, including paid content on Facebook and Twitter, attacking Republican candidates for being wrong on important issues like women's health, national security, and immigration.[21]

Priorities attacked Trump, directly, before he was even the Republican nominee. Its first ad against him, aired jointly with Planned Parenthood Votes, aired in late March. The two Super PACs hit the eventual GOP standard bearer for his statement that "There has to be some form of punishment" for women who have abortions.[22] (Trump quickly walked that declaration back, but Priorities and Planned Parenthood pounced within 24 hours.)

In April, Priorities announced that it would spend $90 million on television ads in seven battleground states and another $35 million in online advertising in those same states.[23] For at least six months, Priorities generated a relentless onslaught aimed at Trump for the many outrageous things he had said and done over the years. For much of that time, the Super PAC was spending $2 to $3 million per week on television ads.[24] Michael Beckel of the Center for Public Integrity wrote in *Time* magazine that, in August, Priorities was running an ad every 15 minutes in Florida and every 17 minutes in Ohio.[25]

Among the many memorable ads Priorities aired was one titled "Speak" that aired in May. In the ad, a variety of people, mostly women, are shown mouthing some of Trump's most controversial comments while Trump is heard saying the words. The ad ends with an announcer asking, "Does Donald Trump really speak for you?"[26] Perhaps the most powerful of Priorities' ads was "Grace." In it, the parents of a child with spina bifida express their shock at having seen Trump mock a disabled journalist. A clip from the Trump rally at which he ridiculed the reporter is shown in the ad.[27] In countless ads throughout the summer and fall, Priorities attempted to portray Trump as lacking the knowledge, experience, and temperament to be president.

Several other organizations, such as the League of Conservation Voters and Tom Steyer's NextGen Climate Action, also ran ads during the campaign, but none had as large a presence on the air as Priorities. Indeed, Priorities USA was referred to as the "Democrats' tentpole" because it was at the center of most of the pro-Clinton outside activity.[28] Some groups partnered with Priorities to extend their reach or to help Priorities perfect its targeting efforts. For instance, Women Vote!, the Super PAC of EMILY's List, joined forces with Priorities to target millennial women with their "Give 'Em Hill" digital advertising campaign.[29] Similarly, Priorities worked with two groups—the Latino Victory Project and El Super PAC Voto Latino—to air Spanish language ads in battleground states with large numbers of Latino voters.[30] The Latino Victory Fund reportedly briefed Priorities on which Spanish accents to use in particular states.[31] Even when they didn't officially partner with Priorities, most pro-Clinton groups relied on Priorities for guidance. As the *New York Times* wrote in late October, "In twice-monthly meetings at a Democratic law firm in downtown Washington, officials at Priorities have convened representatives of a dozen Super PACs and progressive

196   Part III: The General Election

organizations to carve out swing-state turf and share intelligence from organizers on the ground."[32]

Several organizations focused on mobilizing particular demographic groups. Immigrant Voters Win PAC, funded in large part by billionaire George Soros, urged immigrant communities to go to the polls for Clinton.[33] Steyer's NextGen Climate pledged $25 million to target young voters, primarily with a focus on environmental issues.[34] The billionaire environmentalist also teamed up with the AFL-CIO and three public sector unions—the American Federation of Teachers, the National Education Association, and the American Federation of State, County and Municipal Employees (AFSCME)—to form a Super PAC called For Our Future.[35] Steyer's opposition to the Keystone XL Pipeline, however, caused some in the labor movement to object to the new Super PAC. Presidents of several building trade unions complained to the president of the AFL-CIO and one accused Steyer of being "a job-killing hedge fund manager with a bag of cash" who was using For Our Future "to advance his own agenda, promote his own views, and further his own political ambitions."[36] Still, union activity in 2016 was unprecedented; through August, union spending was up 38 percent over the same period in 2012 and almost double what it had been in 2008.[37] The vast majority of this spending, of course, was in support of Clinton (or opposed to Trump).

Advertising and voter mobilization weren't the only activities outside groups undertook. Correct the Record, an initiative that was originally part of the opposition research organization American Bridge 21st Century, was reestablished as a standalone Super PAC to serve as "a pro-Clinton rapid response operation."[38] Its purpose was to counter negative information about Clinton that appeared online. Because it posted information on its website and through social media, and did not make independent expenditures for television ads, the group argued that it could legally coordinate with the Clinton campaign.[39] Many legal experts were skeptical of that argument, but Correct the Record nonetheless appeared to be in close contact with the Clinton campaign throughout the race.

Another entity that pushed back against anti-Clinton information was Shareblue. In this case, the negative information originated in the news media. According to *The New York Times*, "Shareblue's bread-and-butter content is exposing what it considers to be news coverage stacked against Mrs. Clinton."[40] It also attempted to pressure the media into covering Trump more critically. Like Correct the Record, Shareblue was founded by David Brock, a one-time critic of the Clintons who became one of their staunchest allies. It's hard to know whether Shareblue or Correct the Record had much impact. Nevertheless, they were part of a network of allies that did all they could to boost Clinton's chances of victory.

Donald Trump's Allies

If Clinton's relationship with her party was sometimes a bit rocky, Donald Trump's relationship with his appeared at times to be nonexistent. He had won the nomination of the Republican Party over the objection of most of the party establishment and, indeed, had won by running against that very establishment. It's no surprise, then, that party insiders had a hard time warming up to their presidential nominee.

The Republican Party and Joint Fundraising Committees

Trump had largely self-funded his campaign during the primaries and he suggested that he would self-fund his general election campaign as well. However, he quickly decided against paying for the fall campaign out of his own pocket. In early May, after securing enough delegates to the national convention to become the Republican nominee, Trump entered into negotiations with the RNC over a joint fundraising agreement.[41] Because the presumptive nominee had virtually no fundraising operation of his own, he would have to rely heavily on the RNC for the infrastructure required to raise the hundreds of millions of dollars that would be necessary to mount a competitive campaign.

Ultimately, Trump and the RNC agreed to form two JFCs. One—the Trump Victory Fund—was formed between the Trump campaign, the RNC, and eleven state parties. A donor could give up to $449,400 to the Trump Victory Fund.[42] The other—the Trump Make America Great Again Committee—consisted solely of the Trump campaign and the RNC.[43] Although the joint agreement was critical if Trump was going to have any chance of closing the enormous gap between his fundraising totals and Clinton's, the fact that it was formed only after the primary season had ended meant Clinton's JFC (which was formed in August of 2015) had a nine month head start over Trump's. Nevertheless, Trump claimed at the outset that the joint effort would raise $1 billion.[44]

It quickly became clear that that goal was far too optimistic, as many Republican donors appeared unwilling to give to Trump. As one news story on the Trump campaign's fundraising problems put it, "Trump is reviled by much of the donor class, who consider him as an unpredictable bomb-thrower. Many say they simply don't want to have anything to do with him."[45] To make matters worse, Trump himself was reluctant to take an active role in fundraising. According to media reports, Trump had promised the RNC chair Reince Priebus that he would personally call top donors. However, at least initially he called only three.[46] Later in the campaign, Trump would simply stop attending fundraisers; his last formal fundraiser was held on October 19, nearly three full weeks before Election Day.[47]

As a result of these problems—donor reluctance to give and candidate unwillingness to ask—the RNC began "privately encouraging major donors who are leery of Trump to steer their cash to the party instead of his campaign."[48] RNC officials denied this, of course, but *Politico* obtained fundraising documents that appear to inform potential donors about how to designate contributions to the party and not the Trump campaign.[49] Perhaps not surprisingly, the relationship

198 Part III: The General Election

between the Trump campaign and the RNC was "increasingly plagued by distrust, power struggles and strategic differences."[50] Tensions would flare several times throughout the course of the campaign.

While carrying much of the fundraising burden, the RNC was also forced to shoulder the weight of the voter contact and mobilization activity for its nominee. In the wake of the 2012 election, the party issued the "Growth and Opportunity Project" report in which it examined its shortcomings and developed a series of suggestions for how to build a national majority.[51] In addition to recommending more (and better) outreach to communities traditionally overlooked by Republicans (e.g., Hispanics), the report proposed significant investments in data collection and analytics as well as technology and digital capacity. These new resources, intended to enhance the party's voter contact and targeting abilities, reportedly cost the RNC $100 million.[52] They would be tested in the 2014 midterm elections and be fully operational for the 2016 cycle.

Still, the Trump campaign and the RNC had difficulty jelling. The nominee was skeptical that data mattered and he thought much of the party's spending was unnecessary. His argument, in essence, was "I only spent $56 million in the primary and I beat sixteen opponents—why do I need all this?"[53] Yet the Trump campaign asked the RNC to open offices in all fifty states, a move one party staffer called a "complete waste of resources" because so many of those states simply weren't going to be competitive.[54] The RNC, for its part, was annoyed at having "to extinguish the regular political brush fires set off by the unpredictable candidate."[55]

As Trump began to fall in the polls following the Democratic National Convention (and his prolonged row with the Gold Star parents of a Muslim American Army captain killed in Iraq), frustration within the Republican Party reached new levels. Priebus reportedly called Trump to warn that his campaign was collapsing and that the race would soon be over if he didn't change his behavior.[56] At the same time, more than seventy Republicans sent a letter to the RNC asking that the committee stop spending money on Trump and, instead, protect down-ballot candidates. The letter said, in part,

> We believe that Donald Trump's divisiveness, recklessness, incompetence, and record-breaking unpopularity risk turning this election into a Democratic landslide, and only the immediate shift of all available RNC resources to vulnerable Senate and House races will prevent the GOP from drowning with a Trump-emblazoned anchor around its neck ... This should not be a difficult decision, as Donald Trump's chances of being elected president are evaporating by the day.[57]

In private discussions "at the highest levels" of the party, RNC officials seriously considered doing exactly what the letter suggested. Astonishingly, the RNC also began to make the case to political insiders, including donors and journalists, that the party was doing all it could to help the nominee and that only he would be to blame should he lose.[58]

For a few weeks following Labor Day, Republican jitters began to subside. Trump and his campaign seemed to have heeded Priebus's warning, Clinton's lead had narrowed, and the race settled into a holding pattern as the presidential debates approached. On the eve of the second debate, however, a bombshell landed in the race. A 2005 *Access Hollywood* video was made public on which Trump was heard making disturbing comments that amounted to claims of sexual assault. The day after the release of this video, the RNC reportedly ordered a mail vendor working on the Trump Victory JFC to "put a hold/stop on all mail projects right now."[59] In addition, the RNC was said to be redirecting money from the presidential race to down-ballot races and leading Republican elected officials were calling on Trump to step down as the party's nominee.[60]

Trump survived, of course, and the Republicans made the best of a difficult situation. Through the late summer and fall, regardless of the distractions caused by their nominee, the RNC continued to build the robust GOTV operation they had been planning since 2013. Doing so, of course, would help down-ballot Republicans as much as it would help Trump. Although the combined efforts of the Trump campaign, the RNC, and Republican state parties would not match the organization built by the Democratic team, the Republicans would eventually have over 1,400 paid staffers in sixteen states.[61]

As part of the party's emphasis on voter mobilization, very little was spent by the RNC on television advertising for Trump. This was a decision made before the RNC knew who their nominee would be and it was a dramatic departure from past practice. In 2012, for instance, the RNC ran 242,833 ads in support of Mitt Romney between early June and the end of October.[62] During the same period in 2016, the Republican Party did not air a single ad. However, in the last week of the campaign, when the race appeared to be tightening, the RNC did spend $3 million in coordination with the Trump campaign to air ads.[63]

Some of the same difficulties the party faced in trying to assist Trump also affected the role Super PACs and other outside groups could play in 2016. Because Trump was so critical of such organizations during the primaries, and because he eschewed fundraising throughout that process, there was no entity equipped to receive large contributions when the general election began.[64] In addition, many big donors either wanted nothing to do with Trump or thought he was likely to lose and, thus, sent their money to House and Senate races.[65]

Super Pac Allies

By the end of the nomination process, two groups—Great America PAC and the Committee for American Sovereignty—were competing to become the primary pro-Trump Super PACs, but Republican donors viewed both skeptically. As a Republican insider explained to BuzzFeed,

200 Part III: The General Election

One has had top operatives convicted of felonies and is currently led by a 1980s-era figure with little to show for the last two decades. The other is led by a leader of the poorly run Ben Carson campaign and has a title that sounds weirdly nationalistic.[66]

With more established players like American Crossroads and Americans for Prosperity sitting on the sidelines in the presidential race, even those willing to support Trump had difficulty knowing where to send their money. To make matters worse, many of the more than two dozen groups claiming to back Trump that had formed by the middle of May appeared to be "scam PACs."[67]

Eventually, three groups would emerge as Trump's legitimate outside backers. One of these, Rebuilding America Now, was a Super PAC formed in June by a long-time associate of the candidate. Although the group claimed commitments of $32 million, it would spend just over $21 million in independent expenditures.[68] It was the first organization (including Trump's own campaign) to run a general election ad for Trump.[69] That ad, called "Hillary Clinton: More of the Same," was perhaps the group's most memorable ad of the campaign. It alternated between clips of a Clinton news conference in which she denied sending or receiving classified documents on the private email server she used as Secretary of State, with clips of Bill Clinton in 1998 denying he had had "sexual relations" with White House intern Monica Lewinsky.[70] Additional ads suggested that Clinton had gotten rich as a result of donations to her foundation and showed clips of a Clinton speech in India in which she said that outsourcing jobs from America cannot realistically be restricted.[71]

The second significant pro-Trump Super PAC, Future45, had been formed in 2015 as an anti-Clinton group but was relaunched in September of 2016. Most of its funding came from two families—the Ricketts, who own the Chicago Cubs, and the Adelsons, owners of Las Vegas casinos.[72] The group also had an affiliated 501(c)(4) organization, 45Committee, that could accept contributions in unlimited amounts but did not have to disclose donors' names.[73] The group's first ad in the general election, "Crook," compared Clinton to Richard Nixon; another spot, "Responsible," called the American intervention in Libya a "disaster" and placed blame solely on Clinton.[74] In the last few days of the fall campaign, Future45 aired Spanish-language ads with audio clips of Clinton proclaiming her opposition to illegal immigration. The ads use Spanish subtitles to translate Clinton's words.[75]

The last of the trio of Trump-supporting organizations was the National Rifle Association (NRA). The NRA endorsed Trump in May of 2016, five months earlier in the process than it had endorsed either Romney in 2012 or John McCain in 2008.[76] Because of that early endorsement, the Second Amendment advocacy group could begin airing ads in the summer, at time when the Trump campaign itself was not running ads. The NRA's first spot, "Stop Clinton, Vote Trump," features a former Marine who served in Benghazi, Libya. He urges voters, presumably Republicans who did not support Trump in the primaries, to do their part to defeat Clinton.[77] The ad was controversial because it appeared to have been filmed in a national cemetery, which is prohibited by government policy.[78] In one ad, "Hypocrite Hillary Leaves You Defenseless," Clinton is accused of being a hypocrite because, while she receives protection from armed guards, she allegedly doesn't believe Americans have a right to keep a gun at home for their defense.[79] The message of being left defenseless was used in another NRA ad in which a woman is depicted as having only a phone with which to defend herself against an intruder because Clinton and her likely Supreme Court nominees would have eliminated Second Amendment rights.[80] In the end, the NRA may have been Trump's staunchest outside supporter; they might even have been more steadfast than the nominee's own national party committee.

Guccifer 2.0

This chapter has been about the campaign activity of actors who are outside the campaign organizations of the presidential nominees. Typically, these entities are the party committees and various interest groups, non-profit organizations, PACs, and Super PACs. In 2016, an unusual actor, one residing very far outside the candidates' campaigns, became involved in the election. In June, DNC officials announced that hackers had compromised the party's computer network. According to the cyber security firm the DNC hired to investigate, the perpetrators were Russian government hackers.[81] The next day, someone using the moniker "Guccifer 2.0" claimed credit for the attack.[82] When WikiLeaks released its first batch of hacked DNC emails in July, which proved embarrassing to the party and the Clinton campaign and led to the resignation of the DNC chair on the eve of the Democratic National Convention, American intelligence agencies informed the White House that they had "high confidence" that the source of those emails was, indeed, the Russian government. Investigators reportedly had come to believe that Guccifer 2.0 "was an agent of the G.R.U., Russia's military intelligence service."[83]

On October 7, the Obama administration released a statement accusing the Russian government of hacking the DNC, among other institutions and individuals. The statement read, in part, "We believe, based on the scope and sensitivity of these efforts, that only Russia's senior-most officials could have authorized these activities."[84] Ordinarily, of course, such a statement would have received an enormous amount of media attention. However, the incendiary *Access Hollywood* video was also released on October 7.

For his part, Trump denied that there was evidence of Russian involvement in the DNC hacks. During the first presidential debate, Trump suggested the hacker could just as easily have been Chinese or "somebody sitting on their bed that weighs 400 pounds."[85] At one point, he had even seemed to encourage the Russians to snoop around for Clinton's infamous 30,000 deleted emails.[86]

202 Part III: The General Election

Following the election, the *Washington Post* reported that the Central Intelligence Agency (CIA) had "concluded in a secret assessment that Russia intervened in the 2016 election to help Donald Trump win the presidency, rather than just to undermine confidence in the U.S. electoral system."[87] In initial reporting, the Federal Bureau of Investigation (FBI) had not reached the same conclusion.[88] Eventually, however, both the FBI and the Director of National Intelligence were reported to be in agreement with the CIA's assessment.[89] Trump, perhaps not surprisingly, continued to voice skepticism about not only Russia's intentions but their very involvement in the hacking operation.

There is reason to doubt that Russian interference in the presidential election had an effect on the outcome of the election. The email revelations were more of an embarrassment to the DNC and its leadership than to the Clinton campaign and nothing scandalous was revealed about Clinton herself. Nevertheless, to the extent that it cast a pall on the Clinton campaign, or damaged Clinton's standing with Sanders supporters who might have become, as a result, less likely to vote for Clinton, Russia's actions may have mattered at least at the margins. Regardless of its effect on the results, interference in the election by a foreign (and not altogether friendly) government is disturbing and should be alarming to all Americans.

Conclusion

How much did the outside activity in the 2016 presidential campaign matter? On the one hand, we could reasonably conclude that it hardly mattered at all. Clinton and her allies in the Democratic Party had a much more extensive field operation than did team Trump. In addition, Clinton had a 2-to-1 advantage over Trump in outside money.[90] From early June to October 30, Clinton outside groups ran 90,032 television commercials compared to just 30,636 from Trump's allies.[91] Furthermore, Clinton's message was reinforced by, for the most part, just one outside voice—Priorities USA. Trump's outside reinforcement was split between three groups—Rebuilding American Now, Future45, and the NRA. If nothing else, this gave Clinton the advantage of consistency. Yet Trump was able to win the election. Perhaps his appeal to voters was strong enough to overcome the disadvantages he faced in terms of traditional campaign activity.

On the other hand, it could well be the case that Trump would have lost without the RNC's efforts. Trump had very little campaign infrastructure of his own and took an extraordinarily unconventional approach to running for office. Indeed, his campaign spent more on "Make America Great Again" hats than on polling.[92] Without the RNC's sophisticated voter mobilization operation, Trump might have fallen short in Wisconsin, Michigan, and Pennsylvania, which would have meant defeat rather than victory in the Electoral College.

It's also worth mentioning that Clinton won the popular vote by nearly 3 million votes. Perhaps the campaign support she received from the party and her outside allies helped her secure that consolation prize. Or perhaps she would have

Chapter 10: Outside Voices **203**

lost by an even greater margin in Wisconsin, Michigan, and Pennsylvania had she not had as robust a network of campaign support. We cannot conclude that outside efforts on Clinton's behalf were futile simply because she did not become president.

Measuring campaign effects is always difficult. Given the unusual nature of the 2016 presidential election, trying to determine how much an effect outside actors had on the outcome seems especially hard. If we were to speculate, however, it does seem likely that the RNC's role in the campaign was critical for Trump's success. The selection of RNC Chairman Reince Priebus as White House chief of staff by the President-elect may be a tacit acknowledgment of this conclusion.

Notes

1 Michael D. Shear and Matthew Rosenberg, "Released Emails Suggest the D.N.C. Derided the Sanders Campaign," *New York Times*, July 22, 2016, www.nytimes.com/2016/07/23/us/politics/dnc-emails-sanders-clinton.html?_r=0 (accessed December 4, 2016).

2 Anne Gearan, Philip Rucker, and Abby Phillip, "DNC Chairwoman Will Resign in Aftermath of Committee Email Controversy," *Washington Post*, July 24, 2016, www.washingtonpost.com/politics/hacked-emails-cast-doubt-on-hopes-for-party-unity-at-democratic-convention/2016/07/24/a446c260-51a9-11e6-b7de-dfe509430c39_story.html?utm_term=.9dd1b4aed543 (accessed December 6, 2016).

3 Edward-Isaac Dovere and Gabriel Debenedetti, "DNC Announces Fundraising Agreement with Clinton Campaign," *Politico*, August 27, 2016, www.politico.com/story/2015/08/dnc-democratic-committee-hillary-clinton-fundraising-agreement-2016-121813 (accessed December 6, 2016).

4 Kenneth P. Vogel and Isaac Arnsdorf, "Clinton Fundraising Leaves Little for State Parties," *Politico*, May 2, 2016, www.politico.com/story/2016/04/clinton-fundraising-leaves-little-for-state-parties-222670 (accessed December 4, 2016); Matea Gold, "Here's How a Wealthy Trump Supporter Could Give $783,400 to Support His Campaign and the RNC," *Washington Post*, May 19, 2016, www.washingtonpost.com/news/post-politics/wp/2016/05/19/heres-how-a-wealthy-trump-supporter-could-give-783400-to-support-his-campaign-and-the-rnc/?utm_term=.4eac0f717a5a (accessed December 12, 2016).

5 Clare Foran, "Did the Hillary Victory Fund Break the Law?" *The Atlantic*, April 19, 2016, www.theatlantic.com/politics/archive/2016/04/bernie-sanders-hillary-clinton-dnc/478875/ (accessed December 4, 2016).

6 Kenneth P. Vogel and Isaac Arnsdorf, "DNC Sought to Hide Details of Clinton Funding Deal," *Politico*, July 26, 2016, www.politico.com/story/2016/07/dnc-leak-clinton-team-deflected-state-cash-concerns-226191 (accessed December 4, 2016).

7 Ken Thomas, "Eyeing Senate, Clinton Directing Money to 2016 Battlegrounds," Associated Press, May 19, 2016, http://bigstory.ap.org/article/5b30b97a7406469ca28 cf04a14089a4e/eyeing-senate-clinton-directing-money-2016-battlegrounds (accessed December 6, 2016).

8 Shane Goldmacher and Gabriel Debenedetti, "Inside Clinton's Fragile Relationship with Fellow Democrats," *Politico*, October 13, 2016, www.politico.com/story/2016/10/hillary-clinton-democrats-downballot-229718 (accessed December 6, 2016).

204 Part III: The General Election

9 Ibid.

10 Ibid.

11 David Catanese, "DNC Staff: Arrogance Cost Clinton the Election," *U.S. News and World Report*, November 11, 2016, www.usnews.com/news/the-run-2016/articles/2016-11-11/dnc-staff-arrogance-cost-hillary-clinton-the-election-vs-donald-trump (accessed December 2, 2016).

12 Ibid.

13 Reid Wilson and Joe DiSipio, "Clinton Holds Huge Ground Game Advantage Over Team Trump," *The Hill*, October 22, 2016, http://thehill.com/campaign/302231-clinton-holds-huge-ground-game-advantage-over-team-trump (accessed October 25, 2016).

14 Darren Sand and Adrian Carrasquillo, "Democratic Party Targets Minority Coalition With New Michelle Obama Ad," *BuzzFeed News*, October 3, 2016, www.buzzfeed.com/darrensands/democratic-party-targets-minority-coalition-with-new-michell?utm_term=.nb8jK2yZ6#.wy1yO3xVd (accessed December 6, 2016).

15 Hillary for America, "Show Up," www.youtube.com/watch?v=1p6Y4_6iVts&feature=youtu.be (accessed December 6, 2016).

16 Wesleyan Media Project, "Clinton Crushes Trump 3:1 in Air War," November 3, 2016, http://mediaproject.wesleyan.edu/releases/nov-2016/ (accessed December 4, 2016).

17 Matt Friedman, "Democrats: RNC Violating Anti-voter Intimidation Agreement," *Politico*, October 27, 2016, www.politico.com/story/2016/10/voter-intimidation-democrats-rnc-230352 (accessed December 8, 2016).

18 "Federal Judge Rejects Democrats' Voter Intimidation Arguments Against RNC," Associated Press, November 5, 2016, www.chicagotribune.com/news/nationworld/politics/ct-ruling-voter-intimidation-dnc-rnc-20161105-story.html (accessed December 4, 2016).

19 Center for Responsive Politics, "Priorities USA Action: Independent Expenditures," [n.d.], www.opensecrets.org/pacs/indexpend.php?strID=C00495861&cycle=2016 (accessed December 8, 2016).

20 Ben Kamisar, "Super-PAC Ad Defends Clinton Ahead of Benghazi Testimony," *The Hill*, October 21, 2015, http://origin-nyi.thehill.com/blogs/ballot-box/presidential-races/257574-super-pac-ad-defends-clinton-ahead-of-benghazi-testimony (accessed December 8, 2016).

21 Annie Karni, "Pro-Clinton Super PAC Launches Biggest Ad Buy Yet," *Politico*, October 27, 2015, www.politico.com/story/2015/10/priorities-usa-super-pac-ad-attacks-republicans-215183 (accessed December 8, 2016).

22 Amy Chozick, "Pro-Hillary Clinton Groups Plan First Ad Against Donald Trump," *The New York Times*, March 31, 2016, www.nytimes.com/politics/first-draft/2016/03/31/pro-hillary-clinton-groups-plan-first-ad-against-donald-trump/?_r=0 (accessed December 10, 2016).

23 Gabriel Debenedetti, "Pro-Clinton Super PAC Ups Swing State Ad Campaign to $90 Million," *Politico*, April 15, 2016, www.politico.com/story/2016/04/hillary-clinton-super-pac-backing-swing-state-ad-spending-221974 (accessed December 8, 2016); Ed O'Keefe, "Hillary Clinton's Super PAC Planning Multimillion-dollar Online Ad Buy," *Washington Post*, April 18, 2016, www.washingtonpost.com/news/

Chapter 10: Outside Voices **205**

post-politics/wp/2016/04/18/hillary-clintons-super-pac-planning-multimillion-dollar-online-ad-buy/?utm_term=.63d02a702c7b (accessed December 8, 2016).

24 John McCormick, "Clinton Spending Big on Olympics Ads With Trump on Sidelines," *Bloomberg Politics*, August 5, 2016, www.bloomberg.com/politics/articles/2016-08-05/clinton-spending-big-on-olympics-ads-with-trump-on-sidelines (accessed December 8, 2016).

25 Michael Beckel, "Meet the Super PAC Airing an Ad in Florida Every 15 Minutes," *Time*, August 24, 2016, http://time.com/4464921/priorities-usa-campaign-ads/ (accessed December 10, 2016).

26 Amy Chozick and Nick Corasaniti, "Hillary Clinton 'Super PAC' to Air First Attack Ads Aimed at Donald Trump," *New York Times*, May 17, 2016, www.nytimes.com/2016/05/18/us/politics/ad-super-pac-clinton-trump.html (accessed December 10, 2016).

27 Nick Corasaniti, "'Super PAC' Highlights Donald Trump's Mockery of Disabled Journalist." *New York Times*, June 6, 2016, www.nytimes.com/2016/06/07/us/politics/super-pac-highlights-donald-trumps-mockery-of-disabled-journalist.html (accessed December 10, 2016).

28 Nicholas Confessore and Rachel Shorey, "Outside Money Favors Hillary Clinton at a 2-to-1 Rate Over Donald Trump," *New York Times*, October 22, 2016, www.nytimes.com/2016/10/23/us/politics/clinton-trump-gop-money.html (accessed December 11, 2016).

29 Abby Phillip, "Pro-Clinton Groups Launch New Ads Targeted at Female Millennials," *Washington Post*, August 22, 2016, www.washingtonpost.com/politics/pro-clinton-groups-launch-new-ads-targeted-at-millennial-women/2016/08/21/4bd2a638-6740-11e6-8b27-bb8ba39497a2_story.html?utm_term=.6c1f62caae34 (accessed December 11, 2016).

30 Ed O'Keefe, "Clinton Super PAC Is Going On the Air in Spanish in Three Key States," *Washington Post*, September 7, 2016, www.washingtonpost.com/news/post-politics/wp/2016/09/07/clinton-super-pac-is-going-on-the-air-in-spanish-in-three-key-states/?utm_term=.8f1d919f982c (accessed December 11, 2016).

31 Confessore and Shorey, "Outside Money Favors Hillary Clinton at a 2-to-1 Rate Over Donald Trump."

32 Ibid.

33 Nicholas Confessore and Julia Preston, "Soros and Other Liberal Donors to Fund Bid to Spur Latino Voters," *New York Times*, March 10, 2016, www.nytimes.com/2016/03/10/us/politics/george-soros-and-other-liberal-donors-to-fund-bid-to-spur-latino-voters.html (accessed December 11, 2016).

34 Coral Davenport, "Billionaire Environmentalist to Spend $25 Million to Turn Out Young Voters," *New York Times*, April 25, 2016, www.nytimes.com/2016/04/26/us/politics/thomas-steyer-nextgen-climate-change-voters.html (accessed December 11, 2016).

35 Body Mullins and Melanie Trottman, "Some Big Democratic Party Backers to Pool Spending to Support Hillary Clinton and Others," *The Wall Street Journal*, May 12, 2016,www.wsj.com/articles/some-big-democratic-party-backers-to-pool-spending-1463083688 (accessed December 11, 2016).

206 Part III: The General Election

36 Matea Gold, "Building Trade Unions Denounce Labor Partnership with Billionaire Environmentalist Tom Steyer," *Washington Post*, May 16, 2016, www.washingtonpost. com/news/post-politics/wp/2016/05/16/building-trade-unions-denounce-labor-partnership-with-billionaire-environmentalist-tom-steyer/?utm_term=.f90c263adab0 (accessed December 11, 2016).

37 Brody Mullins, Rebecca Ballhaus, and Michelle Hackman, "Big Labor Unions Step Up Presidential-Election Spending," *Wall Street Journal*, October 18, 2016, www.wsj. com/articles/big-labor-unions-step-up-presidential-election-spending-1476783002 (accessed December 11, 2016).

38 Matea Gold, "How a Super PAC Plans to Coordinate Directly with Hillary Clinton's Campaign," *Washington Post*, May 12, 2015, www.washingtonpost.com/news/post-politics/wp/2015/05/12/how-a-super-pac-plans-to-coordinate-directly-with-hillary-clintons-campaign/?utm_term=.594cd46dcfe7 (accessed December 11, 2016).

39 Ibid.

40 Jason Horowitz, "Inside Hillary Clinton's Outrage Machine, Allies Push the Buttons," *New York Times*, September 22, 2016, www.nytimes.com/2016/09/23/us/politics/hillary-clinton-media-david-brock.html (accessed December 11, 2016).

41 Maggie Haberman, Ashley Parker, and Nick Corasaniti, "Donald Trump, in Switch, Turns to Republican Party for Fund-Raising Help," *New York Times*, May 9, 2016, www.nytimes.com/2016/05/10/us/politics/donald-trump-campaign.html (accessed December 12, 2016).

42 Matea Gold, "Donors Can Give Nearly $500,000 to New Joint Fundraising Effort Between Trump and RNC," *Washington Post*, May 17, 2016, www.washingtonpost. com/news/post-politics/wp/2016/05/17/donors-can-give-nearly-500000-to-new-joint-fundraising-effort-between-trump-and-rnc/?utm_term=.871405d9b60a (accessed December 12, 2016).

43 Ibid.

44 Haberman, Parker, and Corasaniti, "Donald Trump, in Switch, Turns to Republican Party for Fund-Raising Help."

45 Alex Isenstadt, "Trump's Fundraisers See No Chance of Hitting $1 Billion," *Politico*, June 8, 2016, www.politico.com/story/2016/06/donald-trump-donors-billion-224080 (accessed December 14, 2016).

46 Kenneth P. Vogel, Eli Stokols, and Alex Isenstadt, "Trump's Relationship with RNC Sours," *Politico*, June 15, 2016, www.politico.com/story/2016/06/donald-trump-republican-national-committee-224403 (accessed December 13, 2016).

47 Matea Gold, "Trump Stops Holding High-dollar Fundraisers That Were Raising Big Cash for the GOP," *Washington Post*, October 25, 2016, www.washingtonpost.com/news/post-politics/wp/2016/10/25/trump-halts-big-money-fundraising-cutting-off-cash-to-the-party/?utm_term=.bbe9037acfcf (accessed December 13, 2016).

48 Kenneth P. Vogel and Alex Isenstadt, "RNC fundraisers hedge on Trump," *Politico*, June 23, 2016, www.politico.com/story/2016/06/rnc-raising-big-moneybut-not-for-trump-224700 (accessed December 13, 2016).

49 Ibid.

50 Vogel, Stokols, and Isenstadt, "Trump's Relationship with RNC Sours."

Chapter 10: Outside Voices **207**

51 Republican National Committee, "Growth and Opportunity Project," 2013, http:// goproject.gop.com/rnc_growth_opportunity_book_2013.pdf (accessed December 13, 2016).

52 David M. Drucker, "RNC to Spend $100m to Get Out Vote," *Washington Examiner*, August 28, 2014, www.washingtonexaminer.com/rnc-to-spend-100m-to-get-out-vote/article/2552530 (accessed December 13, 2016).

53 Matea Gold, "Trump Doesn't Have a National Campaign. So the GOP Is Trying to Run One For Him," *Washington Post*, June 10, 2016, www.washingtonpost.com/politics/trump-doesnt-have-a-national-campaign-so-the-gop-is-trying-to-run-one-for-him/2016/06/09/a9e1f488-2df0-11e6-9b37-42985f6a265c_story.html (accessed December 13, 2016).

54 Jake Sherman, Anna Palmer, and Daniel Lippman, "Playbook," *Politico*, August 12, 2016, www.politico.com/tipsheets/playbook/2016/08/new-narrative-trump-republicans-concede-they-could-lose-election-rnc-to-open-offices-in-all-50-states-in-move-to-help-trump-photos-of-bernies-new-lakefront-home-bday-kelley-mccormick-215838 (accessed December 13, 2016).

55 Ibid.

56 Zeke J. Miller, "Exclusive: The Republican Party's Chairman's Warning to Donald Trump," *Time*, August 11, 2016, http://time.com/4447527/donald-trump-republican-national-committee/ (accessed December 13, 2016).

57 Anna Palmer, "Dozens of Republicans to Urge RNC to Cut Off Funds for Trump," *Politico*, August 11, 2016, www.politico.com/story/2016/08/republicans-urge-rnc-cut-funds-trump-226918 (accessed December 13, 2016).

58 Eli Stokols and Kenneth P. Vogel, "RNC Considers Cutting Cash to Trump," *Politico*, August 14, 2016, www.politico.com/story/2016/08/donald-trump-rnc-support-226987 (accessed December 13, 2016).

59 Alex Isenstadt, "RNC Halts Victory Project Work for Trump," *Politico*, October 8, 2016, www.politico.com/story/2016/10/rnc-halts-all-victory-project-work-for-trump-229363 (accessed December 14, 2016).

60 Evelyn Rupert and Ben Kamisar, "Report: RNC Redirecting Funds Away From Trump," *The Hill*, October 8, 2016, http://thehill.com/blogs/blog-briefing-room/news/300048-report-rnc-redirecting-funds-away-from-trump (accessed December 14, 2016).

61 Wilson and DiSipio, "Clinton Holds Huge Ground Game Advantage Over Team Trump."

62 Wesleyan Media Project, "Clinton Crushes Trump 3:1 in Air War."

63 Kenneth P. Vogel, "RNC Starts Spending on Trump TV Ads," *Politico*, November 2, 2016, www.politico.com/story/2016/11/rnc-trump-tv-ads-230632 (accessed December 14, 2016).

64 Matea Gold, "Billionaires Lining Up for Trump Aren't Sure Where to Send Their Money," *Washington Post*, May 16, 2016, www.washingtonpost.com/politics/billionaires-lining-up-for-trump-arent-sure-where-to-send-their-money/2016/05/15/aa7896e2-1953-11e6-9e16-2e5a123aac62_story.html?utm_term=.d77bc7fbaed0 (accessed December 14, 2016).

65 Nick Corasaniti and Ashley Parker, "G.O.P. Donors Shift Focus From Top of Ticket to Senate Races," *New York Times*, May 20, 2016, www.nytimes.com/2016/05/21/

208 Part III: The General Election

us/politics/republican-donors-trump-senate-house.html (accessed December 14, 2016).

66 Tarini Parti and Rosie Gray, "Donald Trump's Dysfunctional Super PAC Family," *BuzzFeed*, May 24, 2016, www.buzzfeed.com/tariniparti/donald-trumps-dysfunctional-super-pac-family?utm_term=.xbnE9kLA8#.iqJJobM0W (accessed December 14, 2016).

67 Isaac Arnsdorf and Kenneth P. Vogel, "Trump Backers Face 'Scam PAC' Charges," *Politico*, May 16, 2016, www.politico.com/story/2016/05/scammers-feast-of-trump-fundraising-disarray-223141 (accessed December 14, 2016).

68 Center for Responsive Politics, "Rebuilding America Now: Independent Expenditures," www.opensecrets.org/pacs/indexpend.php?strID=C00618876&cycle=2016 (accessed December 14, 2016).

69 Maggie Haberman and Ashley Parker, "New 'Super PAC' Backing Donald Trump Hires Strategist Once Critical of Him," *New York Times*, June 5, 2016, www.nytimes.com/2016/06/06/us/politics/trump-super-pac-alex-castellanos.html (accessed December 14, 2016).

70 Rebuilding America Now, "Hillary Clinton: More of the Same," www.youtube.com/watch?v=9t54Ly_mvuk (accessed December 14, 2016).

71 Rebuilding America Now, "Dead Broke," www.youtube.com/watch?v=4mRwXTMcQS8 (accessed December 14, 2016); and "Outsourcing," www.youtube.com/watch?v=IL-WRErxYRI (accessed December 14, 2016).

72 Theodore Schleifer, "Ricketts, Adelson Families Compare Clinton to Nixon in First Super PAC Ad," *CNN*, September 23, 2016, www.cnn.com/2016/09/23/politics/future-45-first-ad/ (accessed December 14, 2016).

73 Kenneth P. Vogel, "Secret Money to Boost Trump," *Politico*, September 28, 2016, www.politico.com/story/2016/09/secret-money-to-boost-trump-228817 (accessed December 14, 2016).

74 Future45, "Crook," www.youtube.com/watch?v=ztmF73bri_s (accessed December 14, 2016); and "Responsible," www.youtube.com/watch?v=haRxZkne3dg (accessed December 14, 2016).

75 Theodore Schleifer, "Adelson-backed Super PAC Attacks Clinton in Spanish-language Ads," *CNN*, November 1, 2016, www.cnn.com/2016/11/01/politics/future45-spanish-language-ads/ (accessed December 14, 2016).

76 Sarah Wheaton, "NRA Facing Member Backlash Over Trump Endorsement," *Politico*, May 21, 2016, www.politico.com/story/2016/05/nra-donald-trump-endorsement-backlash-223442 (accessed December 14, 2016).

77 NRA Political Victory Fund, "Stop Clinton, Vote Trump," www.youtube.com/watch?v=SIl20jItjHY (accessed December 14, 2016).

78 Justin Fishel and Veronica Stracqualursi, "NRA's Pro-Trump Ad Appears Filmed in National Cemetery Despite Restrictions," *ABC News*, June 29, 2016, http://abcnews.go.com/US/nra-ad-supporting-donald-trump-appears-filmed-inside/story?id=40227403 (accessed December 14, 2016).

79 NRA Political Victory Fund, "Hypocrite Hillary Leaves You Defenseless," www.youtube.com/watch?v=Wxqx5CjfrgE (accessed December 14, 2016).

80 NRA Political Victory Fund, "Don't Let Hillary Clinton Leave you Defenseless," www.youtube.com/watch?v=hPM8e_DauUw (accessed December 14, 2016).

Chapter 10: Outside Voices **209**

81 Ellen Nakashima, "Russian Government Hackers Penetrated DNC, Stole Opposition Research on Trump," *Washington Post*, June 14, 2016, www.washingtonpost.com/world/national-security/russian-government-hackers-penetrated-dnc-stole-opposition-research-on-trump/2016/06/14/cf006cb4-316e-11e6-8ff7-7b6c1998b7a0_story.html?utm_term=.cbd038fa06f6 (accessed December 14, 2016).

82 Guccifer 2.0, "Guccifer 2.0 DNC's Servers Hacked By a Lone Hacker," June 15, 2016, https://guccifer2.wordpress.com/page/3/ (accessed December 14, 2016).

83 David E. Sanger and Eric Schmitt, "Spy Agency Consensus Grows That Russia Hacked D.N.C," *New York Times*, July 26, 2016, www.nytimes.com/2016/07/27/us/politics/spy-agency-consensus-grows-that-russia-hacked-dnc.html (accessed December 14, 2016).

84 David E. Sanger and Charlie Savage, "U.S. Says Russia Directed Hacks to Influence Elections," *New York Times*, October 7, 2016, www.nytimes.com/2016/10/08/us/politics/us-formally-accuses-russia-of-stealing-dnc-emails.html (accessed December 14, 2016).

85 Ibid.

86 Ashley Parker and David E. Sanger, "Donald Trump Calls on Russia to Find Hillary Clinton's Missing Emails," *New York Times*, July 27, 2016, www.nytimes.com/2016/07/28/us/politics/donald-trump-russia-clinton-emails.html (accessed December 15, 2016).

87 Adam Entous, Ellen Nakashima, and Greg Miller, "Secret CIA Assessment Says Russia Was Trying to Help Trump Win White House," *Washington Post*, December 9, 2016, www.washingtonpost.com/world/national-security/obama-orders-review-of-russian-hacking-during-presidential-campaign/2016/12/09/31d6b300-be2a-11e6-94ac-3d324840106c_story.html?utm_term=.27354d3d14b7 (accessed December 15, 2016).

88 Ellen Nakashima and Adam Entous, "FBI and CIA Give Differing Accounts to Lawmakers on Russia's Motives in 2016 Hacks," *Washington Post*, December 10, 2016 www.washingtonpost.com/world/national-security/fbi-and-cia-give-differing-accounts-to-lawmakers-on-russias-motives-in-2016-hacks/2016/12/10/c6dfadfa-bef0-11e6-94ac-3d324840106c_story.html?utm_term=.fd0d65dd7e17 (accessed December 15, 2016).

89 Adam Entous and Ellen Nakashima, "FBI in Agreement with CIA that Russia Aimed to Help Trump Win White House," *Washington Post*, December 16, 2016, www.washingtonpost.com/politics/clinton-blames-putins-personal-grudge-against-her-for-election-interference/2016/12/16/12f36250-c3be-11e6-8422-eac61c0ef74d_story.html?hpid=hp_hp-top-table-main_clintonrussia-0755pm%3Ahomepage%2Fstory&utm_term=.ee841c67bbd7 (accessed December 16, 2016).

90 Nicholas Confessore and Rachel Shorey, "Outside Money Favors Hillary Clinton at a 2-to-1 Rate Over Donald Trump," *New York Times*, October 22, 2016, www.nytimes.com/2016/10/23/us/politics/clinton-trump-gop-money.html (accessed December 15, 2016).

91 Wesleyan Media Project, "Clinton Crushes Trump 3:1 in Air War."

92 Philip Bump, "Donald Trump's Campaign Has Spent More on Hats Than on Polling," *Washington Post*, October 25, 2016, www.washingtonpost.com/news/the-fix/wp/2016/10/25/donald-trumps-campaign-has-spent-more-on-hats-than-on-polling/?utm_term=.b1c7cb5fba79 (accessed December 15, 2016).

11

REPUBLICAN STRATEGY AND TACTICS DURING THE GENERAL ELECTION

Katie Packer

On the morning of July 29, 2016 the world seemed to be Hillary Clinton's oyster. She had emerged from the Democratic National Convention victorious as the first female, major party nominee in history, the first former First Lady of the United States to run for president, and her party's convention had met with rave reviews.

Aftermath of the Nominating Conventions

The week had gotten off to a rocky start with Democratic National Committee leaks which had shown staff and leadership at the DNC actively putting their fingers on the scale to ensure Clinton's primary victory over Bernie Sanders. The ensuing scandal had forced the resignation of DNC chairwoman Debbie Wasserman Schultz and threatened to cast a pall over the convention and the message that the Clinton campaign was attempting to project: a message of hope and inclusion for all. Instead it was further reminder to voters that Clinton and her team felt that the rules didn't apply to them and that they could rig things to benefit them.

But the swift placement of Donna Brazile, a former aide to Al Gore and a respected Democrat operative, at the helm of the DNC did much to quell the uproar and the convention continued and was met with rave reviews. Speeches by President Obama and First Lady Michelle Obama were highlights, along with speeches by former president and husband of the nominee, Bill Clinton. The candidate herself gave a stirring speech intending to unite the party and lift the nation as she referenced the 2016 election as "a moment of reckoning." But perhaps the most memorable speech had come from Dr. Khizr Khan, the father of Muslim U.S. soldier Captain Humayun Khan who was killed in combat. He

Chapter 11: Republican Strategy **211**

spoke with his wife, Ghazala Khan, standing silently by his side. His words asking Donald Trump if he "had ever read the Constitution" were harsh but perhaps the most powerful sentence he uttered was "you have sacrificed nothing and no one." They were powerful words from a very sympathetic individual and Donald Trump could not resist the urge to respond by attacking him. It was political manna from heaven for the Clinton campaign.

Donald Trump was an unconventional politician to say the least. He ran his primary campaign as if it was the ultimate reality TV show: bullying and belittling his opponents, mocking the establishment, attacking the media and always, *always* playing to the crowds. He had been underestimated repeatedly by those who first thought he wouldn't enter the race, then thought he wouldn't stick it out, then thought he certainly wouldn't win the primaries. But time and time again he had surprised his critics (this author included) and the country as a whole by speaking to voters in a language few politicians could understand, let alone speak. He spoke to the silliness of Washington, the ridiculous political correctness that had overtaken our culture, the anxiety of economic despair that many working Americans were feeling, and promised to "Make America Great Again." For many Americans he seemed like the political savior they had been waiting for and many others saw him as a lottery ticket: not likely to win or to make any real difference if he did, but it was worth a shot. He had won the most divisive primary in recent memory. He received more votes than any Republican candidate in history, 13.3 million, but 16 million votes were cast for some other primary opponent.[1] He still had not united the Republican party behind his candidacy, but he had come a long way. A final effort to deny him the nomination on the floor of the GOP convention had been quashed and he had emerged from the convention with a bounce that brought him to a dead heat with Clinton.[2]

There were still many Republican establishment holdouts who were appalled by Trump and refused to support him, including both Presidents Bush, candidates Jeb Bush and John Kasich, and former governor and 2012 GOP standard bearer, Mitt Romney. But his choice of Indiana governor Mike Pence had done much to reassure establishment and conservative Republicans that there would be some balance at the top and the warm embrace by RNC chairman Reince Priebus had helped to bring the Republican National Committee and its donors to the Trump camp with increasing enthusiasm.

But the wild card continued to be the candidate. And many questions loomed large over the Republican Party: Could the candidate control his impulse to say crude and crass things? Could the candidate rein in his Twitter habit which put his erratic thinking on display to the world? Could his campaign develop into the kind of professional operation that would be necessary to win a national election or would it continue to be chaotic and full of infighting as it had been in the primary? What skeletons were lurking in Trump's closet that had not yet been made public? Did the candidate believe any of the things he was saying or was it all just a big show?

212 Part III: The General Election

As the DNC convention wrapped up, the Clinton campaign seemed to be on a glide path. There was no reason to think that the convention wouldn't produce a bump that would once again propel Clinton to the lead. Clinton was every bit as disciplined as Trump was erratic. As long as Democrats followed their playbook and turned out their voters, Trump would lose this election all on his own.

Response to Khizr Khan

His response to Mr. Khan was a perfect example of this, even better than the Clinton campaign had hoped. First he dismissed it to George Stephanopoulos of ABC News saying, "Who wrote that? Hillary's script writers?"[3] Then he seemed to characterize his sacrifices in business as somehow on par with the sacrifices of those who have lost loved ones in service to our country. Then he seemed to attack Mrs. Khan for not speaking, implying that, as a Muslim woman, she had not been permitted to speak.

The story wouldn't go away. Not because the media or the Clinton campaign held on, but because Trump and some of his senior spokesmen couldn't seem to stop stoking the story. Republicans across the country did a collective eye roll and thought "buckle up, this is going to be a loooong three months."

As August progressed Trump seemed unable to get away from Khan and his story. And Republicans across the country, up and down the ballot, were forced to answer for Trump's comments, including Senator John McCain who was up for re-election, Senate Majority Leader Mitch McConnell, and Speaker of the House Paul Ryan, who denounced them strongly, saying

> As I have said on numerous occasions, a religious test for entering our country is not reflective of these fundamental values. I reject it. Many Muslim Americans have served valiantly in our military and made the ultimate sacrifice. Captain Khan was one such brave example.[4]

Paul Manafort

Republicans believed that this was what the fall campaign was going to look like every week: Trump making outrageous comments and Republicans having to defend them or, at a minimum, respond to them. The other story that was beginning to unfold in August involved Paul Manafort, Trump's second campaign manager. Manafort had been brought into the campaign in the spring in an effort to professionalize the operation. He took the reins from Corey Lewandowski, a campaign operative with no national experience and little respect from within the political ranks, who seemed to ride the wave of the campaign led by Trump, as opposed to actually managing the campaign or the candidate. Manafort had been brought in at the urging of the Trump family and some Trump loyalists, like Rudy Giuliani, who believed that Trump could win, but needed a pro to take

Chapter 11: Republican Strategy **213**

the campaign to the next level. Manafort's reputation paved the way for other professional operatives, who until then were reticent to join an organization with Lewandowski at the helm, to join the campaign. Things changed dramatically with Manafort running the show. The campaign's relationship with the media improved, coordination with the RNC began humming along, and the convention came together. But hanging over Manafort was his involvement in Ukraine with a pro-Russia/pro-Putin political party. During the platform committee meetings prior to the RNC convention, when a member of the committee proposed language calling for the U.S. to provide weapons to the Ukrainian government to oppose Russia-backed separatists, the Trump forces showed unusual interest. The language was weakened considerably and many began asking questions as to why. A giant spotlight was trained on Manafort.

As August wore on, more and more questions began emerging about Manafort's ties to Putin and Russia. This was a sensitive issue because Trump himself had come under criticism for being too cozy with Russian President Vladimir Putin. At the same time there was a growing feeling that Manafort was trying to force Trump into the role of a much more traditional candidate and was no longer letting "Trump be Trump." By the third week in August the writing was on the wall: Manafort was out. In place of Manafort, Trump elevated pollster Kellyanne Conway, who had previously run a Super PAC attacking Trump, to the role of campaign manager. He also added to the team conservative activist David Bossie and Breitbart News CEO Stephen Bannon, a controversial figure who was viewed by many as too cozy with the white nationalist/alt-right movement. While Conway was viewed as a calming influence within the campaign, Bossie and Bannon were seen as individuals who stoked the candidate's worst instincts. None were viewed as voices that could smooth the rocky relationship Trump had with other Republican leaders. That role was left entirely to RNC chairman Reince Priebus.

Beginning of the General Election

The Alt-Right and "Deplorables"

As the Trump campaign rode a roller coaster from one bad news story to the next, the Clinton campaign seemed to be humming along with little drama, making little news. The Clinton team desperately tried to insert its campaign into news cycles which were dominated by Trump's antics at rallies and on Twitter, but couldn't seem to make news that was compelling to the media which was desperate to win the ratings/clicks game. Clinton was still dogged by stories about her private email server and whether she had compromised national security, which had hovered over her for over a year, along with stories about improper overlap between the Clinton Foundation and her State Department role which were a constant headache. But none of these stories had the kind of

214 Part III: The General Election

"newsy" quality to them that would catapult them to the top of cable news headers on a daily basis by that point in the campaign.

Clinton consistently led in national and battleground state polls, so her team seemed to decide on a strategy of keeping their heads down, raising tons of money in order to dominate the airwaves, and giving their candidate a lighter public schedule than in previous campaigns, using those public events for significant speeches. On August 25 in Reno, Nevada, Clinton delivered a major speech accusing Trump of "taking hate groups mainstream." In that speech she specifically targeted newly appointed Trump senior strategist, Stephen Bannon:

> Bannon has nasty things to say about pretty much everyone … here are a few of the headlines that they've published [at Breitbart]. And I'm not making this up. "Birth control makes women unattractive and crazy," "Would you rather your child had feminism or cancer?," "Gabby Giffords, the gun control movement's human shield." Just imagine, Donald Trump reading that and thinking: this is what I need more of in my campaign.[5]

The speech was widely applauded and reflected what many Democrats, Independent, and even mainstream Republicans were thinking, including many Republican elected officials and candidates who were increasingly concerned not only with what this might mean on Election Day but what it might mean for the Republican party brand for years to come.

But Hillary Clinton seemed to have an uncanny ability to snatch defeat from the jaws of victory. In a fundraiser on September 9, Clinton made the comment that "you can put half of Trump supporters into what I call the basket of deplorables. Racist, sexist, homophobic, xenophobic, Islamophobic, you name it. And unfortunately there are people like that and he has lifted them up."[6]

Now Hillary Clinton certainly was not the first candidate to make comments in a public forum which offended many of the very voters she was seeking to win over (remember Barack Obama's "clinging to their guns"; Michelle Obama's "for the first time in my life I'm proud of my country"; Mitt Romney's "47 percent") but in a campaign that seemed hers to lose, where just not making any mistakes would likely result in a win, it was viewed by most as an unforced error.

Clinton's Health

Just two days later the Clinton campaign experienced another setback which couldn't be helped, but nevertheless forced them to confront some new realities of the 2016 campaign. At a 9/11 memorial ceremony in New York City, Hillary Clinton began to feel faint and was quietly making an early exit. As she made her way to her campaign van, she appeared to go limp and collapse, and her Secret Service agents had to lift her from the ground into the van. As the van sped away with no media to cover her actions or her whereabouts, the Internet went wild.

Chapter 11: Republican Strategy **215**

For months there had been speculation on right wing blogs and "fake news" sites regarding Hillary Clinton's health. In particular there were accusations that she had multiple sclerosis ("Blackouts and Blood Clots! Hillary Clinton's Secret Multiple Sclerosis Crisis,"[7] and "Multiple Sources: Hillary Clinton has MS"[8]) and was not being forthright with the American people. The video of her collapsing threw a vat of gasoline onto the fire being stoked by right wing media. When she appeared a few hours later in front of her daughter Chelsea's apartment building, seemingly in good spirits, right wing blogs began perpetuating the idea that, in fact, Clinton had a body double.[9] These stories had jumped containment to the small universe of right wing blogs and "fake news" sites and were now being circulated in Republican circles on Facebook and moved around Twitter by senior figures in Trump world and even Trump himself.

The Clinton campaign communicated to the world that Clinton had been experiencing pneumonia but had foolishly tried to push through and keep up her demanding schedule, resulting in exhaustion and a need for the candidate to take some time off from campaigning while she rested and regained her strength.

In the past, an opponent would have handled this situation delicately, offering "thoughts and prayers" and perhaps taking a day or two off from attacking their adversary. But Trump openly mocked Clinton in his rally speeches, making fun of her need for rest compared to his boundless energy, depicting her as a tired, sick, old lady. And the crowds ate it up. The stories that Clinton had been ill but hadn't shared that information with anyone but her closest staffers, reinforced the impression that Clinton had something to hide. It reinforced the impression that voters had that she was aloof, distant, and so driven by ambition that she would do ANYTHING to win.

Republican Operatives Behind the Scenes: The Data Teams

Meanwhile, as all of this was going on under the media glare, there was a team of unsung heroes back at the Republican National Committee working the mechanics of a presidential campaign and keeping its eye on the prize.

In 2012, the Romney campaign and the Republican Party had lost a close race to incumbent President Barack Obama, a race many Republicans expected to win. In the days following the 2012 election there was much written about the data and analytic superiority of the Obama operation and its ability to identify the voters most available to them, message to those voters with very specific and targeted messaging, and deliver those voters to the polls on Election Day. The Obama team was heralded as smarter, more forward thinking, and more innovative than its Republican counterparts.

But Republican operatives knew the truth: they were just as smart, and had forward thinking innovation as well, but two factors had hindered their success. First, the debt that Reince Priebus had inherited when he took office in 2011 from the outgoing chairman was so crippling that he spent the entire year

216 Part III: The General Election

climbing out of it instead of building the programs needed to win a modern general election. Second, whereas the Obama team had the luxury of building their apparatus for four years, and building on an existing successful operation, the Romney campaign had six months to build a winning campaign. It was a huge disadvantage.

Priebus vowed not to make that mistake again. In January 2013 the RNC began working to develop a program that was built to succeed. By January 2015 they had built the infrastructure to make it work for a national presidential campaign, no matter who the candidate was. By September 2016, Katie Walsh, RNC chief of staff and Chris Carr, RNC political director and voter targeting guru, had assembled some of the best minds in the business to focus on the goal of finding potential Trump voters, locking them down, and turning them out to vote. Bill Skelly of Causeway Solutions, Brent Seaborn of TargetPoint Consulting, and Brent McGoldrick of Deep Root Analytics had all come together to create a data "dream team" called Needle Drop. While the common perception among the media was that the Clinton campaign was light years ahead of Trump and the RNC, these data brainiacs plodded along, knowing they were on to something. "We'd been building this massive database," said Seaborn, "we kind of kept sitting on this data, waiting." In the assessment of Brad Parscale, digital director for the Trump campaign, "The RNC had built a data and voter contact program that was really plug-and-play ready for the next candidate."[10]

They determined that there were three segments of voters that would need to be convinced if their candidate was going to be successful: unallocated voters, defined as people who were predisposed to listen to the Trump campaign and the GOP's message; "DJT Underperform" voters, or Republicans still unconvinced about supporting Trump; and "HRC Change" voters, defined as people leaning toward Clinton but also craving change in government.

According to an analysis by Kate Kaye in AdAge, the television targeting firm, Deep Root Analytics, working with two other targeting firms, TargetPoint and Causeway, determined the probable votes expected in each county, and translated that information into a television marketing plan, determining which ads to run, when to run them, and to whom they were targeted. With this information, National Media, a Republican media consulting firm, bought television ad time, in strategic markets. This analytics driven approach "led the Trump camp to place ads in thirteen markets that Mitt Romney's 2012 campaign never bought, including Flint, Michigan, Greenville, North Carolina, and Tallahassee, Florida."[11]

Ads varied with audience and geographic location. For example, in Toledo, Ohio, a Trump ad "Deals" emphasized in strong, clear language how Trump would renegotiate "bad trade deals pushed by the Clintons."[12] To help persuade the "HRC Change" women, there was a softer tone, with an ad called "Builder," which ran in several markets including Milwaukee during "The Ellen DeGeneres Show." The ad hits on themes particularly of interest to women, with Trump

Chapter 11: Republican Strategy **217**

promising to provide child care tax relief and paid maternity leave.[13] Later in the campaign, this early planning and targeted strategy would prove to be a game changer.

The Presidential Debates

As summer gave way to fall, all eyes were on the presidential debates. Hillary Clinton was known to be a master at debating with a full command of virtually any issue that might come her way. But there was uncertainty about how to handle a debate opponent, like Trump, who doesn't play by the rules.

The Clinton strategists came to the first debate at Hofstra University on September 26 with three goals: to present their candidate as the most stable, most qualified, most capable candidate on the stage; to force Trump into a defensive posture; and to create several days of bad news for Trump by causing him to react badly to their attacks.

And they succeeded. The candidates' positions on public policy barely made news. The news emerging from the debate can be captured in four words: "interruptions," "taxes," and "Miss Universe."

Trump regularly cut in on Clinton when he did not agree with what she was saying, coming off as overly aggressive and even bullying. Video clips of his interruptions played over and over on cable news. It was the kind of behavior that he had exhibited in the primary debates, however it came off as far more menacing when there was only one other person on the stage, and she was a woman. Focus groups voiced their disapproval. And the Clinton campaign was only too happy to give the story legs.

The Clinton camp had sought to make an issue of the fact that Trump had still not released his tax returns despite promising earlier in the campaign to do so. It was no longer news that he hadn't released them and they were outraged that he wasn't being held accountable by the media when every major party nominee in modern history had done so. So at the debate Clinton tried a new tactic: to accuse Trump of not paying federal income taxes and force him to release the returns in order to prove them wrong. They were stunned when he responded in the debate to the allegation that he had not paid federal income tax by saying "that would make me very smart." They very quickly characterized this as an admission and released a list of items that get paid for with federal funds, including Social Security, the military, education, health care, the list goes on. They also forced the Trump campaign to answer the question over and over in interviews, giving a variety of different answers in the process.

Trump's Treatment of Women and Minorities

The Clinton campaign had also sought to make Trump's treatment of women and ethnic minorities an issue. And they found the poster child for his bad

218 Part III: The General Election

behavior in Alicia Machado. Machado had been crowned Miss Universe in 1996 at the age of nineteen. As the owner of the Miss Universe Pageant, Trump took more than a passing interest in the competition and its winner. Clinton raised Machado's name and told the audience that he had referred to her as "Miss Piggy" due to her weight gain during her reign, and also "Miss Housekeeping" due to her Hispanic heritage. Trump seemed stunned by the attack, and seemed agitated as he shouted "Where did you find this??? Where did you find this???" Clinton's response was stern: "She has become an American citizen and you can bet that she's going to vote this November."[14]

In fact, the Machado story was well publicized at the time and the Clinton campaign made good use of the footage. In a web video released moments after the debate ended, the Clinton campaign told Machado's story with headlines, a one on one interview of Machado, and video clips of Trump saying she had gained 40–50 pounds (Machado claims it was more like 12 pounds), and Machado exercising at the gym (which she claims was orchestrated by Trump to "humiliate her").[15] It was powerful to say the least. The Clinton campaign was thrilled with the result. They had executed perfectly. And the Trump campaign had seemed to come to the debate with no discernible plan, other than to "let Trump be Trump" and wing the rest. But then it got even better ... for Clinton.

When asked about the issue the following morning on *Fox and Friends*, Trump seemed to double down, saying Machado had gained "a massive amount of weight, it was a real problem" and that she was "the worst we've ever had." Trump said he was irritated by Clinton playing the Machado card and that he had thought about bringing up Bill Clinton's poor treatment of women and "many infidelities" and how Mrs. Clinton treated those women, but felt it wasn't worth the shot because Chelsea Clinton was in the audience, so it "wasn't nice."[16]

Meanwhile Machado was doing her own interviews and was a perfect poster child: a beautiful, articulate, Hispanic woman. She claimed that he had bullied her and that the public humiliation had caused her to be "bulimic and anorexic for years to come."[17]

Never once did Trump seek to quell the discussion by apologizing and expressing regret for his treatment of her. Many women were outraged. Many in the Latino community were outraged. And they were very vocal in the media to express their outrage. The Clinton campaign felt they had hit their target: two groups that were seen by experts as critical to winning a general election were furious with the Republican candidate. Bullseye. They could not wait for the next debate.

What they didn't realize was that Trump's bombastic style, his brutal honesty, his refusal to play by the rules, and his portrayal of Clinton as a typical politician beholden to special interests was hitting its mark with a segment of the electorate that the Clinton campaign was all but ignoring.

Chapter 11: Republican Strategy **219**

Vice Presidential Debate

A week later on October 4 in Farmville, Virginia, the only vice presidential debate of the election took place. Democratic nominee, Virginia senator Tim Kaine and Republican nominee, Indiana governor Mike Pence took the stage. Instead of attacking Pence for his own controversial public policy actions which he had taken as governor of Indiana, Kaine tried to force him to explain and take responsibility for Trump's outrageous words. Pence successfully deflected virtually every attack and Kaine found himself interrupting and speaking over Pence, the very tactic the Clinton campaign had criticized Trump for. Unfortunately for the Clinton campaign, that was the only story coming out of the debate. Unfortunately for the Trump campaign, it was not much of a story. But a few days later a real story popped.

Access Hollywood *Tape*

It was October 7, two days before the second presidential debate and the Trump campaign was still fighting back against charges of sexism and racism stemming from the Alicia Machado story and a follow up story published by the Associated Press quoting former *The Apprentice* employees saying that Trump had made lewd remarks during the filming of the show, on which he was the star.[18] On that afternoon, the *Washington Post* published a story by reporter David Fahrenthold, with accompanying video, quoting a newly remarried Trump in a 2005 "hot mic" moment.[19] On a production bus, with *Access Hollywood* host Billy Bush, Trump made lewd remarks similar to what had been alleged by *The Apprentice* staffers. Trump's comments referred to his efforts to try to have sex with *Access Hollywood* co-host Nancy O'Dell, saying "I moved on her like a bitch." It also quoted him appearing to admit to the sexual assault of women, saying

> I'm automatically attracted to beautiful. I just start kissing them. It's like a magnet. Just kiss. I don't even wait. And when you're a star they let you do it. You can do anything ... Grab them by the pussy. You can do anything.[20]

The media went wild. Several Republican elected officials, who had previously endorsed Trump, like Senator Kelly Ayotte of New Hampshire, Senator John McCain of Arizona, and Representative Martha Roby of Alabama, withdrew their support for his candidacy, and calls for Trump to withdraw his candidacy grew louder.

But Trump was a street fighter. He quickly issued a statement regretting his words and dispatched surrogates, like his wife Melania, to characterize the comments as "locker room talk." And the campaign began minimizing his comments by suggesting that while these were lewd words, former President Bill

220 Part III: The General Election

Clinton's adultery and alleged sexual assault of women, and Hillary Clinton's defense of him, were far worse.

In order to emphasize their point, they did what would have been unthinkable in previous campaigns: Trump invited Bill Clinton's accusers to attend the second debate in St. Louis as his guests. Kathleen Willey and Paula Jones, who had accused Bill Clinton of sexual assault, and Juanita Broaddrick, who claimed Clinton had raped her during his time as Arkansas attorney general, joined Trump at a press conference prior to the debate. The women made strong statements in defense of Trump and made strong accusations against Hillary Clinton for defending her husband's actions and protecting him, allowing him to continue to prey on women.

The Bill Clinton accusers story stepped on any significant news coming out of the debate. And the Clinton campaign was outraged. The media elite mostly believed that Trump had overreached and that this tactic, seen by most as bullying and humiliating a woman, would backfire, especially with women.

But again, they were ignoring an important segment of the electorate which saw a street fighter in Trump, and they liked it. And they had little sympathy for Hillary Clinton who had become the symbol of out of touch Washington politicians who overpromised and underdelivered election after election.

Final Debate

In the final Presidential debate, held at the University of Nevada, Las Vegas on October 16, the two candidates could barely contain their contempt for one another. They refused to shake hands both before and after the debate. Trump referred to Clinton as a "nasty woman." Clinton accused Trump of "choking" in his conversation regarding a border wall with the president of Mexico. The exchanges seemed to be a snapshot of a general election campaign which had sunk to new lows.

The Clinton team was satisfied with their candidate's performance and felt confident as they moved into the final three week stretch. Their candidate led in virtually every national poll, and in most swing state polls. Their math had them so confident that they began sending her to campaign in places like Arizona, which had voted Republican in eleven of the last twelve elections. The truth was, everyone's math said the same thing: this was Hillary Clinton's campaign to lose.

Conclusion

The last two weeks of the campaign, unexpectedly, injected new drama and surprises, thanks to FBI director James Comey. The Trump team honed in on vulnerable Democratic leaning Midwestern industrial states, while the Clinton team hoped to expand the playing field. On election night, against seemingly all odds, reality began to set in, as Trump picked off battleground state after state

Chapter 11: Republican Strategy **221**

previously won by Obama, and remarkably, won Midwestern states thought to be secure Democratic territory.

Comey and His Letter to Congress

On Friday, October 28, eleven days prior to the election, FBI director James Comey sent a letter to Congress indicating that new emails from a separate investigation had been uncovered and might be relevant to the investigation of Hillary Clinton, which had been previously been closed."We don't ordinarily tell Congress about ongoing investigations," Comey told his agents in an email later that day. Nevertheless, he said, "I feel an obligation to do so given that I testified repeatedly in recent months that our investigation was completed. I also think it would be misleading to the American people were we not to supplement the record."[21]

This was unprecedented. And many within the FBI had warned Comey that the agency typically did not release inconclusive evidence so close to an election so as to not inadvertently sway the results, particularly if the information turned out to be irrelevant to the candidate and the election.

The Trump campaign took the Comey letter and ran with it. The Clinton campaign went nuclear. They saw their poll numbers begin to sink and, believing that their candidate was innocent of any wrongdoing, demanded that Comey release the full details of the investigation immediately.

Depending on where you got your news, there were two very different impressions of James Comey, a once highly respected law enforcement officer. Right wing news sites, which had publicly ridiculed Comey after he cleared Clinton earlier in the summer, were singing his praises as a patriot for doing the right thing and informing the American people in time for the information to affect their decision. Left wing news sites and much of the mainstream media saw Comey's actions as irresponsible.

It took Comey eight days to release another statement related to the Clinton investigation, two days before the election. The letter stated that they had reviewed all of the relevant emails and "we have not changed our conclusions that we expressed in July with respect to Hillary Clinton."[22] But the damage was already done.

The Hail Mary: Focus on Michigan, Pennsylvania, Wisconsin

Just two days before the Comey letter and two weeks from Election Day, the Republican team at Needle Drop was not feeling optimistic. The damage that had been done to Trump with women and ethnic minorities seemed significant. Even Speaker of the House Paul Ryan, the highest ranking Republican in Washington, said he would no longer address questions about Trump. The only hope was for Trump to win white working class voters who had previously voted

222 Part III: The General Election

for Democrats or had not voted at all. It was a long shot, but they were recommending that the campaign focus their energy in places like Pennsylvania, Wisconsin, and Michigan, states that had not gone Republican for many years. It was a Hail Mary, to be sure, but it was their only hope. And they were running out of time. Then came the Comey bombshell.

On the Thursday before Election Day, the Republican consulting firm Causeway sent a data set of 699,146 undecided Florida voters to the RNC. This was among other data sets that were prepared for Florida and other states, trying to determine which voters to contact in the last minute efforts to woo the undecided. Through their canvassing and polling, Republicans saw the movement they had been hoping for. Bill Skelly, partner and co-founder at Causeway, watched as the data showed accelerated voter migration into Trump territory. "I don't know that I've ever seen anything like it from a data perspective," he said.[23]

The Republicans and the Trump team focused on battleground states, infusion of millions of dollars of advertising, big data analysis of undecided voters, and thousands of hours of legwork by Trump campaign paid staff, thousands of volunteers, and RNC campaign operatives. Democrats, to be sure, were furiously doing the same. All sides were seeking that elusive voter still undecided or not motivated enough to go to the polls.

Election Night

On November 8, election night, most of America had settled in to watch Hillary Clinton declare victory and become the first female President. Her impressive venue, the Javits Convention Center in New York City, was chosen for its symbolism—it had a massive glass ceiling. The hall was filled with enthusiastic supporters. As media personalities and political operatives began seeing exit polling they believed that Clinton would coast to victory and the U.S. Senate would be controlled by the Democrats. But that began to unravel quickly when the numbers from Florida began coming in. Then Michigan, Pennsylvania, Wisconsin. The major cities were undervoting and the blue collar firewall that Democrats had relied on for two decades had fallen. By midnight eastern time it was clear that, against all odds, Donald J. Trump would become the forty-fifth President of the United States.

Notes

1 Will Doran, "Donald Trump Set the Record for the Most GOP Primary Votes Ever. But That's Not His Only Record," *PolitiFact North Carolina*, July 8, 2016, www.politifact.com/north-carolina/statements/2016/jul/08/donald-trump/donald-trump-set-record-most-gop-primary-votes-eve/ (accessed December 3, 2016).

2 Nate Silver, "Trump Gets Convention Bounce, Drawing Polls to Dead Heat," *FiveThirtyEight.com*, July 25, 2016, http://fivethirtyeight.com/features/election-

update-trump-gets-convention-bounce-drawing-polls-to-dead-heat/ (accessed December 4, 2016).

3 See Maggie Haberman and Richard A. Oppel, Jr., "Donald Trump Criticizes Muslim Family of Slain U.S. Soldier, Drawing Ire," *New York Times*, July 30, 2016, www.nytimes.com/2016/07/31/us/politics/donald-trump-khizr-khan-wife-ghazala.html (accessed December 4, 2016).

4 Larry Buchanan, Alicia Parlapiano, and Karen Yourish, "Paul Ryan and Mitch McConnell Reject Trump's Words, Over and Over, But Not His Candidacy," *New York Times*, October 10, 2016, www.nytimes.com/interactive/2016/10/08/us/politics/how-paul-ryan-and-mitch-mcconnell-have-disavowed-trumps-words-but-not-their-support.html?_r=0 (accessed December 5, 2016).

5 "Transcript: Hillary Clinton's Full Remarks in Reno, Nevada," *Politico*, August 25, 2016, www.politico.com/story/2016/08/transcript-hillary-clinton-alt-right-reno-227419 (accessed December 2, 2016).

6 Reena Flores, "Hillary Clinton: Half of Donald Trump Supporters in 'Basket of Deplorables'," *CBS News*, September 10, 2016, www.cbsnews.com/news/hillary-clinton-half-donald-trump-supporters-basket-of-deplorables/ (accessed November 28, 2016).

7 "Blackouts & Bloodclots: Hillary Clinton's Secret Multiple Sclerosis Crisis REVEALED," *RadarOnline.com*, August 22, 2016, http://radaronline.com/celebrity-news/hillary-clinton-medical-crisis-multiple-sclerosis-claims/ (accessed December 4, 2016).

8 "Multiple Sources: Hillary Clinton Has MS," *Catholic Online*, August 25, 2016, www.catholic.org/news/politics/story.php?id=70539 (accessed December 4, 2016).

9 Ashley May, "The Internet Thinks That Hillary Clinton Had a Body Double," *USA Today*, September 13, 2016, www.usatoday.com/story/news/nation-now/2016/09/13/internet-thinks-hillary-clinton-has-body-double/90297312/ (accessed December 4, 2016).

10 Kate Kaye, "How the Trump Camp's Data Inexperience Helped Propel His Win," *AdAge*, December 14, 2016, http://adage.com/article/campaign-trail/trump-camp-s-inexperience-set-stage-rnc-data-win/307105/ (accessed December 27, 2016).

11 Ibid.

12 Trump for President, "Deals," October 18, 2016, www.youtube.com/watch?v=KLbRcfOQCTM (accessed December 2, 2016).

13 Trump for President, "The Builder," July 22, 2016, www.youtube.com/watch?v=hD6DCW33PQs (accessed December 2, 2016).

14 Michael Barbaro and Megan Twohey, "Shamed and Angry: Alicia Machado, a Miss Universe Mocked by Donald Trump," *New York Times*, www.nytimes.com/2016/09/28/us/politics/alicia-machado-donald-trump.html?_r=0 (accessed January 2, 2017).

15 Clinton Campaign, "Alicia Machado," on YouTube, September 26, 2016, www.youtube.com/watch?v=U8ZM58O_gBo (accessed December 2, 2016).

16 "Donald Trump: Miss Universe Alicia Machado Was 'The Absolute Worst'," Fox News, September 27, 2016, www.foxnews.com/entertainment/2016/09/27/donald-trump-miss-universe-alicia-machado-was-absolute-worst.html (accessed December 2, 2016).

224 Part III: The General Election

17 Evan Real, "Former Miss Universe Alicia Machado Says Donald Trump's Insults Contributed to Her Eating Disorders," *US Weekly*, September 28, 2016, www.usmagazine.com/celebrity-news/news/alicia-machado-donald-trumps-insults-caused-my-eating-disorder-w442444 (accessed December 3, 2016).

18 Garance Burke, "'Apprentice' Cast and Crew Say Trump Was Lewd and Sexist," Associated Press, October 3, 2016, http://bigstory.ap.org/article/2778a6ab7 2ea49558445337865289508/ap-how-trumps-apprentice-moved-capitalism-sexism (accessed December 4, 2016).

19 David A. Fahrenthold, "Trump Recorded Having Extremely Lewd Conversations About Women in 2005," *Washington Post*, October 8, 2016, www.washingtonpost.com/politics/trump-recorded-having-extremely-lewd-conversation-about-women-in-2005/2016/10/07/3b9ce776-8cb4-11e6-bf8a-3d26847eeed4_story.html?tid=a_inl& utm_term=.d36444b74cff (accessed December 5, 2016).

20 Video accompanying Fahrenthold story, ibid.

21 Sari Horwitz, "Read the Letter Comey Sent to FBI Employees Explaining His Controversial Decision on the Clinton Email Investigation," *Washington Post*, October 28, 2016, www.washingtonpost.com/news/post-nation/wp/2016/10/28/read-the-letter-comey-sent-to-fbi-employees-explaining-his-controversial-decision-on-the-clinton-email-investigation/?utm_term=.eb4b190d20fb (accessed December 2, 2016).

22 "FBI Affirms July Decision Not to Charge Clinton, After Review of Weiner Emails," *NPR*, November 6, 2016, www.npr.org/sections/thetwo-way/2016/11/06/500929164/comey-we-have-not-changed-our-conclusions-as-fbi-finishes-clinton-email-review (accessed December 2, 2016).

23 Kaye, "How the Trump Camp's Data Inexperience Helped Propel His Win."

12

DEMOCRATIC STRATEGY AND TACTICS DURING THE GENERAL ELECTION

Maria Cardona

It is the summer of 2016, the Democratic primaries and caucuses are over, and Hillary Clinton has won her party's nomination for president of the United States. It was a long, contentious, and at times heated primary that many, especially in the media, did not expect. Many thought it would be a cake-walk for Clinton, and just about everyone thought her campaign also expected an easy time. But the reality was that the Clinton campaign always knew it would be a challenge. What they were not expecting was that the formidable competition would be the Independent-turned-Democratic senator from Vermont, Bernie Sanders, who inspired young hearts and minds even at the dusk of his political career of more than forty years.

The talk was always about Massachusetts senator Elizabeth Warren or perhaps even Vice President Joe Biden. But it was Sanders who caught progressive fire and embarked on a campaign that he would take until almost the end, fighting hard for progressive values, ensuring that Clinton took nothing and no one for granted. He made her fight for it, and he made her a better candidate in the process. Clinton finally achieved the number of delegates needed to claim the nomination for the Democratic Party.

This chapter explores the strategy, the tactics—real and perceived—and how the Clinton campaign and the Democratic Party laid out and implemented its strategy hoping to elect the first woman president.

The "Woman Card"

There are a couple of things to keep in mind that were important for the Clinton campaign this time around that were not the case in 2008. In 2008, when Hillary Clinton ran against then Senator Barack Obama, the campaign team blatantly did

226 Part III: The General Election

not want to focus on her historic run as a woman candidate vying for the presidency. Clinton's senior campaign aides wanted her to show her strength, backbone, and steeliness.

She was criticized for not being "warm enough," "engaging enough," especially as she ran against a younger, much more charismatic, new-on-the-scene senator from Illinois, who, if elected, also would make his mark in history. She finally did connect with voters, showing her emotional vulnerability, when she teared up at an event in New Hampshire in early 2008. But it was too late. The die had been cast. It was very close but not good enough.

In 2016, however, her campaign was ready for her to play the "woman card." And she did so willingly and often, to the chagrin of her opponents. The reason for this about-face was that it became clear the country had progressed from looking at women's issues as simply affecting women. Women's issues—good paying jobs, wanting to make ends meet for the family, providing a good education for the kids, ensuring health care coverage is affordable and accessible, raising wages, strengthening reproductive rights—are all issues that affect all Americans.

It became clear that one of the key strategies was to communicate that in championing the issues that women care about, Hillary Clinton would be the champion for the American family and America's children. In this vein, she gladly and enthusiastically embraced the "woman card" and often used it as a rallying cry in her speeches by saying that if playing the woman card meant she would be fighting for equal pay for equal work, for raising the minimum wage (important for women since two-thirds of minimum wage workers are women), defending reproductive rights, advocating for affordable health care and education, then "deal her in!" It was a very effective message that enabled her in the end to keep and win the majority of support among women voters.

The message geared towards women also became particularly effective as she ran against a male opponent who had historically and consistently degraded and demeaned women throughout his life, and whose own offensive comments towards women would be used against him during the general election.

This issue came to a crescendo in October when the *Access Hollywood* tape of Donald Trump describing how he likes to sexually assault women became public. This particular moment was perhaps the most damning moment of the election for Donald Trump. The Clinton campaign took advantage of this by releasing perhaps one of the most effective ads of the campaign. Called "Mirrors," the ad features adolescent girls, many of color, looking at themselves in the mirror while the voice-over is Trump in his own words as he insults women calling them ugly, fat pigs, dogs, and treating them as objects.[1]

Hillary Clinton's support among all women spiked around this time in the campaign, leading analysts to conclude that she would win women by a larger margin than any Democrat had thus far, especially since her support among college-educated white women was also soaring, a group that traditionally had

Chapter 12: Democratic Strategy **227**

been won by Republicans, but which Clinton was winning at this point in the election.

While her margin among women was formidable, it ended up equaling what President Obama's was in 2012, not enough to erase the margin among men and white voters that Trump won against Clinton. At this point, FBI director James Comey's letter, released eleven days before the election announcing the discovery of another trove of emails in the Clinton email investigation, was damaging enough to bring white moderate Republican women who had fled Trump, back to his side, albeit begrudgingly. It also allowed women and men who perhaps were not comfortable voting for a woman for president, but did not like Donald Trump, to vote for him anyway because they could use the excuse that her email transgressions, highlighted by Comey's letter (even though nothing new was found and nothing to prosecute) were a bridge too far. They could not accept Clinton.

WikiLeaks and Emails

Clinton left the Democratic Convention on a high note, and enjoyed quite a steep convention bump coming out of that spectacularly successful week for the Democrats. The Clinton campaign felt the email issue was behind them, and that the vast majority of voters had already resolved the issue, deciding one way or the other about how strongly it would play in their support for Hillary.

There was one ominous and ultimately detrimental event that happened at the Democratic Convention that would prove to be the first of a death by a thousand cuts, and the opening salvo in what we now know was the Russians' successful attempt at meddling in our internal elections. The first day of the Democratic Convention also was the first release by WikiLeaks of the stolen, private emails of Democratic National Committee staffers.

Hillary Clinton seemed to weather that storm in the short term; it did minimal damage to her during the Democratic Convention. It riled up Sanders's supporters particularly when they saw evidence in some of the emails that seemed to indicate some DNC staffers were taking sides privately against him and in favor of Clinton. The person who took the fall for the content of these emails, however ill-gotten they were, was DNC chairwoman Debbie Wasserman Schultz, who took responsibility for the whole affair, stepped down for the good of the Party, and allowed the focus to continue to be Clinton and the beginning of the 2016 presidential general election campaign.

It seemed to have worked. On the WikiLeaks emails as well as Clinton's own emails, the consensus was that the majority of voters had made up their minds, for or against her, and that not many swing voters would find this further information important enough to change their minds. That consensus seemed to hold at that time. Clinton was ahead in the polls and the conclusion drawn by me and many fellow supporters and political analysts was that the controversy had

228 Part III: The General Election

been "baked into the Clinton cake." We did not think it would play an oversized role in voters' decision come November.

However, no one could have foreseen Comey's interjection, which was so blatant and political, eleven days before voters went to the polls on Election Day. Hillary Clinton never recovered from the damage caused by the Comey letter to Congress. But up to that point, it seemed that the Clinton campaign had actually managed to neutralize the issue and not have it be front and center of the campaign.

Trump Temperamentally Unfit

Trump's behavior immediately after the Democratic Convention gave Democrats the occasion to crystallize a theme that had started to mature during the primary season when he started his campaign by insulting Mexican immigrants. That insult was quickly followed throughout the campaign by insults against women (whom he has insulted throughout this life) and which came to a head with his caustic remarks against Megan Kelly during the first Republican debate.

Trump also continued insulting Hispanics, stating that Judge Gonzalo P. Curiel—a Mexican American judge assigned to a Trump University class action lawsuit—could not do his job without bias because of his Mexican heritage.

Many of his fellow rivals during the Republican primaries tried to use these insults against him, but to no avail. Jeb Bush repeatedly said that Trump could not insult his way to the presidency. Many of the other candidates tried as well to make Trump's immature behavior a debilitating quality in the eyes of Republican voters. But it seemed that every time Trump hurled an insult, his poll numbers would either stay the same or actually go up.

Democrats were convinced that while that tactic may have worked for the Republican primary electorate, it would backfire badly for the general election because of the much more diverse and moderate electorate Trump would face. That assumption was for the most part correct. Trump stumbled out of his convention, not enjoying any kind of noticeable bump in popularity as is normally the case for most candidates during their conventions.

After the Democratic Convention, Hillary's numbers started to skyrocket. Trump had stepped in it again with his insults. This time he decided to go after the Khan family, a Gold Star family who had lost their son during an IED attack in Iraq. The father had spoken up courageously and forcefully at the Democratic Convention accusing Donald Trump of not respecting or knowing the Constitution of the United States. Mr. Khan was focused on another one of the more egregious insults Mr. Trump unveiled during his primary campaign— the Muslim Ban. It was one of the more popular policies among his base, and it was also one that enabled the Democrats and most Americans to underscore how temperamentally unfit Donald Trump was to be commander in chief of the United States. Mr. Khan and a slew of the other Democratic speakers at the

Democratic Convention slammed Donald Trump on this theme of his lack of temperament to hold the highest office in the land.

In fact, they were all paving the way for the slam dunk of the Democratic Convention when Hillary Clinton took apart Mr. Trump, using his own words against him. Part of that strategy was to criticize the way Trump had used social media, tweeting insults against his rivals, degrading them with 140 characters or less. While Trump's supporters loved the attacks and insults hurled against mere politicians, this also gave Hillary a terrific opportunity to define Trump as someone who should not have access to the nuclear codes if he is so easily baited with a tweet, "A man you can bait with a tweet is not a man we can trust with nuclear weapons."

Clinton's baiting was incredibly effective. It baited Trump into one of the nastiest and most self-destructive episodes of the general election campaign. Trump was in meltdown mode, against Clinton, against Mr. Khan, and it helped solidify the image of Trump as someone who was so thin-skinned, he would be a danger to our county in the Oval Office.

Trump's poll numbers started tanking and Hillary's bump was one of the largest of a candidate after a convention in a long time. The theme of Donald Trump as being too dangerous a gamble to put in the Oval Office was one that was working with exactly the people that Trump needed to gain with and whom he was losing in droves—moderate, Republican-leaning college-educated white women.

College-educated white voters have always been a demographic that Republicans have won. But this year, they were supporting Clinton in numbers that spelled danger for the Republican nominee, especially college-educated white women who went for Romney in 2012, but even with their help, he still lost the election. Democrats were looking at this number as a key to a Hillary Clinton victory. And it seemed that every time Donald Trump opened his mouth, he helped push them to her side.

The Alt Right

Another tactic Clinton used during the general election was to underscore Trump's ties to the Alt Right. Clinton had already given a major speech exposing the Trump campaign and Trump himself as a safe haven and, essentially, a promoter of the Alt Right—a term used to describe right wing conservatives tied to white nationalists, white supremacists, and/or white power leaders or movements.

The tactic was embraced fully after Mr. Trump announced he would hire Steve Bannon, the former head of the right wing website Breitbart.com, who became a senior advisor and confidante to Donald Trump shortly after the conventions. Bannon himself described Breitbart.com as a platform for the Alt Right movement, thereby handing the Clinton campaign a powerful tool and

230 Part III: The General Election

bludgeon with which to bash Trump and highlight his affinity for racists and bigots. It became a powerful strategy throughout the general election, as it also played into what most voters in communities of color already thought about Donald Trump—that he was a dangerous, unstable, racist and bigot who would continue to divide, demean, and degrade women and communities of color not only throughout the campaign but certainly if he won the White House.

Mr. Trump did not do himself any favors throughout the campaign when he was slow to disavow the well-known and pretty universally hated white supremacist leaders such as David Duke. Mr. Trump hesitated to unequivocally condemn David Duke and everything he stood for. It took several media questions for Trump to finally distance himself from David Duke. But it came too late and at that point, several white nationalist leaders had already staked claim on Donald Trump: According to them, Trump was going to help mainstream the message of the Alt Right, and that he had already made them more acceptable.

The Clinton campaign's message of connecting Trump to white nationalists every time they got a chance to was a smart one. Ultimately it fell short, but it proved to be a powerful message and an image that Trump still to this day struggles to shake off.

The Debates

After the political conventions, the next three defining moments that could help make or break a candidate are the three scheduled presidential debates. Hillary Clinton went into these debates in a position of strength and, as anticipated, downplayed expectations for her debate performance; Trump, did the same. Hillary took some days off the campaign trail to prepare for the first debate but Trump was not getting any traditional debate prep time. He clearly felt he didn't need any. He continued to hold his campaign rallies, push on the themes that his supporters loved and thrived on, witnessing chants of "lock her up," and reminding rally goers of her supposed criminality and bad judgment.

The Clinton campaign was singularly focused on winning all three debates outright, on substance, command of the issues, and an unrelenting attack on Trump's character, or lack thereof, underscoring how woefully unprepared he was to take on the responsibilities of being president of the United States. That part worked. Clinton won every single debate according to all legitimate polls and most unbiased analyses.

The first debate showed that Clinton possessed a far greater understanding of the issues facing the country, she possessed the knowledge and the nuance needed to be leader of the free world, and an ability to deflect and answer questions on her own terms. The Clinton campaign's strategy of baiting Trump also worked, pointing out his ineptitude. Towards the end of the debate, Clinton brought up Trump's treatment of a former Miss Universe from Venezuela who had recently publicly shared her story that Trump had fat-shamed her during her tenure as the beauty queen because she had gained some weight.

Clinton retold the story in the context that this is a man who does not hold women in very high regard, that he has historically and continually disrespected women, using vulgar language to describe them and belittling and demeaning them. This tactic got under Trump's skin and he started to tweet out offensive statements about the former Miss Universe, in essence proving Mrs. Clinton right.

What followed were a couple of rough weeks for Donald Trump that he could not seem to put behind him. The strategy was to paint Trump as a bully, a man-child who could not help himself when he received even the smallest of slights, whether real or perceived. He hit hard if he was hit first, as his supporters liked to state. The problem was, many times he was the first to hit.

The second and third debates were both equally effective in showing Trump as incapable of the kind of measured and thoughtful responses, based on experience and facts that most people value in their presidents. In fact, the third debate proved consequential because it happened right after the release of the *Access Hollywood* tape where Donald Trump is heard saying that he could grab women by their genitals and they would let him do it because he was a "celebrity."

It was perhaps the most damning turn of events at that point for the Trump campaign since the beginning of the election cycle. He started losing support, especially among traditional Republicans and especially among college-educated white women as well as men. It seemed hearing Mr. Trump brag about committing sexual assault was a bridge too far for many voters. During the third debate, Clinton was able to solidify the impression that Trump was much too dangerous, much too inexperienced, and much too thin-skinned to become the Leader of the Free World.

All in all, the debates proved a huge boost for Clinton. She won all three by all major public accounts and major polls done by the news media. Most voters saw a distinct difference between someone who had dedicated her life to the betterment of women, girls, children, and the under-represented, versus someone who had made a fortune by many times taking advantage of the more vulnerable people among us, and someone who was all bluster, braggadocio, and bark, but void of substance, conscience, and character.

Fundraising

Hillary Clinton outraised and outspent her opponent. Many times, she would get criticized for raising money from the "Coastal Elites" and Hollywood, while Mr. Trump was going from rally to rally boasting about how he didn't need any sleep or rest. The fact is, she was trouncing him in fundraising, both with big donors as well the smaller donations that make up the bread and butter of a campaign.

But she was unapologetic about taking the time to do the high-dollar fundraising events. While they did get a lot of play in the media, they also brought

232 Part III: The General Election

in the dough that will be what allows for the expansion of a campaign into perhaps some changing but still red states like Georgia and Arizona, which remained competitive until the end and where Democrats seemed to make gains that they can build on in the coming election cycles. For more elaboration on Clinton's campaign fundraising, see Chapter 5 by Anthony Corrado and Tassin Braverman.

Voter Targeting—the "Clinton Coalition"

There was much talk about whether Clinton would be able to hold on to the "Obama Coalition," that demographic group of voters that helped elect President Obama to office twice. It comprises mostly minority voters—African-Americans, Latinos, Asian-Americans, immigrants-turned-citizens, millennials, and single women.

The strategy for the Clinton campaign was not to necessarily hold the exact Obama Coalition but to bring forth the Clinton Coalition that would comprise mostly these groups of voters along with more women voters, specifically college-educated white women, and moderate suburban Republican women who considered Trump as a completely unacceptable choice to be our commander in chief.

The Clinton campaign also realized it would be completely unrealistic to expect the African-American community to show up in the same record numbers as they did for Obama. But they did expect African-Americans to show up in sufficient numbers to be able to hold the coalition together if more women and Latinos joined in support of Clinton.

As such, the Clinton campaign focused much of its efforts at bringing out what would be the Clinton Coalition. Early into the general election the challenge seemed to be trying to get millennials excited about coming out to vote for Hillary, especially as many of them had seen their favorite candidate vanquished by her and were not convinced she represented them and their expansive progressive values.

As the election got closer, polls indicated young people were mostly supporting Clinton and that the nasty hangover of the primary campaign between her and Sanders had subsided. There were still a handful of holdouts that would not support Clinton but, for the most part, millennials knew that Trump—for all his attempts to lure them to his side—did not and would not represent a brighter future for them as he did not support the policies that would lead to that better future—a raise in the minimum wage, debt-free college, affordable housing, health care, good paying jobs, an unwavering commitment to protecting our environment, and a belief that no matter who you are, what color your skin is, who you love, or the economic circumstances of your birth, you could get ahead, succeed, and thrive in this country of opportunity and fairness for all.

#StrongerTogether

Sanders, President Obama, and Michelle Obama all had an important role to play in helping to bring out the key components of the Clinton Coalition, and underscoring her critical message—that we are #StrongerTogether. They fanned out to critical battleground states for the final months of the election, speaking to college students, African-American communities, suburban women, Latinos, and yes, even white working class voters, and making the case that Clinton would be the standard bearer for all Americans' hopes and dreams to have a better life for themselves and their children.

The contrast was stark of having a candidate like Hillary Clinton who celebrated the country's unique differences, diversity of background, thought, economic status, race, ethnicity, gender, sexual orientation, and religion compared to Donald Trump who had done nothing but hurl insults to America's diverse communities from the moment he announced his campaign by calling Mexican immigrants rapists, criminals, and drug dealers.

This would be a tactic Clinton would revisit time and again since Trump gave her ample opportunities to do so. Insulting Hispanics was not the end. It was only the beginning. He followed that up by proposing the Muslim ban in the name of protecting our country from "radical Islamic terrorists." But by putting every single Muslim-American and Muslim around the world in that category, he opened up a rift within America's Muslim communities that would not be easily mended—even to this day.

Trump continually used rhetoric to divide and slice up the electorate between an "us"—presumably the predominantly white working class voters who had been feeling victimized for so many years by the loss of manufacturing jobs, automation, free trade, and the "browning" of America, and the "them" who were the ones changing the face of the country in which many working class whites no longer felt like the predominant group.

To be sure, the sentiment of these white working class voters was real, and raw, and Trump did a masterful job of speaking to their angst and worries for themselves, their future, and their children. But instead of talking about the virtues of all of our communities and uniting into One America, Trump used their fear to focus on lifting them up by tearing everyone else down. Clinton's strategy was to do completely the opposite.

She would remind Americans—all Americans—that our country always is at its best when we are focusing on the strengths of all of our communities. She underscored that hateful rhetoric, fear mongering, and divisive language was what her opponent used in order to tear us down instead of building us up. She used a play on words by using Trump's own words about building a wall on our southern border by saying that Trump was clearly very good at building walls. But that we need to instead build bridges to one another.

234 Part III: The General Election

Clinton's was a message of inclusion and strength through unity. And she would pit that message against Trump's message of demonizing communities of color in order to scapegoat certain demographics. It was particularly effective as she was able to use Trump's own words against him when it came to Latinos, African-Americans, Muslims, women, even veterans and people with disabilities were all the objects of Trump's scorn throughout his campaign at one point or another.

Policies and Proposals

One of the big myths of the 2016 election cycle was that it was completely void of substance. While there was certainly a preponderance of hype, scandal, and personality-driven news cycles, there was also a wealth of substantive, well-thought-out proposals that were offered by Clinton on a myriad of issues facing the American people.

These proposals ranged from how to graduate from college debt-free, to helping parents deal with drug and opiates addiction, to immigration, to how to continue to bring back manufacturing jobs, to raising the minimum wage, to ensuring women get equal pay for equal work, to nurturing and growing small businesses, to how to give families affordable child care options, to how to keep American jobs here at home, to protecting health care rights for women. Clinton's overall message throughout all of her evidence-based policy proposals was that if you had the will to work hard and play by the rules, this country should give you the opportunity to have a good paying job, professional or vocational, that would allow you to raise a family, have an affordable home, access quality health care, give your children the opportunity to go to college, and be able to put something away for retirement. In essence, Clinton wanted to ensure the American Dream was alive and well for everyone, no matter the circumstances of your birth.

But no matter what she did, how many speeches she gave to highlight these detailed proposals, it seemed that the day-to-day drama of Donald Trump's outrageous statements and antics, his over-the-top tweets, and his cult of personality, seemed to always overshadow the substance and heft of Hillary's policies that she was offering the American people. But it did not deter her from continuing to fight to break through on these policies, whether in debates, one-on-one interviews, candidate forums, town halls, or in her daily interactions and conversations with real voters. These policies are what drove her.

I always used to say that Hillary may not be a woman who wears her heart on her sleeve, but she was certainly a public servant who put her heart in the four decades of service for the betterment of the lives of children and families, and her policy proposals reflected the best of her life's work, her real commitment, and true grit.

The majority of voters saw and understood that on a pure policy level, to have a command of the grave issues that faced the country and having the experience

Chapter 12: Democratic Strategy **235**

and temperament to be commander in chief, were critical qualities in a candidate. And that Secretary Clinton was hands down the most qualified candidate. Poll after poll showed this to be true. In any other year, in any other election, that perhaps would have been enough to win the Electoral College vote in addition to the popular vote. It wasn't in 2016. There was a big reason why.

FBI Director James Comey

Earlier, I briefly mentioned that FBI director James Comey injected himself into this election in an egregiously political way as he conducted and announced the findings of his almost year-long investigation into Secretary Clinton's private email server.

To be sure, the whole email server fiasco was all Clinton's doing. She is the first one to admit that and understood that it was a big mistake. She took responsibility for it, and asked for transparency at the highest levels by pushing the State Department to share all of her work-related emails with the public. Many Democrats wish she had apologized sooner, in fact, as soon as it became known she had set up a private email server, she should have shown regret immediately and offered to turn over all of her emails that were work related. She took a bit too long but she finally got there.

The Clinton campaign and the candidate herself never for a second doubted that she would be exonerated by the FBI, and that there was no evidence that she had endangered our national security in any way, or that she had knowingly sent or received any classified material (that was marked classified at the time) on her private email server. Director Comey said as much when he announced his findings of the investigation in July of 2016. But then he did something that was completely unprecedented and seemingly, at least it was perceived as such, blatantly political.

Instead of simply passing on his recommendations to the Department of Justice, that there was not sufficient evidence to prosecute Clinton, he staged a press conference to editorialize his decision, to reprimand Clinton for her use of a private email server, and proceed to completely politicize a bombshell issue that should have and could have been very straightforward.

But he didn't stop there. He later offered to share with Congress his team's notes taken during the investigation of Clinton. This was another blatantly political and unprecedented move that made Mr. Comey seem more interested in providing political cover for his decision than to stay out of a process that is normally deemed off limits to the FBI and its director. If Comey had stopped there, the damage could have been contained. The Clinton campaign's strategy of neutralizing the trust issue on the emails was succeeding, thanks in no small part, to her debate performances, Trump's own disastrous words throughout the campaign, and the gut instinct of voters that Trump was simply unfit for the highest office in the land.

236 Part III: The General Election

But then eleven days before the election, Comey came out with an announcement that the Clinton campaign could not have prepared for, and from which Clinton never recovered. Comey announced that a new batch of emails had been found on a device belonging to former congressman Anthony Weiner, estranged husband of one of Clinton's top aides, Huma Abedin. The Comey announcement changed the trajectory of the election, in the opinion of many strategists both inside and outside of the Clinton campaign.

Should Clinton have visited Wisconsin at least once during the general election? Of course. She should have gone multiple times. Should the Clinton campaign have spent more money on the ground and on ads in Michigan? No question. Should it have focused more on getting white working class voters to Hillary's side? Of course it should have. Any one of these if done better, one could argue, could have allowed Clinton to prevail in spite of Comey's intrusion. But the fact remains that the polls started slipping after the FBI's announcement of a new trove of emails.

It didn't matter that those new emails were most likely not new at all. The FBI didn't even know what was in them before Comey made the announcement. Which makes his action seem even more blatantly political. Then five days before the election, Comey came out and announced that in fact no new emails or material were found in the emails from Anthony Weiner's computer and that his conclusion from the summer still stood intact: that there was no evidence to move forward with any additional action against Clinton. But the damage had been done.

Comey's letter was the death knell for Clinton's campaign. I believe that if he had not come out with his announcement eleven days prior to the election, we would be inaugurating the first woman president of the United States on January 20, 2017. While it still seemed even into the evening hours of Election Day that Hillary Clinton would pull off a win, in hindsight, the Comey letter allowed for depressed turnout among Democrats, for moderate Republican suburban women who did not want to support Trump to give him a second look, for progressives who were already leaning towards supporting a third party candidate to go ahead and do so, and ultimately for Trump to turn out just enough more votes in Pennsylvania, Michigan, and Wisconsin, to win the electoral votes in each state, and therefore the presidency.

Conclusion

In the end, what separated Donald Trump and Hillary Clinton were less than 80,000 votes in these three states. The closeness of the election does not make Trump's win illegitimate in any way. But it also doesn't mean that Hillary's strategies and tactics were failures or that the American people roundly rejected her candidacy and her message. They did not. She got almost 3 million more votes than Trump. That is not a mandate for him and he should not see it as such.

Clinton's strategy and tactics worked as more Americans voted for her than voted for Trump. Just not in the right states.

If Donald Trump really does want to be the president for all Americans and not just for the 46 percent who voted for him, he should adopt some of Clinton's tactics and strategies of inclusion, celebrating diversity instead of vilifying it, understanding the real fears felt in communities of color because of his win, and work to unify the country and divide us no longer. Donald Trump's strategies and tactics worked to win him the presidency. But if he continues to feed the fear and the angst and the divisions in this country, those tactics that won him the Oval Office will lose him the opportunity to become a successful president.

Note

1 Clinton campaign ad, "Mirrors," September 23, 2016, available from YouTube, www.youtube.com/watch?v=vHGPbl-werw (accessed December 22, 2016).

13

THE DEFINING FAULT LINES IN ONE OF THE DARKEST CAMPAIGNS IN POLITICAL HISTORY

Matthew Dallek

The 2016 election was one of the potentially most consequential campaigns in the recent history of presidential politics. Vermont Senator Bernie Sanders, an Independent-Socialist running on a populist, anti-Wall-Street platform, nearly toppled the candidacy of the Democratic Party's frontrunner Hillary Clinton during a hard-fought primary campaign. Real estate mogul and reality TV star Donald Trump, who had earned political notoriety for having questioned whether the nation's first African-American president was born in the United States, defeated sixteen Republican rivals to win the Republican presidential nomination and, ultimately, the presidency.

During the general election, Hillary Clinton was swept up in a never-ending controversy about her use of a private email server as Secretary of State. Russia was accused by U.S. intelligence agencies of hacking the Democratic National Committee's emails and Clinton campaign chairman John Podesta's emails in order to influence the election contest.

Donald Trump generated big headlines and controversies. He ridiculed military generals, war heroes, women, Mexican immigrants, and defied convention when his incendiary comments did not seem to harm him politically. During the general election, virtually every major national and battleground state poll showed Hillary Clinton with a sure path to an Electoral College and popular vote victory. On Election Day, however, Trump won numerous swing states, including Florida and North Carolina, and smashed through Democrats' Midwestern "firewall" when he defeated Clinton in the traditionally blue states of Michigan, Wisconsin, and Pennsylvania to win the White House.

The campaign's myriad turns generated enormous attention around the world. As of this writing, the election results are still being tallied and observers are still struggling to analyze what had just happened and why Trump was able to prevail

Chapter 13: The Defining Fault Lines **239**

in the Electoral College. My colleagues in this book have taken on that challenge, but the debate will rage for years to come.

But too often, the news media described the campaign based on the latest sensational attack leveled by a candidate. More fundamental social and economic divisions revealed by this campaign received too little attention. The election showcased the shifting nature of partisan polarization in early twenty-first century America.

In spite of the GOP's sweeping victories on Election Day, Trump's candidacy challenged the conservative philosophy and movement, sowing a crisis on the right. Race, class, and gender also emerged as hot-button issues in ways that few observers anticipated prior to the presidential primaries. Also on vivid display in the 2016 election was just how fragile American democracy had become.

The Crisis of Conservatism

The GOP's sweeping victory in 2016 has papered over big differences in the Republican Party and the conservative movement. Trump just recently became a Republican. Lacking any fixed ideology, he ran as a populist anti-Washington businessman outsider and brandished a nativist streak to boot. He railed against immigration and free trade accords. At times, his campaign trafficked in racist, misogynistic, conspiratorial, and anti-Semitic tweets, comments, and policies. Just as he belittled Hillary Clinton as a corrupt symbol of the political establishment, he also gleefully denounced elected leaders of his own party including Speaker Paul Ryan, Gov. John Kasich, and Senators Ben Sasse, Marco Rubio, and Lindsay Graham as failed politicians. Trump seemed to have little affinity for conservatives' commitment to free market economics, calling instead for $1 trillion in infrastructure spending and vowing to rip up free trade agreements. On foreign policy, Trump embraced isolationism, vowing to put "America First," echoing the isolationist creed of the pre-World-War II America First Committee. Trump demonstrated little policy fidelity to defending social conservatives' commitment to opposing same-sex marriage, abortions, and giving religion primacy in public policy.[1]

Conservative journalists and intellectuals, along with a handful of principled politicians, denounced Trump as a threat to conservative ideology and even to democracy itself. A #NeverTrump movement took flight. Although it failed to stop Trump's nomination, the breadth of conservative opposition to Trump was a sign of fissures within the conservative cause that Trump's victory has papered over but that nonetheless remain strong.

Conservatives attacked Trump's proposal to build a deportation force and ban Muslims from entering the United States. Some conservatives blanched at Trump's caustic denunciations of free trade agreements. Others criticized his warm words for Russian authoritarian ruler Vladimir Putin. And Trump's belittling of women, Gold Star families, Mexican-Americans, and Muslim-Americans drew conservative fire.[2]

240 Part III: The General Election

Indeed, the 2012 GOP presidential nominee Mitt Romney; Wisconsin talk radio kingpin Charlie Sykes; *Weekly Standard* editor Bill Kristol; independent presidential candidate Evan McMullin; Nebraska Senator Ben Sasse, and *Washington Post* columnists Jennifer Rubin and Michael Gerson were all conservatives who characterized Trump's candidacy as a crisis in conservative thought, style, and policy. Fifty years from now, historians will likely be debating how 2016 affected the future of the conservative movement as an intellectual and political force.[3]

Former George W. Bush speechwriter David Frum captured the conservative agonistes. Writing just a few days prior to the election, Frum questioned how any conservative could in good conscience vote for

> a man who boasts of his delight in sexual assault? Who mocks the disabled, who denounces immigrant parents whose son laid down his life for this country, who endorses religious bigotry, and who denies the Americanism of everyone from the judge hearing the fraud case against Trump University to the 44th president of the United States?

Amanda Carpenter, who served as a press aide to Senator Ted Cruz, a leading conservative, called Trump a "raging sexist." Ohio governor John Kasich and the last two Republican presidents (George H.W. Bush and George W. Bush) all reportedly refused to vote for their party's nominee.[4]

This conservative crisis can be traced to President George W. Bush's second White House term. From 2005 to 2009, Iraq broke into a civil war, and Americans soured on the initial invasion and the failure of the Bush administration to win the peace there. In 2005, the Bush administration failed to save lives during Hurricane Katrina in New Orleans, casting doubts on the ability of conservatives— who were supposed to be known for efficient leadership and competent government—to keep Americans safe inside of their communities. And the 2008 Great Recession—coming after nearly eight years of Republican rule in the White House and Congress—not only left Bush with approval ratings in the mid-twenties but also cast doubt on conservatives' free market supply side approach as a viable path to shared prosperity.[5]

In these ways, Trump's movement was a reaction not only to President Obama's two terms but also to the perceived failures of President Bush. In the wake of Trump's victory, traditional conservatives including Speaker Paul Ryan face some tough challenges. Will they push for smaller government (something Trump has not really championed), internationalism, and a more civil tone especially around issues of race and gender? What will traditional conservatives do about members of the so-called Alt-Right, including the many white supremacists peopling its ranks? Will conservatives challenge the conspiracy theorists whom Trump welcomed into the GOP's tent?

The Republicans' electoral victory in 2016 is likely to delay some of these questions from being answered immediately. Eventually, though, conservatives

Chapter 13: The Defining Fault Lines **241**

will need to confront them—and the debate among historians and the country is likely to focus in part on the impact of 2016 on the conservative movement.

Race and Class

It is hard to discuss the 2016 election results without studying how both race and class shaped its arguments, tone, and outcome. Of course, issues of race and class in politics are as old as the American Republic. But these twin issues, it is also true, manifested themselves with unexpected force in 2016.

More than anybody, Trump inserted race and class into the campaign. He characterized inner-city America as a living "hell" for African-Americans. His years-long "birther" effort questioned the patriotism and American-ness of America's first African-American president. Trump attacked a Mexican-American judge hearing a civil suit against him as biased due to the judge's Mexican heritage (the judge was born and raised in Indiana). Other issues surfaced during the campaign. Trump had allegedly referred to the 1996 Miss Universe winner who was Latina as "Miss Housekeeping," and during the general election he called her "an eating machine." Trump said he might have supported the Japanese-American World War II internment camps as necessary for national security, and he proposed banning Muslims who were not U.S. citizens from coming to the United States. To dismiss Trump's appeals on racial and religious grounds as inconsequential side issues would be to ignore centuries of American politics, in which race especially accounted for many of the country's greatest political divisions. From the Constitution to the Civil War to the civil rights revolution of the 1960s, race and racial appeals have stood at the center of the electoral experience, and Trump's hateful rhetoric and his "Make America Great Again" slogan harked to a pre-civil rights era, a world in which economic and social opportunities were primarily restricted to white men.[6]

Take, for instance, Trump's now-famous announcement speech. It trafficked in racial stereotypes. "When Mexico sends its people, they're not sending their best. They're not sending you," he warned. "They're not sending you. They're sending people that have lots of problems and they're bringing those problems with us. They're bringing drugs, they're bringing crime, they're rapists."[7]

Throughout the campaign, Trump leaned into issues of race with uncommon venom for a major-party nominee. He at first refused to denounce the best-known American Ku Klux Klan leader David Duke. Trump retweeted white supremacists and spread anti-Semitic imagery with an ad, for example, featuring the faces of a trio of wealthy Jews atop a "global power structure" that was conspiring to rip off America's workers.[8]

Often in the same rally speeches where he targeted racial minorities with unsubtle epithets, Trump pitched his message with a brilliant flair for theatrics to working-class whites. Class, as much as race then, was a core part of his message and a key to his political resonance. He insisted that China was "raping" the

242 Part III: The General Election

United States through unfair trade deals. Politicians, reporters, and corporate elites were conspiring to enrich themselves and deny the fruits of their labor to hard-working Americans. Trump derided Clinton and other politicians (Republican and Democrat) as corrupt, feckless, and unable to champion working people's needs—a Washington "establishment" so removed from people's lives that they were blind to the economic pain and suffering that millions of citizens had experienced for decades.

Addressing thousands at a rally in Henderson, Nevada, Trump said, "We are living through the greatest job theft in the history of the world. Our jobs are being stolen. I will be the greatest jobs President that God ever created."[9]

Already in the days since the election ended, a debate has erupted about the factors that propelled Trump's victory. Were his white supporters mainly drawn to his promise of creating good jobs and restoring economic opportunity for them and their families? To what extent were his voters motivated by anger toward immigrants, Muslims, and African-Americans whom Trump, at times, suggested were not authentically American and overrunning the United States with drugs, crime, and terrorism? Was Trump's appeal primarily economic, primarily racial, or some combination of these factors?

Put differently: Was 2016 an earthquake caused by deindustrialization and globalization that had wreaked economic havoc on the lives of millions of once-secure and mostly white Americans? Was the historic vote in the Electoral College an economic voice of protest against U.S. policies and structural economic factors? Or, was a substantial part of his victory driven by his uncanny ability to tap white identity politics and the little-recognized but still intense resistance to America's increasing racial diversity and ethnic heterogeneity?

His victory reflects a long trend in which non–college-educated white voters— once termed "Reagan Democrats"—had come to see the Democratic Party as elitist and more sympathetic to Wall Street than Main Street. Some felt the Democrats favored racial minorities through government programs at the expense of lower-income whites. Trump put an exclamation point on this trend, winning non–college-educated white voters by nearly 40 percentage points. Just as non–college-educated whites overwhelmingly voted for Trump, African-Americans, Latinos, and Asian-Americans voted against him.[10]

Thus, President Trump will have an opportunity to cement the support of working- and middle-class whites behind him. If he can fulfill his vow to restore economic growth in areas left behind by the loss of manufacturing jobs, for example, he might be able to win for the GOP the support of such voters for years to come. Yet if he is unable to jump-start the American economy and reduce income inequality, he risks a backlash from his most fervent supporters.

Ultimately, race (and racism) were a core part of his appeal, while legitimate economic grievances and long-simmering economic frustrations also played a role. Arguing that he alone could take on a corrupt Washington and bring back good jobs in communities decimated by deindustrialization and globalization,

Chapter 13: The Defining Fault Lines **243**

Trump struck a chord among white workers who felt left behind by so-called "elites" in both parties.

This fundamental tension—pitting an ever-more diverse electorate against non-college-educated whites who have lost good jobs in recent decades—is unlikely to disappear any time soon. For the years ahead, the country will likely be debating how issues of race and class helped transform Trump's movement into an electoral juggernaut, at least in 2016.

Gender

The issue of gender in this election will also likely be hotly debated fifty years from this writing. One reason why so many prognosticators believed that Hillary Clinton would win (aside from the polls) was the assumption that social progress was linear: If the United States could twice vote for an African-American to be the president, then surely Americans would be ready, at long last, to elect a woman as president. That, in a nutshell, was the assumption held by numerous progressives.

Ultimately, however, it turned out not to be so. The 2016 election may be seen less as a step forward for gender equality than as a step back. Clinton's campaign at first appeared to be a sure sign of social progress. She became the first woman nominee of a major party. It was assumed that white suburban women would be drawn to her path-breaking candidacy, and that gender might enable her to peel off support of Republican women.

That faith was also, as it turned out, misguided. In fact, Trump ran as arguably the most misogynistic candidate in modern American history. By engaging in gender-fueled attacks on his rivals and critics, Trump was willing to demean women based on their looks, their bodies, and what he saw as their inherent weaknesses. Trump attacked Fox News host Megyn Kelly for having "blood coming out of her wherever," widely construed as a reference to her menstruation. Trump ridiculed GOP primary candidate Carly Fiorina's face and claimed that Hillary Clinton only won the nomination because Clinton had played the "gender card." ("Deal me in," Clinton responded.) During the third presidential debate, Trump called Clinton a "nasty woman," and in the final months he questioned her stamina in an advertisement showing her stumbling while she was sick with pneumonia. More than a dozen women emerged during the general election to describe instances in which Trump sexually harassed or assaulted them. According to exit polls, Hillary Clinton only slightly improved on Obama's 2012 performance among women voters: she won them by twelve points; Obama won them by ten.[11]

Thus, in spite of the ceiling-shattering nature of her candidacy, and in spite of Trump's gendered broadsides, Trump won support from the majority of male voters and performed well enough among women to win the White House. Clinton was a deeply flawed candidate: the email scandal that dogged her for more than a year; the speeches she had given to Goldman Sachs for hundreds of

244 Part III: The General Election

thousands of dollars in fees; her lack of a succinct economic slogan at the core of her campaign; and the impression among many Americans that she had political dynastic ties because of her husband's two White House terms combined to undercut her hoped-for image as a change agent. The Russia hacking of John Podesta's and the Democratic National Committee's emails, coupled with FBI Director James Comey's decision to issue public statements about the investigation into Clinton's email practices, hurt Clinton, too.

These attacks and her political flaws enabled Trump, in retrospect, to claim the mantle of change and tap people's desire for something radically different than a typical politician. But it's impossible to disentangle her flaws as a candidate from the gendered attacks leveled against her during the campaign. What will probably be debated in the years ahead is why so many Americans didn't reject Trump's offensive comments about women and whether or not some Americans were reluctant to elect a woman president—or whether they simply did not want to elect Clinton. It's likely that in the centuries-long struggle for gender equality, the 2016 campaign will be characterized as a setback rather than what progressives expected to be a triumph.

The Fragility of American Democracy

At the close of the campaign, Trump went to Gettysburg, Pennsylvania, where he delivered what his campaign promised would be a major policy address. Gettysburg, the site where President Abraham Lincoln paid tribute to the soldiers who had died in the Civil War, became known for something different on this day. Trump devoted the first fifteen minutes of his speech to attacking women who had charged that he had sexually assaulted them. Trump said he was going to sue them after the election was over. This moment captured a debased discourse that marred the 2016 contest.

Presidential politics has almost always been brutish and personal. During the 1800 presidential election pitting Thomas Jefferson against John Adams, one newspaper warned that "murder, robbery, rape, adultery and incest will openly be taught and practiced" if Jefferson were to win the White House.[12]

But the Trump–Clinton contest was especially rancorous. The election stands out for the depth of the voters' discontent fueled partly by each candidates' blistering attacks on one another. Armed with a Twitter feed and access to cable news shows, Trump attacked so many individuals with so much bile that the *New York Times* actually tracked the more than 280 people and places that he had insulted on Twitter. He coined derogatory nicknames for his opponents ("Crooked Hillary," "Lyin' Ted," "Little Marco"), charged that President Obama was a founder of the terrorist group ISIS, and boasted of Senator Lindsey Graham, "I ran him out of the race like a little boy."[13]

Chapter 13: The Defining Fault Lines **245**

Hillary Clinton's campaign trashed Trump as an erratic, temperamentally unfit bully who must never be given access to the nuclear codes. This election's charges and counter-charges repulsed a majority of the American public.

Yet, although the discourse was shrill, it was the issue of Trump's authoritarian tendencies that cast light on the fragility of American democracy. Trump championed conspiracy theories and he challenged much of the news media as essentially liars. The 2016 campaign went beyond the typical spin engaged in by partisans. Trump seemed not to suffer politically when, for example, he said Clinton was guilty of massive crimes (the FBI cleared her during an exhaustive investigation of her email practices as Secretary of State). He wasn't politically damaged when he charged that Ted Cruz's father was complicit in John F. Kennedy's assassination; or when he asserted with no facts that terrorists were pouring over the southern border; or when he claimed that the media, the Clinton campaign, and unnamed global powers were conspiring against him and throwing the election to Clinton.

The well-regarded *Washington Post* Fact-Checker column found that Trump had "amassed such a collection of Four-Pinocchio ratings [the worst possible]— fifty-nine in all—that by himself he's earned as many in this campaign as all other Republicans (or Democrats) combined in the past three years."[14]

Trump's embrace of authoritarian norms and ideas raised deeper questions about the durability of America's democracy. Trump praised Russian dictator Vladimir Putin as a stronger leader than President Obama. His breaching of democratic norms included his re-tweeting a quote from Italian fascist Benito Mussolini. His convention address featured the line that "I alone can fix it," a statement in the spirit of *Caudillos*, Latin American strongmen. Further flouting democratic traditions, Trump vowed that he would name a special prosecutor and put his rival Hillary Clinton in jail if he were to win the White House. When asked whether he planned to concede the election if he lost, Trump demurred. He said he wanted to keep people in suspense, raising the specter that he would encourage his supporters to revolt against what he called a rigged, corrupt political system.[15]

Conclusion

American democracy has survived crises worse than the one triggered by the 2016 election, of course. The 1860 presidential election and the Civil War that ensued is a case in point. The assassinations of the Rev. Martin Luther King, Jr., and Democratic presidential candidate Robert F. Kennedy in 1968 sowed doubts about democracy's capacity to settle differences through non-violent means. In both moments, democracy itself—the American experiment—seemed to be unraveling.

Nonetheless, the 2016 campaign may be seen fifty years from now as another crisis in the ongoing project of American democracy. Trump's campaign forced

246 Part III: The General Election

numerous conservatives and progressives alike to question Trump's faith in democracy. Millions of Americans worried during the election, and remain worried, that Trump will take power and rule as an authoritarian, punishing his enemies, constraining the free press, suppressing civil liberties, and defying the Constitution's separation of powers. Trump is going to be the forty-fifth president, and the United States will soon begin to know the answers to these most urgent questions. American democracy is going to face perhaps its sternest test since the September 11, 2001 terrorist attacks.

Notes

1 For instances of Trump's racism, misogyny, and anti-Semitism, see Cheryl Greenberg, "Donald Trump's Conspiracy Theories Sound Anti-Semitic. Doesn't He Even Realize It?" *Washington Post*, October 26, 2016, www.washingtonpost.com/posteverything/wp/2016/10/26/donald-trumps-conspiracy-theories-sound-anti-semitic-does-he-even-realize-it/?utm_term=.4a63e4a39881; Tracy Jan, "How the Racism Unleashed in the Aftermath of the Trump Campaign Could Get You Fired," *Washington Post*, December 16, 2016, www.washingtonpost.com/news/wonk/wp/2016/12/16/how-the-racism-unleashed-in-the-aftermath-of-trumps-campaign-could-get-you-fired/?utm_term=.62e31952f1d0; Michael D'Antonio, "Is Donald Trump Racist? Here's What the Record Shows," *Fortune*, August 24, 2016, http://fortune.com/2016/06/07/donald-trump-racism-quotes/; Claire Cohen, "Donald Trump Sexist Tracker: Every Offensive Comment in One Place," *The Telegraph* (UK), November 9, 2016, www.telegraph.co.uk/women/politics/donald-trump-sexism-tracker-every-offensive-comment-in-one-place/. For examples of his breaking with Republican conservative orthodoxy, see Louisa Thomas, "America First for Charles Lindbergh and Donald Trump," *The New Yorker*, July 24, 2016, www.newyorker.com/news/news-desk/america-first-for-charles-lindbergh-and-donald-trump; Kathryn A. Wolfe and Lauren Gardner, "Conservatives vs. Trump's Infrastructure Plan," *Politico*, November 11, 2016, www.politico.com/story/2016/11/conservatives-vs-trumps-infrastructure-plan-231221; Maggie Gallagher, "Four Truths About the Party of Trump," July 22, 2016, www.nationalreview.com/article/438238/donald-trumps-republican-party-will-move-left-social-issues (all accessed December 12, 2016).

2 For examples of conservative criticism of Trump, see Charles C. W. Cooke, "No, Trump's Conservative Critics Have Not Been 'Destroyed' or Silenced," *National Review*, December 14, 2016, www.nationalreview.com/article/443040/never-trump-conservatives-donald-trump-election-ayn-rand-jonathan-chait; Glenn Beck, "Conservatives Against Trump," *National Review*, January 20, 2016, www.nationalreview.com/article/430126/donald-trump-conservatives-oppose-nomination (both accessed December 14, 2016).

3 Charlie Sykes, "Where the Right Went Wrong," *New York Times*, December 15, 2016, www.nytimes.com/2016/12/15/opinion/sunday/charlie-sykes-on-where-the-right-went-wrong.html; Evan McMullin, "Trump's Threat to the Constitution," *New York Times*, December 5, 2016, www.nytimes.com/2016/12/05/opinion/

Chapter 13: The Defining Fault Lines **247**

trumps-threat-to-the-constitution.html; Transcript of Mitt Romney's Speech on Donald Trump, *New York Times*, March 3, 2006, www.nytimes.com/2016/03/04/us/politics/mitt-romney-speech.html (all accessed December 17, 2016).

4 David Frum, "The Conservative Case for Voting for Clinton," *The Atlantic*, November 2, 2016, www.theatlantic.com/politics/archive/2016/11/dont-gamble-on-trump/506207/; Amanda Carpenter, "One GOP Woman Wonders Why the Men in Her Party Won't Defend Her," *Washington Post*, October 25, 2016, www.washingtonpost.com/news/powerpost/wp/2016/10/25/carpenter-op-ed/?utm_term=.ce9dd8f377f1 (both accessed December 18, 2016).

5 "Presidential Approval Ratings, George W. Bush," *Gallup* [n.d.], www.gallup.com/poll/116500/presidential-approval-ratings-george-bush.aspx (accessed December 2, 2016).

6 Ilan Stavans, "Alicia Machado vs. Donald Trump's Machismo," *New York Times*, October 2, 2016, www.nytimes.com/2016/09/28/us/politics/alicia-machado-donald-trump.html; Lindsey Bever, "Intern Camps? 'I Certainly Hate the Concept,' Trump Says," *Washington Post*, December 8, 2015, www.washingtonpost.com/news/post-politics/wp/2015/12/08/trump-on-internment-camps-i-certainly-hate-the-concept/?utm_term=.5df891c121cd; Rebecca Kaplan, "Donald Trump Defends Muslim Plan by Comparing Himself to FDR," *CBS News*, December 8, 2015, www.cbsnews.com/news/donald-trump-defends-muslim-plan-by-comparing-himself-to-fdr/ (all accessed December 16, 2016).

7 "Donald Trump's Announcement Speech," *Time*, June 15, 2016, http://time.com/3923128/donald-trump-announcement-speech/ (accessed December 5, 2016).

8 "New Trump Ad Features Prominent Jews in Deriding International Bankers," *Jewish Telegraphic Agency*, November 6, 2016, www.jta.org/2016/11/06/news-opinion/politics/new-trump-ad-focuses-on-prominent-jews-in-deriding-international-bankers; Harper Neidig, "Trump Retweets Another Apparent White Supremacist," *The Hill*, April 19, 2016, http://thehill.com/blogs/ballot-box/gop-primaries/276919-trump-retweets-another-apparent-white-supremacist; Eugene Kiely, "Trump's David Duke Amnesia," *Factcheck.org*, March 1, 2016, www.factcheck.org/2016/03/trumps-david-duke-amnesia/ (all accessed December 18, 2016).

9 Jeff Gillan and Craig Feigener, "Donald Trump Rallies, Thrills Thousands in Henderson," *News 3*, Las Vegas, October 5, 2016, http://news3lv.com/news/local/supporters-get-in-line-before-midnight-to-attend-trump-henderson-rally (accessed December 4, 2016).

10 Jim Tankersley, "How Trump Won: The Revenge of Working-Class Whites," *Washington Post*, November 9, 2016, www.washingtonpost.com/news/wonk/wp/2016/11/09/how-trump-won-the-revenge-of-working-class-whites/?utm_term=.86a4ea4ae2a9 (accessed December 7, 2016).

11 Hannah Levintova, "The Stunningly Long List of Women Who've Accused Trump of Sexual Assault," *Mother Jones*, October 14, 2016, www.motherjones.com/politics/2016/10/all-women-whove-accused-trump-sexual-assault; Richa Chaturvedi, "A Closer Look at the Gender Gap in Presidential Voting," Pew Research Center, July 28, 2016, www.pewresearch.org/fact-tank/2016/07/28/a-closer-look-at-the-gender-gap-in-presidential-voting/ (both accessed December 12, 2016).

248 Part III: The General Election

12 "Thomas Jefferson: Campaigns and Elections," Miller Center of Public Affairs, University of Virginia, [n.d.], http://millercenter.org/president/biography/jefferson-campaigns-and-elections (accessed December 27, 2016).

13 Jasmine C. Lee and Kevin Quealy, "The 289 People, Places and Things Donald Trump Has Insulted on Twitter: A Complete List," *New York Times*, updated December 6, 2016, www.nytimes.com/interactive/2016/01/28/upshot/donald-trump-twitter-insults.html?_r=0#jeb-bush (accessed December 15, 2016).

14 James Warren, "Washington Post Fact-Checker Says Trump Lies Way More Than Clinton," Poynter Institute, November 7, 2016, www.poynter.org/2016/washington-post-fact-checker-says-trump-lies-way-more-than-clinton/437802/ (accessed December 3, 2016).

15 For various takes on Trump as a threat to democracy, see, for example, Steve Livetsky and Daniel Ziblatt, "Is Donald Trump a Threat to Democracy?" *New York Times*, December 16, 2016, www.nytimes.com/2016/12/16/opinion/sunday/is-donald-trump-a-threat-to-democracy.html; Editorial board, "Donald Trump is a Unique Threat to Democracy," *Washington Post*, July 22, 2016, www.washingtonpost.com/opinions/donald-trump-is-a-unique-threat-to-american-democracy/2016/07/22/a6d823cc-4f4f-11e6-aa14-e0c1087f7583_story.html?utm_term=.7e980f06bb14; David Frum, "The Seven Broken Guardrails of Democracy," *The Atlantic*, May 31, 2016, www.theatlantic.com/politics/archive/2016/05/the-seven-broken-guardrails-of-democracy/484829/ (all accessed December 18, 2016).

Appendix A

TIMELINE

Pre-Primary Phase (2015)

January 2015

29 Mitt Romney, after toying with the idea of a third run for the Republican nomination, publicly decided not to pursue it.

March

22 Ted Cruz, senator from Texas, announced that he was a candidate for the Republican nomination for president. His is the first formal declaration on the Republican side.

April

6 Rand Paul, senator from Kentucky, became the second Republican candidate.

12 Marco Rubio, senator from Florida, became the third Republican candidate.

12 Hillary Clinton, former senator from New York, former Secretary of State, and 2008 presidential aspirant, announced that she was a candidate for the Democratic nomination for president. She was the first Democratic candidate to announce.

May

4 Ben Carson, neurosurgeon and conservative activist, became the fourth Republican candidate.

5 Carly Fiorina, former CEO of Hewlett-Packard, became the fifth Republican candidate.

5 Mike Huckabee, former governor of Arkansas and 2008 presidential aspirant, became the sixth Republican candidate.

250 Appendix A: Timeline

25 Bernie Sanders, senator from Vermont, became the second Democratic candidate.
26 Rick Santorum, former senator from Pennsylvania and 2008 presidential aspirant, became the seventh Republican candidate.
28 George Pataki, former governor of New York, announced via YouTube, became the eighth Republican candidate.
29 Martin O'Malley, former governor of Maryland, became the third Democratic candidate.
31 Lindsey Graham, senator from South Carolina, became the ninth Republican candidate.

June
3 Lincoln Chafee, former governor of Rhode Island, became the fourth Democratic candidate.
3 Rick Perry, former governor of Texas and 2012 presidential candidate, became the tenth Republican candidate.
14 Jeb Bush, former governor of Florida, after a long period of waiting in the wings, became the eleventh Republican candidate.
16 Donald Trump, New York City businessman and entrepreneur, became the twelfth Republican candidate.
23 Bobby Jindal, governor of Louisiana, became the thirteenth Republican candidate. Jill Stein announced as the Green Party candidate.
30 Chris Christie, governor of New Jersey, became the fourteenth Republican candidate.

July
2 Jim Webb, former senator from Virginia, became the fifth Democratic candidate.
12 Scott Walker, governor of Wisconsin, became the fifteenth Republican candidate.
20 John Kasich, governor of Ohio, became the sixteenth Republican candidate.
29 Jim Gilmore, former governor of Virginia and 2008 candidate, became the seventeenth and final Republican candidate.

August
6 First Republican debate, sponsored by Fox television, held in Cleveland, Ohio. The undercard debate featured Fiorina, Gilmore, Graham, Jindal, Pataki, Perry, and Santorum. The top ten event featured Bush, Carson, Christie, Cruz, Huckabee, Paul, Rubio, Trump, Walker, and Kasich. All-time television viewing record for main event.

September
6 Professor Lawrence Lessig became the sixth Democratic candidate.

Appendix A: Timeline **251**

12 Rick Perry suspended his presidential campaign.
16 Second Republican debate, sponsored by CNN, held at the Reagan Presidential Library. Fiorina added to list, making this an eleven-candidate debate.

October
13 First Democratic debate, hosted by CNN, held in Las Vegas, with the five candidates: Clinton, Sanders, O'Malley, Webb, and Chafee.
19 Webb dropped out of the Democratic primaries; pondered a third-party bid.
20 After months of speculation, Vice President Joe Biden announced that he would not be a candidate for the Democratic nomination.
22 Hillary Clinton grilled by House special committee on Benghazi.
23 Chafee dropped out of the Democratic primaries.

November
2 Lessig dropped out of the Democratic primaries.
10 Third Republican debate, held in Milwaukee, Wisconsin, with Trump, Carson, Rubio, Cruz, Fiorina, Bush, Kasich, and Paul. The earlier debate featured Christie, Jindal, Huckabee, and Santorum. (Neither Pataki nor Gilmore had enough popular recognition to reach the second-tier round.)
12 Terrorist attacks in Paris.
14 Second Democratic debate, held at Drake University, Des Moines, Iowa, with three candidates: Clinton, Sanders, and O'Malley.
17 Jindal dropped out of the Republican nomination race.

December
15 Fifth Republican debate, Las Vegas, Nevada.
19 Third Democratic debate hosted by ABC News, held at Saint Anselm College, Manchester, NH, with Clinton, Sanders, and O'Malley.
21 Graham dropped out of the Republican race.
29 Pataki dropped out of the Republican race.

January 2016
6 Gary Johnson, former governor of New Mexico and 2012 presidential candidate, announced candidacy through the Libertarian Party.
14 Republican debate in North Charleston, South Carolina, hosted by Fox Business Network, with Trump, Cruz, Rubio, Bush, Kasich, Christie, and Carson. The undercard debate featured Santorum, Huckabee, and Fiorina. Rand Paul chose not to participate in the undercard debate.
17 Final Democratic debate before beginning of primaries, Charleston, SC, hosted by NBC News, with Clinton, Sanders, and O'Malley.
29 Final Republican debate before Iowa caucus, in Des Moines, Iowa, hosted by Fox News, with Cruz, Rubio, Bush, Kasich, Christie, Carson, and Paul.

252   Appendix A: Timeline

The undercard featured Santorum, Huckabee, and Fiorina. Trump made the biggest splash by refusing to participate, holding his own rally and fundraiser for veterans a few blocks away.

Primary and Caucus Phase (February–June 2016)

February

1   Iowa caucus, closed (52-D delegates, Clinton won; 30-R delegates, Cruz won. (See Appendix D for more detail on primaries and caucuses results.) O'Malley suspended campaign; Huckabee dropped out.

3   Santorum and Paul dropped out. Remaining nine Republican candidates are Bush, Carson, Christie, Cruz, Fiorina, Gilmore, Kasich, Trump, and Rubio. Gilmore, who received just twelve votes in Iowa, bragged on Twitter that he had outlasted Paul.

9   New Hampshire primary, mixed (32-D, Sanders; 23-R, Trump).

10   Fiorina dropped out; Christie suspended his campaign. Seven Republican candidates remained: Bush, Carson, Cruz, Gilmore, Kasich, Rubio, and Trump. Gilmore, with 0.0 percent of the New Hampshire vote, remained a candidate.

11   Democratic debate at the University of Wisconsin-Milwaukee, sponsored by PBS and Facebook between Sanders and Clinton.

12   Gilmore dropped out.

20   South Carolina Republican primary, open (50, Trump); Nevada Democratic caucus, closed (43, Clinton).
Bush dropped out. Remaining five Republican candidates: Carson, Cruz, Kasich, Rubio, and Trump.

23   Nevada Republican caucus, closed (30, Trump).

26   Chris Christie endorsed Trump.

27   South Carolina Democratic primary, open (59, Clinton).

March

1   Super Tuesday, with fifteen primaries and caucuses. Alabama primary, open (60-D, Clinton; 50-R, Trump); Alaska Republican caucus, closed (28, Cruz); American Samoa Democratic caucus, open (10, Clinton); Arkansas primary, open (37-D, Clinton; 40-R, Trump); Colorado caucus, closed (79-D, Sanders; 37-R, Cruz); Georgia primary, open (116-D, Clinton; 76-R, Trump); Massachusetts primary, mixed (116-D, Clinton; 42-R, Trump); Minnesota caucus, open (93-D, Sanders; 38-R, Rubio); Oklahoma primary, closed (42-D, Sanders; 43-R, Cruz); Tennessee primary, open (76-D, Clinton; 58-R, Trump); Texas primary, open (252-D, Clinton; 155-R, Cruz); Vermont primary, open (26-D, Sanders; 16-R, Trump).

2   Carson suspended campaign. The remaining Republican candidates are Cruz, Kasich, Rubio, and Trump.

Appendix A: Timeline **253**

3 Republican debate in Detroit. Romney denounced Trump; Trump fired back. Intense criticism of Trump from establishment Republicans, including Paul Ryan and others.

5 Kansas caucus, closed (37-D, Sanders; 40-R, Cruz); Kentucky caucus, closed (45-R, Trump); Louisiana primary, closed (58-D, Clinton; 47-R, Trump); Maine Republican caucus, closed (23, Cruz); Nebraska Democratic caucus, closed (30, Sanders).

6 Maine Democratic caucus, closed (30, Sanders); Puerto Rico Republican primary, open (23, Rubio).

8 Hawaii Republican caucus, closed (19, Trump); Idaho Republican primary, closed (32, Cruz); Michigan primary, open (148-D, Sanders; 59-R, Trump); Mississippi primary, open (41-D Clinton; 40-R Trump); Democrats Abroad (17-D).

9 Guam Republican convention, closed (9, Trump).

11 Carson endorsed Trump.

12 Northern Marianas Islands Democratic caucus, closed (11, Clinton); District of Columbia Republican caucus, closed (18, Rubio).

15 Florida primary, closed (246-D, Clinton; 99-R, Trump); Illinois primary, open (182-D, Clinton; 69-R, Trump); Missouri primary, open (84-D, Clinton; 52-R, Trump); North Carolina primary, mixed (121-D, Clinton; 72-R, Trump); Northern Mariana Islands Republican caucus, closed (9, Trump); Ohio primary, mixed (159-D, Clinton; 66-R, Kasich).
Rubio suspended his campaign, leaving three GOP candidates: Cruz, Kasich, and Trump.

19 Virgin Islands Republican caucus (9, Trump).

22 American Samoa Republican convention, open (9, Trump); Arizona primary, closed (85-D, Clinton; 58-R, Trump); Idaho Democratic caucus, closed (27, Sanders); Utah primary, closed (37-D, Sanders; 40-R, Cruz).
Jeb Bush endorsed Cruz.

26 Alaska Democratic caucus, closed (20, Sanders); Hawaii Democratic caucus, closed (34, Sanders); Washington Democratic caucus, closed (118, Sanders).

April

5 Wisconsin primary, open (96-D, Sanders; 42-R, Cruz).

9 Wyoming Democratic caucus, closed (18, Sanders).

19 New York primary, closed (291-D, Clinton; 95-R, Trump).

26 Connecticut primary, closed (70-D, Clinton; 28-R, Trump); Delaware primary, closed (31-D, Clinton; 16-R, Trump); Maryland primary, closed (118-D, Clinton; 38-R, Trump); Pennsylvania primary, closed (210-D, Clinton; 71-R, Trump); Rhode Island primary, mixed (33-D, Sanders; 19-R, Trump).

27 Cruz announced that Carly Fiorina would be his choice for vice president.

254 Appendix A: Timeline

May

3   Indiana primary, open (92-D, Sanders; 57-R, Trump).

4   Cruz suspended campaign.

5   Kasich suspended campaign, leaving only Trump as Republican candidate.

7   Guam Democratic primary, closed (12, Clinton).

10   Nebraska Republican primary, closed (36, Trump); West Virginia primary, mixed (34-D, Sanders; 37-R, Trump).

17   Kentucky Democratic primary, closed (61, Clinton); Oregon, closed (73-D, Sanders; 28-R, Trump).

24   Washington Republican primary, closed (44, Trump).

June

4   Virgin Islands Democratic caucus, open (12, Clinton).

5   Puerto Rico Democratic caucus, open (67, Clinton).

6   Associated Press declared that Clinton has enough delegates to secure the Democratic nomination.

7   California primary, mixed (546-D, Clinton; 172-R, Trump); Montana primary, open (27-D, Sanders; 27-R, Trump); New Jersey primary, mixed (142-D, Clinton; 51-R, Trump); New Mexico primary, closed (43-D, Clinton; 24-R, Trump); North Dakota Democratic caucus, closed (23, Sanders); South Dakota primary, closed (25-D, Clinton; 29-R, Trump).

12   Orlando nightclub massacre.

14   District of Columbia Democratic primary, closed (46, Clinton).

23   British voted to exit from the European Union (Brexit).

Nominating Conventions and General Elections (July–November, 2016)

July

16   Trump announced that Indiana governor Mike Pence would be his running mate.

18–21   Republican Party Nominating Convention, choosing the ticket of Donald Trump and Mike Pence.

22   Clinton announced that Virginia senator Tim Kaine would be her running mate.

25–28   Democratic Party Nominating Convention, choosing the ticket of Hillary Clinton and Tim Kaine. WikiLeaks of Democratic National Committee emails; DNC chair Debbie Wasserman Schultz resigned.

August

30   Trump made a quick trip to Mexico, meeting with President Enrico Peña Nieto.

September

11 Clinton cut short an appearance in New York; doctors revealed she had pneumonia and dehydration.

26 First presidential debate, held at Hofstra University, Hempstead, LI, New York. Lester Holt of NBC moderated.

October

4 Vice presidential debate, held at Longwood College, Farmville, Virginia. Elaine Quijano, CBS News, moderated.

8 *Washington Post* published audio and video of Trump making salacious remarks about women; soon to be called the *Access Hollywood* tape.

9 Second presidential debate, held at Washington University, St. Louis, Missouri. Martha Raddatz, ABC News, and Anderson Cooper, CNN, moderate.

Flurry of Republican officials denounced Trump, some called on him to step down from the race.

19 At least ten women have come forward to claim they had been groped or inappropriately touched by Trump in past years. Trump vowed to sue them. Third presidential debate, held at University of Nevada-Las Vegas. Chris Wallace, Fox News, moderated.

24 Federal government announced that Obamacare premiums would increase by 22 percent for benchmark plan.

28 FBI director James Comey announced that more Clinton emails have been discovered.

November

6 Comey announced that no indictments would be as a result of the new emails.

8 Election Day. Trump prevailed with 304 electoral votes and 46 percent of the popular vote; Clinton won 232 electoral votes and 48.1 percent of the popular vote.

December

19 Electors meeting in respective states; officially selecting Trump as the next president.

2017

January

6 Results of the Electoral College are read in the House of Representatives, and formally certified.

20 Inauguration Day.

Appendix B
PRESIDENTIAL AND VICE PRESIDENTIAL CANDIDATES

The Republicans

For President
Donald J. Trump, Sr.
Born June 14, 1946 in Queens, New York City. Education: B.S., Wharton School of Finance and Commerce, University of Pennsylvania. Businessman principally in real estate, golf courses, and resorts; entrepreneur, author, and television host of *The Apprentice*.

For Vice President
Michael Richard (Mike) Pence
Born July 7, 1959 in Columbus, Indiana. Education: B.A., Hanover College; J.D., Indiana University School of Law. Attorney in private practice and radio talk show host. Unsuccessful candidate for Congress, 1988 and 1990. Member of Congress, 2001–2013, representing Indiana's Second and then Sixth congressional districts; Indiana governor, 2013 to present. Conservative Republican and supporter of the Tea Party faction.

Declared Candidates for Republican Presidential Nomination
John Ellis (Jeb) Bush
Born February 11, 1953 in Midland, Texas. Education: B.A., University of Texas, Austin. Entrepreneur in Florida, then elected as Florida's secretary of commerce, 1988; unsuccessful candidate for Florida governor's office in 1994. Elected governor in 1998, and re-elected in 2002. After leaving office, Bush served as an advisor and consultant in health care and investment banking.

Appendix B: Candidates **257**

Benjamin Solomon (Ben) Carson, Sr.
Born September 18, 1951 in Detroit, Michigan. Education: B.S., Yale University; M.D., University of Michigan. Director of pediatric neurosurgery at Johns Hopkins University and pioneer in several path-breaking surgical techniques. Recipient of more than sixty honorary degrees and awarded the Presidential Medal of Freedom in 2008. Best-selling author and conservative activist.

Christopher James (Chris) Christie
Born September 6, 1962 in Newark, New Jersey. Education: B.A., University of Delaware; J.D., Seton Hall University Law School. U.S. Attorney for New Jersey, 2002–2008. Elected governor of New Jersey in 2009, and re-elected in 2013. Elected chairman of the Republican Governors Association in 2013. For many months, Christie was considered as a potential candidate for the Republican presidential nomination in 2012, before backing away.

Raphael Edward (Ted) Cruz
Born December 22, 1970 in Calgary, Alberta, Canada. Education: B.A., Princeton University; J.D., Harvard University Law School. Associate deputy attorney general, U.S. Department of Justice; solicitor general of Texas, 2003–2008; elected U.S. Senator, Texas, 2013–present.

C. Carleton (Carly) Fiorina
Born September 6, 1964 in Austin, Texas. Education: B.A., Stanford University; M.B.A., University of Maryland; M.S., Sloan School of Business, MIT. Corporate leadership positions at Lucent and chief executive officer at Hewlett-Packard (HP), 1999–2005. Named tenth most powerful businesswoman in the world by *Forbes* magazine. Ran unsuccessfully for the U.S. Senate seat in California in 2010.

James Stuart (Jim) Gilmore, III
Born October 6, 1949 in Richmond, Virginia. Education: Bachelor's degree, University of Virginia; law degree, University of Virginia. Gilmore served in the U.S. Army and was an attorney in private practice. He was Virginia attorney general, 1993–1997, and governor of the state 2007–2001. Gilmore was a candidate for the 2008 Republican presidential nomination, then ran unsuccessfully for the U.S. Senate that year. He is also president and CEO of the Free Congress Foundation.

Michael Dale (Mike) Huckabee
Born August 24, 1955 in Hope, Arkansas. Education: Bachelor's degree, Ouachita Baptist University; attended Southwest Baptist Theological Seminary. Baptist minister, 1980–1992. Ran unsuccessfully for the U.S. Senate seat from Arkansas in 1992, then was elected lieutenant governor in 1993. Huckabee was elected

258 Appendix B: Candidates

governor and served from 1993 through 2007 and was a candidate for the Republican presidential nomination in 2008.

Piyush (Bobby) Jindal
Born June 10, 1971 in Baton Rouge, Louisiana. Education: B.S., Brown University; MLitt, Oxford University, where he was a Rhodes Scholar. Secretary of Louisiana Department of Health in 1996, then president of the University of Louisiana System in 1999; Assistant Secretary of U.S. Health and Human Services Department, 2001–2003. He was elected to U.S. House of Representatives in 2004, re-elected in 2006. He became governor of Louisiana in 2008, serving until January, 2016.

John Richard Kasich
Born May 13, 1952 in McKees Rocks, Pennsylvania. Education: B.A., Ohio State University. Member, U.S. House of Representatives, 1983–2001, serving as chairman of the Budget Committee. Ran unsuccessfully for Republican presidential nomination in 2000. Elected governor of Ohio, 2010, and re-elected in 2014. Author of three books.

George Elmer Pataki
Born June 24, 1945 in Peekskill, New York. Education: B.A., Yale University; J.D., Columbia University Law School. New York state assemblyman (1985–1992) and senator (1993–1994); governor of New York for three consecutive terms, 1995–2007.

Randall Howard (Rand) Paul
Born January 7, 1963 in Pittsburgh, Pennsylvania. Education: Bachelor's degree, Baylor University; M.D., Duke University. Ophthalmologist most of his career; active in Young Conservatives of Texas movement. Elected as U.S. Senator from Kentucky, 2011. His father, Ron Paul, was a Texas congressman and three-time candidate for the presidency.

James Richard (Rick) Perry
Born March 4, 1950 in Paint Branch, Texas. Education: B.S., Texas A&M University. Served as captain in the Air Force, then elected as a Democrat to the Texas House of Representatives in 1984, switching to the Republican Party in 1987. He was state agricultural commissioner then lieutenant governor of Texas in 1998, and became governor when George W. Bush resigned that position in December 2000. Perry was re-elected in 2002, 2006, and 2010, becoming the longest-serving governor of the state. In 2012 he sought the Republican nomination for president.

Appendix B: Candidates **259**

Marco Antonio Rubio
Born May 28, 1971 in Miami, Florida. Education: B.A., University of Florida; J.D., University of Miami Law School. Elected to Florida House of Representatives, 1999–2008, and became House speaker in 2005. Elected to U.S. Senate from Florida in 2010; re-elected in 2016.

Richard John (Rick) Santorum
Born May 10, 1958 in Winchester, Virginia. Education: B.A., Pennsylvania State University in 1980; MBA from the University of Pittsburgh; and J.D. from Dickinson Law School. Elected to the U.S. House of Representatives (1990–1994). He was elected to the U.S. Senate that year and won re-election in 2000, but defeated in 2006. In 2012, he sought the Republican nomination for president, winning eleven state primaries.

Scott Kevin Walker
Born November 2, 1967 in Colorado Springs, Colorado. Education: attended Marquette University. Elected to the Wisconsin State Assembly (1993–2002) then became Milwaukee County Executive (2002–2007). Elected governor of Wisconsin, 2011; survived a recall election in 2012, and was re-elected in 2014.

The Democrats

For President
Hillary Rodham Clinton
Born October 26, 1947 in Chicago, Illinois. Education: B.A., Wellesley College; J.D., Yale University. First Lady of Arkansas, 1979–1981, 1983–1992; First Lady of the United States, 1993–2001. Elected to the U.S. Senate from New York (2000) and re-elected in 2006. Candidate for 2008 Democratic presidential nomination. U.S. Secretary of State (2009–2013).

For Vice President
Timothy Michael (Tim) Kaine
Born February 27, 1958 in St. Paul, Minnesota. Education: B.A., University of Missouri; J.D., Harvard University Law School. City councilman and mayor (1998–2001) of Richmond, Virginia. Elected lieutenant governor (2002–2006), then governor of Virginia (2006–2010). Kaine was chairman of the Democratic National Committee (2009–2011), and was elected to the U.S. Senate from Virginia in 2012.

Declared Candidates for Democratic Presidential Nomination
Lincoln Davenport Chafee
Born March 26, 1953 in Providence, Rhode Island. Education: B.A., Brown University. The only presidential candidate who was a farrier (horseshoeing). (1953),

260 Appendix B: Candidates

former governor, Rhode Island; former U.S. senator, Rhode Island. Elected mayor of Warwick, Rhode Island (1993–1999); U.S. Senate from Rhode Island (1999–2007, as a Republican); elected governor of the state (2011–2015, as a Democrat).

Martin Joseph O'Malley
Born January 18, 1963 in Washington, D.C. Education: B.A., Catholic University of America; J.D., University of Maryland-Baltimore. Elected mayor of Baltimore (1999–2007), then elected governor of Maryland (2007) and re-elected in 2011. Chosen as chairman of the Democratic Governors Association (2011–2013).

Bernard (Bernie) Sanders
Born September 8, 1941 in New York City. Education: B.A., University of Chicago. Elected mayor of Burlington, Vermont (1981–1989); U.S. House of Representatives, 1991–2007. Elected to the U.S. Senate in 2006 and re-elected in 2012.

James Henry (Jim) Webb, Jr.
Born February 9, 1946 in St. Joseph, Missouri. Education: B.S., U.S. Naval Academy; J.D., Georgetown University. Decorated Vietnam War veteran, attaining rank of captain in U.S. Marine Corps (1968–1972); Assistant Secretary of Defense under Ronald Reagan (1984–1987); Secretary of the Navy (1987–1988); elected U.S. Senator from Virginia (2007–2013). Author of several fiction and non-fiction works.

Lester Lawrence (Larry) Lessig III
Born June 3, 1961 in Rapid City, South Dakota. Education: B.A. and B.S., University of Pennsylvania Wharton School; M.A., Cambridge University Trinity College; J.D., Yale University Law School. Academician, activist, and professor of law, Harvard University Law School.

Principal Third Party Candidates

Gary Johnson (Libertarian Party)
Born January 1, 1953, in Minot, North Dakota. Education: B.S. from University of New Mexico. Founder of Big J Enterprises, a multi-million dollar construction company. Two-term governor of New Mexico (1995–2003). The only presidential candidate to have scaled Mount Everest. He also was a presidential candidate in 2012 for the Libertarian Party.

Jill Ellen Stein (Green Party)
Born May 14, 1950, in Chicago, Illinois. Education: B.A. and M.D., Harvard University. Physician and activist, a candidate for governor of Massachusetts in 2002 and 2010, and presidential candidate for the Green Party in 2012.

Appendix C
CAMPAIGN OPERATIVES AND CONSULTANTS

Trump–Pence Campaign

Kellyanne Conway, campaign manager
Stephen Bannon, chief executive officer
David Bossie, deputy campaign manager
Michael Glassner, deputy campaign manger
Cory Lewandowski, campaign manager (fired, June 2016)
Paul Manafort, campaign chairman and chief strategist (resigned, August 2016)
Rick Wiley, political director (fired, May 2016)
Jim Murphy, national political director
Mike Biundo, senior political advisor
Bill Stepien, national field director
Hope Hicks, press secretary
Jason Miller, senior communications advisor
Brad Parscale, digital director
Stephen Miller, national director of policy
Tony Fabrizio, pollster
Jared Kushner, Trump's son-in-law and unofficial advisor
Ivanka Trump, Trump's daughter (married to Kushner) and unofficial advisor

Clinton–Kaine Campaign

Roby Mook, campaign manager
Joel Benenson, pollster and chief strategist
Jennifer Palmieri, communications director
Brian Fallon, lead press secretary

262 Appendix C: Campaign Operatives

Jim Margolis, media advisor
Jake Sullivan, senior policy advisor
Cheryl Mills, senior advisor
John Anzalone, pollster
David Binder, pollster
Mandy Grunwald, media advisor
Charlie Baker, chief administrative officer
Tony Carr, director of research
Teddy Goff, senior adviser for digital strategy
Stephanie Hannon, chief technology officer
Shane Hable, chief information officer
Marlon Marshall, director of state campaigns
Maya Harris, senior policy advisor
LaDavia Drane, congressional liaison
Amanda Renteria, national political director
Beth Jones, chief operating officer
John Podesta, campaign chair
Huma Abedin, campaign vice chair
Minyon Moore, senior advisor
Dennis Cheng, national finance director
Marc Elias, general counsel

Sources: Eric Appleman, Democracy in Action website, www.p2016.org; Ballotpedia.org, *Politico*, and various news sources.

Appendix D
PRIMARY AND CAUCUS RESULTS

Republican Primary and Caucus Results

February

Date	State (Caucus/Primary)	Top Vote Getters (Percentage of Vote/Delegates Received)
1	Iowa Caucus: 30 delegates	Cruz (27%/8); Trump (24%/7); Rubio (23%/7)
9	N. Hampshire Primary: 23	Trump (35%/10); Kasich (16%/4); Cruz (12%/3)
20	South Carolina Primary: 50	Trump (32%/50); Rubio (23%/0); Cruz (23%/0)
23	Nevada Caucus: 30	Trump (46%/14); Rubio (24%/7); Cruz (21%/6)

March

Date	State (Caucus/Primary)	Top Vote Getters (Percentage of Vote/Delegates Received)
1	Alabama Primary: 50	Trump (43%/36); Cruz (21%/13); Rubio (19%/1)
1	Alaska Caucus: 28	Cruz (36%/12); Trump (34%/11); Rubio (15%/5)

264 Appendix D: Primary and Caucus Results

Date	State (Caucus/Primary)	Top Vote Getters (Percentage of Vote/Delegates Received)
1	Arkansas Primary: 40	Trump (33%/16); Cruz (31%/14); Rubio (25%/9)
1	Georgia Primary: 76	Trump (39%/40); Rubio (24%/14); Cruz (24%/18)
1	Mass. Primary: 42	Trump (49%/22); Kasich (18%/8); Rubio (18%/8)
1	Minnesota Caucus: 38	Rubio (36%/17); Cruz (29%/13); Trump (21%/8)
1	Oklahoma Primary: 43	Cruz (34%/14); Trump (28%/12); Rubio (26%/11)
1	Tennessee Primary: 58	Trump (39%/31); Cruz (25%/14); Rubio (21%/9)
1	Texas Primary: 155	Cruz (44%/99); Trump (27%/38); Rubio (18%/4)
1	Vermont Primary: 16	Trump (33%/6); Kasich (30%/6); Rubio (19%/0)
1	Virginia Primary: 49	Trump (35%/17); Rubio (32%/16); Cruz (17%/8)
5	Kansas Caucus: 40	Cruz (48%/24); Trump (23%/9); Rubio (17%/6)
5	Kentucky Caucus: 45	Trump (36%/17); Cruz (32%/15); Rubio (16%/7)
5	Louisiana Primary: 47	Trump (41%/18); Cruz (38%/18); Rubio (11%/5)
5	Maine Caucus: 23	Cruz (46%/12); Trump (32%/9); Kasich (12%/2)
6	Puerto Rico Primary: 23	Rubio (74%/23); Trump (14%/0); Cruz (9%/0)
8	Hawaii Caucus: 19	Trump (42%/10); Cruz (33%/6); Rubio (13%/0)
8	Idaho Primary: 32	Cruz (45%/20); Trump (28%/12); Rubio (16%/0)
8	Michigan Primary: 59	Trump (37%/25); Cruz (25%/17); Kasich (24%/17)
8	Mississippi Primary: 40	Trump (47%/24); Cruz (36%/13); Kasich (9%/0)
9	Guam Convention: 9	Trump (9); Cruz (0); Kasich (0)
10	Virgin Islands Caucus: 9	Trump (6%/9); Uncommitted (65%/0); Cruz (12%/0)

Appendix D: Primary and Caucus Results **265**

Date	State (Caucus/Primary)	Top Vote Getters (Percentage of Vote/Delegates Received)
12	D.C. Caucus: 18	Rubio (33%/10); Kasich (36%/9); Trump (14%/0)
15	Florida Primary: 99	Trump (46%/99); Rubio (27%/0); Cruz (17%/0)
15	Illinois Primary: 69	Trump (39%/53); Cruz (30%/9); Kasich (20%/5)
15	Missouri Primary: 52	Trump (41%/25); Cruz (41%/15); Kasich (10%/0)
15	N.C. Primary: 72	Trump (40%/29); Cruz (37%/27); Kasich (13%/9)
15	N. Mariana Caucus: 9	Trump (73%/9); Cruz (24%/0); Kasich (2%/0)
15	Ohio Primary: 66	Kasich (47%/66); Trump (36%/0); Cruz (13%/0)
22	Am. Samoa Conven.: 9	Trump (9); Cruz (0)
22	Arizona Primary: 58	Trump (47%/58); Cruz (25%/0); Kasich (10%/0)
22	Utah Primary: 40	Cruz (69%/40); Kasich (17%/0); Trump (14%/0)

April

Date	State (Caucus/Primary)	Top Vote Getters (Percentage of Vote/Delegates Received)
5	Wisconsin Primary: 42	Cruz (48%/36); Trump (35%/6); Kasich (14%/0)
19	New York Primary: 95	Trump (61%/89); Kasich (25%/3); Cruz (15%/0)
26	Connecticut Primary: 28	Trump (58%/28); Kasich (28%/0); Cruz (12%/0)
26	Delaware Primary: 16	Trump (61%/16); Kasich (20%/0); Cruz (16%/0)
26	Maryland Primary: 38	Trump (54%/38); Kasich (23%/0); Cruz (19%/0)
26	Pennsylvania Primary: 71	Trump (57%/17); Cruz (22%/0); Kasich (20%/0)
26	Rhode Island Primary: 19	Trump (64%/10); Kasich (24%/5); Cruz (10%/3)

266 Appendix D: Primary and Caucus Results

May

Date	State (Caucus/Primary)	Top Vote Getters (Percentage of Vote/Delegates Received)
3	Indiana Primary: 57	Trump (53%/57); Cruz (37%/0); Kasich (8%/0)
10	Nebraska Primary: 36	Trump (61%/36); Cruz (18%/0); Kasich (11%/0)
10	W. Virginia Primary: 37	Trump (77%/30); Cruz (9%/0); Kasich (7%/1)
17	Oregon Primary: 28	Trump (67%/17); Cruz (17%/3); Kasich (16%/3)
24	Washington Primary: 44	Trump (76%/40); Cruz (11%/0); Kasich (10%/0)

June

Date	State (Caucus/Primary)	Top Vote Getters (Percentage of Vote/Delegates Received)
7	California Primary: 172	Trump (75%/172); Kasich (11%/0); Cruz (9%/0)
7	Montana Primary: 27	Trump (74%/27); Cruz (9%/0); Kasich (7%/0)
7	New Jersey Primary: 51	Trump (81%/53); Cruz 13%/0); Kasich (6%/0)
7	New Mexico Primary: 24	Trump (71%/24); Cruz (13%/0); Kasich (8%/0)
7	South Dakota Primary: 29	Trump (67%/29); Cruz (17%/0); Kasich (16%/0)

Summary of Republican Primaries and Caucuses

Candidate	Pledged Delegates	Votes
Donald Trump	1,457	14.0 million (45% of total)
Ted Cruz	553	7.8 million
Marco Rubio	166	3.5 million
John Kasich	160	4.3 million
Ben Carson	7	0.8 million
Jeb Bush	4	0.3 million

Delegates needed to win: 1,237

Democratic Primary and Caucus Results

February

Date	State (Caucus/Primary)	Top Vote Getters (Percentage of Vote/Delegates Received)
1	Iowa Caucus: 52 delegates	Clinton (49.9%/23); Sanders (49.6%/21)
9	N. Hampshire Primary: 32	Sanders (60.4%/15); Clinton (38.0%/9)
20	Nevada Caucus: 43	Clinton (52.6%/19); Sanders (47.3%/15)
27	South Carolina Primary: 59	Clinton (73%/39); Sanders (26%/14)

March

Date	State (Caucus/Primary)	Top Vote Getters (Percentage of Vote/Delegates Received)
1	Alabama Primary: 60	Clinton (78%/19); Sanders (19%/9)
1	Am. Samoa Caucus: 10	Clinton (68%/4); Sanders (25%/2)
1	Arkansas Primary: 37	Clinton (66%/22); Sanders (30%/10)
1	Colorado Caucus: 79	Sanders (59%/38); Clinton (40%/28)
1	Georgia Primary: 116	Clinton (71%/72); Sanders (28%/28)
1	Massachusetts Primary: 116	Clinton (50%/46); Sanders (49%/45)
1	Minnesota Caucus: 93	Sanders (62%/46); Clinton (38%/29)
1	Oklahoma Primary: 42	Sanders (52%/21); Clinton (42%/17)
1	Tennessee Primary: 76	Clinton (66%/42); Sanders (32%/22)
1	Texas Primary: 252	Clinton (65%/145); Sanders (33%/74)
1	Vermont Primary: 16	Sanders (86%/16); Clinton (14%/0)
1	Virginia Primary: 110	Clinton (64%/61); Sanders (35%/32)
5	Kansas Caucus: 37	Sanders (68%/23); Clinton (32%/10)
5	Louisiana Primary: 58	Clinton (71%/37); Sanders (23%/14)
5	Nebraska Caucus: 30	Sanders (57%/15); Clinton (43%/10)
6	Maine Caucus: 30	Sanders (64%/15); Clinton (36%/7)
8	Michigan Primary: 148	Sanders (50%/65); Clinton (48%/58)
8	Mississippi Primary: 41	Clinton (83%/29); Sanders (17%/4)
8	Democrats Abroad: 17	Sanders (69%/9); Clinton (31%/4)
12	N. Mariana Caucus: 11	Clinton (54%/5); Sanders (34%/2)
15	Florida Primary: 246	Clinton (64%/130); Sanders (33%/63)
15	Illinois Primary: 182	Clinton (50%/68); Sanders (49%/67)
15	Missouri Primary: 84	Clinton (50%/31); Sanders (49%/32)
15	N.C. Primary: 121	Clinton (55%/59); Sanders (41%/45)
15	Ohio Primary: 159	Clinton (57%/76); Sanders (43%/57)
22	Arizona Primary: 85	Clinton (58%/41); Sanders (40%/26)

268 Appendix D: Primary and Caucus Results

Date	State (Caucus/Primary)	Top Vote Getters (Percentage of Vote/Delegates Received)
22	Idaho Caucus: 27	Sanders (78%/17); Clinton (21%/5)
22	Utah Primary: 37	Sanders (80%/24); Clinton (20%/5)
26	Alaska Caucus: 20	Sanders (80%/14); Clinton (20%/4)
26	Hawaii Caucus: 34	Sanders (70%/18); Clinton (30%/13)
26	Washington Caucus: 118	Sanders (73%/25); Clinton (27%/19)

April

Date	State (Caucus/Primary)	Top Vote Getters (Percentage of Vote/Delegates Received)
5	Wisconsin Primary: 96	Sanders (57%/48); Clinton (43%/43)
9	Wyoming Caucus: 18	Sanders (56%/7); Clinton (44%/7)
19	New York Primary: 291	Clinton (58%/139); Sanders (42%/106)
26	Connecticut Primary: 70	Clinton (52%/28); Sanders (46%/27)
26	Delaware Primary: 31	Clinton (60%/12); Sanders (40%/9)
26	Maryland Primary: 118	Clinton (63%/61); Sanders (33%/33)
26	Pennsylvania Primary: 210	Clinton (56%/105); Sanders (44%/83)
26	Rhode Island Primary: 33	Sanders (55%/13); Clinton (43%/11)

May

Date	State (Caucus/Primary)	Top Vote Getters (Percentage of Vote/Delegates Received)
3	Indiana Primary: 92	Sanders (53%/44); Clinton (47%/39)
7	Guam Primary: 12	Clinton (60%/9); Sanders (40%/3)
10	W. Virginia Primary: 34	Sanders (51%/18); Clinton (36%/11)
10	Nebraska Caucuses: 25	Sanders (57%/15); Clinton (43%/10)
17	Kentucky Primary: 61	Clinton (47%/27); Sanders (46%/27)
17	Oregon Primary: 73	Sanders (56%/34); Clinton (33%/25)

June

Date	State (Caucus/Primary)	Top Vote Getters (Percentage of Vote/ Delegates Received)
4	Virgin Islands Caucus: 12	Clinton (87%/12); Sanders (13%/0)
5	Puerto Rico Caucus: 67	Clinton (60%/42); Sanders (38%/24)
7	California Primary: 546	Clinton (53%/254); Sanders (46%/221)
7	Montana Primary: 27	Sanders (52%/11); Clinton (44%/10)
7	New Jersey Primary: 142	Clinton (63%/79); Sanders (37%/47)
7	New Mexico Primary: 43	Clinton (52%/18); Sanders (48%/16)
7	North Dakota Caucus: 23	Sanders (64%/13); Clinton (25%/5)
7	South Dakota Primary: 25	Clinton (51%/10); Sanders (49%/10)
14	D.C. Primary: 46	Clinton (78%/39); Sanders (21%/6)

Summary of Democratic Primaries and Caucuses

Candidate	Delegates + Super Delegates	Votes
Hillary Clinton	2,205 + 570.5	16.8 million (55% of total)
Bernie Sanders	1,846 + 43.5	13.1 million (43% of total)

Delegates needed to win: 2,382

Appendix E
GENERAL ELECTION RESULTS

To win the presidency, a candidate must have 270 Electoral College votes.

Clinton: 227 Electoral votes; 65,844,610 popular votes (48.1 percent)
Trump: 304 Electoral votes; 62,979,636 popular votes (46.0 percent)
Seven electors voted for someone other than Trump or Clinton.

Results by State

This appendix indicates the Electoral votes, popular votes, and percentage of popular votes gained by the two principal candidates, Donald Trump and Hillary Clinton. It also indicates the voting preference of each state through the past six election cycles (1992–2012). Further, it displays the popular vote and percentage of popular vote for Romney and Obama in the 2012 election.

Winning candidates in each state are noted in *italics*.

+   indicates that Clinton had higher percentage than Obama; Trump had higher percentage than Romney
-    indicates that Clinton had lower percentage than Obama; Trump had lower percentage than Romney
★   indicates that the votes gained by third party candidates Johnson (McMullin, Stein, or others) made difference between Trump and Clinton

When a state and the candidates are in CAPITAL LETTERS, that indicates that the vote had flipped from the results in the 2012 election.

State	Electoral Votes	Popular Votes	Percentage of Popular Vote	Comparison with 2012 Election		
Alabama (last six elections, 1992, 1996, 2000, 2004, 2008, 2012: R–R–R–R–R–R)						
- Clinton	—	729,547	(34.4)	Obama	793,620	(37.6)
+ *Trump*	9	1,318,255	(62.1)	*Romney*	1,252,453	(60.7)
Johnson	—	44,467	(2.1)			
Alaska (R–R–R–R–R–R)						
- Clinton	—	116,454	(36.6)	Obama	102,138	(41.3)
- *Trump*	3	163,387	(51.3)	*Romney*	136,848	(55.3)
Johnson	—	18,725	(5.9)			
Arizona (R–R–R–R–R–R)						
+ Clinton	—	1,161,167	(44.6)	Obama	930,669	(44.1)
- *Trump*	11	1,252,401	(48.1)	*Romney*	1,143,051	(54.2)
★ Johnson	—	106,327	(4.1)			
Arkansas (D–D–R–R–R–R)						
- Clinton	—	380,494	(33.7)	Obama	389,699	(36.9)
+ *Trump*	6	684,872	(60.6)	*Romney*	638,467	(60.5)
Johnson	—	29,829	(2.6)			
California (D–D–D–D–D–D)						
+ *Clinton*	55	5,481,885	(61.5)	*Obama*	6,493,095	(59.3)
- Trump	—	2,965,704	(33.2)	Romney	4,202,127	(38.3)
Johnson	—	281,467	(3.2)			
McMullin	—	13,255	(1.2)			
Colorado (D–R–R–R–D–D)						
- *Clinton*	9	1,338,870	(48.2)	*Obama*	1,238,490	(51.2)
- Trump	—	1,202,484	(43.3)	Romney	1,125,391	(46.5)
★ Johnson	—	144,121	(5.2)			
Stein	—	38,437	(1.4)			

State	Electoral Votes	Popular Votes	Percentage of Popular Vote	Comparison with 2012 Election		
Connecticut (D-D-D-D-D-D)						
- *Clinton*	7	897,572	(54.6)	*Obama*	912,531	(58.4)
+ Trump	—	73,215	(40.9)	Romney	631,432	(40.4)
Johnson	—	48,676	(3.0)			
Stein	—	22,841	(1.4)			
Delaware (D-D-D-D-D-D)						
- *Clinton*	3	235,603	(53.4)	*Obama*	242,547	(58.6)
+ Trump	—	185,127	(41.9)	Romney	165,476	(40.0)
Johnson	—	14,757	(3.3)			
Stein	—	6,103	(1.4)			
District of Columbia (D-D-D-D-D-D)						
- *Clinton*	3	282,830	(90.9)	*Obama*	222,332	(91.4)
- Trump	—	12,723	(4.1)	Romney	17,337	(7.1)
Johnson	—	4,906	(1.6)			
Stein	—	4,258	(1.4)			
FLORIDA (R-D-R-R-D-D)						
-CLINTON	—	4,504,975	(47.4)	*Obama*	4,235,470	(50.0)
+ *TRUMP*	29	4,617,886	(48.6)	Romney	4,162,081	(49.1)
★JOHNSON	—	207,043	(2.2)			
Georgia (D-R-R-R-R-R)						
+ Clinton	—	1,877,963	(45.4)	Obama	1,761,761	(45.4)
- *Trump*	16	2,089,104	(50.5)	*Romney*	2,070,221	(53.4)
Johnson	—	125,306	(3.0)			

State	Electoral Votes	Popular Votes	Percentage of Popular Vote	Comparison with 2012 Election		
Hawaii (D-D-D-D-D-D)						
- *Clinton*	4	266,891	(62.2)	*Obama*	303,090	(70.6)
+ Trump	—	128,847	(30.0)	Romney	119,494	(27.8)
Johnson	—	15,954	(3.7)			
Stein	—	12,737	(3.0)			
Idaho (R-R-R-R-R-R)						
- Clinton	—	189,765	(27.5)	Obama	212,560	(32.6)
- *Trump*	4	409,055	(59.2)	*Romney*	420,750	(64.5)
McMullin	—	46,476	(6.7)			
Johnson	—	28,331	(4.1)			
Illinois (D-D-D-D-D-D)						
- *Clinton*	20	3,090,729	(55.5)	*Obama*	2,916,811	(57.3)
- Trump	—	2,146,015	(38.5)	Romney	2,090,116	(41.1)
Johnson	—	209,596	(3.8)			
Stein	—	76,802	(1.4)			
Indiana (R-R-R-R-D-R)						
- Clinton	—	1,033,126	(37.8)	Obama	1,140,425	(43.8)
+ *Trump*	11	1,557,286	(56.9)	*Romney*	1,412,620	(54.3)
Johnson	—	133,993	(4.9)			
IOWA (D-D-D-R-D-D)						
- CLINTON	—	653,669	(41.7)	*Obama*	816,429	(52.1)
+ *TRUMP*	6	800,983	(51.1)	Romney	727,928	(46.5)
Johnson	—	59,186	(3.8)			

State	Electoral Votes	Popular Votes	Percentage of Popular Vote	Comparison with 2012 Election		
Kansas (R–R–R–R–R–R)						
- Clinton	—	427,005	(36.1)	Obama	427,918	(37.8)
- Trump	6	671,018	(56.7)	Romney	678,719	(60.0)
Johnson	—	55,406	(4.7)			
Stein	—	23,506	(2.0)			
Kentucky (D–D–R–R–R–R)						
- Clinton	—	628,854	(32.7)	Obama	679,340	(37.8)
+ Trump	8	1,202,971	(62.5)	Romney	1,087,127	(60.5)
Johnson	—	53,752	(2.8)			
McMullin	—	22,780	(1.2)			
Louisiana (D–D–R–R–R–R)						
- Clinton	—	780,154	(38.4)	Obama	808,496	(40.6)
+ Trump	8	1,178,638	(58.1)	Romney	1,152,460	(57.8)
Johnson	—	37,978	(1.9)			
Maine (D–D–D–D–D–D)						
- Clinton	3	357,735	(47.8)	Obama	397,754	(56.0)
+ Trump	1	335,593	(44.9)	Romney	290,437	(40.9)
★ Johnson	—	38,105	(5.1)			
★ Stein	—	14,251	(1.9)			
Maryland (D–D–D–D–D–D)						
- Clinton	10	1,677,928	(60.3)	Obama	1,527,686	(61.7)
- Trump	—	943,169	(33.9)	Romney	904,970	(36.6)
Johnson	—	79,605	(2.9)			
Stein	—	44,799	(1.6)			

State	Electoral Votes	Popular Votes	Percentage of Popular Vote	Comparison with 2012 Election		
Massachusetts (D-D-D-D-D-D)						
- *Clinton*	11	1,995,196	(60.0)	*Obama*	1,900,575	(60.8)
- Trump	—	1,090,893	(32.8)	Romney	1,177,370	(37.6)
Johnson	—	138,018	(4.2)			
Stein	—	74,661	(1.4)			
MICHIGAN (D-D-D-D-D-D)						
- CLINTON	16	2,268,839	(47.0)	*Obama*	2,561,911	(54.3)
+ *TRUMP*	—	2,279,543	(47.3)	Romney	2,112,673	(44.8)
★ JOHNSON	—	72,136	(3.6)			
★ STEIN	—	51,463	(1.1)			
Minnesota (D-D-D-D-D-D)						
- *Clinton*	10	1,367,716	(46.4)	*Obama*	1,547,668	(52.8)
- Trump	—	1,322,951	(44.9)	Romney	1,321,575	(45.1)
★ Johnson	—	112,994	(3.8)			
★ McMullin	—	53,106	(1.8)			
Mississippi (R-R-R-R-R-R)						
- Clinton	—	485,131	(40.1)	Obama	528,620	(44.5)
+ *Trump*	6	700,714	(57.9)	*Romney*	670,302	(55.5)
Johnson	—	13,789	(1.2)			
Missouri (D-D-R-R-R-R)						
- Clinton	—	1,071,068	(37.9)	Obama	1,215,031	(44.3)
+ *Trump*	10	1,594,511	(56.4)	*Romney*	1,478,961	(53.9)
Johnson	—	97,359	(3.5)			

State	Electoral Votes	Popular Votes	Percentage of Popular Vote	Comparison with 2012 Election		
Montana (D–R–R–R–R–R)						
– Clinton	—	177,709	(35.4)	Obama	200,489	(41.8)
+ *Trump*	3	279,240	(55.6)	*Romney*	264,974	(55.3)
Johnson	—	28,037	(5.6)			
Stein	—	7,970	(1.6)			
Nebraska (R–R–R–R–R–R)						
– Clinton	—	284,494	(33.7)	Obama	289,154	(37.8)
– *Trump*	5	495,961	(58.7)	*Romney*	462,972	(60.5)
Johnson	—	38,946	(4.7)			
Stein	—	8,775	(1.0)			
Nevada (D–D–R–R–D–D)						
– *Clinton*	6	539,260	(47.9)	*Obama*	528,801	(52.3)
–Trump	—	512,058	(45.5)	Romney	462,422	(45.7)
★ Johnson	—	37,384	(3.3)			
★ Others	—	36,663	(3.3)			
New Hampshire (D–D–R–D–D–D)						
– *Clinton*	4	348,526	(46.8)	*Obama*	368,529	(52.2)
+ Trump	—	345,790	(46.5)	Romney	327,870	(46.4)
★ Johnson	—	30,777	(4.1)			
★ Others	—	19,203	(2.6)			
New Jersey (D–D–D–D–D–D)						
– *Clinton*	14	2,148,278	(55.0)	*Obama*	1,960,744	(58.0)
+ Trump	—	1,601,933	(41.0)	Romney	1,383,233	(40.9)
Johnson	—	72,477	(1.9)			
Stein	—	37,772	(1.0)			

State	Electoral Votes	Popular Votes	Percentage of Popular Vote	Comparison with 2012 Election		
New Mexico (D-D-D-R-D-D)						
- *Clinton*	5	385,234	(48.3)	*Obama*	408,312	(52.9)
- Trump	—	319,666	(40.0)	Romney	331,915	(41.0)
★ Johnson	—	74,541	(9.3)			
★ Stein	—	9,879	(1.2)			
New York (D-D-D-D-D-D)						
- *Clinton*	29	4,547,218	(59.0)	*Obama*	3,875,826	(62.6)
+ Trump	—	2,814,346	(36.5)	Romney	2,226,637	(36.0)
Johnson	—	161,836	(2.3)			
Stein	—	107,756	(1.4)			
North Carolina (R-R-R-R-D-R)						
- Clinton	—	2,189,316	(46.2)	Obama	2,178,388	(48.4)
- *Trump*	15	2,362,631	(49.8)	*Romney*	2,275,853	(50.6)
Johnson	—	130,126	(2.7)			
North Dakota (R-R-R-R-R-R)						
- Clinton	—	93,758	(27.2)	Obama	124,490	(38.9)
+ *Trump*	3	216,794	(63.0)	*Romney*	187,586	(58.7)
Johnson	—	21,434	(6.2)			
OHIO (D-D-R-R-D-D)						
- CLINTON	—	2,394,154	(43.2)	*Obama*	2,697,260	(50.1)
+ *TRUMP*	18	2,841,005	(51.3)	Romney	2,593,779	(48.2)
Johnson	—	174,498	(3.2)			

State	Electoral Votes	Popular Votes	Percentage of Popular Vote	Comparison with 2012 Election		
Oklahoma (R–R–R–R–R–R)						
- Clinton	—	420,375	(28.9)	Obama	442,647	(33.2)
- *Trump*	7	949,136	(65.3)	*Romney*	889,372	(66.8)
Johnson	—	83,481	(5.7)			
Oregon (D–D–D–D–D–D)						
- *Clinton*	7	1,002,106	(50.1)	*Obama*	937,321	(54.5)
- Trump	—	782,403	(39.1)	Romney	733,743	(42.7)
Johnson	—	94,231	(4.7)			
Stein	—	50,002	(2.5)			
Others	—	72,594	(3.6)			
PENNSYLVANIA (D–D–D–D–D–D)						
- CLINTON	—	2,926,441	(47.5)	*Obama*	2,907,448	(52.0)
+ *TRUMP*	20	2,970,733	(48.2)	Romney	2,619,583	(46.8)
★ Johnson	—	146,715	(2.4)			
★ Stein	—	49,941	(0.8)			
★ Others	—	69,182	(1.1)			
Rhode Island (D–D–D–D–D–D)						
- *Clinton*	4	252,525	(55.4)	*Obama*	274,342	(62.7)
+ Trump	—	180,543	(38.9)	Romney	155,355	(35.5)
Johnson	—	14,746	(3.2)			
South Carolina (R–R–R–R–R–R)						
- Clinton	—	855,373	(40.7)	Obama	845,756	(44.0)
+ *Trump*	9	1,155,389	(54.9)	*Romney*	1,049,507	(54.6)
Johnson	—	49,204	(3.2)			
McMullin	—	21,016	(1.0)			

State	Electoral Votes	Popular Votes	Percentage of Popular Vote	Comparison with 2012 Election		
South Dakota (R-R-R-R-R-R)						
- Clinton	—	117,458	(31.7)	Obama	144,984	(39.9)
+ *Trump*	3	227,721	(61.5)	*Romney*	210,541	(57.9)
Johnson	—	20,850	(5.6)			
Castle	—	4,064	(1.1)			
Tennessee (D-D-R-R-R-R)						
- Clinton	—	870,695	(34.7)	Obama	953,043	(39.0)
+ *Trump*	11	1,522,925	(60.7)	*Romney*	1,453,097	(59.5)
Johnson	—	70,397	(2.8)			
Texas (R-R-R-R-R-R)						
+ Clinton	—	3,877,868	(43.2)	Obama	3,294,440	(41.4)
- *Trump*	38	4,685,047	(52.2)	*Romney*	4,555,799	(57.2)
Johnson	—	283,492	(3.2)			
Utah (R-R-R-R-R-R)						
+ Clinton	—	310,676	(27.2)	Obama	229,463	(24.9)
- *Trump*	6	515,231	(45.1)	*Romney*	671,747	(72.8)
★ McMullin	—	243,690	(21.3)			
★ Johnson	—	39,608	(3.5)			
Vermont (D-D-D-D-D-D)						
- *Clinton*	3	178,573	(56.7)	*Obama*	199,259	(67.0)
+ Trump	—	95,369	(30.3)	Romney	92,700	(31.2)
Johnson	—	10,078	(3.2)			
Others	—	31,047	(9.9)			

State	Electoral Votes	Popular Votes	Percentage of Popular Vote	Comparison with 2012 Election		
Virginia (R-R-R-R-D-D)						
-*Clinton*	13	1,981,473	(49.8)	*Obama*	1,905,528	(50.8)
-Trump	—	1,769,443	(44.4)	Romney	1,789,618	(47.8)
Johnson	—	118,274	(3.0)			
McMullin	—	54,054	(1.4)			
Washington (D-D-D-D-D-D)						
-*Clinton*	12	1,742,718	(52.6)	*Obama*	1,620,432	(55.8)
-Trump	—	1,221,747	(36.9)	Romney	1,210,369	(41.7)
Johnson	—	160,879	(4.9)			
Other	—	186,116	(5.6)			
West Virginia (D-D-R-R-R-R)						
- Clinton	—	188,794	(26.2)	Obama	234,925	(35.5)
+ *Trump*	5	489,371	(67.9)	*Romney*	412,406	(62.3)
Johnson	—	23,004	(3.2)			
WISCONSIN (D-D-D-D-D-D)						
- CLINTON	—	1,382,536	(46.5)	*Obama*	1,613,950	(52.8)
+ *TRUMP*	10	1,405,284	(47.2)	Romney	1,408,745	(46.1)
★ JOHNSON	—	106,674	(3.6)			
★ STEIN	—	31,072	(1.0)			
Wyoming (R-R-R-R-R-R)						
- Clinton	—	55,973	(21.9)	Obama	68,780	(28.0)
+ *Trump*	3	174,419	(68.2)	*Romney*	170,265	(69.3)
Johnson	—	13,287	(5.2)			

Along with third party candidate Gary Johnson (Libertarian), several others were on various state ballots. Jill Stein (Green Party), Evan McMullin (Independent), and Darrell Castle (Constitutional) were the only other third party candidates who received more than 1 percent in any of the state balloting.

Appendix F
EXIT POLLS

		Clinton	*Trump*
Gender	Male (47%)	41%	53%
	Female (53%)	54%	42%
Race	White (71%)	37%	57%
	Black (12%)	88%	8%
	Hispanic (11%)	66%	29%
	Asian (4%)	65%	29%
Race and Gender	White Men (34%)	31%	62%
	White Women (37%)	43%	52%
	Black Men (5%)	82%	13%
	Black Women (7%)	94%	4%
	Latino Men (5%)	63%	32%
	Latino Women (6%)	69%	25%
Age	18–29 (19%)	55%	36%
	30–44 (25%)	51%	41%
	45–64 (40%)	44%	52%
	65+ (16%)	45%	52%
Education	High School or less (18%)	46%	51%
	Some college (32%)	43%	52%
	College grad. (32%)	49%	44%
	Postgrad. (18%)	58%	37%

		Clinton	*Trump*
Education among Whites by Gender	College grad. women (20%)	51%	44%
	Non-college women (17%)	34%	61%
	College grad. men (17%)	39%	53%
	Non-college men (16%)	23%	71%
Income	Under $30k (17%)	53%	40%
	$30k–$49k (19%)	52%	41%
	$50k–$99.99k (30%)	46%	49%
	$100k–$199.99k (24%)	47%	48%
	$200k–$249.99k (4%)	49%	47%
	$250k and more (6%)	46%	46%
Ideology	Liberal (26%)	84%	10%
	Moderate (39%)	52%	40%
	Conservative (35%)	16%	81%
Which Candidate Quality Mattered Most?	Cares about me (15%)	57%	34%
	Can bring change (39%)	14%	82%
	Right experience (22%)	90%	7%
	Good judgment (20%)	65%	25%

Source: Edison Research for the National Election Poll, a consortium of ABC News, Associated Press, CBS News, CNN, Fox News, and NBC News. November 8, 2016. 24,558 respondents.

Appendix G
CAMPAIGN SPENDING, BY CANDIDATES, PARTIES, AND MAJOR SUPER PACS

Clinton Campaign Team

Hillary Clinton campaign	$623.1 million
Party and Joint Fundraising Committees	$595.4 million
Super PACs	$204.2 million

Trump Campaign Team

Donald Trump campaign	$329.4 million
Party and Joint Fundraising Committees	$524.0 million
Super PACs	$70.0 million

Comparison with Obama and Romney in 2012

Obama	$726 million
Clinton	*$623 million*
Romney	$471 million
Trump	*$329 million*

Other candidates	Raised	Super PACs
Democrats		
Bernie Sanders (left race, July 12)	$234.3 m.	$6.3 m.
Martin O'Malley (left Feb. 2)	$6.3 m.	$0.8 m.
Jim Webb (left Nov. 17, 2015)	$0.8 m.	$0.0 m.
Larry Lessing (left Nov. 2, 2015)	$1.0 m.	$0.0 m.
Lincoln Chafee (left Oct. 23, 2015)	$0.4 m.	$0.0 m.

Appendix G: Campaign Spending · **285**

Republicans

Ted Cruz (left May 2)	$92.7 m.	$89.2 m.
Ben Carson (left March 4)	$59.5 m.	$19.0 m.
Jeb Bush (left Feb. 20)	$34.7 m.	$124.6 m.
Marco Rubio (left March 15)	$50.7 m.	$77.7 m.
John Kasich (left May 4)	$19.3 m.	$30.5 m.
Chris Christie (left Feb. 10)	$8.6 m.	$23.7 m.
Carly Fiorina (left Feb. 10)	$12.1 m.	$15.2 m.
Rand Paul (left Feb. 3)	$12.3 m.	$11.4 m.
Mike Huckabee (left Feb. 12)	$4.2 m.	$7.4 m.
Rick Santorum (left Feb. 3)	$1.8 m.	$0.4 m.
Jim Gilmore (left Feb. 12)	$0.4 m.	$0.4 m
Scott Walker (left Sept. 21, 2015)	$9.0 m.	$31.4 m.
Bobby Jindal (left Nov. 17, 2015)	$1.6 m.	$8.6 m.
Lindsey Graham (left Dec. 21, 2015)	$4.9 m.	$4.2 m.
Rick Perry (left Sept. 11, 2015)	$1.3 m.	$14.1 m.
George Pataki (left Dec. 29, 2015)	$0.5 m.	$0.8 m.

Top Ten Super PACS and Affiliation

Group	*Raised*	*Supports/Opposes*
Priorities USA Action	$192.0 m.	supports Clinton
Senate Leadership Fund	$115.3 m.	conservatives
Right to Rise USA	$121.7 m.	supports Bush
Senate Majority PAC	$92.6 m.	liberals
Conservative Solutions PAC	$60.5 m.	supports Rubio
Get Our Jobs Back	$50.3 m.	conservatives
House Majority PAC	$55.7 m.	liberals
Congressional Leadership	$50.9 m.	conservatives
Women Vote!	$36.7 m.	liberals
Freedom Partners Action	$28.2 m.	conservatives

Source: Federal Election Commission data, as of November 28, 2016, compiled by the Center for Responsive Politics, www.opensecrets.org/outsidespending/summ.php?chrt=V&type=S; *Washington Post*, November 28, 2016, www.washingtonpost.com/graphics/politics/2016-election/campaign-finance/ (accessed December 12, 2016).

INDEX

50 Cent Party 23
527 groups 2
503(c)(4) groups 2

Abedin, Huma 236, 262
"Access Hollywood" video 11, 199, 201,
  219–20, 226, 231, 255
ActBlue 115
Adelson, Sheldon 3, 8, 200; "Sheldon
  Primary" 8
advertising 196, 222; digital 114, 131,
  138, 153, 157, 195; evolution of
  presidential advertising 146–8; Google
  and Facebook policies 23; "Native"
  advertising 174–5; television 153–4;
  Super PAC spending 110, 118
advertising, general election 152–3;
  Clinton 120; Trump 134, 138, 175,
  199
advertising, primaries 148–52; Democrats
  48, 114, 116, 151–2; Republicans 118,
  148–50
Affordable Care Act (Obamacare) 53, 83,
  152, 162
Ailes, Roger 7
Alexander, Lawrence 176
Alt-Right 26, 213, 214, 240
American Bridge 21st Century 196

American Crossroads Super PAC 200
American Dream 25, 234
Americans for Prosperity Super PAC 200
Angry American, The (Tolchin) 24
Anzalone, John 7, 262
Arizona 220, 232
Arizona Republic 25
Art of the Deal (Trump with Schwartz) 28
Atlantic, The 14, 18
authoritarianism, as voter determinant 91,
  94, 98, 164
aversion to change 82, 86, 94, 98
aversion to difference 82, 91–4, 98
aversion to government 82, 85–6
Axelrod, David xiii, 7
Ayotte, Kelly 32, 219

Bannon, Stephen K. xv, 7, 26, 153, 213,
  214, 229, 261
Baron, Martin 178
"basket of deplorables" 26, 168
#BasketofDeplorables 168–9
Bates, Stephen 146
Beckel, Michael 195
Benenson, Joel 7, 132, 261
Benghazi investigations 12, 54, 96, 184,
  194
Bennett, William 13

Index 287

"Bernie Bro" 58
Biden, Joe 5, 49, 51, 52, 60, 194, 225, 251
Big Sort, The (Bishop) 29
"billionaire bounce" 95
Binder, David 7, 262
Bishop, Bill 29
Black, Allida 111
Bloomberg, Michael 17
Bloomberg Politics 83, 132
Bond, Paul 177
Bossie, David 7, 213, 261
bots 157, 158, 160–1
Braverman, Tassin ix, xvii, 9, 105, 232
Brazile, Donna 210
BreitbartNews.com 23, 26, 153, 214, 229
Brennan Center on Social Justice, New York University 16
Brock, David 196
Brooklyn (Clinton headquarters) 49, 193
Brown, Lara M. ix
Buchanan, Patrick 10
bundlers 113, 114
Burke, Edmund 86
Bush, Billy 219
Bush, George H. W. 4, 15, 240
Bush, George W. 14, 16, 50, 240
Bush, Jeb 5, 8, 68–9, 71–3, 166, 167, 176, 211, 228, 256 (*see also* Right to Rise Super PAC)
Buzzfeed 22, 138, 176, 199

cable television coverage of primaries 176
Cambridge Analytica 140
Campaign Finance Institute 111
Campbell, James E. 28
Cardona, Maria x, xvii, 30, 225
Carr, Chris 216
Carson, Ben 68, 69, 71, 72, 116–17; grassroots fundraising 71, 108
Causeway Solutions 216, 222
celebrity news and candidate 174–5
Center for Responsive Politics 152
Central Intelligence Agency (CIA) 23, 202

Chafee, Lincoln 5, 50, 51, 52, 260–1
Chetty, Raj 25
Chisholm, Shirley 10, 95
Christie, Chris xv, 5, 65, 68, 69, 72, 73, 257
Cincinnati Enquirer 14
Citizens United v. Federal Election Commission xiv, 7, 8; Post-*Citizens United* era xv, 105, 106, 192, 194
Clinton campaign: advertising, paid 149–50, 151–2, 152–3; and Alt Right 229–30; and "basket of deplorables" 26, 168, 213–14; and battleground states 30–1; and "Clinton Coalition" 232; and James Comey 221, 235–6; campaign consultants 7; debate performance 217, 220, 230–1; Democratic party and joint fundraising 192–4; emails and wikileaks 23, 227–8; endorsements 14, 25; fake news stories 21–2; fundraising, primaries 105, 107, 108, 111–14; fundraising, general 118, 119–21, 232–3; general election 1, 2, 9, 15, 21, 30; hashtag slogans and Twitter 161, 162–4, 165–6, 167; historic candidacy 10; and Barack Obama 3, 14–15; popular vote 2, 9, 31; press coverage 18, 184; primaries 5, 9, 48–50, 53–4, 55–61; and social media 47, 130, 131–3, 135–7, 140, 153, 160; Super PAC fundraising 110, 194–6; vilification of xv, 11–12, 21; why she lost 30–2, 81, 82, 84–5, 88–9, 96–7; "woman card" 225–7
Clinton, Hillary xiv, 259; 2008 primaries 47; health 214–15, 217; unpopularity 3, 10, 81, 96–7
Clinton, William J. (Bill) 11, 55, 200, 210, 218, 220
Clyburn, James 56
Cohen, Michael x, xvii, 18, 153, 156
Cohen, Nate 30, 31
Cohen, Sara 8
Comey, James 21, 30, 220, 221, 222, 227, 228, 235–6, 244
Confessore, Nicholas 8, 30

288 Index

congressional elections 3, 32–3, 193
Connally, John B. 8
conservatism: crisis of 239–41; different measures of 85–91, 91–5
Conway, Kellyanne 7, 213, 261
Corasaniti, Nick 138–9
Cornfield, Michael x, xvii, 18, 153, 156
Corrado, Anthony x, xvii, 9, 105, 232
Correct the Record 196
Cramer, Katherine J. 24
Crimson Hexagon 157
Cronkite, Walter 20
#CrookedHillary 166–7, 168, 169
Cruz, Ted 5, 8, 9, 11, 108, 111, 176, 245; fundraising 148–9; primaries 65, 67, 69, 71–5
Curiel, Gonzalo P. 228

Dale, Daniel 182
Dallas Morning News 14
Dallek, Matthew x–xi, xviii, 238
"dark money" 106
debates 21, 182, 217, 230–1, 235; Democratic primary 50, 52–4, 58, 115, 151; first presidential 168, 182, 201, 217–18; Republican primary 59, 73, 149; second presidential 17, 199; third presidential 11, 15, 219, 220, 243; Vice Presidential 219
#debatewithBernie 170
#DeleteYourAccount 167–8
democracy, fragility of 244–5
Democratic National Committee 191; fundraising 119, 192–4; hacked emails 23, 227–8, 238, 244
Democratic National Convention 15, 92, 198, 201, 210
Democratic Party digital advantage 132
Democrats' advantages 2
Democrats' warning signs 2–4
Diamond, Edwin 146
DiGiacomo, Frank 175
digital advertising (*see* advertising)
digital technology 115, 116, 121
Dinan, Stephen 129
Dionne, E. J., Jr. 24

dispossession, as voter determinant 90, 91
Dowd, Jim 135
Dowd, Katie 136
Duke, David 230, 241

economic dislocation, as voting determinant 94, 95
Economist/YouGov poll 90
economy, as factor in election 84
Edwards, John 48, 49
Eisenhower, Dwight D. 3, 12, 15, 36, 61–2, 146
Election Day 96, 222, 236, 238, 239
elections, presidential of: 1948 12, 28, 146; 1964 12; 1972 12; 2008 xiii, 7, 21, 30, 47, 48, 49, 53, 54, 58, 115, 117, 129, 226; 2012 4, 5, 8, 9, 21, 29, 107, 108, 129, 131, 138, 148, 198, 215
Electoral College 1, 5, 31–2, 147; Clinton strategies 232–3; results 1, 2, 31, 81; Trump strategies 202, 213–17
Elmer-DeWitt, Philip 19
El Super PAC Voto Latino 195
emails of Hillary Clinton (*see* Hillary Clinton Campaign)
EMILY's List 113, 195
Erickson, Erick 13
"Equality of Opportunity Project" 25

Fabrizio, Tony 7, 261
Facebook 135, 145, 195; and fake news 215; and fundraising 114, 138, 158; and links 133; and Trump campaign 135, 138, 154, 177
Fahrenthold, David 219
fake news xiv, 17, 19–23, 81, 171, 176–7, 215; during 2008 election 21; during 2012 election 21; Macedonian teenagers 22; Pizzagate 21–2
feminists 88–9
Fenn, Peter xi, xvii, 145, 175
finances, campaign (*see* fundraising)
Fiorina, Carly 5, 8, 10, 11, 68, 73, 243
Flynn, Michael T. 22,
For Our Future Super PAC 196

Fox News 243
Fox News poll 83, 96
Frank, Thomas 24
French, David 19
Frum, David 240
fundraising 106–10, 121; candidate fundraising strategies 110–14; efficiency and delegates 8–9; general election fundraising 118–21; online 116, 119, 139; personal money 117–18; small donor 11, 106, 108, 114–17, 119–20, 121; "smart money" 8; Trump problems, donor reluctance 197
Future45 Super PAC 8, 200, 202

Gallup polls 12, 17, 88, 96, 179
Garrett, Major xi, xvii, 18, 173, 181, 182
gender, as determinant in voting 88–9
Gerson, Michael 240
Gilmore, Jim 5, 68, 71, 257
Goff, Teddy 139, 262
Goldwater, Barry 12
Gore, Al 15, 16, 30, 31, 36
Goren, Lilly J. xi, xvii, 5, 47
GOTV efforts 61, 193, 194, 199
Graham, Lindsay 5, 18, 67, 71
Greenberg, Stanley 24, 30
"Growth and Opportunity Project" 198, 207
Guccifer 2.0 201–2 (see also Russia hacking of emails)
Gun control 2, 54

Hannity, Sean 13
Hannon, Stephanie 139, 262
hashtags 156–70 (see also Twitter); hashtag phrases in election 161–9; political magic of hashtagged phrases 156; Twitter #debates hashtag 159
Hibbing, John 26
Hillary for America 192
"Hillary Primary" 48–60
Hillary Victory Fund (HVF) 119, 192, 193
Hillbilly Elegy (Vance) 25
HillBlazers 113

Hispanic voters 30, 57, 62, 198
Hochschild, Arlie Russell 24
Huckabee, Mike 5, 8, 18, 68, 72
Hughes, Scottie Nell 180
Humphrey, Hubert H. 15

"I'm With Her" 49, 161, 165
immigrants 21, 26, 67, 70, 76, 92, 93, 98, 152, 228, 242
Immigrant Voters Win PAC 196
immigration 21, 67, 68, 75, 76, 92, 93, 98, 150, 234, 239
Indiana Republican primary 74, 139, 266
Ingraham, Laura 13
"invisible primary" 50, 70–2
Iowa caucuses 49, 50, 70, 263, 267; Democratic 52, 54–5, 56, 106, 115, 267; Republican 72–3, 116, 263
issues 2, 137, 152, 173, 183, 226, 230, 234, 240–1; media failure to cover 19

Jindal, Bobby 5, 18, 68, 71, 258
Johnson, Dennis W. ix, 1
Johnson, Gary 1, 18, 31, 260
joint fundraising committees 119, 284; Democratic 119, 192–6; Republican 120, 121, 197–9

Kaine, Tim 14, 219, 259
Kantor Media/CMAG 152
Kasich, John 5, 68, 69, 71, 73, 74, 75, 111, 150, 211, 239, 240, 258
Kelly, Megyn 11, 228, 243
Kessler, Glenn 182, 183
Khan, Khizr 92, 210, 212, 228, 229
Kinder, Donald 90
King, Gary 23
Kludt, Tom 178
Koch brothers xv, 2, 8
Koch, David 8
Krauthammer, Charles 13
Kreiss, Daniel 132
Kristol, Bill 240
Krohn, Cyrus 141
Kruse, Michael 175
Kushner, Jared 7, 139, 261

290 Index

Lansing, Gerritt 139
Latino Victory Project Super PAC 195
Lessig, Lawrence (Larry) 5, 50, 260
Lewandowski, Corey 7, 180, 212, 213, 261
LGBT rights 87
Liberty Writers News 22
Listen, Liberal (Frank) 24, 41
#LockHerUp 166–7
Lockwood, Belva A. 10
Lowenstein, Jenna 136

Machado, Alicia 218, 219
Macomb County, Michigan 24, 30
Mahler, Jonathan 20
"Make America Great Again" 7, 27, 86, 148, 164, 202, 211, 241
#MakeAmericaGreatAgain (also #MAGA) 156, 164–5, 169
Make America Great Again Committee 120, 197
Making presidential election history 9–24
Manafort, Paul 7, 17, 212–13, 261
Margolis, Jim 7, 262
Market Watch 149
McCain, John xiii, 11, 14, 15, 32, 50, 107, 120, 200, 212, 219
McConaghy, John 90
McConney, Justin 134
McCutcheon v. Federal Elections Commission 8, 119, 192
McGoldrick, Brent 216
McMullin, Evan 31, 240, 270
media 59, 70, 71, 71, 72, 75, 153–4, 160; attacks by Trump 27–8, 66, 178–80; Clinton interaction with press 184; complicity and collapse 17–18; culture of modern media 129, 130, 132; Democratic media buys, general election 194–6; Democratic media buys, primaries 151–2; digital 129–30; failure to cover issues (*see* issues); free media coverage of Trump 18, 23, 24, 50, 59, 71, 120, 175; general election media buys 152–3; Republican media buys, general election 194–6, 196–201;

Republican media buys, primaries 148–50; social (*see* social media); Trump interaction with press 173–5, 176–7, 177–8, 180–4
MediaQuant 149
Media tracker 18
Medvic, Stephen K. xi, xvii, 9, 106, 191
Mellman, Mark S. xi, xii, xvii, 27, 81
Mellman Group xii, 81
Men Without Work (Eberstadt) 25
Michigan 29, 97, 181; general election vote 29, 31, 81, 147, 152, 153, 203, 221–2, 236; primaries 57, 74
Miranda, Luis 193
Mitchell, Andrea 132
Moffett, Zac 132
Money in 2016 campaign 95, 121, 152, 202–3; Clinton allies 192–4, 194–6, 231–2; Democratic primaries 47, 48, 49, 51, 61; fundraising strategies 110–14; general election 121; impact of *Citizens United* 105–6; outside groups (*see also*, Super PACs) 107–8, 110, 191–2; personal funds 117–18; Republican primaries 68, 70–1, 108; small donors 114–17; Trump allies 196–9, 199–201
Monnat, Shannon M. 25
Montanaro, Domenico 15
Mook, Robby 7, 261
Moonves, Leslie 18, 177
Moore, Gordon 137
Moore, Michael xvi, 29
Moore's Law 137
Muslims 32, 233; ban 212, 228, 238; Trump's statements on 11, 19, 70, 198, 212, 228, 238, 241; voter attitudes towards 76, 94, 239, 242

Nader, Ralph 30–1
#NastyWoman 168
National Review, The 73
National Rifle Association 200, 201, 202
National security officials denouncing Trump 13
Needle Drop 216, 221

Nevada caucuses 52, 55, 56
#NeverTrump 73, 161, 167, 168, 239
New Hampshire primary 50; Democrat 49, 50, 52, 55, 56, 61, 115; Republican 72–4, 150
New media (*see also* social media) 145, 176
New York Times, The 8, 11, 22, 96, 149, 166, 179, 195, 196, 244
NextGen Climate Action Super PAC 195, 196
Nixon, Richard M. 3, 15, 36, 148, 200
North American Free Trade Agreement (NAFTA) 53, 57
North Carolina Republican Party 16

Obama, Barack xvi, 2, 3, 10, 54, 60, 68, 176; 2008 presidential campaign xiii, 9, 21, 30, 47, 48, 53, 58, 59, 115, 129; 2012 presidential campaign 7, 8, 9, 107, 114, 121, 129, 131, 215; 2016 presidential campaign 14–15, 194, 201; on Donald Trump 10; on Hillary Clinton 15, 210
Obamacare (*see* Affordable Care Act)
Obama coalition 2, 49, 54, 56, 152, 227, 232, 243
Obama, Michelle 14, 194, 210, 214, 233
Obama presidency 2, 3, 21, 68, 83, 108
Oczkowski, Matt 140
O'Malley, Martin 5, 49, 51, 52, 53, 54, 106, 151, 260
Overton, Joseph P. 19
Overton Window 19, 26
Oxford, Kelly 168

Packer, George 24
Packer, Katie xii, xvii, 30, 210
Palin, Sarah 17
Palmieri, Jennifer 136, 261
Pan, Jennifer 23
Parkhomenko, Adam 111
Parscale, Brad 138, 139, 216, 261
Partisanship 81, 84, 98
Pataki, George 5, 68, 71, 258

Patterson, Dan 138
Patterson, Thomas E. 17
Paul Rand 5, 18, 67, 69, 72, 258
Pence, Mike 169, 211, 219, 256
Pennsylvania 1, 29, 31, 152, 153, 202, 203, 221–2, 236; Democratic primary 57, 59; Republican primary 74
PEORIA Project 157, 160
Perot, Ross 10, 17, 27, 117
Perry, Rick 5, 18, 68, 71, 258
Pew Research Center 2, 69, 75, 130, 133, 153, 169
Pfeiffer, Dan 134
Podesta, John 22, 129, 238, 244, 262
political advertising (*see* advertising)
political science predictions 28–9
Politico 149, 197
Politics of Resentment, The (Cramer) 24
"post-truth" era 19–23
PPP poll 90
Priebus, Reince 197, 198, 199, 203, 211, 213, 215, 216
primaries and caucuses (*see also* individual state primaries and caucuses) 5–6, 47–61, 65–76; 2008 Democratic primaries 47, 48, 56–8, 108; Clinton strategy 48–50, 58–60; Democratic candidates 50–2; invisible primary, the 50, 51, 52, 69, 70–2; Republican candidates 66–9; rules for selecting nominees 66–7; Sanders strategy 54–6, 58–60; Trump strategy 73–4
Priorities USA Action Super PAC 60, 110, 120, 194, 195, 202
Putin, Vladimir 213, 239, 245

Quinnipiac University Poll 83

race and class 241–3
Rasiej, Andrew 136
Rauch, Jonathan 4
Ready for Hillary Super PAC 111, 113, 165
Ready PAC (*see* Ready for Hillary Super PAC)
Reagan Democrats 242

292 Index

Reagan, Ronald 4, 12, 15, 85, 164, 176, 177; Reagan and Trump media similarities 177–8
Real Clear Politics poll 152
Rebuilding America Now Super PAC 200
Reed, Harper 131
Remnick, David 176
reporters 28, 173, 174–5, 183, 184; harassment and assaults on 10, 17, 173, 178–80, 242
Republican National Committee (RNC) 8, 216; assistance for Trump campaign 30, 120, 138, 194, 197–9, 202, 203, 211, 213, 222
Republican National Convention xv, 12, 166
Republican Party 2, 5, 9, 24, 65, 167, 193, 197–9, 211, 214, 239–41; hostility toward party establishment 69–70
"rigged" elections xiv, 15, 21, 194, 245
Right to Rise Super PAC 8, 71, 110
risk taking, as voter determinant 97–8
Roberts, Margaret E. 23
Romney, Mitt 5, 9, 14; 2012 presidential campaign 9, 67, 107, 108, 117, 131, 138, 148, 214–16; comparisons with Trump campaign 25, 29, 82; criticizing Trump 13, 73, 240
Roosevelt, Eleanor 12, 14
Roper, Elmo 28
Rosenblatt, Alan 137
Rove, Karl 7, 73
Rubin, Jennifer 240
Rubio, Marco 69, 71, 72, 73, 74, 75, 90, 111, 117, 118, 259
Russia xiv; hacking of emails 23–4, 81, 191, 201–2, 238, 244 (see also Guccifer 2.0); manipulation of election xiv, 192, 202, 227
Rutenberg, Jim 149
Ryan, Paul 4, 202, 221, 239, 240

Sabato, Larry J. 3
Sanders, Bernie xiv, xvii, 3, 5, 9, 225, 227, 232, 233, 238, 260; fundraising

successes xv, 9, 105–6, 108, 110, 114–16, 192; primary elections, 9, 48, 49, 50–2, 52–4, 54–8, 149, 151–2, 170; surge in primaries 58–60, 121
Santorum, Rick 5, 18, 68, 71, 72, 148, 259
Sasse, Ben 239, 240
Scola, Nancy 166
Seaborn, Brent 216
Sears, David 90
Shareblue 196
Shelby County v. Holder (2013) 16
Sheridan, Pete 138
Sides, John 25
Sigala, Hector 170
Silverman, Craig 176
Skelly, Bill 216, 222
Skopcol, Theda 25
"Snapchat election" 130
social identity, as voting determinant 81, 82, 94
social media 23, 130–4 (see also Twitter); Clinton's use of 113, 115, 135–7, 228–9; emergence in 2016 election 18–19, 137–42; in 2008 presidential campaign 48, 130; millennials use of 21; Sanders' use of 58; Trump's use of xv, 65 , 71, 119, 121, 134–5, 153–4, 164, 177, 179, 184 (see also Trump, use of Twitter)
Soll, Jacob 20
Soros, George 196
South Carolina 52, 90; Democratic primary 52, 55, 56; Republican primary 73, 74, 83, 168
Southern Poverty Law Center 26
Stealth Democracy (Hibbing and Theiss-Morse) 26
Steger, Wayne xii, xvii, 5, 65
Stein, Jill 1, 10, 18, 30–1, 106, 260
Stenner, Karen 82, 91
stereotypes 94, 95, 241
Stetler, Brian 178
Steyer, Tom 195, 196
Strangers in Their Own Land (Hochschild) 24

Stromer-Galley, Jennifer 140
#StrongerTogether 156, 163, 165–6, 169, 233–4
Super PACs xv, 4, 8, 106–11, 117, 118, 150, 191–2, 202–3, 284–5; candidate-specific PACs 8, 60 (*see also* Right to Rise Super PAC; *see also* Priorities USA Super PAC; *see also* Ready for Hillary Super PAC); Clinton Super PAC allies 194–7; Trump Super PAC allies 199–201
Super Tuesday 50; Democratic primaries 56–8, 59, 61; Republican primaries 73, 74
Sykes, Charlie 240

Tankersley, Jim 24
Tea Party and the Remaking of Republican Conservatism, The (Skopcol and Williamson) 25
Tea Party movement 24, 25, 67, 69, 70, 148
Television spending (*see* advertising)
Tesler, Michael 25
texting 139
Theiss-Morse, Elizabeth 26
Time 23, 195
Tolchin, Susan 24
Traister, Rebecca 58
Trans-Pacific Partnership (TPP) 53, 54, 57
Trump, Donald xiii, 1; appeal of 4, 24–7, 81–3, 84–95, 96–7; challenging election results (*see* rigged election); criticism by conservatives 4, 12, 13, 14, 25, 26, 27, 69, 70, 73, 239, 240, 246; criticism of press 17, 18; dislike of 3, 89, 96, 97; fighting with RNC 12–14, 69–70; fundraising strategy (*see* fundraising); insults and taunts xiv, xv, 10–11, 20, 21; lack of experience xiv, 195, 231; on Hillary Clinton 11, 12; on Russian hacking 23; opportunistic genius of 27–8; saturated media coverage 71; and social media xiv, 134–5; use of Twitter 11, 13, 27, 133, 134–5, 168–70, 177, 179, 244; Was he even a Republican? 4

Trump campaign: free media coverage (*see* media); general election 30, 105, 211–12, 212–15 (*see also* debates; *see also* Access Hollywood tape); political consultants xv, 7; primaries 65–6, 68, 72–6
Trump Effect, The 173–85
Trump, Ivanka 7, 261
Trump Make America Great Again Committee 197
Trump, Melania 219
#TrumpThatBitch 167
Trumptwitterarchive.com 157
Trump Victory Fund 197
trust in media xiv, 17, 179, 180
"truthful hyperbole" 28
Twitter xiv, 18–19, 23, 114, 145; as a campaign venue 18–19, 158–9; followers and following 23, 58, 153–4, 161, 162–9
TwitterAudit.com 161
Tyndall, Andrew 19

union activity 107, 176, 196
Unwinding, The (Packer) 24

Vance, J.D. 25
voter mobilization 191, 194, 196, 199, 202
voter protection activities 194

Walker, Scott 5, 18, 68, 72, 140, 176, 259
Wallace, Chris 15
Wallace, George 10, 11, 17
Walsh, Katie 216
Warren, Elizabeth 60, 225
Washington Post, The 168, 179, 202, 219, 245; revocation of press credentials by Trump 178
Washington Post/ABC News polls 92, 94, 96
Wasserman Schultz, Debbie 52, 192, 210, 227
Webb, Jim 5, 50, 51, 52, 260
Weiner, Anthony 236
Wesleyan Media Project 118, 149, 194

294 Index

What's the Matter With Kansas? (Frank) 24
white Americans xvi, 94, 242
Why Americans Hate Politics (Dionne) 24
WikiLeaks xiv, 23, 169, 192, 193, 201,
    227–8
Wiley, Rick 7, 261
Will, George 12, 13, 73
Williamson, Vanessa 25
Wisconsin 1, 16, 29, 30, 31, 57, 59, 68,
    81, 97; Clinton and 147, 152, 202, 203,
    221, 222, 236, 238

"woman card", the 225–6
woman heading the ticket 10
Women Vote! Super PAC 195

Yourish, Karen 8

Zito, Salena 25
Zucker, Jeff 149
Zurn, Suzanne xii, xvii, 18, 129